Methods for Development Work and Research

D1377415

Methods for Development Work and Research

A New Guide for Practitioners

Second Edition

Britha Mikkelsen

SAGE Publications
New Delhi ❖ Thousand Oaks ❖ London

Copyright © Britha Mikkelsen, 1995, 2005

All rights reserved. No part of this book may be reproduced or utilized in any form or by any means, electronic or mechanical, including photocopying, recording or by any information storage or retrieval system, without permission in writing from the publisher.

First published in 1995

This edition published in 2005 by

Sage Publications India Pvt Ltd
B-42, Panchsheel Enclave
New Delhi 110 017

Sage Publications Inc.
2455 Teller Road
Thousand Oaks, California 91320

Sage Publications Ltd
1 Oliver's Yard, 55 City Road
London EC1Y 1SP

Published by Tejeshwar Singh for Sage Publications India Pvt Ltd, phototypeset in 10 pt Calisto MT by Star Compugraphics Private Limited, Delhi and printed at Chaman Enterprises, New Delhi.

Library of Congress Cataloging-in-Publication Data

Mikkelsen, Britha.
  Methods for development work and research: a new guide for practitioners/Britha Mikkelsen.—2nd ed.
    p. cm.
  Includes bibliographical references and index.
1. Economic development—Research—Methodology.   I. Title.
  HD77.M55   330'.072—dc22   2005   2004028917

ISBN: 0–7619–3327–1 (Hb)   81–7829–481–8 (India–Hb)
          0–7619–3328–X (Pb)   81–7829–482–6 (India–Pb)

Sage Production Team: Proteeti Banerjee, Mathew P.J. and Santosh Rawat

Contents

List of Boxes

List of Figures

List of Abbreviations

ABC	Attitudes and Behaviour Change
ACPDT	African Community Publishing and Development Trust
ADR	Alternative Dispute Resolution
AI	Appreciative Inquiry
AIC	Appreciation-Influence-Control
AKIS	Agricultural Knowledge and Information System
ASPS	Agricultural Sector Programme Support
BA	Beneficiary Assessment
BMN	Basic Minimum Needs
BRIDGE	Development—Gender (Non-profit Unit at IDS)
CAP	Community Action Planning
CAPEQM	Administrative Unit in Thailand
CBO	Community Based Organization
CDD	Community Development Department
CDF	Comprehensive Development Framework
CEDAW	Convention on the Elimination of all Forms of Discrimination Against Women
CERD	International Convention on the Elimination of all Forms of Racial Discrimination
CIAT	International Centre for Tropical Agriculture
CIMMYT	International Maize and Wheat Improvement Centre
CIP	Community Infrastructure Project
COWI	Danish Consultants
CRC	Convention on the Rights of the Child
CUDOS	Communalism, Universalism, Disinterestedness, Organized Scepticism
D&P	Decentralization & Participation
DAC	Development Assistance Committee
DANIDA	Danish Development Assistance (Part of MFA)
DFID	Department for International Development
DGIS	Dutch Directorate General for International Cooperation
DIIS	Danish Institute for International Studies
DIP	Deliberate Democracy and Inclusionary Processes
DISHA	Development Initiatives for Social and Human Action
DNA	Deoxyribonucleic acid
EC	European Commission
ECD	Evaluation Capacity Development
ENRECA	Danish Programme for Enhancement of Research Capacity
ESA	Economic Stakeholder Analysis

ESPS   Environmental Sector Programme Support
ESSD   Environmentally and Socially Sustainable Development
FAO   Food and Agriculture Organization of the United Nations
GA   Gender Analysis
GAD   Gender and Development
GDI   Gender-related Development Index
GIS   Geographical Information System
GLM   Generalized Linear Model
GM   Genetically Modified
GNP   Gross National Product
GPS   Global Positioning System
HDI   Human Development Index
HDR   Human Development Report
HFI   Human Freedom Index
HIPC   Highly Indebted Poor Countries
HPI   Human Poverty Index
IBIS   Danish NGO
ICCPR   International Covenant on Civil and Political Rights
ICESCR   International Covenant on Economic, Social and Cultural Rights
ICT   Information and Communication Technology
IDA   International Development Association
IDEA   International Development Ethics Association
IDR   Institute for Dispute Resolution (University of Khon Khaen, Thailand)
IDS   Institute of Development Studies
IFAD   International Fund for Agricultural Development
IIED   International Institute for Environment and Development
IMF   International Monetary Fund
INGO   International Non-governmental Organization
IT   Information Technology
KIDP   Kitui Integrated Development Programme
KPI   Key Performance Indicators
LFA   Logical Framework Analysis/Approach
LIFT   Local Initiative for Farmer's Training (Bangladesh)
LIS   Land Information System
LLL   Linked Local Learning
M&E   Monitoring & Evaluation
MDG   Millennium Development Goals
MFA   Ministry of Foreign Affairs (Denmark)
MFEP   Ministry of Finance and Economic Planning
MLA   Member of Legislative Assembly
MSC   Most Significant Change

NAFSA	National Association for Foreign Student Affairs
NGO	Non-governmental Organization
NORAD	Norwegian Agency for Development Cooperation
NRD2C	Ministry of Interior
NRM	Natural Resource Management
NUD*IST	Non-numerical Unstructured Data Indexing Searching and Theorizing
ODA	Official Development Assistance
ODA	Overseas Development Agency
OECD	Organization for Economic Cooperation and Development
OED	Operations Evaluation Department
OHCHR	Office of the High Commissioner for Human Rights
PALM	Participatory Appraisal and Learning Methods
PAME	Participatory Assessment, Monitoring and Evaluation
PANOS	Name of an International Non-governmental Organization
PFI	Political Freedom Index
PFM	Participatory Forest Management
PIM	Participatory Impact Monitoring
PLA	Participatory Learning and Action
PM&E/PME	Participatory Monitoring and Evaluation
PPA	Participatory Poverty Assessment
PRA	Participatory Rural Appraisal
PROWWESS	Promotion of the Role of Women in Water and Environment Sanitation Services
PRS	Poverty Reduction Strategy
PRSP	Poverty Reduction Strategy Paper
PSI	Poverty Strategies Initiative
PSIA	Poverty and Social Impact Analysis
QA	Quality Assurance
QPES	Qualitative Poverty and Exclusion Studies
RAP	Rapid Assessment Procedure
RBA	Rights Based Approach
RBM	Results Based Management
RRA	Rapid Rural Appraisal
RS	Remote Sensing
SA	Social Assessment
SARAR	Self-esteem, Associative Strengths, Resourcefulness, Action Planning, Responsibility
SAREC	Swedish Programme for Strengthening Research Capacity
SCC	Systematic Client Consulting
SCOT	Social Construction of Technology
SDC	Swiss Development Cooperation
SIA	Social Impact Assessment
SIDA	Swedish International Development Cooperation Agency

SMART	Specific, Measurable, Attainable/Realistic, Relevant, Time-bound
SOAS	School of Oriental and African Studies
SOCAT	Social Capital Assessment Tool
SORO	Special Operations Research Office (U.S. Army)
SPS	Sector Programme Support
SPSS	Statistical Package for the Social Sciences
SSI	Semi Structured Interviews
SWAP	Sector Wide Approach
SWOT	Strengths, Weaknesses, Opportunities and Threats
TOR	Terms of Reference
TQQ	Time, Quantity and Quality
UN	United Nations
UNCHS	United Nations Centre for Human Settlement—Habitat
UNDESA	United Nations Development of Social and Economic Affairs
UNDP	United Nations Development Programme
UNHCR	United Nations High Commissioner for Refugees
WB	World Bank
WCARRD	World Conference on Agrarian Reform and Rural Development
WDR	World Development Reports
WIDER	World Institute for Development Economics Research
WTO	World Trade Organization

The current Guide is an update of *Methods for Development Work and Research: A Guide for Practitioners*, published in 1995 (Mikkelsen, 1995). By spreading knowledge about participation in development and participatory methods, and presenting them as a complement to common, globally practised social science methods rather than as stand-alone ones, the 1995 version seemed to hit a gap in the literature on methods for development work and research. The **'complementary' perspective** is retained as well as the target groups—development practitioners and researchers in the South and North—in this updated version.

In the meantime many lessons have been learned on the merits and pitfalls of development work, including **lessons on practising participatory methods and participatory development.** A substantial update was required. Where lessons have been learned on better practices, they are reflected in this book, while it is acknowledged that new lessons are significant only if development issues are understood in the **context of a wider development discourse.** Many issues remain painfully unresolved even after decades of development cooperation. **Poverty** is by far the most serious issue for international development cooperation, and the issue runs as a red thread through the book, recognizing that poverty reduction is not primarily a question of the right methods but one of political will.

In chronological order, the significant updates and changes to this new edition are: Chapter 1 outlines some significant traits of international development cooperation with reference to **change and continuity.** *Change* in development cooperation in **a globalizing world** fosters an emphasis on holistic and cross-disciplinary approaches. *Continuity* is manifest at the level of approach, e.g., in the continued application of the **planning cycle** and the **objectives-based logical framework planning approach**—with a renewed focus more on **programme and policy support** than on projects, and on **processes as much as on results.**

My attempt to leave out a general introduction to participatory methods by referring the reader to more recent, excellent guides which concentrate on 'community participation' and offers a more in-depth study of single participatory techniques and tools (e.g., Kumar, 2002; IFAD, 2001) than this Guide intended to do was not particularly supported by my co-readers. An introduction to the **concept of participation in development** is therefore retained and updated in Chapter 2, while **critical perspectives on participation** have been given substantial space for practitioners to reflect on the theoretical as well as practical and ethical implications of their work. Examples of **participatory methods in use** are illustrated in more detail in Chapter 3, with an emphasis on **spreading uses** where the application of **participatory methods in macro-policy, budgeting and poverty reduction strategy studies** have gained momentum.

Feedback from many users of the 1995 version in the South and the North as well as advice from co-readers in the revision process have given me highly-valued suggestions for this update. As a consequence

Chapter 4 alerts the reader to the **linkages between research purpose, methods and design of development studies,** and **research questions for quantitative and qualitative style of research** in different types of development studies, while Chapter 5 tries to capture the request for more guidance on **theory-based data generation and analysis.** Important **philosophy of science underpinnings of methods** are introduced. Illustrations are given of **analysis of qualitative data** originating from different sources, **interviews, text analysis, using indicators and IT tools.** A new issue is how to set standards of **quality** of qualitative research when the traditional criteria of validity and reliability are less suitable.

As mentioned, many key issues in development cooperation remain painfully unsettled. Sometimes agencies propose and manage to induce new ways for all to address overarching problems. The current **Poverty Reduction Strategy Paper, PRSP, approach** is one recent example which has far reaching policy **and** methodological implications, e.g., in terms of **'stakeholder participation',** as reflected in Sections 3.2.3 and 6.2 in particular. Chapter 6 also provides an update on gender perspectives in development work and on **gender mainstreaming** and related **gender analysis.** The contesting discourse on **women's empowerment** is an additional dimension. Chapter 6 is the place for the introduction of issues and approaches which are given renewed attention in the current development cooperation discourse: A **Rights Based Approach, RBA,** to development is elaborated in Section 6.1, because the RBA is currently substituting the conventional needs based approach, for want of acceptable results, in several agencies. A rights perspective has been reflected in the policies of many agencies, NGOs and UN organizations in particular, for several decades, but an explanation, not least of *how* to implement the approach, is warranted and an appetizer is given in Section 6.1. **Appreciative Inquiry, AI** (Section 6.4.2) adds a constructive perspective to the predominant problem-focus of much development work. AI is included for its alternative approach to strategic planning, evaluation and change, which builds on the positive forces that foster strength within an organization, partnership or project to learn from its own practice. While appreciative inquiry is basically an explorative investigation method, the **Social Capital Analysis Tool (SOCAT)** illustrates how participatory methods can be applied to investigate the presence, absence and potential of social capital in connection with poverty alleviation initiatives—an issue which was not paid much attention until the preparation of the World Development Report on Poverty Reduction (World Bank, 2000). The **spatial approach, Geomatics** (Section 6.4.3) extends space related participatory methods (Section 2.2.3), as it focuses on combining high-tech remote sensing and geographical information systems, GIS, with people's knowledge 'on and of the ground'. In recent years Geomatics has brought technical planners and anthropologists together for eliciting local knowledge in longitudinal studies with a historical perspective, and has functioned as a weapon in the hands of disfavoured ethnic groups.

Other approaches in focus in this updated version reflect the fact that issues and approaches which have been part of the development discourse for long are gaining new momentum. The current focus on **Monitoring and Evaluation, M&E,** Chapter 7, is a sign that the world is moving towards an audit culture. M&E have always been part of the project cycle, but never as much an 'industry' as today. Despite the current move of development planning away from projects towards policy and sector-wide interventions, monitoring and evaluation are there to stay—certainly for a considerable time and irrespective of the 'tyranny of evaluation' claim from some circles. The chapter on monitoring and evaluation has been considerably extended from the 1995 version, supported with nine case illustrations of different M&E methods including participatory monitoring and evaluation, to give the reader a broad basis of inspiration.

Intervention in other people's lives through development work and research fosters a continuous attention to the ethical implications. Chapter 8 elaborates on **ethics, methods and development interventions** and illustrates **regulations and codes of conduct.** With the expansion of participatory development, the question of **images of 'the others' and cultural encounters** remain no less urgent, not least due to the risk that practitioners of participatory methods might themselves fall into the trap of the patronizing they want to counter.

All in all the updated version of *Methods for Development Work and Research* is a substantial revision based on many people's and my own hands-on experience. With the additional experience reflected, it will hopefully continue to offer valuable, practical guidance and critical reflection on methods for development work and research in a non-orthodox spirit.

Britha Mikkelsen
COWI Denmark, April 2004

At certain moments in your life you suddenly see your work in a new and revealing light. You realize you have established inexpedient routines and that you do your work according to formulas you have long forgotten to question.

This happened to me when I almost lost the chance to undertake what I thought would be an interesting study of people's communication patterns—A Study of the Use of Public Telephones in Kenya. The job was to be my initiation as a sociologist in a large engineering consultancy firm. Together with the company's foremost statistician, I was asked to design the user study of public telephones. Our zealous interpretation of the terms of reference (TOR), almost killed the event.

The TOR were as ambitious as TORs always are, I later learned. Our interpretation told us that the TOR asked for assessment of public telephone (PT) use in urban, semi-urban and rural areas; in high-potential, medium- and low-potential rural areas; in residential, commercial, administrative and industrial areas; in areas with long-term coverage, with recent installation of public telephones and areas not yet provided with the service. Profiles of users, potential users and non-users were asked for. Gender, age and ethnicity, social status and much more were relevant.

Keeping to our text-book learning, honouring rules for respresentativeness and sampling, we presented our client with a proposal for a sample survey of some 3,700 interviews. I am glad I was not present when the roaring laughter must have shaken our client's halls: 3,700 interviews to assess the use of 2,700 phones! Our reference to scientific sampling rules and statistical significance must have drowned in laughter.

It was our fortune we were not dismissed on the spot. Our client accepted a reduced sample survey of 2,300 interviews, which broke with our 'scientific principles' but was likely to provide significant information anyway! Together with a team of local sociologists and staff of the telephone agency we undertook a comprehensive questionnaire sample survey with precoded questions and a few open-ended questions, besides intensive observations.

In retrospect—had I known then what I know today—the field study design and methods would have looked quite different. There would be reason to consider a variety of the methods presented in this book: observation—more observation—than we actually carried out; focus group interviews with different groups, semi-structured interviews with key persons in and outside the organization; indicators for use, non-use and potential use; gender analysis and possibly ranking and scoring by selected groups, supplemented with short, targeted questionnaires if required. Mapping for selection of preferential sites for new PTs would also be relevant, scenario workshops a possibility and cross-disciplinary approaches a necessity. An attempt would be made to make the study a participatory event, knowing its limitations, since participation by users, potential users and local telephone corporation staff had been non-existent from the outset. Surely, the results would compare favourably with the outcome of the comprehensive questionnaire survey we actually did undertake.

I am extremely grateful for the encouragement I have received to write down some of my field study experience and reflections. The introductory anecdote tells that you learn better from own experience than from others'. Yet I hope readers will find some parts in this book which may help them to gain that experience in a less painful way than what might otherwise have been the case.

But first of all I am grateful for the opportunity to review my own experience in light of the experience of many other people. The major parts of this book stem from the contributions of others as they have been recorded in textbooks, reports, in fiction and visual forms, and from personal communication and observation in the field.

I have attempted to give an introduction to a variety of field study methods from which the reader may combine her/his own mixture to suit the problem, time and resources available. It should be possible to dig in at relevant places without going through the whole book.

Some may think the book should have left out conventional field study methods altogether and gone into more detail on how to apply participatory methods. If the result is somwhat schizoid and suffers from many sceptical considerations, this only reflects the dilemmas and contradictions I personally experience when doing field studies. As practitioner or as researcher of the North or the South we can at best make field studies a continuous learning process. The time is not ripe to skip long-time practices. Let us instead carefully reflect on what are relevant problems to study and make the best of methodological pluralism.

Britha Mikkelsen
Copenhagen, January 1994

Acknowledgements

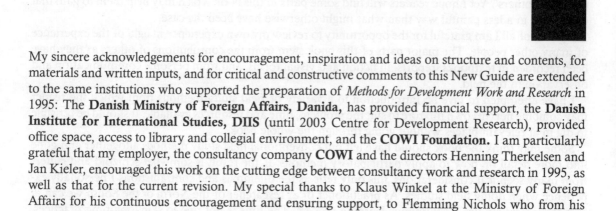

My sincere acknowledgements for encouragement, inspiration and ideas on structure and contents, for materials and written inputs, and for critical and constructive comments to this New Guide are extended to the same institutions who supported the preparation of *Methods for Development Work and Research* in 1995: The **Danish Ministry of Foreign Affairs, Danida,** has provided financial support, the **Danish Institute for International Studies, DIIS** (until 2003 Centre for Development Research), provided office space, access to library and collegial environment, and the **COWI Foundation.** I am particularly grateful that my employer, the consultancy company **COWI** and the directors Henning Therkelsen and Jan Kieler, encouraged this work on the cutting edge between consultancy work and research in 1995, as well as that for the current revision. My special thanks to Klaus Winkel at the Ministry of Foreign Affairs for his continuous encouragement and ensuring support, to Flemming Nichols who from his secondment at IFAD provided constructive suggestions on early drafts on Participatory Development and Monitoring and Evaluation, and to Margrethe Holm Andersen and Kurt Mørck Jensen for confirming the need for an updated version.

At DIIS my sincere appreciation to Jannik Boesen, Ellen Buch-Hansen, Steen Folke, Peter Gibbon, Amanda Hammer, Esbern Friis Hansen, Søren Hvalkof, Ravinder Kaur, Julie Koch, Jesper Linell, Henrik Nielsen, Rie Odgaard, Susanne Possing, Helle Munk Ravnborg, Lisa Richey, Ninna Nyberg Sørensen, Pernille Sørensen, Ole Therkildsen, Finn Stepputat, Niel Webster, Kirsten Westergaard, Olaf Westermann, Fiona Wilson, and the librarians Svend Erik Lindberg-Hansen, Ole Nørgaard and Marianne Thrane. While associated with the DIIS, an enthusiastic young candidate from the Danish Veterinary and Agricultural University, Maria Andreassen, who shared the fate of unemployment with many young academics, joined me on a voluntary basis and took the main responsibility for preparing the Bibliography on Participation and Participatory Methods in Development Work and Research (DIIS 03.3). Thanks and congratulations to Maria who is now an active Development Worker and instructor of young farmers in Zambia with the Danish Association for International Cooperation.

My warm appreciation to colleagues at COWI, with several of whom I have spent time conducting field studies: Cecilia Ljungman, Sarah Forti, Søren Skou Rasmussen, Charles J. Pendley, Morten G. Poulsen, and Thomas J. Thomsen in particular have provided significant inputs and constructive comments, while inspiration has been gained from discussions or the works of Anette Aarestrup, Robin Bloch, Ane Bonde, Knud Erik Christensen, Lars Peter Christensen, Peter Christensen, Kim Clausen, Jes Clauson-Kaas, Tom Dahl-Østergaard, Søren Dreyer, Kristian R. Duus, Per K. Hansen, Caroline Hartoft, Claudia Heim, Carsten H. Laugesen, Mette Jacobsgaard, Rikke I. Jensen, Jasmine A. Jessen, Henrik Brade Johansen, Peter Jørgensen, Louise Kjær, Mikkel Kliim, Daniel la Cour, Hans-Norbert Lahme, Annelies Leemanns, Vincent Martino, David Moore, Hanne Nielsen, Dorthe K. Nordentoft, Henrik Grooss Olesen, Niels E. Olesen, Thyge Poulsen, Claus C. Rebien, Vagn Rehøj, Arne Kvist

Rønnest, Henrik Steen Pedersen, Palle Smith-Petersen, Suzanne Steensen, Susanne Vedsted, Rasmus Ødum—and special and technical support from Anja M. Rasmussen, Susanne Krogh Hansen, Gunvor Velser, Dorthe G. Kok and Richard Thrane.

Valuable exchanges and contacts were forged with individuals and a number of external institutions during the process: Professor Prakash Reddy, the Department of Anthropology, Sri Venkateswara University, Tirupati, Berry Underwood, and Rekha Dayal, India; Meryl Williams, WorldFish Center, Malaysia; Kgotso Schoeman, Kagiso Trust, South Africa; Irene Guijt, Learning by Design, Jens Lerche, SOAS, University of London, Alanagh Raikes, Sussex; Mariken Vaa, the Nordic Africa Institute Uppsala, Sweden; Prudence Woodford-Berger and Eva Lovgren, Sida; Gunnar Sorbo, Johan Helland and Tone Bleie, Christian Michelsen Institute, Bergen, Norway; Ole Dybbroe, Mikkel Funder, Claus Heinberg, Jan Kirstein, Roger Leys, Søren Lund, Kurt Aagaard Nielsen, University of Roskilde; Jens Müller, University of Aalborg; Ida E. Andersen, the Danish Council for Technology; Finn Tobiesen, Organisation for Renewable Energy; and the Department of Political Science at the University of Copenhagen, where Merete Watt Boolsen tested draft sections in her courses on New Methodology and contributed generously with inspiration and inputs on 'Data and Analysis' in this Guide. Targeted input and comment was received on various sections from Virginie Lafleur Thige, Lisbeth Boye, Katalyst, and Peter Sigsgaard, the Danish Association for International Cooperation. I was delighted that Josephine Obel 'tested' the section on Monitoring and Evaluation for DanChurchAid in the field in Tanzania.

The rich sources on Participation in Development available in the United Kingdom are unmatched anywhere in the world. The 'Reading Room' at the Institute for Development Studies, University of Sussex, was generously at disposal with inspirational guidance from Robert Chambers and John Gaventa. Other sources of inspiration at the IDS are Bob Baulch, and Hazel Reeves and Emma Bell from the BRIDGE Gender-development network. At the International Institute for Environment and Development, IIED, my appreciation to David Satterthwaite and Camilla Toulmin and to IIED's reading room on Participation.

Last, but not least, I would like to thank Ms Omita Goyal, Sage Publications, New Delhi, for her persistent encouragement to make this revision materialize.

Britha Mikkelsen
April 2004

CHAPTER

1

Issues in development cooperation change, and methods are adjusted and scrapped and new ones invented as lessons are being learnt. Many challenges and contradictions remain in the minefield where practitioners and researches meet with other development actors. Conflicting traits and trends of the development discourse form the context for the changing approaches presented throughout the book, amongst which people-oriented participatory approaches are central. Despite many changes, the prevalent way of analysing and designing development interventions is still the planning cycle, departing from problem analysis and following an objectives-oriented logical framework approach. These tools are introduced up front with a discussion of the pros and cons.

1.1 Issues and Approaches in Current Development Cooperation

1.1.1 Introduction

This book can be read as an input into a discourse on adequate methods for addressing current development cooperation issues in field studies. It provides an introduction to a variety of methods and methodological considerations which may help guide the 'development practitioner' to match issues and approaches in development studies.

A vast and differentiated group of development workers, including technical assistants of public and private aid organizations, consultants, information workers and researchers, are continuously occupied in short or longer-term development activities which require studies of different kinds. Cooperation and dialogue between the development workers from outside and local planners, administrators, researchers and ordinary people should be straightforward, but does not always seem to be the case. There is a continuous need for reflection on *how* development cooperation is undertaken and could be improved, at least in one important area—field work.

Dialogue, flexibility and participatory methods are central concepts when we talk about interventions in social processes and other people's cultures. None of these are panaceas. Development is not a technical fix. Even the best of methods, attitudes and intentions do not always help to meet the goals for development cooperation with which the development worker is engaged. Development work and field studies are subject to many stifling conventions that do not change overnight. It is an aim of the book to encourage reflection on what we are doing when we intervene in other people's worlds in the name of development.

Reflection is enhanced through practice, and guidance is provided on alternative ways to generate and analyse data for development studies in cooperation with the affected and concerned people.

Access to *secondary* information and data on specific sectors and particular countries is generally thought to be simple, but this is the case only if it is published in national or international reports.[1] *If* accessible, secondary data are often unreliable. When it comes to guidance on which *primary data* and information to collect and by which methods, ways to analyse data and how to apply results, it cannot be taken for granted that each individual will find a way. The ethics of doing development work and re-search—for many in a foreign country—is often handled as a peripheral concern, though it is increasingly being addressed in the literature (see Chapter 8).

The education that development workers receive does not always provide them with adequate tools and methods for the type of research and field studies with which they become involved. Field research methods have been developed for specific disciplines and sciences, often long ago when the research questions were different from today's issues. History adds new questions to development thinking, and adequate research tools tend to lag behind.

Participatory research methods, for micro studies initially but increasingly also for policy-related studies, are continuously in the making. The major part of this book is devoted to the discourse on participation in the broadest sense—from elaboration of the 'politically correct' concept to participatory approaches to development and application of participatory methods, techniques and tools. These are all too often taken for granted even in milieus and agencies which subscribe to 'people's participation'. The selection presented in the book is made on the presumption that several field study methods can be shared by development researchers and practitioners alike, despite their different roles and approaches to develop-ment work. Regardless of whether the methods are new or adjustments of conventional research methods, they are a reflection of a changed perception of North-South and outsider-insider relations. The resulting 'new development issues' and participatory approaches to development work and studies, which are in the making, are the main topics of this book. It may be seen as a complement to, but in no way as a substitute for, individual discipline methods.

This is not a cookbook for the study of all possible development issues. There is no ambition to deal with 'it all'. By spreading knowledge about participatory methods and presenting them as a complement to common, globally practised social science methods for development studies, this updated Guide will hopefully contribute to a useful overview of well-established and newer techniques and tools, without exhausting all possible field study methods. The reader will find a variety of practical suggestions in the many illustrations in the text, boxes and figures. It should be possible to read relevant parts of the book selectively. If more detailed guidance is required, the reference literature should be of assistance.

This chapter continues to outline traits and trends of international development cooperation which provide the context for the issues and approaches presented in the following chapters. A message with methodological implications is that despite many changes, international development aid cooperation continues to be interpreted as a planning cycle, departing from problem identification and following an objectives-oriented logical framework approach. These are therefore introduced up front. Alternative models and approaches are discussed in later chapters, e.g. a Rights Based Approach (section 6.1) and

---

[1] For a discussion of a data *black hole,* i.e., missing data on key indicators such as infant mortality rates and maternal mortality rates see Sumner, 2004 and UNDESA, 1999.

Appreciative Inquiry (section 6.4.1). The reader who wants to start with a more narrow outline of the book may jump to Section 1.3.

1.1.2 Development Cooperation in a Globalizing World— Continuity and Change

Issues in development cooperation change, and methods and approaches to deal with them are adjusted, scrapped and invented as lessons are gained. Yet most of the problems addressed in development co-operation over the last 50 years have remained or escalated. Issues change because the contexts change. The 'empire' of today's global markets (Hardt and Negri, 2003) differs significantly from the colonial empires and the context of the new nation states in which development cooperation was set in the post-colonial era.

Frequent adjustments and reversals have been made in policies and approaches to international development cooperation from the national to the grass-roots level since the beginning in the 1960s. Welfare and basic needs approaches of the 1970s were surpassed by structural adjustment and neo-liberal policies of the 1980s and 1990s, reflecting different theoretical interpretations by and political interests of powerful actors on the development scene (Degnbol-Martinussen and Engberg-Pedersen, 2003). In the process lessons about better practices have been learned—but not always well reflected in later strategies.

An important lesson on better practices is captured in the 'participatory development approach', which this book makes a point of sharing. After several decades on the agenda, it is evident that the participatory approach is still in the making despite adherence to the idea of 'popular participation' in wider and wider circles of development agencies. The participatory approach has many dimensions and there are many pitfalls before it significantly influences the top-down approach which continues to characterize much development work and research. It requires sound and critical consideration by the practitioner to compose the optimal approach to the issues s/he wants to study. Lessons must continuously be shared, as this book attempts, to improve development cooperation.

Though lessons **have** been learnt, it must be questioned how much the situation has changed from the 1960s to date concerning enhanced understanding of the dynamics and conditions of development and change. Many challenges and contradictions remain in the minefield where practitioners and development researchers meet with other development actors—partners, users, 'beneficiaries', etc. For example:

- World poverty remains devastating, natural resources are being depleted, political and social conflicts are escalating, and four decades of substantial aid input in the developing countries is accompanied by a net transfer of resources from the poor to the rich countries, and growing scepticism in the Third World about the objectives of international development assistance. Is there a connection between these and the fact that the interpretation of what development is all about—how it can be defined and accomplished, for whom, by whom and why—is still very much determined by the 'haves', by representatives of the international 'aid business', and legitimized by development researchers, as suggested by Tvedt more than a decade ago (Tvedt, 1990)?

- Development practitioners and researchers alike better understand that they are part of a learning process. However, a learning process, to be real learning, also contributes to its opposite, i.e., a recognition that the problems unsolved escalate even faster than the problems solved. There is a continuous challenge in making the process a shared learning one with people whose lives are affected by the interventions undertaken by development workers of all kinds. New tools have been developed for the analysis of development problems. While some enhance dialogue, others run the risk of being tools for the busy 'practitioner' and consolidating the isolation between the 'experts' and the users.

- The more it is realized that the same reality can appear completely different through different lenses, the more are reductionist perspectives being replaced by holistic and interdisciplinary ones. Yet there is still a tendency to have quantitative research dominate the macro development discourse and policy arena, whilst qualitative research drives the micro and project work. Econometrics and ethnographic methods, for example, are not easy complements, but a productive synergy is possible both between methods and between disciplines (White, 2002). Methodological inventions are required to improve approaches which involve several disciplines and methods to make them more applicable.

- The obvious shortcomings in misconceived aid interventions and analytical capacity contribute to disillusionment and threaten to result in demands for more control, more accountability, 'quality assurance', etc. Conditionalities may be necessary as development cooperation is becoming more political, moving from micro interventions to macro processes, to budget support and donor harmonization; but without a simultaneous promotion of dialogue and a climate of mutual listening and learning in the new partnerships, additional control may be counterproductive.

- There is a struggle, but rarely an open one, between different 'aid models' for development cooperation. According to one perspective, they are 'blueprints' set out to guide how development interventions ought to take place. According to another, the aid model brings together different interests and social actors linked through the aid relationship and provides an arena for negotiation and consensus-building—the latter still relatively unexplored, but could open up a promising line of enquiry (Wilson, 2004). Amidst the aid models, the question remains as to whether it is possible to balance goals that seek to provide conditions which are more conducive to local and regional experiments based on autonomous, hybrid models by taking into account peoples' own models (Escobar, 1995), and the goal of healthier regimes of accumulation and development.

- The embryonic 'participatory development paradigm' holds prospects for the future but requires further analysis and application to be a convincing way ahead. In the process, it is necessary that a critical distinction be made between rhetoric and analytical and operational participatory concepts as convincingly argued by Rosander (1992)—that the further one is removed from the field, the stronger is the rhetoric about 'people's participation'!

- It is argued by development researchers in particular that current development concepts such as sustainability, participation, empowerment, ownership, etc., are unscientific. But if the concepts are used to describe issues that are widely recognized as relevant in a context which is global as much as it is local, the challenge seems to be to look for appropriate ways to interpret, operationalize and apply them until better concepts have been invented.

It is an aim of this Guide to alert the user to be critical and inventive in adopting approaches to development work based on such 'rubbery' concepts, not least the concept of participation. This rests on the assumptions that,

> development is an idea, an objective and an activity—all interrelated .... Its character and results are determined by relations of power, not by the rhetoric of fashionable populist labels such as 'participation', 'empowerment', 'civil society' or 'poverty reduction'. (Kothari and Minogue, 2002: 12–13)

'Participation' is not a technical fix but an approach which promotes democratic mechanisms and helps to deal with 'power relations'—whether these are embedded in foreign, national or local structures—*provided participation is sensibly applied.*

1.1.3 Practice, Process and Knowledge in Development Studies

Convergence in Development Work and Research

The recognized need for research and studies to enhance preparation, performance and sustainability of aid interventions, projects, programmes or policy support has fostered a profession of 'development specialists'. Generation of information about the pre-conditions and contexts, interpretation of processes of development interventions and their effects, and utilization of 'knowledge' about the impacts is the pivot for international development cooperation. Development work has become a para-scientific event, not without tensions, as indicated by McNeill (Box 1.1). There is a convergence of tasks in the development arena, but also a feeling of discomfort amongst many development researchers at finding themselves in the same compartment as the development practitioners, and discovering they have adopted the practitioners' vocabulary and 'development language' (Sørbø, 2001). The dubious quality of work by practitioners (consultants) which development agencies let pass is questioned (Vaa, 1997). The researchers are being challenged to reconsider their role and take advantage of the scope for critical studies, and not just for studies legitimizing established concepts and procedures (see Box 1.1).

The convergence between development work and research goes both ways. Development workers and practitioners increasingly demand better knowledge and up-to-date approaches to development 'paradigms'—or issues—with which they work. Repeated failures of blueprint planning have prompted an interest in and increasing adoption of alternative perspectives and approaches:

- Holistic perspectives on development issues—e.g., poverty reduction, gender equality, inclusion, accountability, sustainability, capacity, partnership, etc., including macro (global/national), meso (regional/sector) and micro (community/household) perspectives.
- Cross-disciplinary perspectives—for which appropriate methodologies are developing as important complements to methodologies applied by individual disciplines.

> **Box 1.1   Development Research—Policy-oriented and Interdisciplinary: A Challenge to Quality**
>
> A distinguishing feature of development studies is that it is very often linked, directly or indirectly, to policy—to action. This need not necessarily be the case, but experience shows that it has very largely been so. Indeed the very word 'development' has, as we know, been taken over by the development business, to the extent that not only does it have strong moral connotations (who can question that it is a good thing?), but it is also linked very closely with policies (what should countries do in order to develop?). Further, it has been so much a part of the aid business that development and aid have become almost inextricably linked, with the result that development studies have, to an excessive extent, been concerned not with the empirical study of social change, but with how aid donors can or should encourage development.
>
> But this link can be dangerous because there can be a direct conflict between the demands of good research and those of good policy.
>
> The real world is complex, as any good researcher knows. And researchers distinguish themselves not by confirming conventional wisdom, but by questioning it.
>
> Policy makers, by contrast, require that the world be very simple .... Neither the politician nor the bureaucrat wishes to be told that the world is complex. And, as busy people with lots of things to do, they are—in a sense—quite right. They are simply not able to take account of complexity....
>
> I suggest that researchers, as researchers, should be wary of policy-making. They should analyse the world as they perceive it to be, untainted by how they would like it to be. They may of course take on a role as advisers, consultants, but they should recognize that they are then crossing a line—between analysis and action—and that this is likely to draw them into unwarranted generalization, unjustified simplification. In short, being too close to policy-making constitutes a threat to good research. Policy-makers need high quality analysis carried out by good researchers, but both would do well to recognize that there is an inevitable tension, sometimes amounting even to a conflict of interest, between them.
>
> *After* McNeill, 1992.

- A demand for results and impact from interventions combine in a challenge to balance planning by objectives with getting the processes of change right.
- Interpretive iteration—i.e., continuous analysis—is accepted as a valid research method and qualitative data and information is fully accepted. Methodologies to handle and analyse qualitative data have developed considerably.
- A belief in 'popular knowledge' and experimentation with different forms of 'people's participation' in action-oriented research and development interventions provides continuous inputs to learning from development cooperation.

Alternative perspectives and approaches in development cooperation face their own challenges. As Minogue points out in his article 'Power to the People? Good Governance and the Reshaping of the State' (2002): 'Given the complex nature of the interaction of economic, social and political systems, and the varied cultural contexts this interaction produces, it is to be expected that at the very least problems of policy transfer and application will occur.' Popular participation is not a panacea.

Practice and Process Orientation and 'Popular Knowledge'

To get things moving towards participatory planning, development planners, practitioners and researchers alike have to give up one of their fundamental self-established rights—the right to define **what** the problem is, **whose** problem it is, **how** to solve it, and **why** (see Box 1.2).

Box 1.2   Whose Interpretation? Excerpts from 'The Development Game'

The Social Researcher on the Team

These people are poor. Very poor. They scratch a living without enough land or water. Every year the government distributes subsidized wheat at great expense, but many are too remote to be reached. The men have to leave their homes to look for work elsewhere. The ecology is collapsing. Because the trees have been destroyed, there are deadly mud-slides which bury villages, and floods which destroy the crops. Three and a half million Afghan refugees make the situation worse—but they are not our concern. The refugees are under separate administration and for us they hardly exist. We pass their camps and caravans, and the officials direct our attention elsewhere. We are skilled at not seeing.

The Official to the Donor

We are very interested in the mountain area. We want to do something for our people quickly. We don't want your six-year project; we want two years, three years. The people up there hardly know the government exists. They wonder what the government is doing for them. They see the refugees receiving all sorts of international aid and they wonder why they are not getting anything. It is a restless place. You should not think so small. We want to make an impact. You should be building tunnels through the mountains and making truckable roads. There are huge barren areas you could irrigate with large-scale irrigation schemes. Agricultural research and improved farming are not enough. We want results. The government is ready to move. You do not need to work it out in detail. Just release the money and we will do the rest.

The Donor to the Authorities

Look, we want to lend you the money, but one valley is not enough. One valley doesn't have the absorption capacity. We need a minimum of two valleys. We want at least a million people. Otherwise Geneva won't like it. We want to give you a project but you will have to take away some valleys from someone else and give them to us.

After Frank, 1986: 234, 238, 241 (in GRANTA, No. 20). Reprinted with permission from Granta Publications.

Conflicting perspectives on what the issues are (Box 1.2) are mirrored in different perspectives on approach. Thus, Storgaard describes how already in the late 1970s The Danish International Development Agency, Danida, together with Indian federal authorities and professional health workers, engaged in a process-oriented planning model with a 'bottom-up' approach using participatory methods for a primary health care project (Storgaard, 1991: 199).

The advantages of the process-oriented, bottom-up approach to project planning were:

- Data are collected, analysed and tested directly by the users.
- Problem-solutions can be tried out during the planning process itself.
- Appreciation of the stakeholders' problems, cultural context, possibilities and conditions of change is enhanced.
- Weaknesses and strengths are perceived by the participants directly.
- People's motivation to participate actively in project implementation is enhanced through their participation in decision-making and better understanding of the problems.

The planning model was a process that included workshops, data collection and analysis, problem analysis, preparation of recommendations and plans, new workshops, etc. Anthropological approaches inspired the model in several ways: (a) the participatory planning approach; (b) the holistic approach to problem identification, analysis and action; (c) the focus on relationships; (d) a demand for information about local people's knowledge, attitudes and practices concerning illness and health; and (e) insistence on cross-disciplinary cooperation with architects and construction engineers. One and a half years were set aside for planning the project.

With hindsight it is possible to find many explanations for why the planning model ran into difficulties and has been superseded by more conventional blueprint planning. Basically, it was a conflict between the donor's and government's demand for quick and visible results and the uncertainties involved in the flexible, process-oriented planning approach. The participatory, process-oriented planning model and research approach are gaining momentum but ambivalence is apparent from many sides (e.g., Cooke and Kothari, 2000, and Chapter 2, this book).

The concern for development problems and their solutions based on the incorporation of popular knowledge must be placed in the context of people's own expressions of identity, problems and needs. This is also a question of power relations, i.e., who has the power to define problems? To define what the facts are? (see Boxes 1.2 and 1.3).

Box 1.3   Whose Knowledge Counts?

'I know you do not know what I know, but why do you not want to know that I too know what you do not know? You may have quite a lot of book knowledge, but I still believe (*olul ok puonj dhok mit chiemo*) the anus does not teach the mouth the sweetness of food'.

This was an exasperated statement made by Mzee Joel Kithene Mhinga of Buganjo village in Northern Tanzania, after a long discussion in which I was trying to prove to him that he had got his historical facts wrong about the genesis of the Buganjo clan.

After Anacleti, 1992.

The unfolding of popular knowledge can be used for the formulation of genuine participation strategies, hence the increasing interest in the concept from designers of development projects. But participation can also be (mis)used for the purpose of legitimation (see Section 2.3). To let the voices of the people themselves be heard (e.g., Epstein, 1998; Narayan, 2000 and 2002; Stiefel and Wolfe, 1994)—for example, to let women speak for themselves as a primary source of information—was a radical break with earlier paradigms of development. To quote Wilson:

> ... we should like to argue for the primacy of the utterances and practices of Third World people themselves. Not that what they say is sacrosanct or less bound up with power relations than what we say, but because we consider it is vitally important to remember that they have the right to define themselves and what they believe (Wilson, 1990: 16).

However ambivalent development agencies and many of their partners remain with regard to the participatory planning model, repeated failures of blueprint planning models have opened up their interest in the participatory approach, though admittedly more on paper than in practice. Considerable adjustments have been made since the time when the guiding principle for participatory planning and data collection was 'popular knowledge'—equated with grass-roots knowledge. Today participatory planning means 'stakeholder participation' at all levels.

Many development researchers and practitioners have found inspiration and comfort in applying the grounded theory approach—explicitly or implicitly when generating 'data' and 'knowledge'. In grounded theory it is necessary to keep the empirical material in constant dialogue with theoretical generalization. This suits the explorative element which is part of most development studies. Research becomes an iterative process between observation and analysis, and both are influenced by the researcher's political and ideological standpoints. It is a break with the previously almost universal demand for value-free objectivity.

Another sound perspective on knowledge is increasingly reflected in development studies—the reflexivity of one's own role and its potential influence on the interpretation of observations and data.

The learning process indicates that adjustments of approaches and familiarity with practice are required, which depend, inter alia, on a better understanding of participatory techniques and tools by all parties involved. Examples and illustrations are given in this book.

1.2   Dialogue, Problem Identification and Planning Cycle

1.2.1 Problem Identification in Dialogue

The era of international development cooperation involved years of building up management and planning systems. Detailed planning, with a focus on results and physical output rather than on the development **process,** has tended to counteract flexibility and people's participation. Ironically, the increased interest in participatory planning is set within a management culture, not without consequences for how participatory development is perceived (see Chapters 2 and 3).

In the cacophony of approaches which nevertheless reign in the planning arena, there are signs that the 'planning phobia' may be relaxed in many spheres of society and substituted with flexible learning processes with more room for imagination and creativity. To give an example from social studies, Flyvbjerg's path-breaking studies (1998, 2001) call attention to a tradition long forgotten—phronetic investigation. The concept of phronesis has disappeared from contemporary social science terminology, the closest concept being 'action research'. Since the concept has much relevance to the interface between development research and practice with which this book is concerned, a short summary of the characteristics is presented in Box 1.4.

Box 1.4   Characteristics of the Science of Concreteness (Phronetic Research)

1. **Values.** Phronetic research focuses on values, asking questions like: Where are we heading? Is that desirable? What should be done?
2. **Power.** Relevant questions are: Who wins? Who loses? By which means of power? What are the prospects of changing existing power relations? Is concrete research activity itself part of a power relationship?
3. **Presence/Engagement.** The analyst seeks nearness to the subject/s of what is being studied during all phases from data collection, analysis and reporting to sharing results. Reactions, positive or negative, to one's studies are consciously sought. This creates 'stakeholders' who take an interest in the research. The analyst becomes part of the problems being researched without 'going native'. Profound empirical data from a variety of sources are required (cf. the 'Dig Where You Stand' tradition, Lindqvist et al., 1982).
4. **Minutiae.** Start by asking 'small questions'. This principle seems to contradict conventional wisdom about 'important problems' or 'big questions'. The aim is a balance between detail and generalization.
5. **Practice.** Focus is on everyday activities and practical knowledge. Practice is more fundamental than discourse and theory.
6. **Concrete Cases.** Interpretation and judgements are best drawn from profound case experience and communicated through exposure of cases.
7. **Context.** Everyday practice and cases can be understood only in the relevant context.
8. **How?** Focus is more on the dynamic question HOW? than on the structural question WHY? The result is analysed and interpreted in a process perspective.
9. **Narrative/History.** The narrative story, including actors and events, as well as the historical development perspective, are important.
10. **Actor/Structure.** Focus is on the level of actors and the level of structures and on their interrelations to get beyond dualistic interpretations.
11. **Dialogue.** A fundamental objective of the research is a contribution to practice, which expresses itself as public dialogue. There are four types of dialogue:

    - Dialogue with the subjects of study.
    - Dialogue with other analysts or researchers.
    - Dialogue with decision-makers and key persons.
    - Dialogue with the general public.

Author's interpretation of Flyvbjerg, 1992: 82–86, and 2001.

The last principle, **dialogue,** in Box 1.4 is of particular relevance in connection with problem identification. The participatory perspective maintains that 'problems' are not to be defined by 'experts', but should be based on 'dialogue'. But how far can the dialogue be taken? Must all four groups mentioned by Flyvbjerg be consulted in all circumstances? In practical terms, it is rarely possible to involve 'all persons concerned' as suggested by Altrichter (1991: 90) when he talks of situating research in a democratic context.

Exploratory trips into the field, into existing studies and into a variety of local documentation can help to focus the dialogue with parties concerned with regard to relevant research problems. In all societies a great deal of information exists from where one can start exploration and focusing a study. The 'Dig Where You Stand' (Lindqvist et al., 1982) approach has been mentioned, where oral sources of information in countries in the South are an important supplement (Sillitoe et al., 2002; Vansina, 1985).

If research is not assigned as it is in project-related studies, the first step in problem identification can be to settle on some general area: migration, patron/client networks, selectivity in education, etc. Certain topics are more popular at one period than at another, either because a breakthrough in these seems to be more possible or necessary than in other areas, or because they are simply fads. It is relatively easy to jump on to a bandwagon, to decide to study what many others are studying. A topic that rouses interest and concern in the society to be studied may be a better criterion.

What, then, are 'good' research problems? It depends on the **type** of research, i.e., on the purpose (see Chapters 4 and 5). Sophie Laws (2003), Neuman (2003) and Boolsen (2004) provide a number of ideas and questions to test whether a research problem is good. Enderud's formulation still holds: 'Generally we may say that good research problems are **critical** and **creative** in regard to existing practices. They ask **new, unexpected** and often **provocative** questions about the existing situation and about how improvements can be obtained' (Enderud, 1984: 95, emphasis mine).

A criterion for the development researcher's choice of topic should be that it must be sufficiently flexible to incorporate interests other than his/her private ones. A minimum common understanding of the relevance of a research problem is required, e.g., between the analyst and local researchers, planners or people who will be affected by and involved in the research.

In the field of international development cooperation, *apart from research*, there is a call for a process approach and people's participation. Experience is building up and it is important for development workers and researchers alike to be alert to the current trends and participate in the formulation of adequate approaches. Development agencies (e.g., Oxfam, Save the Children, DFID, World Bank) are increasingly becoming trend setters in **how** development cooperation and related studies are undertaken. Their methodological conditionalities aside, it should be the obligation of everyone engaged in international development cooperation to participate in continuous critical assessments of the approaches applied. Practice prompts experience, which needs to be shared to continuously inform and improve development cooperation.

While experience is being gathered from the scattered experiments with process-oriented, participatory and bottom-up forms of international development cooperation, it is necessary to be well acquainted with the current planning tools. Important alternative approaches to problem identification—and solution—such as the Appreciative Inquiry Approach introduced in Chapter 6 are gaining momentum. Yet development workers should be well acquainted with the *planning cycle* concept and with the *objectives-oriented planning model*, the *Logical Framework Approach*. It is still in the context of these that participatory development is most often practised.

1.2.2 The Planning Cycle and Objectives-oriented Planning

With slight variation and increasing flexibility, the step-wise planning cycle and the Logical Framework Approach are still predominant tools in development cooperation. This despite escalating critique over several decades. They are based on the assumption that,

> Inadequate planning is a persistent fundamental problem in international development aid. Planning documents are often specific and clear as to the physical and financial inputs, personnel, activities and expected physical results. But thorough assessment of the overall objectives, the target groups and the external factors which determine success or failure is often lacking.... Donor organizations repeatedly urge improved planning and project preparation with more emphasis on monitoring, analysis and evaluation during the lifetime of the projects. There is ample evidence to show that a modest investment in improved planning usually pays off in terms of better projects and direct savings (NORAD, 1990: 3).

The Logical Framework Approach, LFA, an objectives-oriented planning tool, was developed in response to some of these problems. The 'logical framework' method is a way of structuring the main elements in a planning process, be this a project or a programme, a policy or strategy, highlighting logical linkages between inputs, planned activities and expected process. The LFA has also introduced 'external factors', assumptions and risks into the planning process (see Box 1.5). This is an important element towards appreciating the importance of *context* and the complexity of societal processes within which development interventions are set. It is a supplement to the project/planning cycle which divides development work into discrete phases (Figure 1.1). Beginning in the 1990s, it was repeatedly claimed by many who work in the field of development that the project focus entails a risk of misconceiving development problems. 'Projects' are influenced by a variety of context-specific factors, ranging from global relations, national policies, interventions by other national or international agencies, to capacities of implementing agencies, and people's interests and attitudes of those in power to decide which interventions are promoted. Projects are artificial units that follow dynamics other than that of the development process in the surrounding society, and yet influence these. It may be possible to integrate a project into a wider development process. This is attempted by development planners, but many of the influential factors remain outside the control of project planners. Institutional reforms, legislative adjustments, etc., are, for example, often identified as necessary elements in addressing a specific development problem, but hard to influence through project support.

To better cope with these problems of project support, Sector Programme Support (SPS) was adopted as an aim for transition by the leading development agencies in the 1990s.

The Sector Programme Support strategy has the following main features:

- relates directly to national sector policies
- focuses on broader-scale capacity development and a longer-term cooperation perspective of 10–20 years

- relates or provides support to various levels in the sector (macro, meso, and micro)
- enables partners to be fully accountable (national ownership and adaptation of aid to national financial management systems, for example)
- applies various modalities of support (e.g., training, technical assistance, operation and maintenance support, investments, commodity and budget support)
- offers room for flexibility within an agreed set of objectives, areas of support, and procedures
- provides effective coordination by the national partner of support from various donors
- provides scope for reduction of the number of external assumptions made for the support, thereby internalizing and addressing risks as part of the SPS.

(*After* Ministry of Foreign Affairs, Danida, 1996 and 1998)

Figure 1.1   The Project/Programme Cycle

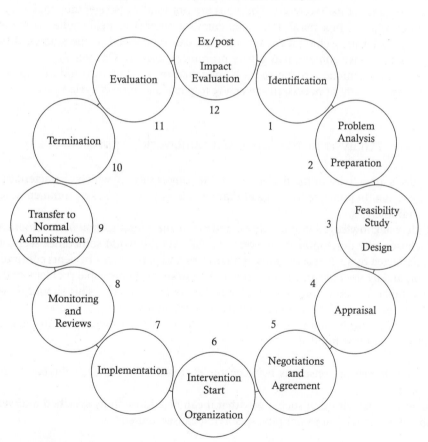

After Hvidt, 1987.

It is realized that the transition from project to sector programme support—called the Sector Wide Approach, SWAP, by some, will take time. After the first decade of harvesting experience, it has become clear that flexibility is required in this area too.

Despite these caveats and overall strategy changes, the concepts and vocabulary used in development planning and in many types of field studies are constructed with the 'project' as the focal concept. Hence, it is still relevant to introduce 'the project cycle', using the word 'project' to signify different types of development interventions, including projects with a defined objective, sector programmes, studies, etc.

Care should be taken when using project/programme cycle terminology because there is no fully consistent project/planning cycle terminology between donor organizations. Some use the word 'evaluation' instead of 'appraisal' (early assessment); others call it 'monitoring', 'review' or 'evaluation', etc. At the same time the individual agencies tend to insist that only their own terminology be used by practitioners.

Figure 1.1, the *project/programme cycle,* shows 12 steps which are typically applied in planning and implementing development interventions. The steps are not totally discrete; they may vary in duration and the cycle may continue in a spiral. Each step entails a number of field studies, some of which are presented with the relevant techniques and tools that can be applied in the studies. *Monitoring* and *evaluation*, for example, have come to play a very prominent role (see Chapter 7).

Participatory study techniques are increasingly made use of in all phases, and examples are given in the remaining chapters without necessarily referring to particular project cycle steps.

1.2.3 Problem Analysis in the Logical Framework Approach

Problem analysis is an activity in the project cycle, the importance of which characterizes the Logical Framework Approach. In principle the Logical Framework Approach gives a prominent role to problem identification and analysis.

It is now widely acknowledged that top-down and erroneous identification of development problems is one of the causes why development interventions fail. Yet the world sometimes seems to carry on, more or less unaffected by such observations, with donors and partner governments continuing to define *where*, for *whom*, and by *what* means to intervene in development. In principle problem analysis can and should be undertaken by representatives of all stakeholders in a project. This should be kept in mind when the LFA is discussed below in connection with problem analysis.

A set of methods for problem analysis has been developed which ensures that, in theory, two fundamental requirements can be fulfilled:

1. A minimum degree of consensus between the stakeholders over what the basic problem to be addressed is.
2. The problem is formulated in such a way that it can be addressed by specified interventions—i.e., the problem is analysed in its entirety, specifying causes and effects.

The LFA can be explained as consisting of activities which enhance planning, analysis of and communication about development interventions. Four sets of activities concentrate on analysis, three on design:

Analysing the Situation
1. Participation analysis (Stakeholder analysis)
2. Problem analysis
3. Objectives analysis
4. Alternatives analysis/Strategy formulation

Designing the Project
5. Identification of project elements
6. Identification of external factors
7. Identification of indicators

To go through all these activities—first identifying the most direct and essential causal relationships, followed by intervention design—is a major task, which is sometimes called the LFA workshop. It is during the workshop exercises that the participants seek to reach a common understanding of *what* the problem to be addressed is, *how* and under *which constraints*. Not only should local stakeholders be represented in the LFA workshop, but the workshop should also be a multidisciplinary event. Inputs from people of different disciplines contribute to a broader analysis of the situation. The joint exercise of preparing an intervention/project matrix entails a clarification of problems, objectives, constraints, etc., which has shown to minimize problems at a later stage, when decisions have to be taken on what to monitor and evaluate. The matrix is the condensed outcome of the LFA workshop. Box 1.5 summarizes the generic elements of the matrix.

The mandate of the LFA workshop may often be restricted to one specific sector programme, e.g. water and sanitation, including policy and sub-projects, or be conducted in connection with one particular project. Whatever the case, problem analysis is the major stepping stone for determining the approach of the particular project or programme.

Box 1.6, Problem Analysis, illustrates that problems must be formulated in a particular way in order to be 'researchable' or for action to be taken vis-à-vis. *A problem is not the absence of a solution but an existing negative state.* The 'cards' referred to in Box 1.6 are the building elements of a problem tree (see Figure 1.2).

The formal requirements of the definition of a problem extend to identification of the cause-effect relationship. Figure 1.2 shows a very simple problem tree. The focal or core problem is placed at the centre. The substantial and direct causes of the core problem are placed below it, and the direct effects are placed above.

The preparation of the problem tree has several purposes:

1. It clarifies for the participants what they themselves think are the main cause-effect relationships characterizing the problem.
2. In the objectives analysis, the problem tree is transformed into a tree of objectives (future solutions of the problems), and analysed. The problems are reformulated as positive statements. Figure 1.3 shows how the problem tree is turned into a means-end relationship.
3. The problem tree, constructed on the basis of brainstorming and card sorting, gives a picture of the complexity of problems.

Box 1.5 The Elements of the Logical Framework Matrix

1. Goal
The higher-level objective towards which the project/intervention is expected to contribute
(Mention target groups)

1. Indicators
(Objectively Verifiable)
Measures (direct or indirect) to verify to what extent the development objective is fulfilled
(Means of verification should be specified)

1. Assumptions
Important events, conditions or decisions necessary for sustaining objectives in the long run

2. Purpose
The effect which is expected to be achieved as the result of the project/intervention.
(Mention target groups)

2. Indicators
Measures (direct or indirect) to verify to what extent the immediate objective is fulfilled.
(Means of verification should be specified)

2. Assumptions
Important events, conditions or decisions outside the control of the project/intervention, which must prevail for the development objective to be attained

3. Outputs
The results that the project/intervention management should be able to guarantee.
(Mention target groups)

3. Indicators
Measures (direct or indirect) which verify to what extent the outputs are produced.
(Means of verification should be specified)

3. Assumptions
Important events, conditions or decisions outside the control of the project/intervention management, necessary for the achievement of the immediate objective.

4. Activities
The activities that have to be undertaken by the project/intervention in order to produce the outputs.

4. Assumptions
Important events, conditions or decisions outside the control of the project/intervention management necessary for the production of the outputs

5. Inputs
Goods and services necessary to undertake the activities.

After NORAD, 1990, 1999: 17.

No further elaboration of the Logical Framework Approach will be attempted here. The main purpose was to show how problems and issues can be analysed in a stringent way by the use of this approach. It is not always easy to comply with the rules, e.g., rules for the formulation of problem cards which require that a problem be stated as an existing state, and not as the absence of a solution. Nor does the LFA matrix in its raw form indicate the many different analyses which a particular intervention, for example a sector programme, requires: *Technology Analysis, Organizational and Institutional Analysis,*

Box 1.6   Problem Analysis

How to formulate problems:
1. Identify **existing** problems—not possible, imagined or future ones.
2. A problem is not the absence of a solution, but an existing **negative state**.

   Example:
   No pesticides are available: **Wrong**
   Crop is infested with pests: **Right**

3. Only one problem per card.

After NORAD, 1990: 35.

Economic and Financial Analysis, Environmental Assessment, Socio-economic Analysis, Analysis of Gender Issues, Analysis of Human Rights, Good Governance, and Democratization/Participation Aspects (Ministry of Foreign Affairs, Danida, 1998).

Figure 1.2   Problem Analysis from a Bus Project

a. Problem Analysis
(Cause-effect relationship)

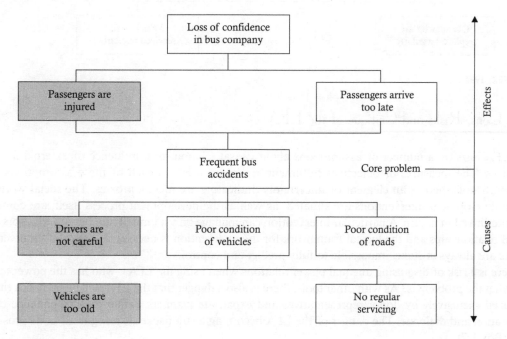

After GTZ, 1991: 8.

Figure 1.3   Objectives Analysis from a Bus Project

b. Objectives Analysis
(Means-end relationship)

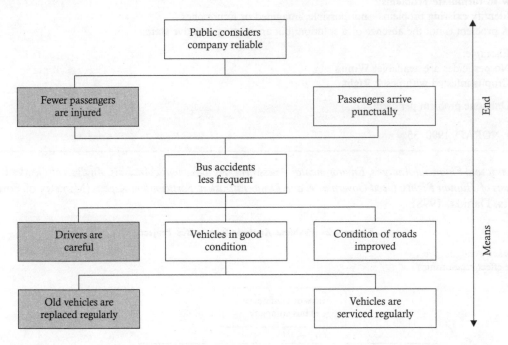

After GTZ, 1991: 9.

Pros, Cons, Risks and Critique of the LFA

The LFA rests on a number of assumptions about causal relationships, influence of external factors, and risks. The measures of objectives fulfilment are 'indicators'. In each of these assumptions and choice of tools there is an element of uncertainty. Indicators are merely proxies. The social world in which development interventions are situated, as well as the development process itself, are complex and interlinked in nature. A particular intervention can manage only a limited number of indicators and causal relationships and the logical framework for the intervention is necessarily selective. Intervening factors are always at stake, impossible to fully predict and control.

There is a risk of disguising unequal power relations when using the LFA—who has the power to define what the problem is? As with other tools, there is also a danger that the LFA will be used as a ritual, and used exclusively by donor representatives and expatriate planners, rather than to enhance communication and dialogue. The danger of the LFA becoming a straitjacket is recognized in its pros and cons (Box 1.7).

Box 1.7   The Pros and Cons of the Logical Framework Approach, LFA

The Advantages of Using LFA are the Following:

1. It ensures that fundamental questions are asked and weaknesses are analysed in order to provide decision-makers with better and more relevant information.
2. It guides systematic and logical analysis of the interrelated key elements which constitute a well designed project.
3. It improves planning by highlighting linkages between project elements and external factors.
4. It provides a better basis for systematic monitoring and analysis of the effects of projects.
5. It facilitates common understanding and better communication between decision-makers, managers and other parties involved in the project.
6. Management and administration benefit from standardized procedures for collecting and assessing information.
7. The use of LFA and systematic monitoring ensures continuity of approach when original project staff are replaced.
8. As more institutions adopt the LFA concept, it may facilitate communication between governments and donor agencies.
9. Widespread use of the LFA format makes it easier to undertake both sectoral studies and comparative studies in general.

The Limitations of LFA are the Following:

1. Rigidity in project administration may arise when objectives and external factors specified at the outset are over-emphasized. This can be avoided by regular project reviews where the key elements can be re-evaluated and adjusted.
2. LFA is a general, analytic tool. It is policy-neutral on questions of income distribution, employment opportunities, access to resources, local participation, cost and feasibility of strategies and technology, or effects on the environment.
3. LFA is therefore only one of several tools to be used during project preparation, implementation and evaluation, and it does not replace target-group analysis, cost-benefit analysis, time planning, impact analysis, etc.
4. The full benefits of utilizing LFA can be achieved only through systematic training of all parties involved and methodological follow-up.

After NORAD, 1990: 8.

A major weakness of the LFA is the danger that it could be turned into the 'experts' tool of control'. The LFA is not an optimal tool for coping with power relations, different interests and diverging interpretations of development problems. It does not necessarily contradict the people-oriented principles and interactive study approaches which have been mentioned above and which are described in more detail in the following chapters. However, it has a particular aim, i.e., to plan according to well-defined objectives—a principle which, if strictly retained, may block the flexibility that has been advocated. The odd highly skilled development planner may be able to detect the inherent contradictions between these principles and avoid clashes by ensuring participatory approaches to the LFA, for example. Instead, experience shows that the LFA tends to become another management tool in the hands of development planners, removed from the potential users of a project.

After these introductory comments on issues and approaches in development cooperation, the following sections should guide the utilization of the book.

1.3   Target Groups, Readership and Terminology

1.3.1 Target Groups

The methods illustrated in this book may be embryonic, in the making and in the process of being tried out in real life situations, but the potentials of different field work methodologies, in particular the different participatory methods, justify dissemination to a larger audience, to the benefit of many types of development work. For the greater benefit of the reader, guidance is given on data generation and analysis, and on conduct when doing development work and research.

The book is written with students in mind who are prospective development workers or researchers and for junior development planners and practitioners. The main target groups of this book are:

- Development researchers, especially from disciplines where field work methodologies are only sporadically taught.
- Development workers, including staff of bilateral and multilateral aid organizations and NGO personnel, consultants and others who will be working for shorter or longer periods with field studies and who need or want to investigate particular problems.

It is believed that the book will be useful for development researchers, planners and practitioners in the South as well as in the North.

Development planners and practitioners can use the book as inspiration and as a source book for reference to more elaborate texts and research networks. A number of more experienced development workers and researchers would look for more sophisticated writings to satisfy their needs. It is largely they who have contributed with their experience to this book.

The book should be useful for teaching development studies. It provides an overview of a variety of traditional and newer field study methods and refers the reader to much additional literature. It does not replace more elaborate texts, but will serve as a supplement to the basic methodology texts of sociology, anthropology, human geography and related disciplines. International development organizations and NGOs may find parts or all of it useful for preparation courses for their field staff.

The main author is a sociologist who has worked with people from a variety of disciplines and different cultures in cross-disciplinary and cross-cultural teams, primarily in South and East Asia and Africa South of the Sahara, for several decades. Her personal experience is from development work and research with a focus on different policies, sectors and cross-cutting issues, e.g. rural infrastructure, environment, water and sanitation, education and health, poverty and gender analysis. The perspective is the social scientist's, the spirit is cross-disciplinary and cross-cultural.

The level and language anticipates a general familiarity with development terminology, and acquaintance with the basics of research vocabulary. The illustrations in the form of supporting text examples are collected from many corners of the world. These and the visualized participatory techniques, e.g. graphs, maps, diagrams, etc., should make the text more approachable.

1.3.2 Related Publications

The book has taken inspiration from a variety of sources. Foremost amongst them are theoretical presentations and reflections on the development discourse, and practical illustrations and results of development cooperation. The sources which this book resembles most are guides to research for development (e.g. Laws et al., 2003), handbooks and introductions to participatory rural appraisal, PRA methods (e.g. S. Kumar, 2002) and practical guides to development fieldwork (Scheyvens and Storey, 2003), and to planning, implementation, monitoring, evaluation and impact assessment of international development cooperation (e.g. Gosling, 2003), or to monitoring and evaluation in particular (IFAD, 2002). It differs from these by being less of a handbook and more of a contribution to a discourse on adequate methods for different types of development work and research.

Literature on participatory methods, for convenience gathered under the name Participatory Rural Appraisal, PRA sources, often go into more detailed hands-on descriptions of individual techniques than this book does. Inspiration has been gained from the collections in the 'participatory reading room' started by Robert Chambers and continued by John Gaventa at the Institute of Development Studies, IDS, at the University of Sussex, and the comprehensive collection at the International Institute for Environment and Development, IIED, London. This book does not confine itself to rapid and participatory methods, but sees them as an important adjustment of or complement to other qualitative and quantitative conventional field study methods such as formal sample surveys and participant observation. The weight of the Guide is on qualitative methods. Patton's comprehensive works on qualitative field research strategies and evaluation studies (1997 and 2002) and the classics by Denzin and Lincoln (1994 and 2000), Neuman (2003), Bauer and Gaskell (2002), Bryman (2001) and Denscombe (2003) give more detailed guidance in strategies for social research and in the use of qualitative methods and partly in structured surveys than this publication aims to do, but they have been of great inspiration.

The approach used in this book is to highlight different methods for studying selected development issues. The book alerts the reader to retain a critical perspective on different uses and misuses. A wide range of development literature is referred to in which the reader is recommended to seek further guidance.

Much of the inspiration and specific experience originates from the research and practice contexts in which the main author moves, not least from colleagues in COWI who work throughout the world, and from researchers in the South and the North associated with the Danish Institute for International Studies, DIIS (former Centre for Development Research). Many of the reports quoted reflect practical experiences in Asia, Africa and Latin America, but the wealth of experience currently being gained by NGOs and development organizations in the South is far from fully reflected. Since Scandinavia is rich in both analytical and practical experience of development research and aid, having been amongst the larger aid donors since the 1960s, frequent references are made to this. Besides, there is a substantial fund of action research in Scandinavia which has inspired this work (Nielsen, 2002).

1.3.3 Terminology

This book can be criticized head-on for applying a number of value-laden concepts from 'development language'. There are several references in the text to literature which point out the ideological and unscientific nature of the concepts we busily use in development studies. We need only mention concepts such as **development, development aid, developing country, Third World,** to be reminded of an age-old criticism of the Eurocentric definitions of central concepts. A host of concepts prevail in the development vocabulary such as **sustainability, feasibility, good governance, dialogue,** and **participation,** which suffer from these weaknesses. A newer generation of concepts suffering from similar value-laden imprecision has been added: **empowerment, capacity, ownership, partnership, primary stakeholder, transparency, poverty alleviation, cohesion, inclusion,** to mention a few. Since it is impossible to avoid the use of such rubbery concepts, the advice is to be 'transparent' about how one uses them and be explicit about how one interprets, operationalizes and applies the concepts in a given context. Ideas on how this can be done are provided throughout the Guide. An extensive elaboration of the many interpretations and applications of the concepts Monitoring and Evaluation is contained in Chapter 7.

Some of the concepts, e.g. participation, are discussed at length both in a positive and in a critical perspective in this book, since **participation and participatory** are adopted for want of better terms. They designate important field study methods, indicating approaches 'as if people matter'. Other concepts are avoided as much as possible throughout the book. Thus, 'the **South**' is used to designate 'developing', 'poor or poorer' and 'Third World' countries, while 'the **North**' designates the rich countries. This simple dichotomy is problematic, indicating 'rich' and 'poor' in material terms only, and does not capture the distributional dimensions of wealth and poverty or experienced deprivation. No systematic attempt is undertaken to substitute biased terminology with new concepts, but attention is called to the risks and pitfalls of uncritical adoption of 'nice' concepts. It is beyond the scope of this book, however necessary that task seems to be for further theoretical and methodological inventions in development cooperation. Scholars and practitioners will no doubt keep challenging hollow development jargon and substitute it with better theories, concepts and analysis. The approach used in this Guide is to alert the reader to the fact that 'development language' reflects on values and shapes our (mis)interpretation of global inequalities and what we do about them.

A few concepts require clarification:

Field study[2] designates systematic investigation of social situations and social change. It seeks answers to certain questions in a systematic way without following a strictly predetermined route of enquiry. Field study is a learning process, and in the process new questions may arise which require analysis, sometimes by unthought-of methods. Field studies are undertaken with different objectives in mind:

---

[2] The explanation of field studies and field work given here are less profound than Scheyvens and Storey's, who have dedicated their edited book to 'Development Fieldwork' (2003).

e.g., enhanced understanding of a problem, an input to policy formulation or for a particular intervention. The interpretation comes close to the French sociologist Bourdieu's (1992) use of the concept **field** (in relation to habitus), meaning a social arena within which struggles or manoeuvres take place over specific resources or stakes and over access to them. 'Fields are defined by the stakes that are at stake—cultural goods (life-style), housing, intellectual distinction (education), employment, land, power (politics), social class, prestige or whatever—and may be of differing degrees of specificity and concreteness' (Jenkins, 1992: 84).

Field studies are carried out in connection with **development research and development practice** in our terminology. Although they differ considerably in purpose, type, form, contents and duration, development research and development practice have one thing in common: they provide information about people's lives, their ways of organizing themselves and acting in society.

The **analyst** who carries out field studies is normally a **researcher.** A development researcher may be engaged in studies which aim to question conventional concepts and contribute to inventions of development theory. In this book researchers may have this role, but it is rather the researcher who is closer to **development practice** and application of results who is in mind. The development researcher is often a social scientist but may come from almost any field. The analyst may be part of a **multidisciplinary** team which studies problems in a **holistic, cross-disciplinary** perspective.

In some cases **practitioners** undertake or participate in conducting field studies, in which case they are **analysts. Practitioners** are also called **development workers** as are **development researchers** when they participate in **development work, in international development cooperation or aid work.** These phrases are used interchangeably with **development practice.** The analyst is an integral part of the field study process, i.e., an active part in the interactions and human relations that characterize the process. Besides the analyst—the researcher or practitioner—ordinary people and hired assistants can participate in data collection and analysis.

Field work is the actual process of data collection—intertwined with data analysis and possible revision of initial questions (iteration). **Field work** necessarily brings the **analyst** out of the office to engage in empirical data collection and generation (see Chapter 5), whereas **field study** encompasses a number of activities which are not confined to the 'field' but should be carried out in close contact with the field, e.g., theoretical studies, seeking a variety of relevant data sources, documentary studies, preparing instruments and tools for data collection and analysis, theoretical (re)interpretation, final analysis, reporting and dissemination of results.

Micro-level studies are sometimes used synonymously with field studies in contrast to **macro-level studies** that are concerned more with policy studies at national and international levels. The distinction is not quite consistent, since field studies may require—or provide an important input to—higher-level policy studies. Micro-level development studies are usually set in a macro-level context that includes a historical dimension. The challenge is to understand the **linkages between micro** (community, household), **meso** (regional or sector), and **macro** (national and global) **levels,** which poses special demands on the analysts' skills.

Reference literature and sources are quoted with the name of author, year of publication and page number. An *after* has been added when text or figures have been adjusted by the present author, and to indicate that a source text has been used and quoted out of its original context.

A **Glossary** of selected concepts follows after the main text.

1.3.4 Outline of the Book

The globalizing world in which current international development cooperation takes place provides for significant changes, and some continuity. Continuity is retained in much of the development planning approach: The project/programme cycle, departing from problem analysis and objectives-oriented planning, set the framework at a practical level for *how* development issues are addressed through interventions. Due to its omnipresence in development cooperation the Logical Framework Approach, LFA, is introduced in *Chapter 1: Context and Focus,* despite the considerable critique of the rational objectives-based planning 'model'. Changes from project focus to sector programme, budgetary and policy support have significant implications for where the weight is laid in development cooperation. The 'development language': dialogue, process orientation, incorporation of 'popular' knowledge, participation, etc., have taken on multiple and changing connotations in the convergence between development work and research. A new generation of value-laden concepts require explanation and transparency. From the outset it is evident that development work is riddled with paradoxes.

Participation in Development, Chapter 2, is one of the paradoxes. On the one hand participation has been taken on board in the mainstream development discourse and appears as a mandatory approach in strategies of almost all development cooperation agencies. On the other hand, participation has been crowned 'the new tyranny'. However critical one must be of a rubbery concept like participation, it is important to remember its basic meaning, i.e., people taking decisions on their own lives. For want of a better concept, participation and participatory rural appraisal, PRA, are used throughout the book after an elaborate examination of the contested concept in Chapter 2 and of the critical positions in Section 2.4. Critical positions notwithstanding, participation has potentials for reversing a top-down approach to a more democratic bottom-up approach. This requires a critical—and self-critical—approach to how participation is interpreted, applied and followed up in development work and research. Participation is not a panacea, and the participants are not just 'the grass-roots'. Familiarity with the methods, techniques and tools is vital for the practitioner to build on. For that purpose, practical applications of the 'Catalogue' of PRA methods are richly illustrated in *Chapter 3, Participatory Methods in Use*. Special attention is given to ranking and scoring methods, since these are particularly relevant for the study of social inequalities which characterize much development work. A selection of topical applications in new areas such as budget and economic analysis, technology assessment and advocacy are included.

Chapter 4, Different Types of Development Studies, moves from participation in development to alert the practitioner to how the purpose of a study and the questions asked are decisive for study design and selection of methods. Some meta science underpinnings are given. The investigator must consider whether s/he is seeking exploratory, descriptive, explanatory or action-oriented answers, for example, and then seek optimal combinations of research methods—given the constraints of time and resources. Participatory methods are often complements, rather than stand-alone approaches. With new issues coming up in the development discourse—pre- and post-crisis interventions, conflict resolution, health pandemics, etc.—basic or strategic research might help to develop the needed new knowledge. The aim is to alert the reader to basic elements and logics in the research process.

Chapter 5, Data Construction and Analysis of Qualitative Data, goes into more detail about data generation and analysis. 'Data' is the basis on which sometimes far-reaching decisions about interventions are taken, after analysis and interpretation. But data is not just data. Data can originate from many sources and take many forms. In development studies, interviews and documents are key sources of data and illustrations of data generation and analysis in these areas are provided. Attention to different theoretical frameworks helps us to pose relevant questions in a coherent way and select or construct data. Indicators, both qualitative and quantitative, are increasingly used to construct and analyse data. Attention is called to the common mistake of presenting plain data as if data themselves are the same as analysis. Qualitative studies and research require other quality criteria than conventional validity and reliability ones.

Chapter 6, Selected Development Issues and Approaches, is the place for updating central issues and approaches which are given new attention or are relatively new on the development cooperation agenda: **A rights-based approach, RBA** (Section 6.1) currently substitutes the conventional needs-based approach in several agencies. An appetizer is given of *what* RBA is and *how* it can be approached. **Poverty measures and analysis** (Section 6.2) are set in the context of the evolving agenda for addressing the overarching goal of poverty reduction within the framework of the Poverty Reduction Strategy Papers (PRSP) and Millennium Development Goals. Lessons on implementation of the **mainstreaming strategy for promotion of gender equality** (Section 6.3) highlight implications in terms of gender analysis, including identification of gender indicators. The PRSP offers a framework for integrating gender into poverty diagnostics, while gender mainstreaming is being contested in the context of an **empowerment of women** discourse.

Innovative approaches in development cooperation incorporate participatory methods in various ways (Section 6.4): **Appreciative Inquiry, AI** (Section 6.4.1) adds a constructive alternative perspective to the predominant problem focus of much development work. The **Social Capital Analysis Tool (SOCAT)** (Section 6.4.2) illustrates a combined tool where participatory methods have been incorporated to assess the role of social capital in relation to poverty reduction. Lastly, **Geomatics** (Section 6.4.3) illustrates a spatial method combining high-tech Geographic Information Systems, GIS, with anthropological methods and integration of indigenous knowledge. This genuine cross-disciplinary tool illustrates potentials in the hands of not only development planners, but also of indigenous groups, and is currently gaining momentum. The aim of the chapter is to provide the user with inspiration and rich illustrations of newer approaches, including for example cross-disciplinary approaches that combine high-tech methods with participatory ones.

The rich illustrations of *Chapter 7, Monitoring and Evaluation,* serve a similar purpose. Monitoring and Evaluation, M&E, are separate steps in the planning cycle but are treated together unless otherwise stated, since monitoring and evaluation have much in common—as management tools, a basis for learning, and in methods applied. The chapter is set in context of escalating demands for documentation of performance, accountability, results, effects and impact—some talk of an 'audit culture' and 'tyranny of evaluation'. The espistemological questions: 'What *can* be measured and what can be attributed to the ever moving target of development interventions' have prompted an interest in evaluating processes as much as outcomes. The movement seems to be from evaluation studies to streams. A variety of approaches to M&E are presented, indicator or narrative-based, for example, reflecting that there are different purposes and intellectual and practical skills required to carry out good evaluations. Guidance is provided on participatory M&E including stakeholder and beneficiary analysis, and nine cases are included to illustrate the richness and inspire the prospective evaluator.

The **ethical questions** related to doing research and intervening in society and other people's worlds are in focus in *Chapter 8*. They should concern all who participate as 'agents of change' in the process, whether as planners, practitioners and researchers, and whether expatriates or indigenous participants. It has been an age-old discussion since missionaries first paved the way for imperialist interests and anthropologists laid open the saliencies of 'primitive man and his culture'. When anthropology joined the applied sciences, the concern about ethics expressed itself in codes of conduct. Such codes may help the development practitioner to reflect on what s/he is doing to whom, but cannot solve all ethical questions. The forms of intervention are different today—some may think they are more civilized, others that they are more subtle and dangerous. At the root of our behaviour lie images of 'the others' and of 'ourselves'. The concept 'participation' itself raises the suspicion of an unequal relationship—i.e., who participates on whose conditions is not always clear. Interpretation by whom, about whom, with whom, for whom and why, are basic ethical questions in development cooperation. 'Dialogue' has the connotation of an equal relationship, but even the dialogue may be defined by the party who controls knowledge and resources.

CHAPTER

2

Development work is riddled with paradoxes. 'Participation' in development work is a particularly contested concept and approach. On the one hand participation has been taken on board in the mainstream development discourse and appears as a mandatory approach in strategies for development cooperation globally. On the other, participation has been crowned 'the new tyranny'. And in the midst of different positions practitioners are struggling with better practices for development cooperation, for example testing participatory methods and tools. The situation calls for a critical assessment of participation—how it has been used and interpreted over the last few decades. Perspectives of practitioners and of the critics as well as those of people on the ground who are involved in participatory development resound in this chapter with more concrete illustrations provided in Chapter 3. This is based on a review of different meanings of participation and strategic considerations for using participatory methods. Critical positions notwithstanding, it is maintained that 'participation is here to stay', not least because it constitutes a potential democratic mechanism where others may be weak.

2.1 Perceptions of Participation

2.1.1 Participation—A Contested Concept

The concept of participation has been subject to lengthy debates regarding its historical origin, its theoretical grounding and practical applicability, and its critical connotations. The more experienced development worker and researcher will know that 'participation' is so widely and so loosely used (like many other catchwords in development jargon), that the meaning of the concept has become blurred. Yet participation is one of the most important concepts in development cooperation because it is potentially a vehicle for different stakeholders to influence development strategies and interventions. Rather than dismissing participation for being blurred, the challenge for the development researcher and practitioner is to define what s/he means.

Some of the common meanings attached to 'participation' and 'participatory' are:

- Participation is the voluntary contribution by people in projects, but without their taking part in decision-making.
- Participation is the sensitization of people to increase their receptivity and ability to respond to development projects.

- Participation is an active process, meaning that the person or group in question takes initiatives and asserts the autonomy to do so.
- Participation is the fostering of a dialogue between the local people and the project or programme preparation, implementation, monitoring and evaluation staff in order to obtain information on the local context and on social impacts.
- Participation is the voluntary involvement of people in self-determined change.
- Participation is involvement in people's development of themselves, their lives, their environment.

This conceptual diversity indicates that 'participation' may amount to little more than a catchword devoid of real content. 'Genuine' participation, initiated and managed by people themselves, is a goal in the democratic process. But few societies rely on voluntary approaches alone to activate people for major development activities. *Coercion* and *positive motivation* are very different approaches, yet in the literature both concepts are used to designate participatory methods.

Participatory development is a relatively new frontier. Different interpretations can be expected. A precise, global definition may not emerge, nor may one even be desirable. Some clarification of the different meanings can, nevertheless, help the practitioners towards 'optimal' participation in development (see Section 2.1.4), and is necessary to justify the claim of participatory development. In other words, 'seeking clarity through specificity' helps to distinguish more or less successful participatory frameworks (Cohen and Uphoff, 1980; Uphoff et al., 1998).

The language of development rhetoric changes fast. Sometimes words prevail, regardless of whatever happens to the field reality. 'Participation' is one such word which has remained in the development discourse, perhaps because 'participation' conveniently takes on a variety of meanings (see Boxes 2.1 and 2.2).

Box 2.1   Three Main Uses of 'Participation'

There are three main ways in which 'participation' is used.

First, it is used as a *cosmetic label,* to make whatever is proposed appear good. Donor agencies and governments require participatory approaches and consultants and managers say that they will be used, and then later that they have been used, while the reality has often been top-down in a traditional style.

Second, it describes a *co-opting practice,* to mobilize local labour and reduce costs. Communities contribute their time and effort to self-help projects with some outside assistance. Often this means 'they' (local people) participate in 'our' project.

Third, it is used to describe an *empowering process* which enables local people to do their own analysis, to take command, to gain in confidence, and to make their own decisions. In theory, this means that 'we' participate in 'their' project, not 'they' in 'ours'. [It implies] a commitment to equity, empowering those who are marginalized, excluded and deprived, often especially women.

After R. Chambers, 2002b and 1995: 30.

Development practitioners generally agree that participation is inevitable in order to get nearer to lasting development results or sustainability. Consequently most development agencies and NGOs today have incorporated a participatory approach in their strategies for development cooperation. But there is no consensus on what this implies. So contested is the concept that after the first decade of practising participation, 'participation as tyranny' has been crowned as one of the recent standpoints in the discourse. What may sound as a devastating critique covers a set of legitimate challenges of the theoretical, political, conceptual and technical limitations of participation. For the proponents of participation, it seems absolutely necessary to reflect on the critique if participation is to obtain a lasting and fruitful role in development cooperation. We shall return to some of the arguments in Section 2.4 in this chapter.

2.1.2 Participation in Development—The New Mainstream 'Paradigm'?

The practical implications of a participatory approach have been expressed as follows:

> It will have to begin with the people who know most about their own livelihood systems. It will have to value and develop their knowledge and skills, and put into their hands the means to achieve self-development. This will require a reshaping of all practices and thinking associated with development assistance. In short, it will require the adoption of a new paradigm (Pretty and Guijt, 1992: 23).

What, then, has come of 'the new paradigm'? And what is in the words and the discourse 'participation in development'?

'Participation' had a renaissance in the 1990s when a whole new set of participatory methods mushroomed under the name Participatory Rural Appraisal, PRA. So widespread was the use of PRA methods with villagers that some, like Pretty and Guijt above, talked of a paradigm shift to participatory development, moving from 'things' to 'people' and reversing power relations from 'uppers' to 'lowers' (Chambers, 1995). Many put their finger on the need for a shift from top-down, blueprint development planning towards bottom-up, participatory processes led by active partners, while at the same time pointing to the pitfalls and problems in achieving participation.

While many development practitioners engaged in 'community participation', 'popular participation', 'people's participation', and similar names for involving partners and users of development interventions, others were busy sharpening the arguments *against* participation, which they saw as a populist, manipulative approach to development. Conflicting trajectories have crystallized—captured in the following quote from perspectives on participation for poverty reduction:

> For some, the proliferation of the language of *'participation' and 'empowerment'* within the mainstream is heralded as the realisation of a long-awaited *paradigm shift* in development thinking. For others, however, there is less cause for celebration. Their concerns centre on the use of participation as a legitimating device that draws on the moral authority of claims to involve the poor to place the pursuit of other agendas beyond reproach. According to this perspective, much of what is hailed as 'participation' is a mere *technical fix* that leaves inequitable global and local relations of power, and with it the root causes of poverty, unchallenged (Cornwall, 2000: 15, my emphasis).

By the turn of the millennium *participation, partnership* and *empowerment* had become central concepts in the *mainstream* development discourse (e.g., MFA/Danida, 2000; Sida, 2002; UNDP, 2003; World Bank, 2002). From constituting an alternative development approach focusing on the **micro level**—the people, the community, the grassroots—and mainly promoted by NGOs, participation and partnership are now central at the **macro level** in mainstream development policy.

In conjunction with the focus on poverty reduction over the last decade, and with it the status of development orthodoxy, participation in development has gained a new respectability and legitimacy. Participation has, so to speak, been *mainstreamed into the development policies* of many development agencies—public or private.

In practice *mainstreaming participation* puts a lot of demands on development agencies and their partners in terms of institutional reforms and methodological approaches:

> **Mainstreaming participation** means adopting the 'institutional reforms and innovations necessary to enable full and systematic incorporation of participatory methodologies into the work of the institution so that meaningful primary stakeholder participation becomes a regular part of a project and policy development, implementation and evaluation' (Long, 1999: 11 in Blackburn et al., 2000).

The assumption seems to be that if development cooperation takes place in a participatory partnership at a state to state level, then the external donor partner can assume that the 'recipient' government will also incorporate the local level, the civil society and the poor and marginalized groups in a participatory manner, promoting democratization and sustainable development (Buch-Hansen, 2002). This assumption is translated into an explicit approach in the most recent omnipresent policy for international development cooperation, the Poverty Reduction Strategy Papers, PRSPs.[1]

The centrality which participation has acquired in the mainstream development discourse prompts a number of questions: What is actually meant by participation? Have the perceptions changed? What are the benefits—and for whom—of a participatory approach? How can 'quality' participation be practised? Which costs and constraints are involved, not only in terms of resources but also in terms of people's dignity, independence, etc.? Such questions are behind the following sections with the intention to help development practitioners reflect on the justifications, precautions and possible approaches to take when engaging in development work and research.

2.1.3 Perspectives Over Time of Participation in Development Cooperation

A series of changing perceptions of participation in the development discourse can be identified over the decades. They mirror the fact that participation is perceived by some as a paradigm shift and by others as a technical fix (Box 2.2).

---

[1] Countries that are involved in the World Bank and IMF-initiated Poverty Reduction Strategy Paper, PRSP, process (World Bank, 2002) or relate to its forerunner, the UNDP-led Poverty Strategies Initiative, PSI, have adopted participation in various ways, e.g., as Participatory Poverty Assessments (see Chapter 3).

Box 2.2   Changing Perceptions of Participation in Development Cooperation

1960s: Sharing of technologies transferred from outside was considered participation. 'Self-help' groups attract attention.

1970s: 'Popular participation' of the poor and excluded to gain access to and control over development resources and benefits. There are three major perspectives:

1. People participate as the 'beneficiaries' of development and are called upon to help make contributions to interventions so as to increase the effectiveness. Participation is done *for* people: it often consists in people being invited to take part in consultative processes and enjoined to play a role in shouldering costs for their own good.
2. Participation is seen as a process owned and controlled *by* those whom development is supposed to benefit. As such, it can be associated with broader struggles for democracy and equity, in which the otherwise excluded participate in order to gain rights over and entitlements to resources.
3. Participation involves working *with* people, rather than for them. This perspective emphasizes the need for a closer relationship between those who work in development and those whom it is intended to benefit.

1980s: 'Projects with people' and a rapid rise in popularity of the use of participatory approaches in projects and programmes. The perspective entails significant methodological innovations to promote the concept and practice of participation. There are two 'schools':

1. *Methods promoted by official agencies:* Stakeholder analysis, social analysis, beneficiary assessment, logical framework analysis. Essentially toolkits applied by planners and implementers to promote participation by primary or secondary stakeholders in pre-identified initiatives.
2. *Methods promoted by the 'participatory development' school:* The Participatory Rural Appraisal (PRA) family of methods: RRA, PRA, PLA, PALM, etc. Essentially tools to enable people to share, enhance and analyse their knowledge of life and conditions, to plan and to act.

1990s: Participation is viewed more as a partnership, coordination or ownership of programmes leading towards people's control over their resources. Significant shifts of emphasis in mainstream discourses on participation move participation debates beyond the bounds of 'the community', from beneficiary to stakeholder and customer. 'Empowerment' is recast to also mean liberation from an interventionist state, providing a link between 'popular participation' and economic liberalization. 'Scaling out' and 'scaling up' of participation suggest a growing acceptance of an alternative approach to development. Examples from the wide spectrum of perspectives on participation are:

1. Participation is a process through which stakeholders influence and share control over development initiatives, decisions and resources which affect them (World Bank).
2. Participation is intimately bound up with politicized questions of exclusion, rights and control, and with relations of power (ODA/DFID).
3. Participation is a democratic right—personal and cultural dimensions are central for democratic change (Sida).

(Box 2.2 contd)

(Box 2.2 contd)

2000–present: With the move away from projects towards sector programmes and macro policy environments, participation also moves from the micro towards the meso (sector) and macro levels. Forms of 'invited participation' multiply, expanding into spheres—such as policy reform—once virtually closed off to legitimate public involvement. 'Participation *in* the project cycle' is contested by 'participation *outside* the project cycle'—for advocacy. Participation is being *mainstreamed* and institutionalized.

Author's Extension of Cornwall, 2000.

Looking at these changes over time, attention is called to a compelling emerging storyline: One in which consensus on the importance of participation gradually grew and spread from the margins of development practice to the very heart of the development mainstream (Cornwall, 2000). From being linked to projects, and focused mainly on rural development, participation is now linked to larger issues of policy and governance. Tracing discourses of participation reveals both the striking *similarities* (e.g., participation for efficiency and effectiveness) and just as striking *differences* (e.g., participation as a right to inclusion and to counter inequalities) that emerge in the way key terms and concepts of participation have come to be redefined. Participation interpreted as a right, for example, is a perspective forcefully advocated by Ferguson (1999). She argues that people cannot realize things like the right to health unless they can also exercise their democratic right to participate in decision-making processes about service provision. Participation becomes a prerequisite for other claims, and is seen as a basic human right (see also Chapter 6, Section 6. 1).

Efforts in the past decade to bring participation into the development mainstream have yielded a rich harvest of learning. However, a closer inspection of the uses and understanding of participation and associated terms such as 'empowerment' reveals that there is no one a priori strategy for *who* participates in the development mainstream, in *what, why* they participate, and *how,* and on *which conditions.* But quite a bit is known about the opportunities and constraints of participatory approaches to development, some of which are related to how participatory methods are being used.

2.1.4 Different Strategies and Interests in Participation

Before turning to the more specific uses of participatory methods it should be recalled that participatory approaches are used for many purposes. Clarification of purpose is a must to decide on a relevant approach to a given development activity and to foresee possible conflicts of interest. A few analytical tools on different types of participation and interests in participation may assist the practitioner in clarifying the relevance of applying a participatory approach (Boxes 2.3 and 2.4).

It has been common practice to make a distinction between participation as a *means* (*instrumental participation*) to improve development activities, making development interventions more effective and sustainable by involving the users, or participation as an *end* in itself (*transformational participation*), ensuring people's influence on their own situation as *empowerment* (Oakley and Marsden, 1991). As an analytical distinction this may be useful, but in practice the distinction between instrumental and transformational participation often turns out to be less relevant since participation as a goal of democratic involvement and as a means to enhance effective development can be pursued at the same time (e.g., MFA, 1999/11).

More elaborate typologies have been developed, most of them building on the instrumental–transformational dichotomy. Thus, Pretty et al. (1995) developed a 'scale' of seven stages based on experience with participation in rural development projects and research, each stage describing varying levels of involvement of the community. If at all different types of participation are made explicit in specific studies, exercises or programmes, reference is very often to Pretty's seven 'stages' (e.g., Mikkelsen et al., 2002). Lessons from concrete cases show, however, that the 'scale' can usefully be supplemented with other categories, i.e., participation as 'Catalysing change', 'Optimum participation' and 'participation as manipulation' (Box 2.3):

Box 2.3   A Typology of People's 'Participation' in Development

1. Passive participation

People participate by being told what is going to happen or has already happened, with no ability to change it. The information being shared belongs only to external professionals.

2. Participation in information giving

People participate by answering questions posed by extractive researchers and developers. People do not have the opportunity to influence proceedings, as the findings of the research are neither shared nor checked for accuracy.

3. Participation by consultation

People participate by being consulted, and external people listen to views. External professionals define both problems and solutions, and may modify these in the light of people's responses. The consultative process does not concede any share in decision-making, and professionals are under no obligation to take on board people's views.

4. Participation for material incentives

People participate by providing resources such as labour and land, in return for food, cash or other material incentives. People have no stake in prolonging activities when the incentives end.

5. Functional participation

People participate by forming groups or committees which are externally initiated. Groups/committees are seen as means to achieve predetermined goals. The groups tend to be dependent on external initiations and facilitators, but may eventually become self-dependent.

6. Interactive participation

People participate by being involved in analysis and development of action plans, for example. Participation is seen as a right and not just as a mechanical function. Groups may be formed and together with partners (donor agencies) make use of systematic and structured learning processes. Groups take control over local decisions, and so people have a stake in maintaining structures or practices.

(Box 2.3 contd)

(Box 2.3 contd)

7. Self-mobilization
People participate by taking initiatives to change systems independent of external institutions, although the latter can help with an enabling framework. They retain control over how resources are used. Such self-initiated mobilization and collective action may or may not challenge existing inequitable distribution of wealth and power.
After Pretty et al., 1995.

To the above types of participation the following 'categories' can be added:

8. Catalysing change
The involvement and stakes of community members in influencing others in the environment to participate and initiate change.
After IFAD, 2001.

9. 'Optimum' participation
'Optimum' participation indicates the need to focus closer attention on the different contexts and purposes in order to determine what form of participation makes sense. Paying closer attention to who actually participates in 'participatory' initiatives and who does not, either through exclusion or self-exclusion, may also help determine strategies to optimize the difference externally-initiated participation can make to the lives of the poor and excluded.
After Cornwall, 2000.

10. Manipulation
A pretence of involvement, but no real power, e.g., to 'people's representatives on a board or committee, who are outnumbered by external agents'. 'Participation is a new and more subtle form of manipulation.'
After Rahnema, 1992.

The typology of participation can function as a useful analytical tool as long as it is taken for no more than a description of ideal types. The 7-stage 'scale' of participation has been criticized for attaching values to the different types of participation—with self-mobilization indicating the best form of participation—forgetting that in real life situations there are a number of constraints on who participates and on what type of participation is possible. It is not always possible to choose between such ideal types. The focus, theory and questions of a particular study, for example, influence which categories of participation are relevant (see Chapter 5). Thus the 'Best Practice' study on Community-Driven Rural Development for the Inter-American Development Bank, used four participation categories: (*i*) Eliciting or *gathering information;* (*ii*) *consultation;* (*iii*) *active participation;* (*iv*) *empowerment* (Dahl-Østergaard et al., 2003). The scope and context of a particular intervention likewise influence what is 'optimum' participation. The categories signal different levels of participation, but level is different from quality of participation.

A point to remember when using categories of participation as those included in Box 2.3 is that the categories are not discrete stages or 'degrees' of participation. For example, in the evaluation of Mainstreaming Gender Equality in Swedish development cooperation in Nicaragua, South Africa and

Bangladesh (Mikkelsen et al., 2002), the evaluation team found that participation was rarely implemented as a conscious strategy. By default it happens that many interventions apply 'participation in information giving' and as 'consultations', while 'functional participation' is registered where an intervention-design requires the formation of user groups. This was, for example, the case in the non-formal literacy programme for urban working children in Bangladesh, which requires that parents or guardians participate in 'functional' groups. Participation initiated by the parents and guardians themselves in such groups was rare. When the guardians did participate in 'functional' groups, it fulfilled the expectation on the part of the external agency, Sida, that guardian groups were to be formed. At the same time participation also contributed to the guardians having influence on decisions and resulted in more satisfaction and better quality of the non-formal education centres.

Like this example of 'functional' participation in guardian groups, development cooperation during the 1980s and 1990s bear witness to much externally-initiated participation. With the concern for *sustainability* starting in the 1980s grew the concern for local institutional development and resulted in the formation of user groups around natural resources management, health care services, water supply, etc. Scores of new informal 'institutions' were created: From sector specific user groups to village development committees to ad hoc groups for appraisals or evaluations—each sector and each donor establishing its own groups. For many communities the expectations of their participation in many different groups has been overwhelming. In positive cases participation has contributed to opening up avenues for influence over development interventions for men and women who were previously excluded from participating in decisions. On the other hand, externally initiated participation in many cases resulted in token participation only, not least of women committee members. Box 2.4 points to different—and sometimes conflicting—interests in participation:

Box 2.4 A Typology of Interests in Participation			
Form of participation	What 'participation' means to the implementing agency	What 'participation' means for those on the receiving end	What 'participation' is for (the purpose)
Nominal	Legitimization—to show they are doing something	Inclusion—to retain some access to potential benefits	Display
Instrumental	Efficiency—to limit funders' input and make projects more cost-effective	Cost—of time spent on project-related labour and on other activities	As a means to achieving cost-effectiveness and local facilities
Representative	Sustainability—to avoid creating dependency	Leverage—to influence the shape of the project and its management	To give people a voice in determining their own development
Transformative	Empowerment—to enable people to make their own decisions, work out what to do and take action	Empowerment—to be able to decide and act for themselves	Both as a means and an end, a continuing dynamic
After Nilsson and Woodford-Berger, 2000.			

In development cooperation, participation has come to be seen as both a central project tool and a key outcome of the wider process of social and political transformation. Some have developed guidelines (e.g., World Bank, 1996). It is more surprising that some development agencies which advocate a participatory approach have little to say on *how* they interpret and intend to promote participation in sector programming and partnership cooperation (MFA, 2000, 2003). Participatory planning, research and evaluation have become part of the standard vocabulary in several governmental as well as non-governmental organizations. But often it remains a declared approach which is left to ad hoc measures. A minimum requirement for development planners to decide on optimal approaches and for practitioners to support implementation is to have knowledge of different participatory methods.

2.2   Participatory Methods, Techniques and Tools

2.2.1   Multiple Terminology and Sources

Many names have been coined by individual practitioners and organizations for the participatory methods and activities in which they engage.[2] More than 20 phrases and acronyms were already counted for these related concepts in IIED sources a decade ago (Cornwall et al., 1992; RRA Notes, 13). Some have been abandoned, and new ones adopted. NGOs in particular have developed a certain pietism around such concepts when they represent the organization's ideological stance.

However reluctant one is to be accused of using blurred and imprecise development jargon and ambiguous concepts, the lack of imagination in creating and naming new concepts forces one to adopt a language which is understood by colleagues and others in the 'development community' (but not necessarily by other people). Participatory rural appraisal, PRA, is one such unavoidable concept in development language. Ironically, PRA need not be **rural**; PRA need not be **appraisal**—the 'A' may equally well refer to **assessment, analysis** or **activity.** And 'participatory' covers different forms.

Participatory Rural Appraisal **(PRA)** (Chambers, 1994, 1997), now more commonly known as Participatory Learning and Action **(PLA)**, is a set of tools and techniques for gathering, sharing, and analysing information, and for planning and action. They are 'participatory' as they involve a number of people other than the researcher him-or-herself in the research process. These other participants can be different 'stakeholders' (see Section 2.3.3) in the outcome of the research and actions. Analysis of difference is an

---

[2] There were the previously popular 'rapid' approaches, e.g., Rapid Rural Appraisal (RRA) and Rapid Assessment Procedures (RAP). There are community-based decision making techniques—Participatory Rural Appraisal (PRA), Participatory Appraisal and Learning Methods (PALM), Participatory Learning and Action (PLA), Self-esteem, Associative Strengths, Resourcefulness, Action Planning and Responsibility (SARAR), and Participatory Assessment Monitoring and Education (PAME). Workshop-based methods include Appreciation-Influence-Control (AIC), Logical Framework Analysis (LFA), Appreciative Inquiry (AI), Strengths, Weaknesses, Opportunities and Threats (SWOT) workshops. Acronyms have also been given to different stakeholder consultation methods—Beneficiary Assessment (BA) and Systematic Client Consultation (SCC), and supplementary techniques of Social Assessment (SA) and Gender Analysis (GA).

important underlying theme of participatory learning and action. For the same reason PRA/PLA methods are particularly relevant to the study of social differentiation—exclusion/inclusion and access, deprivation/entitlement, poverty reduction, gender *in*equality and empowerment, human rights, conflict prevention and resolution, to mention a few areas.

Sources of information about participation and development and participatory methods are many,[3] judging by the multiplicity of terms in the participation discourse. The flexibility associated with participatory learning and action has led to the invention and further development of a variety of participatory methods, techniques and tools, of which the core methods are captured in the 'Catalogue' of PRA methods (Box 2.5).

Though many names exist, PRA is the best-known acronym for participatory methods, and is used throughout this book as a generic term, except when specification of particular techniques and tools are vital.

2.2.2 'Catalogue' of Participatory PRA Methods

PRA (Participatory Rural Appraisal) techniques have proved to be of much use in diagnosing specific problems and highlighting possible solutions. Little by little they have come to fill the PRA 'tool-box'. Some methods and techniques have been successfully applied in so many contexts that their persistence justifies their inclusion in a 'catalogue' of PRA methods (see Box 2.5).

Box 2.5   'Catalogue' of Selected PRA Methods, Techniques and Tools

Participatory Data Collection, Data Analyses and Communication Techniques:

1. **Review of secondary sources**
   - Documents, statistics, reports, books, files, aerial photos, maps

2. **Direct observation**

3. **Key indicators**
   - Local, national and global indicators
   - Objectives, performance, outcome and process indicators

4. **Semi-structured interviews**
   - Key individuals
   - Focus groups, homogeneous or mixed groups
   - Chain of interviews, probing questions

(Box 2.5 contd)

---

[3] (1) Lessons from applying participation in practice are reflected in a mushrooming range of publications and recorded in bibliographies, articles and on websites (Andreassen and Mikkelsen, 2003); (2) Written and visual documentation is extensive in the South and North—e.g., at IDS Participation Group, Sussex, and the Participation Resource Centre at the International Institute for Environment and Development, London and Dakar; and (3) Debates on participation are kept alive in large electronic fora (Learning Participation Network, IDS, 2002–ongoing).

(Box 2.5 contd)

5. **Ranking and scoring**
   - Scoring and ranking of options
   - Matrix scoring and ranking
   - Well-being or wealth ranking

6. **Construction and analysis of maps, models and diagrams**
   - Social and resource maps
   - Topic and theme maps
   - Census maps and models
   - GIS-based aerial maps
   - Transects

7. **Diagramming**
   - Causal, linkage and flow diagrams
   - Force field analysis
   - Time lines, trend analysis
   - Seasonal diagrams
   - Activity profiles
   - Daily routines
   - Venn diagrams

8. **Case stories**
   - Life histories, oral or written stories by key people, e.g., school children
   - Narrative

9. **Drama, games and role plays**

10. **Workshops**
    - SWOT, Strengths, Weaknesses, Opportunities, Threats—Workshops
    - AIC—Appreciation Influence Control
    - AI—Appreciative Inquiry
    - Possible future and scenario workshops
    - Consensus workshops and conferences
    - Public hearings

11. **Triangulation**
    - Data triangulation
    - Investigator triangulation
    - Discipline triangulation
    - Theory triangulation
    - Methodological triangulation

12. **Continuous analysis and reporting**
    - With or without software for analysis of quantitative and qualitative data

(Box 2.5 contd)

(Box 2.5 contd)

13. Participatory planning, budgeting, monitoring, evaluation and self-surveys
  • Participation in all project cycle activities

14. Do-it-yourself
  • Outsiders being taught by insiders

The methods included in the 'catalogue' Box 2.5 can be seen as the core of participatory PRA methods that have been tried out in practice on many occasions. They are neither exhaustive, exclusive, nor discrete. New variants are continuously developed, some of which are illustrated in Chapter 3. And several of the methods can be applied in the same study or project. Analysis of the utilization illustrates that although many of these methods are not exactly new, they have been adjusted to become more participatory than they formerly were.

2.2.3 Classification and Typologies of Participatory Methods

Participatory PRA methods serve several purposes: There are PRA methods for (*i*) collecting data and information; (*ii*) analysing information, (*iii*) both collecting and analysing data, e.g., diagrams and workshops; and (*iv*) for communication. In spite of innovations in participatory methods, they seem to appear within certain standard categories. For example, Neela Mukherjee (2002), in her book *Participatory Learning and Action—With 100 Field Methods*, presents the 100 participatory methods in eight groups, based on criteria of direct and indirect support for field participation, and accompanied with notes from her own field experience. These groups are:

• Personal attributes and approaches
• Fostering team spirit and analytical skills
• Building rapport and holding conversations
• Walking together
• Visual portrayal—mapping and sketching
• Revealing priorities—ranking and scoring
• Seasonal calendars
• Visual depiction—diagrams and flow charts

There are those methods, which help us in doing the background work, in preparing our mind-sets and body language as individuals and there are those which help us to organise ourselves and improve our analytical abilities as facilitators ... there are 'verbal' methods, which help in building rapport and holding conversation ... and 'visual' methods of mapping and diagramming ... and methods which help in revealing priorities and preferences such as ranking/scoring, those, which portray seasonality and those, which involve walking together with local women and men (Mukherjee 2002: 10).

Space, time and *relations* are core parameters used by many to categorize PRA/PLA methods, each group—and each method—containing a variety of techniques and tools (Box 2.6).

Box 2.6 Classification of PRA Methods by Space, Time and Relations

Space related PRA Methods
- Social maps
- Resource maps
- Participatory modelling methods
- Mobility maps
- Services and opportunities maps
- Transects
- Participatory Census Methods

Time-related PRA Methods
- Time line
- Trend analysis
- Historical transect
- Seasonal diagram
- Daily activity schedule
- Participatory genealogy method
- Dream map

PRA Relational Methods—incl. Ranking and Prioritizing
- Cause-effect diagram
- Impact diagram
- Systems diagram
- Network diagram
- Process map
- Well-being ranking methods
- Venn diagram
- Pair-wise ranking method
- Matrix ranking/scoring method
- Force field analysis
- Pie diagram
- Livelihood analysis
- Spider diagram
- Body mapping

After Kumar, 2002.

Specific participatory studies and situations may suggest the application of methods and tools mentioned in Boxes 2.5 and 2.6. The challenge for the practitioner, who should also have the capacity to apply and critically analyse the results, is to choose methods which are relevant in a particular situation and for a particular group.

Kumar provides assistance in this direction. He systematically describes each of the PRA methods with lots of illustrations, some of which are included in Chapter 3. Kumar presents each PRA method, technique or tool along the following lines:

- Introduction to the method/tool—its origin, distinction from other tools, etc.
- Applications—variety of situations in which the method can be used
- Illustration of how the method can typically be used, and illustrative findings
- Process—*steps* proposed to apply the method/tool, and *sequencing,* i.e., when in the project/programme the method is optimally used
- Materials required—e.g., cards, colours, seeds, chalks, large paper, etc.
- Time required—varies considerably for and between each method
- Scope for improvisation and complementarity with other methods—e.g., gender and socio-economic group perspectives
- Whether the methods can be used as monitoring and evaluation tools
- Advantages and limitations of each method/tool

In addition to this thorough and systematic presentation, Kumar provides a 'ready reckoner' for each method under the three groups listed in Box 2.6. The ready reckoner contains a brief statement of characteristics for the particular method; it distinguishes between people's involvement and scope for improvisation as *high, moderate* or *low;* and advice is given on when in the project/programme cycle each PRA method could best be used. Practitioners will find these novel 'ready reckoners' of PRA methods useful.

Kumar has provided a far more detailed presentation of a variety of PRA methods in use than this book can. What follows is a brief description of the three categories—space, time and relational PRA methods—as discussed by him.

Space-related PRA Methods

Space-related PRA methods are useful for exploring the spatial dimensions of people's reality. These methods deal with mapping and the focus is on how people perceive and relate to space rather than just to the physical aspects, as they exist. The commonly used space-related methods are the social map, resource map, participatory modelling methods, mobility map, services and opportunities map and transect.

The social map is used to depict the habitation pattern while the resource map is focused on the natural resources. Participatory modelling is a three-dimensional depiction of an area. Mobility mapping is used to depict and analyse the mobility patterns of the local people while services and opportunities maps help in presentation of the availability of various services and opportunities in the locality. Transect provides a cross-section of an area and is particularly useful in natural resource management.

Time-related Methods

Time-related PRA methods are used to explore temporal dimensions of people's realities. What is unique about these PRA methods is that they allow people to use their own concept of time. The commonly used time-related methods include time-line, trend analysis, historical transect, seasonal diagram, daily activity schedule, participatory genealogy and dream map.

Time-line is commonly used to depict an aggregate of the various landmark events as perceived by the local people while trend analysis focuses on changes that have taken place across certain time landmarks. Historical transect, 'then and now' and 'past, present and future' methods are variants of trend analysis. The daily activity schedule depicts how the people spend their day from the time they get up till they go to bed. Seasonal diagrams depict the changes in people's lives across the annual cycle and across seasons or months. The participatory genealogy method is helpful in pinpointing the various generations, descent and the changes that have taken place over the generations. A dream map depicts the future vision and aspirations of the people.

Relational Methods

This category of PRA methods includes flow diagrams like cause-effect diagrams, impact diagrams, system diagrams, network diagrams, and process maps; as also well-being ranking method, Venn diagram, pair-wise ranking method, matrix scoring/ranking method, force field analysis, pie diagram, livelihood analysis, spider diagram and body mapping. These methods have been commonly used to study the relationships between various items or various aspects of the same item (Kumar, 2002: 40).

Besides space, time and relational methods, other generic categories are *sampling related methods* and *discussion methods for groups*. These methods are dealt with in Chapter 7 on Monitoring and Evaluation, e.g., Box 7.13 which classifies a large number of Monitoring and Evaluation methods. Many of these are used not only for monitoring and evaluation, but in diagnostic and planning studies as well.

If one tries to summarize some more important developments of participation and participatory methods, a well situated source and frequent PRA practitioner is Robert Chambers, who observes:

Box 2.7   What Has Changed with Participation and PRA over the Past Five Years? (ca. 1997–2002)

- Scale. PRA/PLA-labelled activities in 2002 will probably have been at least ten-fold those of 1997. Participatory methodologies more generally have gained acceptance.
- Participatory language has become obligatory donor-speak. The World Bank, for example, has mainstreamed participation and others are seeking to move in the same direction, but with so far rather disappointing results.
- Boundaries between participatory methodologies have increasingly dissolved.
- PRA-type mapping is very widespread indeed. (Well over a million maps must have been made by local people now.)
- PRA has become required by many donors, projects and programmes. The issue increasingly is not whether it will be used, but how badly or well it will be used. There is lots of bad practice.
- PRA fatigue in some communities. (Some communities have been 'carpet-bombed' with PRA.)
- Applications have multiplied and diversified into many new fields—e.g. drug probations, HIV/AIDS information, institutional analysis …
- PRA and related approaches have spread extensively in the North.
- Networks have multiplied and on the whole strengthened.
- Relationships have changed between North and South, to become more equal.
- Gender and participation has been opened up.
- Participatory Poverty Assessments, PPAs, have evolved and spread. Participation is now linked with Poverty Reduction Strategy Papers, PRSPs.
- Participatory Monitoring and Evaluation, PM&E has spread with huge potentials.[4]
- Children have come into their own PRA.
- Universities and university staff have begun to take PRA seriously and adopt PRA methods (including some enthusiastic and creative social anthropologists).
- Academic critics, mostly without practical PRA or participatory methodology field experience, are describing participation as a new orthodoxy.[5] At the level of rhetoric they have a point. Much of the reality falls short of the words. But critics often point to weaknesses of which PRA practitioners themselves are quite widely aware (e.g., the inherent bias against the participation of busy women). They also tend not to understand some strengths (e.g. democracy of the ground, representations and analysis of complexity, Attitudes and Behaviour Change, ABC, impacts of facilitation, etc.).

After Chambers, 2002b.

---

[4] See Chapter 7.
[5] See Section 2.4.

Among the changes in participation listed in Box 2.5, *scaling up* participation has been pointed out as a major challenge (e.g., Estrella and Gaventa, 1998). *Scaling up participation* means increasing the number of participants or places that participate or expanding people's participation in one activity, such as appraisal, to many types of activities, e.g., to increase civil society's participation in policy dialogue and in 'upwards' accountability measures towards those in power, in programmes or in government. It means involving people throughout the development process in a way that empowers (Pretty and Scoones 1995; Gaventa et al., 2002). A major challenge has been to widen the impact beyond isolated local successes in community-based, participatory and adaptive planning on a scale which goes beyond simply replicating successful projects and moves towards strategic policy changes. The integration of participatory perspectives into *poverty reduction strategies* and into *safeguard policies* (WB/ESSD web) are indications of such strategic changes. But then the challenge is also to increase numbers and uses without undermining the *quality* of participation!

2.3   Considerations for Using Participatory Methods

2.3.1 Overall Principles

Practitioners have long been aware of the many threats to quality and personal integrity in the use of participatory methods (see Section 2.4). For the same reason practitioners are supposed to respect a set of principles for using participatory methods (Box 2.8).

Failing to put *behaviour* and *attitudes* before *methods* is a major threat to the quality of participation. This is often highlighted as the most important of the principles. On the other hand, 'handing over the stick', which Chambers includes in this principle, is used by several critics (Cooke and Kothari, 2000) to pinpoint the rhetoric which they maintain riddles the participation discourse. Indeed, they are right in that the many principles can rarely be honoured in practice, and in pointing to the many paradoxes riddling participation (see Section 2.4). Does this mean that missing out on some principles results in bad participation? Hopefully not, as we are also continuously reminded that *there is no one a priori participatory strategy*.

There is scope for imagination, and the overarching principle for using participatory methods has become mnemonic:

Use your own best judgement at all times!

Lessons from specific situations where participatory methods have been applied prompts the addition of new principles which Rasmussen calls **The right *not* to participate** and **the right to direct representation** (Rasmussen, 2004), i.e., the right to represent your own views only and not to speak on behalf of others or have others speak on your behalf.

Box 2.8   Principles of Applying Participatory Methods, PRA/PLA

- *A reversal of learning,* to learn from people, directly, on the site, and face-to-face, gaining from local physical, technical and social knowledge.
- *Learning rapidly and progressively,* with conscious exploration, flexible use of methods, improvisation, iteration, and cross-checking, not following a blueprint programme but adapting in a learning process.
- *Offsetting biases,* especially those of rural development tourism, by being relaxed and not rushing, listening not lecturing, probing instead of passing on to the next topic, being unimposing instead of important, and seeking out the poorer people and women, and learning their concerns and priorities.
- *Optimizing trade-offs,* relating the costs of learning to the useful truth of information, with trade-offs between quantity, relevance, accuracy and timeliness. This includes the principles of **optimal ignorance**—knowing what is not worth knowing—and of **appropriate imprecision**—not measuring more than needed. We are trained to measure things, but often trends, scores or ranking are all that are required.
- *Triangulation*—using different methods, sources and disciplines, and a range of informants in a range of places, and cross-checking to get closer to the truth through successive approximations.
- *Seeking diversity:* This has been expressed in terms of seeking variability rather than averages, and has been described as the principle of maximum diversity, or 'maximizing the diversity and richness of information'. This can involve sampling in a non statistical sense. It goes beyond the cross-checking of triangulation; it deliberately looks for, notices and investigates contradictions, anomalies and differentness.
- *Facilitating—they do it:* Facilitating investigation, analysis, presentation and learning by rural people themselves, so that they present and own the outcomes, and also learn. This often entails an outsider starting a process and then sitting back and not intervening or interrupting.
- *Critical self-awareness and responsibility:* Meaning that facilitators are continuously examining their behaviour, and trying to do better. This includes embracing error—welcoming error as an opportunity to learn to do better; and using one's own best judgement at all times, meaning accepting personal responsibility rather than vesting it in a manual or a rigid set of rules.
- *Sharing* of information, of methods, of food, of field experiences and ideas between rural people, between them and facilitators, and between different facilitators, and sharing camps and shelter, training and experience between different organizations.
- *Commitment to equity,* empowering those who are marginalized, deprived, excluded and regarded as not capable, often especially women, children and those who are poorer.
- *Changing behaviour and attitudes,* from dominating to facilitating, gaining rapport, asking people, often 'lowers', to teach us, respecting them, having confidence that they can do it, handing over the stick, empowering and enabling them to conduct their own analysis.

After Chambers, 1992 and 2002b.

2.3.2 Gender Sensitivity in Application of Participatory Methods

More specific considerations are required in concrete situations, e.g., the principle of inclusion of marginalized groups, disabled, aged and young people—and gender sensitivity. Many studies have shown that women are particularly vulnerable to being excluded from the rapidly expanding attempts at participatory development (Moser, 1993; Kabeer, 1994). Participatory development programmes, while inclusive of women, may end up silencing them. Many programmes value and privilege public debate and communication. Yet some cultures or socio-political environments devalue women's public roles, moving them to be passive to men. This is all the more the case when sensitive issues such as rape, violence, or sex are discussed publicly (Kapoor, 2002: 469).

Participation is not the panacea many assume because there are limits to what participation alone (even if interactive) can achieve in terms of equity and efficiency, given pre-existing socio-economic inequalities and relations of power. Bina Agarwal (2001) shows how community forestry groups set up as participatory institutions can exclude significant sections such as women. Similar exclusionary processes have also been observed in other arenas, for example, water user associations, village councils, and the many new governance structures being promoted today in the name of decentralized institution building.

Agarwal analyses the factors which determine participation of women and she settles on *bargaining* as a way ahead:

A promising analytical framework for examining the possibilities of positive change is that of bargaining. In terms of this framework, women's ability to change rules, norms, perceptions and endowments in a gender-progressive direction would depend especially on their bargaining power with the State, the community and the family, as the case may be (Agarwal, 2001: 1641)

Reasons to be gender sensitive in participatory research is formulated in Box 2.9.

Box 2.9 Gender Sensitivity in Application of Participatory Methods

Any participatory research methodology should consider the importance of gender. From a practical point of view, this means that researchers should be sure to include participants who play different roles within households, such as women, children, spouses, parents, and female heads of households. This also means paying special attention to interactions among household members. Depending on where the research is being done, it may be necessary to form same-sex groups (i.e., groups of only men or only women), since in mixed groups women may not participate at all. In other contexts, however, mixed groups may provide an excellent opportunity to elicit gender differences and concerns. Even in individual interactions it may be necessary for men to interview or interact only with men, and for women to interact only with women.

In the past, agricultural research focused mainly on male farmers and assumed that all household members shared the same goals, had the same access to resources and outputs, and faced similar constraints. Now it is clear that in most cases this view is incorrect. Just as differences between farmers and households may be attributed to differences in access to resources, knowledge, and information, differences within households also exist and may be attributed to different factors. Household members may have diverse responsibilities, perform different activities, and have varying work loads and access to resources. They may also have conflicting interests ....

Regardless of where the research is being undertaken, gender considerations are always important and relevant. Researchers must also be careful to go beyond a simple concern with females or female-headed households and to look carefully at the way household members are organized and interact.

After Bellon, 2001: 22–23.

Participation can be used in *advocacy,* e.g., to enhance people's (in many cases women's) bargaining power in the community (Agarwal, 2001); in other cases to build negotiation power among small farmers who are often women, or for democratic decentralization in urban contexts (Carrión, 2001). Advocacy and negotiation are important perspectives in promotion of gender equality both at the micro (community) level and at the macro (policy) level. Whether this means women's and men's participation should be joint or separate cannot be determined a priori. It has been argued that under some circumstances the poor, like women, may benefit more from heterogeneous associations (Uphoff et al., 1998). The answer must come from working with people and letting them determine what arrangements will be culturally feasible and socio-economically beneficial.

2.3.3 Stakeholder Participation and Practitioner Capabilities

Stakeholder Participation

To identify strategic parameters for participatory development it is important to specify *who* the people are, the stakeholders involved, and not just the population as such (see also Section 7.3.3). The strategic parameters have been suggested to involve: (*a*) the local versus the national level; (*b*) the state versus civil society; and (*c*) the privileged social strata versus the weak and excluded. There are concerned actors, or stakeholders, at each level.

Stakeholders are individual persons, groups or institutions with vested interests in an intervention. **Primary stakeholders** are those who will be directly or ultimately affected by an intervention, either positively (beneficiaries) or negatively. **Secondary stakeholders** are intermediaries such as implementing organisations, or other individuals, persons, groups or institutions involved in interventions, including funders. **Key stakeholders** are those of the primary and secondary stakeholders who can significantly affect or influence an intervention either positively or negatively during its course, and who will share responsibility, quality and sustainability of subsequent effects and impact (Nilsson and Woodford-Berger, 2000: 11).

All agencies concerned with people's participation and 'consultations' have to decide who should participate or be consulted. This requires a stakeholder analysis of *who* are concerned parties with what kind of vested interest, *what* is their interest and which kind of power do they have to influence the outcome of an intervention, and *how* can they be motivated to participate. (Constraints and risks of patronizing are discussed in Section 2.4.) The target group for development aid, i.e., the poorest 40–60 per cent of the population in developing countries—termed 'beneficiaries' by some—are the first stakeholders to consider.

This book, however, attempts not to use the term 'beneficiaries', despite its frequent use in the development vocabulary. 'Beneficiaries' seems to be an ideological and value-laden term. It is a contradiction in terms to not let people themselves decide whether or not they see themselves as beneficiaries, and for someone from outside—the donor, the government—to tag the name beneficiary on to people who may consider themselves in opposition to the project or intervention, or worse, maybe even as losers.

In practice there are many 'stakeholders'—individuals and groups who have a 'stake' in a development programme or intervention, who therefore have different interests in participating and different interests in including or excluding others. The 'target group' has to be specified—moving away from the conglomerate of individuals and taking into account the different social groups determined by economic, political, ethnic, religious, age and gender characteristics.

A second point is that participation should not concern the prospective users (primary stakeholders) of project/intervention services alone. Indeed, for people's participation to be efficient and successful, it will in many cases be a pre-condition that 'officers' of involved authorities themselves participate as a stakeholder group in activities directed at involving the community, or at least support the idea of people's participation. There is also substantial evidence that support is required from top officials for participatory development activities to become successful (Cernea, 1991). To turn hostility on the part of project management into an active demand for participatory process monitoring is an aim in many development interventions, but is not always possible. Box 2.10 illustrates a successful case:

The Community Infrastructure Project case illustrated by Pendley is typical of much participation in development cooperation: It is donor driven and at first met with open or disguised hostility from project management, whose judgement may stem from contempt for 'non-scientific' methods more than from personal exposure to participatory activities. To turn such hostility into active requests for participatory monitoring, etc., is quite an accomplishment. Support from project management is often forgotten but can be eased by informed initial consultations on the scope of participation in development. Stakeholder analysis of the interests and possibilities of different stakeholder groups to participate helps development planners and project management to be more precise and to specify what kind of participatory approaches they may aim to apply, to bring into action, and to effect in cooperation with defined stakeholders.

Practitioner Capabilities

Practitioners use a variety of methods to support participatory development. The 'catalogue' of PRA methods provide for direct application of selected methods or for adaptation to specific tasks and situations. The ability to select, adapt and combine methods, be they participatory or more conventional methods such as surveys, is a primary skill requirement for facilitators of participatory development.

There is no a priori correct selection. A diligent application of any one method can yield good results as long as the facilitators are explicit about the purpose and aim and sensitive to the inclusion of the target groups and differences in opportunities and interests between them. Practising and facilitating participatory methods thus require a variety of skills and capabilities, of which attitudes count as much as technical and pedagogic skills.

Professional facilitation of participatory methods is mandatory if these methods are to constitute a serious approach to development research and practice. To retain credibility, it is important that the practitioners possess sufficient capabilities to practice PRA, and knowledge of the strengths and pitfalls of PRA tools. Participatory methods have spread to practitioners of many disciplines. They are no

---

**Box 2.10   From Hostility to Demand—Opening the Eyes of Project
Management to the Usefulness of Process Monitoring**

The Community Infrastructure Project (CIP) aims to apply a demand-responsive approach to the provision of infrastructure in 55 rural and urban low-income communities implemented in the Northwest Frontier Province of Pakistan. It has been supported by IDA (World Bank), Swiss Development Cooperation (SDC) and UNICEF. This project is unique in that it contains a number of innovative elements referred to collectively as Community Action Planning (CAP). One of these innovative elements is a Process Monitoring Unit attached to the Project. An example of how process monitoring, using a variety of participatory methods, contributed to improving the effectiveness of the project, is given below.

Early in the implementation of the Project, management became concerned about the high drop-out rate of communities identified for receiving assistance from the Project. Project management, supported by the donors, asked the Process Monitoring Unit to look into the reasons for the high drop-out rate. Using participant observation, focus-group discussions, social mapping, transect walks and other methods, the process monitoring team was able to identify possible causes for the high dropout rate. Among the reasons identified by the team were lack of representativeness, particularly of women, but also that so-called 'block representatives' who were important contact points between the Project and the community were not chosen by community members, but appointed by influential persons in the village.

Another reason for the high drop-out rate was poor coordination between the social and technical components and staff in the project. Technical surveys started only after the social surveys were completed, were often delayed and did not build on the contacts and information developed during the social surveys.

As obvious as these findings are, convincing project management to change project roles and rules—and their own attitude—was not easy. In the beginning, project management, mostly civil servants and engineers from the local government and rural development department, did not understand the role and purpose of process monitoring and the participatory methods used. They tended to view the process monitoring team as being critical of the Project, 'finding faults' and generating a negative image of the Project to its donors.

Eventually though, after many meetings and discussions, and some persuasive influence from the main donors, project management came to realize the value of process monitoring and the methods it used. Finally, project management came to view the process monitoring team in a non-threatening manner and even requested the team to investigate and report on other project issues.

Source: Dr Charles J. Pendley, Senior Sociologist, COWI.

---

longer the exclusive domain of sociologists, anthropologists, communication specialists, and related disciplines. Many other practitioners—economists, biologists, foresters, geographers, medical staff, engineers, administrators, etc.—have shown an interest and adopted participatory approaches. The spread of utilization to practitioners from different disciplines enhances the credibility of participatory approaches and is a sign of spreading appreciation (see Box 2.10).

Reflexivity by the researcher and practitioner him/herself over the possible impacts of his/her pre-conceived notions and participation in the research or action process has been slow to penetrate the development arena. Discourse analysis has brought the importance of reflexivity to the surface (see Chapter 5). Indeed, self-reflective perspectives should be the foundation of the participatory practitioner's capabilities.

All development practitioners need not personally practice PRA, but they should know about the ramifications of participatory methods, know how to get hold of professionals who have mastered facilitation, and ensure that the basic principles for using participatory methods are followed. In a globalizing world, new requirements for practising participatory methods imply new capabilities, such as a better understanding of linkages between the local and the global. Few development problems can be resolved in isolation at the local level; they must be understood and addressed in a larger social context and in the context of macro policies.

Participatory methods may best be learnt through practice, but the basic knowledge needs to be obtained from courses or other systematic learning. PRA courses are provided by a variety of institutions, often by NGOs, Agricultural Universities, etc. They are not systematically taught in international development studies around the world, which on the other hand provide important critical perspectives on participation in development (see Section 2.4). Those who practice participatory methods sometimes operate as 'a self-regulating cadre' (Green, 2002) beyond the 'quality assurance' of other professionals. Practitioner capabilities of this 'self-regulating cadre' should therefore be a serious concern for development agencies which employ specialists to facilitate participatory development activities. To avoid the abuse of 'using the label without the substance', a look at the many critical perspectives on Participation in Development and participatory, PRA methods can be a help.

2.4   Critical Perspectives on Participation

2.4.1 Positions in the Critiques of Participation in Development

The messages in this book are: Avoid being dogmatic; be flexible in field study design without losing direction, be sensitive to the context of the field study and adjust your approach accordingly; listen to people's own knowledge, but don't think that only the voice of the grassroots counts—that would be another kind of dogmatism. The variety of stakeholders, and the relations between them, matters. Attempt to create a dialogue with those who will be directly or indirectly affected by your study and intervention, and share decisions and responsibilities where feasible. Respect the will **not** to participate. Use your imagination, but do not impose your views. Reflect on your own role and legitimacy of your encroachment. The list of 'DO's and 'DON'T's could continue for pages!

'Participation in development' is entangled in many dilemmas. Working with participation—participation as a democratic principle, as a right, as methods and tools, etc., raises a variety of theoretical and operational challenges as well as normative and ethical considerations like those just mentioned.

Critical insights into strengths and weaknesses, emanating from 'conceptual and ideological examination of its theory, methods and practices' (Cooke and Kothari, 2000: 2), will facilitate any attempt to understand and address the dilemmas of the participatory development discourse. But listening to the concerns of participants, to those who participate voluntarily or under pressure, may be the best lesson of all. This section attempts to capture major critical positions and arguments in the discourse on participation in development.

Critiques of participation in development tend to be made from one or more of the following positions: (*i*) There are those criticisms which are broadly sympathetic to the participatory 'movement'—a phrase used by Brown et al. (2002b). These critiques are aimed at improving rigor and range. (*ii*) Second, there are the radical critiques, which question what is seen as the proponents' messianic claims that PRA represents a new form of popular empowerment. (*iii*) Third, there are concerns about the predominance of orthodoxy, manipulation and enforcement over authentically participatory realities. (*iv*) Fourth, a blindness to context, leading to mechanistic applications of participatory techniques and the neglect of power differentials within project communities (McGee, 2002).

Critiques of participation in development are generally expressed by scholars and sometimes by practitioners with hands-on experience. Concerns expressed by participants, who willingly or under pressure get involved in participatory development activities, are not often documented. This is not so different from the patterns in development cooperation debates in general—perhaps a reflection of the (im)balance in partnerships of 'donors' and 'recipients'? Nevertheless, open or disguised concerns by partners and participants have contributed to the uneasiness which is reflected in the critiques of the participatory development discourse in general and of participatory methods, PRA, in particular.

Participation—Subtle Forms of Manipulation?

The more radical critiques question both the theoretical foundations of PRA and the class interests it is likely to promote. They tend to see 'participation' as an ideology distorting real democracy, and as an approach which is eminently prone to co-optation by the elite. They go as far as to dub participation the 'new tyranny' (Cooke and Kothari, 2000).

Critically interpreted, the well-intentioned promotion of empowerment and ownership through local participation and take-over of the external 'expert's' role as change agent is a refined and accelerating—yet unconscious—process for 'colonizing the life worlds of villagers'. Or, as Rahnema characterizes participatory methods and conscientization—they are simply new and more subtle forms of manipulation (Rahnema, 1992).

New Forms of Knowledge, Power, Action and Know-How?

Rahnema attaches four functions to how popular participation came about as key elements in creating an alternative, human-centred development, i.e., a *cognitive,* a *social,* an *instrumental* and a *political* function. That is, old knowledge systems had to be replaced by a different popular knowledge system, and new forms of people's power were envisaged by the proponents. Rahnema questions whether the participatory approach has succeed in bringing about such new forms of people's power. Instead, he thinks there are indications that the way many activists interpreted their mission contributed to de-valuing the traditional and vernacular forms of power. He therefore asks the fundamental questions: Did (or can) such methods as dialogical interaction, conscientization and participatory action research really succeed in halting the processes of domination, manipulation and colonization of the mind? Can they really help bring about new forms of knowledge, power, action and know-how, needed to create a different type of society? His is a very pessimistic answer.

Who Participates?

Many note the often highly public orientation of participatory (PRA) exercises, and argue that this may limit their ability to reach the socially marginal and address issues of equity (e.g., Cornwall, 2002 and Mosse, 1993, 1995). Insensitivity regarding *access* and *equity,* pointing to the failure of many attempts to target specific categories, for example women, is frequently mentioned (Guijt and Shah, 1998).

> Participation, while 'now part of the standard toolkit ... may in practice replicate existing social divisions, be appropriated by the elite and the articulate, and exclude poorer and marginalised groups, including women (Green, 2002).

When participation becomes part of the standard toolkit, it is easy to forget to check possible sensitivities involved for the target group/participants. Several development agencies, including NGOs, are prone sometimes to propagate and impose the use of participatory approaches against the wishes of the people.

Chambers warns of the danger of a 'naïve populism in which participation is regarded as good regardless of who participates or who gains' (Chambers, 1994). The high opportunity costs which the use of participatory methods may entail, in particular for the rural poor, tend to be overlooked. A more imaginative usage of the tools and more careful *targeting* is called for.

Responsibility and Accountability?

A widespread concern is that PRA methods allow practitioners to disown responsibility for their own constructs by requiring 'participants' to engage in imposed behaviour, the consequences of which the latter will nevertheless be held accountable for (Sellamna, 1999). In the guise of support for democratic involvement, responsibility may be transferred onto rural communities for decisions in which they have played only a marginal role.

Better Knowledge? True Values?

Participation is often advocated for the recognition of the value of local people's knowledge and its potential contribution to development. While laudable in itself, participation may not solve many of the basic causes of underdevelopment. 'Listening is not the same as acting, although it is an excellent first step' (Buhler et al., 2002). Participatory planning may be viewed as the acquisition and manipulation of a new 'planning knowledge' rather than the incorporation of people's knowledge (Mosse, 2001). The ability of rapid and participatory research tools to provide accurate information is questioned.

The ease with which PRA methods can be manipulated, with no possibility of external checks, is also a concern (Brown, 1990, 1998). Participants themselves can manipulate the participatory process, as happened in a Joint Forest Management Project in India (Hildyard et al., 2001).

The transactional environments in which participatory methods are often employed make for risks of distortion and manipulation of information (Moore et al., 1998). This is for example the case where NGOs are involved in multiplex relationships with village communities, training them in participatory methods at the same time as they provide them with valued goods and services. In such circumstances, the assumption that the methods can reveal the 'true' values and interests of the community must be doubted (Brown et al., 2002a).

Idealizing Community—Over- or Under-estimating NGOs?

Implicit in the participatory approach, the critiques say, is a tendency to idealize the 'community' and a danger of confusing between social and geographical communities (Biggs and Smith, 1998; Francis, 2001; Stirrat, 1996). Others warn of the danger of using the term 'community' as if it covered a homogeneous, idyllic, unified population with which researchers and developers can interact with no problems (Nelson and Wright, 1995).

> A more dynamic vision is needed of 'institutions' and of 'community', one that incorporates social networks and recognises dispersed and contingent power relations, the exclusionary as well as the inclusionary nature of participation. We need a much better understanding of local norms of decision-making and representation, of how these change and are negotiated, of how people may indirectly affect outcomes without direct participation ... I see the need for a radical reassessment of the desirability, practicality and efficacy of development efforts based on community participation. This involves rethinking not just the relationship between differently placed individuals and historically and spatially specific social structures, but also the role of individuals, households, communities, development agencies and the state (Cleaver, 2000: 54–55).

Part of the critique of participation converges around the central role NGOs have come to play. The notion that NGOs are more 'participative' is at risk of becoming received wisdom. Aid donors who often use NGOs as agents have come to realize that NGOs display very different understandings of what participation means and how it might best be achieved. In Costa Rica Laura Macdonald's (1995) analysis revealed that NGOs have contributed to marginalize and de-politicize participation. Participatory initiatives have in several cases been turned on their head and have ensured the promotion of the interest of dominant powers, rather than actually empowering the poor. The explanation, according to Macdonald, seems to be that the ideology of community self-reliance as a basis for NGO activity is perfectly compatible with the current drive towards privatization and the dismantling of Third World states. Thus NGOs—unintentionally perhaps—may come to facilitate 'poorly conceived' participatory strategies, premised on the strategies of the powerful, national or international development agencies, and then reinforce an already ongoing process of 'the system-world's colonization of the life-world' in the affected communities, to use a Habermas inspired phrase (Habermas, 1987).

Does this mean that 'participation' should not be put in the hands of NGOs? Not according to Macdonald. But

> ... participation must be reclaimed, and explicitly linked with national and international processes of democratisation. If this link is not made, even the most participatory of NGO projects runs the risk of following the path of isolated nineteenth century utopian communities in Britain and North America which were eventually extinguished by internal conflict and hostile external forces (Macdonald, 1995: 115).

The dilemma for NGOs concerns their preparation to play a more active part in democratization.

Representation—Structure and Agency

The limitations of project-level participation through agency structures are being increasingly recognized (e.g., McGee, 2002). Imported structures and tools for participation, including PRA methods, contrary to intentions may in practice replicate existing social divisions, be appropriated by the elite and the articulate, and exclude marginalized groups, including women. The fact that participation cannot be equated with representation—who actually represents whom in participatory exercises?—has implications for the quality of social analyses that use participatory methods, whether at the community level or, as in the case of the more ambitious participatory poverty assessments, at the national level.

> Perhaps more significantly, there is a risk that participatory development at the project level, divorced from local structures of political representation and process, will foster the creation of parallel structures for participation that—in a travesty of formal agencies' commitment to transparency and accountability as the essence of good governance—will serve to depoliticise development interventions and remove them from public scrutiny at the local level (Green, 2002: 67).

It is a dilemma that 'participation in projects' is still the most common form of promoting participation, notwithstanding the trend to move away from the project approach.

Further empirical evidence and analysis is needed of whether and *how* the structure of participatory projects include/protect/secure the interests of poor people. What *exactly* are the linkages between the participation of poor individuals and the furthering of their social and economic good? Understanding this requires analyses of 'competent' communities and 'successful' participatory projects that focus on process, on power dynamics, on patterns of inclusion and exclusion. These could be built up through process documentation of the dynamics of conflict, consensus-building and decision-making within communities, and not just the recording of project-related activities (Cleaver, 2000: 54).

Such empirical evidence of strengths and weaknesses from a selection of 'participatory projects' is contained in Box 2.13.

2.4.2 Methodological Concerns and 'Tyranny of Tools'

Tyranny of Tools

A concern has been raised about the 'tyranny of tools'—because of the popularity and high profile of PRA (IFAD, 2002). Methodological concerns and concerns over the quality of use of the PRA tools and techniques are summarized in Box 2.11.

Box 2.11   The Tyranny of Tools—Concerns about PRA from the Field

Fears have been expressed about the following risks and pitfalls of PRA:

- **Legitimization of agendas**—PRA being used to legitimize projects that communities might have challenged given more information, time and political clout
- **Depth of coverage?**—No norms for what are appropriate levels of dis-aggregation of different stakeholder groups, e.g., gender, age, caste, race, ethnicity for PRA analysis
- **Detailed or shallow PRAs?**—is not always honestly documented. Importance of sound and detailed PRA studies are often downplayed
- **'Facipulation'**—Communities are 'helped' to identify a pre-defined project focus as if it were their own primary concern
- **The pressure of deadlines**—PRAs are mandatory in most donor supported programmes but sufficient time not allowed for finding suitable PRA persons, doing the PRA and reporting
- **Varying Competence and Attitudes of Practitioners**—PRA requires communication skills, personality, attitudes and analytical skills—and in many cases un-learning of old practices
- **Vast amounts of qualitative information** generated by PRAs are difficult to sift through, systematize, summarize and assimilate by policy makers and other researchers
- **PRA results are difficult to compare** when different methods and depth of investigation have been applied by different field teams and at different points in time
- **Institutional limitations** are constraints on scaling-up and scaling-out PRA
- **Contracting out PRA**—limits learning, continuity and policy feed-back within organizations by compartmentalizing the participatory element in projects and programmes
- **PRAs focus on the negative**—departs from problems and can be de-motivating, in contrast to the appreciative inquiry method which builds on positive experiences and energies
- **Some PRAs are extractive**—e.g., if done to understand people's need for a particular output, but more likely to lead to **empowerment** if the concern is people's awareness of their rights
- **PRAs raise expectations** that may not be fulfilled either in the short or long term
- **PRA fatigue**—some easily accessible communities are subjected to frequent PRAs and get tired of participating to the detriment of quality of information
- **Personal consequences for information providers** can be serious when those in power are challenged, in particular in faction-ridden locations

After Deshingkar and James, 2001.

The tyranny of tools tends to be exacerbated by those who are not used to being innovative in the field. They have a tendency to follow PRA manuals rigidly and to treat them as commandments. This has led to ridiculous situations where PRA practitioners have insisted on using 'traditional' materials such as dung, leaves, stones and sticks to the amusement of villagers who would have been more comfortable with a blackboard or flipchart.

A different aspect is when 'professionalization' in the use of participatory methods takes place as captured in this quote from a village woman, who had been 'professionalized' in making village maps—social maps, resource maps—when interested development agencies requested the application of participatory mapping:

We are becoming very good at making maps of our village. This is good. It makes it easier for us to make the map again for others (Mikkelsen, 1998).

For the village it may save time to leave the mapping exercises to the 'professional' map makers in the village, but at the cost of participation and dialogue.

Participatory Methods, Participatory Development and Structural Reforms

A fundamental question is the relationship between participatory methods and participatory development. Development practice has witnessed the widespread emergence and sometimes merging of concepts of participation with participatory methods and tools such as PRA.

After a period with much focus on particular PRA methods and tools, some critics have asked to what extent the use of PRA methods is at all critical for participatory development to occur. There is a suspicion that participatory methods have come to supplant the actual practice of participation, and become a convenient and controllable substitute for it (Biggs and Smith, 1998). Promoting participatory development may also become a substitute for more fundamental structural reform (Box 2.12).

Box 2.12   Participation—Substitute for Structural Reforms—Empirical Evidence

Experience from a water supply programme in Northern Ghana feeds a serious concern:

... because of the inherent goodness of the notion of participation, it has become a substitute for the structural reforms needed for social change.

The case study referred to illustrates a form of participation that fails to recognize that people are sometimes so poor that participating in externally initiated community activities makes no sense. Local resources are insufficient to meet local needs and the participatory process introduced does not allow the people to define for themselves—least of all to pursue—their priority needs. The villagers in this case no longer become the progenitors of development but simply a resource to be used for development. What happens is that the constitution of development with its emphasis on participation, empowerment and sustainability reflects a blindness to the

(Box 2.12 contd)

(Box 2.12 contd)

wider socio-economic processes which have contributed to the need for development. Attention is directed away from the internal politics in the village and from questions of the nature of actual social relations and the distribution of wealth and power. Attention is only given to the willingness of the local communities to raise their initial share of contribution for the borehole so that they can possess an indicator of 'modernity'—a hand-pump fitted potable water system. Botchway calls into question how the post-colonial state systematically has co-opted and directed all efforts at community participation in development, as the state is seen to evade its responsibilities. Hence, participation has become a substitute for a necessary structural reform for resource-mobilization involving the community and the state.

After Botchway, 2001.

In a poorly conceived community participation approach, there are risks and abuses in the application of participatory *methods and tools* in addition to concerns over *methodological violations,* i.e., insensitivity to power structures, idealizing community, exclusion of voiceless groups, etc. Empirical evidence from a selection of projects and programmes in the Gambia can further illustrate the case for and against the use of participatory methods (see Box 2.13).

Empirical Support *for* and *against* Participation

An empirical evaluation of selected projects in the Gambia supported by international development agencies is a valuable contribution to learning lessons from experience. The research team (Brown et al., 2002a) undertook a detailed review of participatory approaches, PRA, used by DFID's main NGO partner, ActionAid—The Gambia. The study findings for and against PRA are summarized in Box 2.13.[6]

On the four key criteria: 'utilitarian considerations', 'community mobilization', 'motivational benefits' and 'empowering the poor', the conclusions about the results of having applied participatory method-ologies in the four Gambia cases are not impressive. In general they confirm many of the critiques against participatory approaches.

Criticisms such as those recorded above are sometimes severe, but often stop short of a fundamental questioning of the value of PRA techniques, even if only on utilitarian grounds, and many suggest ways in which the use of PRA can be modified and refined.

---

[6] The four case studies illustrate different approaches to participatory development practice, all of them using PRA tools to a greater or lesser degree. In one case, ActionAid—The Gambia, PRA usage was given a high profile. In two others Support to Decentralized Rural Development and The Gambian-German Forestry Project, PRA was seen as an important component of the strategy, while in the fourth, The Sesame Growers' Associations, PRA was seen as a minor tool in a strategy defined largely in other terms.

Box 2.13 The Case for and against PRA, with Lessons from Four Aid Funded Projects in the Gambia		
The case *for* PRA	The case *against* PRA	Conclusions from four cases
1. Utilitarian considerations More effective and efficient data collection; low overall cost; not perfect but better than the alternatives, particularly in action research and policy-relevant contexts.	**1. Utilitarian considerations** Data suspect; methodologically weak and without adequate safeguards; high opportunity costs to the poor. Undiscriminating.	**1. Utilitarian considerations** Some benefits in this regard, in that a wide range of individuals have become involved in 'formal' data collection (individuals who would probably not otherwise have had the opportunity to do so). But there are still concerns about data quality, and cost-effectiveness (both training costs and opportunity costs for the poor and to field agents).
2. Community mobilization Enhanced participation of the poor in data collection and analysis, and in the control and direction of initiatives intended to benefit them.	**2. Community mobilization** Participation biased to certain categories, not necessarily the poor.	**2. Community mobilization** The balance-sheet probably positive, though some concerns about the idealization of 'the community' and privileging of the literate.
3. Motivational benefits Motivating and a 'spur to action' for development workers and community members alike. Greater empathy and sharing by professionals.	**3. Motivational benefits** Risks over-inflated expectations, with negative repercussions. Encourages just the sort of amateurish development tourism that it was intended to counter.	**3. Motivational benefits** Definite motivational benefits for staff, and—at least in the short term—for villagers, though likely to be diminishing returns, particularly for the latter. There is a danger that the tools will be used in a superficial way, as a form of development tourism, and there are few if any safeguards against this.
4. Empowering the poor An important means of achieving popular empowerment and a vehicle for social change. Offers the prospect of self-sustaining community-based development. May lead to important changes in personal behaviour and attitudes on the part of development agents. At the organizational level also has radical potential.	**4. Empowering the poor** Such claims are overblown. Offers no means, on its own, to challenge power relations. Patronizes the poor in the guise of transformation. Unlikely to be sustainable.	**4. Empowering the poor** Serious concerns in this area. Little evidence of any serious challenge to existing power relations, and the techniques are easily subordinated to the status quo. Major doubts about long-term sustainability, particularly as regards self-initiated use by villagers.

After Brown et al., 2002b.

2.4.3 A Changing Participation Agenda?

International development agencies and their partners alike have adopted participatory practices and policies at multiple levels. Participatory practices are increasingly being linked to issues of policy, of national budgeting, of governance, etc., as much as to projects and community activities. As the participation agenda is changing, new issues arise on top of what has already been discussed in the previous sections. A few of these are discussed below.

Inclusion and Institutionalization

Beyond the above criticism of the PRA 'movement' is a wider concern about the promotion, in aid-funded environments, of notions of participation and 'truly' participatory development. It is asked whether attempts to promote popular participation is supportive or destructive of more fundamental principles of democracy (Ribot, 2002). The development institutions are challenged by inclusionary decisions:

> The challenge for participation over the last decades has been to open spaces for public engagement, by transforming institutions and promoting invited participation at all levels. Lessons from experience indicate that inviting 'the people' to participate as beneficiaries or consumers is not in itself enough to bring about meaningful change. The challenge for the future is *both* to enable those excluded by poverty and discrimination to take up opportunities extended to them for influence and control *and* to exercise agency through the institutions, spaces and strategies they make and shape for themselves (Cornwall, 2002: 78).

Institutional changes of cultures, procedures and rewards are unavoidable.

Trust in Personal Change, Attitudes and Learning

In relation to practising participatory development, convergence in the critique centres on a trust in personal change and attitude. Both a proponent of participatory approaches like Robert Chambers and a staunch critique as Majid Rahnema seem to agree that it is the 'qualities and gifts of learning, relating and listening' which are important for changing the agenda. *These qualities cannot be co-opted.*

However different their positions, they use more or less the same words to state that if whole systems are to shift and transform, it will be because of the sum and interaction of innumerable personal actions and changes in what sort of people we—the practitioners—are.

More recently—some would say in a 'post-tyranny' period (Fransman, 2003), there are notable shifts towards an understanding of participation as a vehicle to build greater voice, accountability and trust in relationships between people and institutions (Shah and Youssef, 2002). Successful innovations and practice are resulting in participation being seen as a desirable end as well as a means, with the potential to reduce poverty and social injustice by strengthening citizen rights and voice, influencing policy making, enhancing local governance, and improving the accountability and responsiveness of institutions (Gaventa et al., 2002).

If participation can deliver such valuable results, it is important to query how participation is learned as a complex body of ideas, concepts, attitudes, behaviour, values, methods and approaches. Learning, including experiential learning through practice, is recognized as creating the ground for effective participation. How the pitfalls of earlier mainstreaming efforts can be avoided and lessons learned from them is, therefore, an important question in the current participation agenda.

Quality Concerns

Concerns about abuses have led to discussions of requirements for some kind of quality control and greater ethical standards in the practice of participatory PRA methods and reporting of results. Probably the most effective check on how PRA is done comes from the peer group of practitioners themselves and from the people who are exposed to participatory PRA activities. To ensure quality of participation requires that the different types of concerns are understood.

Methodological concerns include the reductionism which derives from PRA's preference for the visual over the verbal, and the simplification that this implies (Laier, 1999), as well as the lack of any 'objective' standards of assessment and quality control by which one might know whether a PRA exercise has been well or badly undertaken.

There is no doubt that participatory methods have gone a long way towards making the development process more participatory. However, despite the rapid spread of PRA, there are concerns about the quality of the participatory processes and research, the degree of participation that is actually achieved, and the interpretation of results.

Linkages with concepts of civil society, citizenship and a rights-based approach to development influence the participation agenda in the new millennium. This poses challenges to participation advocates, both in shoring up existing theory and practice—maintaining quality—and in breaking new ground.

Quality is—and must be—a major concern in the current participation agenda. But the pressures are many to violate quality. Donors and governments are maybe the worst abusers, wanting to go instantly to scale, in hundreds, even thousands, of communities. Some donors place outrageous demands, and employ 'expert' consultants who say they can provide PRA and participatory training in however short a time. To these abuses Chambers (2002b) adds that donors and Government Departments, and even NGOs, rarely recognize that they themselves need institutional changes—of cultures, procedures and rewards—if they are to promote and sustain a good participation agenda.

Mainstreaming Participation

There is a continuous uneasiness and concern that participatory processes are co-opted to agendas which are in fact tightly controlled by the centre (Christoplos, 1995). The participatory methodologies aim at 'awareness-raising', 'empowerment', 'mobilizing people to see the need for transformation', and associate with a 'more democratic, equitable, inclusive and pluralist development paradigm' (McGee, 2002). In this dressing participatory methodology is not merely a toolkit, but a possible threat to status quo:

> The threat this approach offered to the political *status quo*, both globally and locally, perhaps explains the 'mainstreaming' of participatory development discourse by major donors, and the linking of it to governance and democratisation agendas .... Nevertheless, donors appear to have accepted many of the principles of the participatory development approach, so this 'subsuming of the radical alternative by the orthodoxy' is genuinely transforming the mainstream development agenda (Kothari and Minogue quoting McGee, 2002: 186).

This raises a questions as to whether a convergence has taken place between a radical participatory alternative and an orthodox mainstream development agenda. McGee finds arguments for convergence between the *participatory development agenda* and the *mainstream development cooperation agenda.* There are apparent similarities in *current participation agendas,* whether in official development agencies, NGOs, or in select academic circles. Does this mean that one agenda has co-opted the other? Not quite. The convergence can be explained in such a way, that 'this is more a sign of the success of the transformative project of "participatory development" than evidence of absorption of the alternative by the orthodoxy' (McGee, 2002: 93). In other words, the convergence can be interpreted as a positive development for both the mainstream and the alternative participation current.

What shall one make of the observation that both the orthodox approach to participation and the suggested alternatives to make good the deficiencies of the orthodoxy have been brought within the mainstream policies and practices of key development agencies? On the one hand it may be regarded positively, as a process whereby criticisms of traditional practice have compelled the major aid agencies to incorporate more innovative ideas into their work. On the other hand, others would see the process as an attempt by powerful institutions to neutralize radical ideas by taking them over, controlling their operation, and emptying them of radical content. Which of these interpretations is right depends on the eyes that see, and lead to the conclusion that development is a terrain upon which these battles of ideas and disputes about action will continue to be fought and reflected in 'the changing participation agenda'.

The extensive discussions and evolving critiques about the many meanings, uses and abuses of participation bear witness to the fact that participation is a living but contested concept. In the absence of fundamental democratic mechanisms can participation sometimes become a substitute, or even a surrogate? Chapter 3 will provide illustrations of selected and innovative uses of participatory methods.

The use of participatory methods has spread to almost every area of development cooperation. From mainly rural development projects, participatory methods—for convenience called participatory rural appraisal (PRA) methods—are now being applied in areas as diverse as policy analysis and planning, poverty reductions strategies, dispute resolution and advocacy. Brief illustrations are given of the most commonly used methods from the 'Catalogue' of PRA methods. Ranking and scoring and social maps get special attention since these are particularly relevant tools for analysis of difference, unequal relationships and prioritization, which are at the core of much development work and research and which many development studies have to address. Examples are given of the spreading uses of participatory methods to policy areas of decentralization and Poverty Reduction Strategies Processes, PRSPs, and to topical applications for participatory budgeting, economic analysis, for technology assessment and advocacy.

3.1   Illustrations of Selected Participatory Methods

A list of participatory methods, techniques and tools were introduced with reference to the 'Catalogue' of PRA methods in Section 2.2.2. In the following sections explanations and illustrations will be given of these. However, it cannot be over-emphasized that the 'Catalogue' should not be understood as the exclusive and mandatory list of participatory methods. On the contrary they should serve as inspiration for application and adjustment to specific situations and contexts. The methods included in the 'Catalogue' represent the more commonly used PRA methods.

3.1.1 Elaboration of the 'Catalogue' of PRA Methods

Review of Secondary Sources

No matter what our research topic is, there is almost always a wealth of information hidden in a variety of sources. Many references are accessible in libraries, in reports and in databases, and many documents may be downloaded from the internet. It is a crime in research and development work to not allocate time for prior documentary studies. It gives a better start and saves time—not only your own, but more importantly valuable time for respondents. There are two major types of sources:

Documents: Research and other official and unofficial studies and reports on socio-cultural, political, ecological conditions, national and area-specific **statistics**, topical and area-specific articles from journals and newspapers, archives and files, aerial and satellite photos and maps.

Folklore: Mythology, oral tradition, local and topical stories, proverbs and poetry (e.g., Hanghe, 1988; Vansina, 1985).

To either of these categories belong films, videos and other relevant audio-visual documentation. The use of images and sound which were earlier confined to exotic anthropological studies has been revitalized (Bauer and Gaskell, 2002).

Development studies make frequent use of secondary data in the form of statistics. Who doesn't make use of the data made available in a variety of UN and World Bank reports on an annual basis? Figures on human development and poverty, on women's and men's participation in education, access to health services, etc., are convincingly presented for groups of more or less developed countries. Statistics are powerful. They look objective, but are seductive and often highly unreliable.

Direct Observation

Observation of physical structures, social differences, behaviour, action and symbols, in solitude or with others with whom observations are discussed, provides important information for posing central questions. Observation during all phases of a study contributes information on persistence and change. The shift in development cooperation from 'top-down' interventions towards 'grassroots' participatory perspectives provides a great demand for up-to-date approaches to appreciate indigenous knowledge in a globalizing world. Participant observation—the classical method of anthropology for understanding indigenous knowledge and symbols—is putting on new gowns, as 'the time has come for anthropology to consolidate its place in development practice' (Sillitoe, 2002).

Key Indicators[1]

An indicator is a qualitative or quantitative factor or 'unit of information' that provides a basis for assessing importance, achievement, change or performance.

Local indicators: Local stakeholders' criteria for what is more and less significant, e.g., criteria for priority crops, of poverty or well-being, of gender roles, of illness, etc., are vital in problem analysis and for posing relevant questions.

National and global indicators: Since development studies are set in contexts where social groups, geographical areas, environmental zones, etc., are analysed, ranked and compared, it is necessary to be familiar with the indicators that are applied at national and global levels. The globally agreed Millennium Development Goals are providing key indicators on a long list of global and national conditions relating

---

[1] For a discussion on 'key' and 'additional' indicators, see Section 7.4.3, and Sections 6.2 and 6.3 on poverty and gender indicators.

to human development, poverty and ecological sensitivity, etc., in the United Nations' annual Human Development Report and in special progress reports.

Indicators for objectives, for achievement, outputs and performance are integral tools when logical framework is applied in planning and monitoring development interventions. Most development agencies attach much importance to indicators without necessarily being able to advise on which indicators to use. How indicators can be identified and used, e.g., in topical applications, are illustrated in Section 1.2.3, Section 5.1.3, and in Chapter 7 on monitoring and evaluation.

Semi-structured Interviews

Increasingly, interviews based on written or memorized checklists are taking the place of or supplementing large-scale structured questionnaire surveys in development studies. In semi-structured interviews (SSI) questions are open-ended. Unexpected, relevant issues are followed up with further questions or probing. Interviewees are typically key individuals, focus groups or mixed groups.

Key individuals are people anticipated to have particular insight into or opinions about the topic under study. They may be ordinary people and not necessarily professional specialists, the better educated, those in power, or the officials. In participatory poverty studies poor people themselves are key people—though not without practical and ethical problems. Issues to be highlighted must determine who the relevant key persons are. Who the key people are is best identified by enquiring from different sources to avoid a biased view.

Focus groups, homogeneous or mixed groups are relevant when the dynamics of the group situation is considered to provide additional useful information. A homogeneous group of farmers may be optimal for in-depth information about farming systems. A group interview with specialists may provide more and better information than could be obtained through a much more time-consuming exercise of individual interviews with the same people. A mixed group of young, middle-aged and elderly women will provide more information about knowledge, attitudes and practice of family planning, for example, than a homogeneous group. Care must be taken not to combine mixed groups with in-built breaks on open discussion, e.g., by mixing caste or ethnic groups in non-appropriate ways.

Chains of interviews between the different key individuals, groups and specialists can be a useful sequencing of data collection.

Probing questions or asking direct questions that lead to key issues without beating around the bush can make an interview more dynamic.

Simple questionnaires, possibly to be managed by selected participants themselves in connection with self-surveys and **self-evaluations**, can be designed to permit **continuous data analysis** in the field. The questionnaires should be short and easy to code. The application of semi-structured interviewing is elaborated in Section 5.2.2.

Ranking and Scoring

In development studies knowledge of difference and inequality is often required, whether in socio-economic conditions or in people's attitudes. The overarching objective of development work is to combat unequal social relations and exploitation, and to reduce poverty through the promotion of economic and social development. People's perception of the most detrimental causes of poverty and inequalities is an important basis for remedial interventions to combat poverty whether at the policy, sector or community level. Had there been consensus between all concerned stakeholders about the causes and remedies of poverty, the world would have looked different than what it does! Ranking and scoring of problems and remedial action reflect different interests between different people; and power relations, whether in small or large forums, in wealth ranking of communities or in national elections, influence the outcome. Attributes such as wealth or economic status, class, caste, race and ethnic group—interlinked with age and gender—are often the bases of social and economic inequality and influence people's perceptions of problems and remedies.

Ranking and scoring have long been used to assess people's expectations, beliefs, judgements, attitudes, preferences, and opinions. Ranking and scoring mean placing something in order. Social marketing research uses ranking and scoring to develop strategies for changing public behaviour (Kotler and Roberto, 1989). Action-oriented development studies use comparative data and rankings for prioritizing actions. Ranking and scoring are the central tools in what is called the *possible future workshop approach* (see point 10 below), practised by many participatory-oriented physical planners and social workers (for more details see Sections 3.1.2. and 3.1.3).

Construction and Analysis of Maps and Models

Participatory mapping is used for providing distribution information relating to limited physical space and settlements, e.g., information on population distribution, demographic data, infrastructure, natural resources, and social services distributions. Maps are drawn collectively on the sand, or on paper if the map is to be saved for later monitoring, for example. The mapping method is quick and reliable as communication between the participating group members has a corrective function.

Construction of models, i.e., three-dimensional models of villages, housing and water sources, etc., may be preferred if the exercise, besides providing collective information, has the objective of longer lasting demonstration.

Joint analysis of **aerial maps** and photographs is a different method for obtaining local knowledge of physical space and natural resources. With the expansion of Remote Sensing and Geographical Information Systems, **GIS**, development planners in cooperation with anthropologists are starting to see the prospects embedded in the GIS tool for participatory planning, e.g., for Natural Resource Management (see Section 6.4.3 on Geomatics).

Transects are cross-sectional maps or diagrams of an area (see Figure 3.1). They are constructed as a joint exercise with local informants during walks through the area for observing, discussing and registering the endowments and problems of the area. Section 3.1.3 shows techniques of mapping.

Diagramming

Participatory diagramming is used for (*i*) summarizing empirical information, for example, in time lines, as well as for (*ii*) summarizing analysed information, for example in bar charts and pie charts. The

Figure 3.1 Agro-ecosystems Transect, Misera (Young Men)

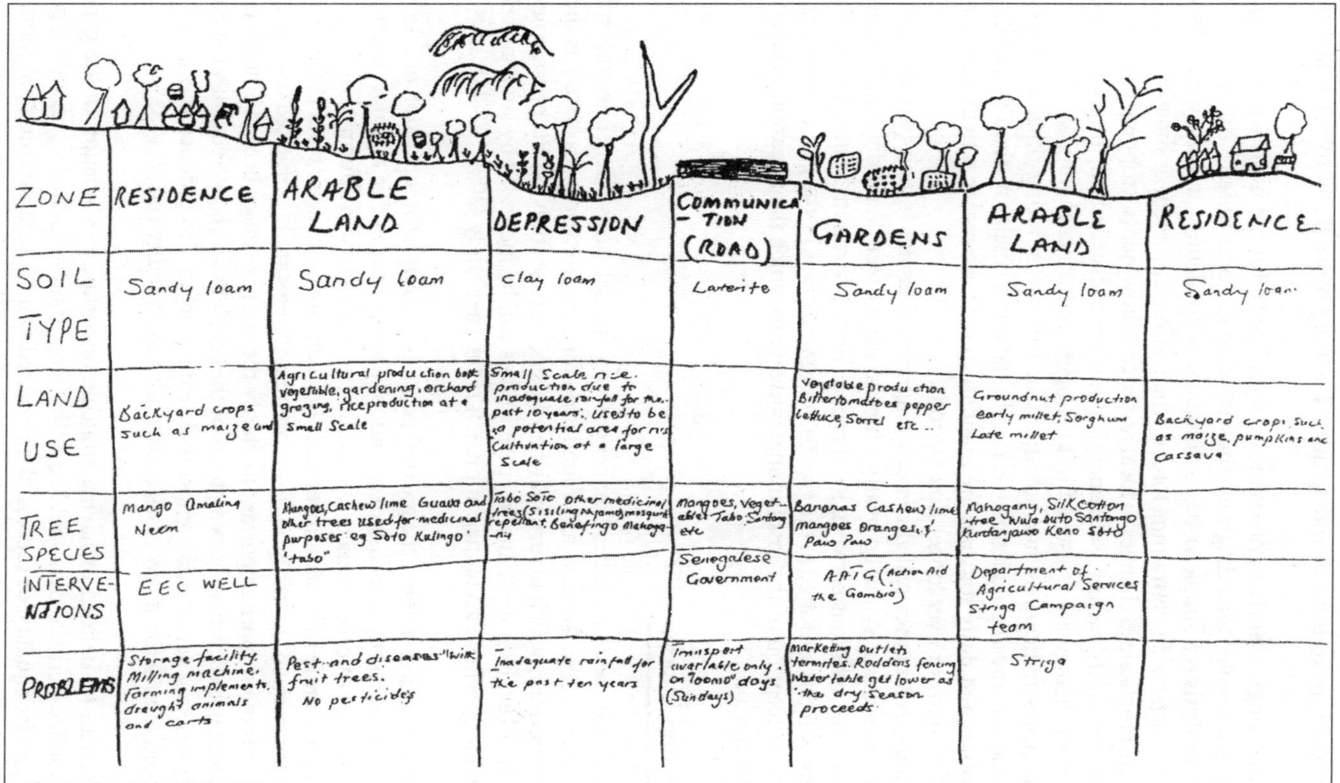

ZONE	RESIDENCE	ARABLE LAND	DEPRESSION	COMMUNICATION (ROAD)	GARDENS	ARABLE LAND	RESIDENCE
SOIL TYPE	Sandy loam	Sandy loam	Clay loam	Laterite	Sandy loam	Sandy loam	Sandy loam
LAND USE	Backyard crops such as maize and	Agricultural production e.g. vegetable, gardening, orchard grazing, Rice production at a Small Scale	Small Scale rice production due to inadequate rainfall for the past 10 years. Used to be so potential area for rice cultivation at a large scale		Vegetable production Bitterball, okra pepper lettuce, Sorrel etc.	Groundnut production early millet, Sorghum Late millet	Backyard crops such as maize, pumpkins and cassava
TREE SPECIES	Mango Orange Neem	Mangoes, Cashew, lime Guava and b&t trees Used for medicinal purposes eg Sorto Kolingo "toto"	Toto Soto after medicinal trees (Sisiling-nyamg-mmsimmi repellant. Sorto Jingo Bainyango etc	Mangoes, Veget- ables Toto Sinbay etc	Bananas Cashew lime mangoes Orange? Pano Pano	Mahogany, Silk Cotton tree Wula Jato Santango Kurto Jambo Kono Sotto	
INTERVENTIONS	EEC WELL			Senegalese Government	APIG (Action Aid ne Gambo)	Department of Agricultural Services Striga Campaign team	
PROBLEMS	Storage facility. Milling machine, farming implement, draught animals and carts	Pest and diseases thunk fruit trees. No pesticides	Inadequate rainfall for the past ten years	Transport available only on Toonid dogs (Sarbays)	Marketing outlets permitted Rondons fencing waterhole get lower as the dry season proceeds.	Striga	

After ActionAid, 1992: 102.

idea is to let people make their own diagrams. They are more likely to use other measures than the outsider.

Time lines are rough overviews of events of significance for the history of the group or the area in question. They are simpler than diagrams showing changes over time.

Force Field Analysis is a simple visual technique used to identify and analyse on the one side 'driving forces', and on the other side 'restraining forces' which affect a problem or situation (e.g., gender equality).

Trend analysis emphasizes changes in local resource endowments, cropping patterns, ecology, climate, physical and social infrastructure, settlements, population distribution, migration, wealth, 'quality of life', etc. Causes of change are registered or kept open for further inquiry.

Seasonal diagrams indicate annual variations or variations during other relevant periods for vital factors of production and reproduction—e.g., rain, labour availability, food availability, or prices.

Activity profiles and daily routines are made to summarize major activity trends for individuals or groups on a daily basis or over longer time periods.

Venn diagrams, sometimes called *chapatti* diagrams after the Indian pancake-shaped bread, place circles of different sizes in symbolic relationships to each other. Venn diagrams are used to depict the participants' sense of relations between local groups or organizations. The size of the *chapatti*s symbolizes the different weights allocated to the groups or organizations by the participants. Figure 3.2 illustrates Wollo peasants' perception of the institutional universe to which their peasant association belongs. It is a subjective delineation.

Case Studies and Stories

Case studies, as the name indicates, concentrate on special cases. Generalizations from case stories must be handled with care. To serve as a foundation for generalizations, case studies should be related to a theoretical framework, which in turn may be adjusted as case study results provide new evidence (Yin, 1989 and 2002). The 'generalizability' of case studies can be increased by strategic selection of *critical cases*. Says Flyvbjerg, whose acclaimed approach is the case study (2001: 77–78):

> When the objective is to achieve the greatest possible amount of information on a given problem or phenomenon, a representative case or a random sample may not be the most appropriate strategy. This is because the typical or average case is often not the richest in information. Atypical or extreme cases often reveal more information because they activate more actors and more basic mechanisms in the situation studied. In addition, from both an understanding-oriented and an action-oriented perspective, it is often more important to clarify the deeper causes behind a given problem and its consequences than to describe the symptoms of the problem and how frequently they occur. Random samples emphasising representativeness will seldom be able to produce this kind of insight; it is more appropriate to select a few cases chosen for their validity (pp. 77–78).

A *critical case* can be defined as having strategic importance in relation to the general problem. In development studies a critical case could be a 'flag-ship' intervention, e.g., regarding poverty reduction, promotion of gender equality, or successful micro-credit and decentralization programmes, etc., and the

Figure 3.2   Venn Diagram of Decision Makers in a Peasant Association in Wollo, Ethiopia

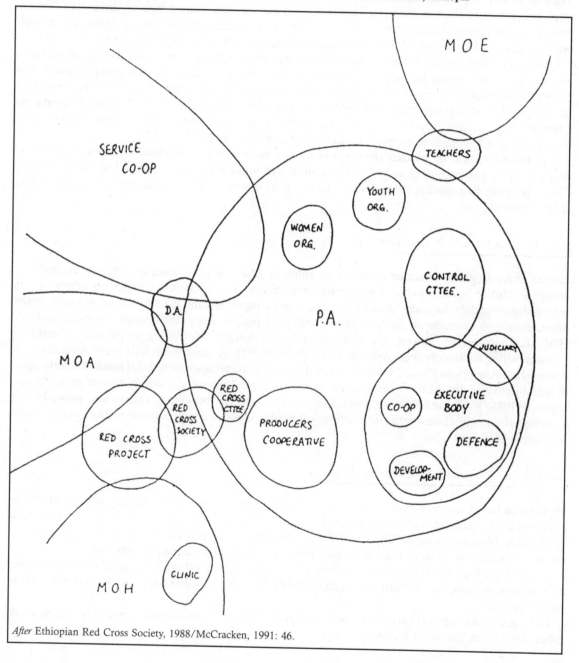

After Ethiopian Red Cross Society, 1988/McCracken, 1991: 46.

focus be on learning the maximum lessons about intervention parameters, their relations, context, etc., from in-depth analysis. For example, Tendler (1997) has an enlightening way of discussing 'Decentralisation, Participation and Other Things Local' by selecting cases where better performance by staff and workers could be attributed to active support and motivation from their employers.

Case studies often contain a substantial element of **narrative**. Asking 'How?' and carrying out narrative analysis are closely linked activities. Narrative inquiries develop descriptions and interpretations of a phenomenon from the perspective of participants, researchers, and others. Narratives not only give meaningful form to experiences already lived through (see for example Section 7.3.7 on **Most Significant Change**), they can also provide a forward glance, helping us to anticipate situations even before we encounter them, allowing us to envision alternative futures (Flyvbjerg, 2001: 137).

Life histories, oral or written stories told by key people, e.g., by school-children, function as supplementary information or as in-depth case studies of households, of groups and of events. The social analyst gives clear guidance to the story teller or informants on how to structure the story, if structuring is at all desired.

Drama, Games and Role Plays

Games and role plays, direct or recorded on video or film, are sometimes the optimal methods for bringing sensitive issues into the open. Professional actors can play sensitive topics for others or join with ordinary people. In many cultures drama is deeply ingrained and used to act out sensitive issues often relating to violation of rights of minorities, poor people, dalits, the landless, women, widows, HIV/AIDS victims, etc., and on how to defend and reclaim rights. Motivating people to act sometimes requires skilled facilitators (e.g., Mlama, 1991; Orkin, 1991). A number of NGOs are specialized in dramatizing development issues. **Games** may be designed in accordance with **social marketing** principles if the objective of the game is to motivate participants for an idea, a product, an aid package, etc. (Epstein, 1988; Kotler and Roberto, 1989; Epstein et al., 1991). Speaking in images and **proverbs** can sometimes bring one closer to the truth, while doing **role plays** can enrich communication and be useful as training exercises.

Workshops, Scenarios and Possible Futures

Workshops have become a most favoured method of communication with different 'stakeholders', for collecting data, and sometimes for jointly analysing data. The book *Participatory Workshops—A Sourcebook of 21 Sets of Ideas and Activities* (Chambers, 2002a) provides useful guidance for facilitators and trainers on how best to conduct workshops and move from 'teaching' to **participatory learning**.

A useful package for facilitation of workshops, including self-adhesive cards of different shapes and colours, posters, sticky cloth, etc., called PARTICIPLAN, is illustrated on the Internet (www.participlan.com).

There are many types of workshops with different forms of participation, some resembling focus group discussions (see point 4 above):

SWOT, Strengths, Weaknesses, Opportunities and Threats Workshops originate in organizational analysis but can easily be adjusted to suit other purposes. SWOT is a useful way to elicit participants' ideas retrospectively on what have been the strengths and weaknesses of an intervention, a learning process, etc., and for identifying priorities (opportunities) with due consideration to threats (controllable or un-controllable conditions) in a given context. Writing statements on cards and sorting these under common denominators can be very participative and entertaining. Simpler and adjusted SWOT approaches, e.g., with only strengths or weaknesses registered on flip-charts, are common. SWOT can be used for planning as well as in evaluations.

AIC—Appreciate-Influence-Control is a workshop-based method which brings diverse stakeholders together. AIC typically involves three phases: looking at present realities and the reasons for present issues and problems; brainstorming as many ideas as possible about the ideal situation; and jointly discussing strategies of how to get from present reality to the ideal vision, prioritizing different options and then setting action plans which participants could commit to implementing, how these would be implemented, including who would be responsible for what and when.

Possible Future Workshops (Future Search) bring people together to elaborate possible strategies for acting on identified problems and issues, e.g., overcrowding and slum upgrading, crime prevention, youth employment. The participants, who preferably represent different experiences, contribute their ideas to change and improve the situation. Future workshops are frequently used in connection with action research, e.g., on work and labour market issues (Nielsen, 2002). In Possible Future Workshops the *participants develop the scenarios* and opt for planning along the lines of one of these. They follow a standard sequence of phases: (*i*) Critical assessment and prioritization of the main critical issues; (*ii*) Phase of imagination: brainstorming of ideas and prioritization of the main positive ideas; (*iii*) Preparation of an implementation plan after selection and critical assessment of ideas for solutions (Jungk and Müllert, 1984). A future workshop may last from one to several days. Lessons from future workshops with resource-poor Tanzanian farmers is documented in Ravnborg (1992). The stepwise approach of future workshops resembles the **Appreciative Inquiry, AI**, approach (Section 6.4.1), but differs in starting out from 'critical issues' while Appreciative Inquiry departs from appreciation of 'what works well'.

Scenario Workshops differ from future workshops in bringing people together to discuss and prioritize scenarios which may have been prepared by specialists or outsiders (Elle, 1992). A typical topic could be a common concern for a community, for example 'ecological sustainable city' relating to a larger project of urban planning. The topic should not be too narrow and should deal with assessment and choices—using, for example, ranking and scoring—between scenarios representing markedly different types of technology. The scenarios are used as visions and as a spur for discussion. The scenario workshop can be a local meeting that includes a dialogue among four local groups of actors: *citizens, policy makers, business representatives* and *experts*. Each group comes with their own experience. It is important that the topic lies within the participants' sphere of action, i.e., that not all decisions have been taken, and there is consensus that local action is a necessity. The current form of scenario workshop tends to let participants meet initially in smaller groups to develop different scenarios. Hence a scenario workshop can be a sequence of workshops. The participants may meet in separate thematic groups according to experience and interest. In the 'urban ecology' scenario workshops conducted by the Danish Board of Technology, the task was to agree on a common vision and produce local action plans for energy, water and waste.

The results from the scenario workshops were evaluated and fed into local political debate. The outcome was a report and a national plan for urban ecology, which was presented at a public conference. Subsequently this was partly implemented by the Danish Ministry of the Environment (Andersen and Jaeger, 2001). In contrast with *citizens' juries* and *consensus conferences,* consensus is not necessarily aimed for.

Consensus Conferences have become a popular form of public consultation, using a technique intended to 'bridge the gap between the general public, experts and politicians' (Grundahl, 1995; Wallace, 2001). Consensus conferences are often initiated by politicians who want civil evidence about sensitive issues of public concern before taking political decisions. For example, an expert panel gives evidence on the topic to a panel of laymen who, after deliberation and negotiation, reach a consensus. The outcome is a report on a possible practical solution. The major challenge as with other (semi) participatory techniques is to make the politicians listen to and act upon the outcome.

Public Hearings, typically about physical planning programmes, are a long-established approach to involve the public in commenting on forthcoming plans. Hearings may use the public media, but will also often include public meeting arrangements where dialogue takes place between decision makers and experts *and* the public audience. Workshops as those mentioned above may be included, but priorities must take into consideration the fact that such workshops and conferences are time-consuming and resource demanding.

Deliberations and negotiations in the participatory workshops, consensus conferences and hearings are different examples of democracy in practice. They help to provide stronger evidence for decision makers, but there is no guarantee that ideas proposed by the public and by participating stakeholders will be adhered to.

Triangulation

Triangulation—looking at things from different points of view—or multiple strategies, is a method to overcome the problems that stem from studies relying upon a single theory, a single method, a single set of data from a limited sample, and from a single investigator. Triangulation helps to validate observations and information. In cross-disciplinary teams in particular, the presence of people with different experiences should be optimized through triangulation; i.e., listening and learning from each member's observations and findings.

There are at least five types of triangulation.

1. **Data triangulation** which can be divided into
   Time triangulation where the influence of time is considered in study design, e.g., using longitudinal research design;
   Space triangulation, a typical form of comparative study;
   Person triangulation, for example comparisons of reactions at three levels of analysis,
   (*a*) the individual level, (*b*) the interactive level among groups, and (*c*) the collective level.
2. **Investigator triangulation** means that more than one person examines the same situation.

3. **Discipline triangulation** means that a problem is studied by different disciplines. It optimizes the experience of the different perspectives if combined with investigator triangulation, i.e., having at least two people of different disciplines study the same problem together.
4. **Theory triangulation**, in which alternative or competing theories are used in any one situation.
5. **Methodological triangulation** involves 'within-method' triangulation, that is, the same method used on different occasions, and 'between-method' triangulation (Christiansen, et al., 2001) when different methods are used in relation to the same object of study.

Continuous Analysis and Reporting

Participatory methods mean potential participation of selected stakeholders in all stages of a study or project, from identification of the problem to evaluation—possibly with different degrees of intensity. The processes of data analysis and interpretation are no exceptions. Continuous data analysis in the field and reporting on the spot can be done in concert with local people, if not **by** and **for** local people themselves. The advantage of early or continuous data analysis is that data gaps, surprising perspectives worth pursuing, etc., are discovered at an early stage. The analyst, who also needs to report to authorities, can start analysing data in the field. **Portable computers** are useful.

Software for analysis of quantitative as well as qualitative data, which do not require large data-space, is available and permits continuous treatment of data (see Section 5.2.4).

Participatory Planning, Budgeting, Monitoring, Evaluation and Other Self-surveys

Participatory approaches to development work rest on the assumptions that (*i*) ordinary people's knowledge is different from but counts as much as the experts', and (*ii*) people's support for a development activity increases when they are actively part of the decision-making process. The ultimate aim of project-specific participatory activities is often that people develop their own **plan or product**. A plan can be a map or a model showing physical structures, a narrative document, a report, a **prioritised budget** (see Section 3.3.1), or a time-chart, all produced with incorporation of the participants' ideas or by the participants themselves. Participants may come from different groups of stakeholders, i.e., users, local officials, NGOs and others.

Participation in all project or programme cycle activities aims at creating dialogue with the stakeholders, getting the necessary information to and from them through convenient communication methods, and to promote stakeholder 'ownership'. **Who participates in which activities** will be determined from case to case. Participation by different stakeholders provides more information than from a narrow group of users.

Self-survey methods, used for example for participatory monitoring and evaluation (see Chapter 7) may include quantitative and qualitative data. Self-surveys entail community members undertaking the basic data collection, typically under the guidance of a facilitator. Survey forms for collection of clearly defined information must be short. Pre-coding permits data processing *in situ*.

Do-it-yourself

Do-it-yourself reverses the classical roles, i.e., outsider-insider, observer-observed, of the researcher and the researched. The outsider gets hands-on knowledge from trying the activities under the insider's instruction. The reversal of roles between the insider and the outsider prompts dialogue.

To conclude, the core methods and techniques in the PRA 'Catalogue' is a good starting point from where to choose and further develop, combine and apply the different techniques. The Catalogue is not a recipe. There is plenty of scope for innovations in PRA methods, spanning from stand alone oral communication and visual exercises to methods which increasingly make use of information and communication technology, ICT.

3.1.2 Ranking and Scoring Techniques

The classics in sociological ranking techniques for making scales are those developed by Thurstone (differential ranking), Likert (summated ranking) and Guttman (cumulative ranking) (Karlsson, 1961; Kumar, 1999). They encompass a variety of ordinal metrics, interval metrics, weighted metrics, pre-set or derived categories, etc. There is a distinction between ranking (ordinal—putting in order) and scoring (cardinal—weighting differences). The scoring techniques vary between multiple choice, choosing between alternatives with or without a fixed reference point, graphical techniques, etc.

The ranking and scoring techniques used in participatory rural appraisal, PRA, differ from the classical approaches in activating respondents to undertake the ranking and leaving more decisions on **what** to be ranked/scored to the participants. Ranking and scoring is therefore relevant for participatory identification of **indicators**.

It is important to emphasize that ranking and scoring exercises are relevant not only for 'users' and community members, but in some cases even more so as exercises for planners and practitioners themselves.

The **types of ranking** that are most common in connection with development studies include:

- Problem, preference and opportunity ranking
- Pair-wise ranking
- Matrix ranking or scoring
- Wealth and well-being ranking—or grouping.

Problem, preference and opportunity ranking can be used to quickly identify main problems, opportunities or preferences as experienced by individuals or groups of stakeholders. In the exploratory stage of a study the divergence of people's rankings will give an impression of different interests or opinions, which may then be compared, and consensus later be approached through discussion. In the Figure 3.3 example six respondents have agreed that drought ranks as the most severe constraint on agricultural production. In descending order pests, weeds, cost of inputs and labour shortage follow. Note, however, that considerable differences exist in the individual scores—something which may be of relevance for follow-up interviews to check on 'correlation' with respondents' individual experience.

The most common technique for ranking, which has been widely used especially for social stratification research, is **card sorting**. Informants sort cards, which represent occupations, into piles. That is, they will sort a cross-section of typical national occupations into social ranks—usually five—with high consistency (Svalastoga and Carlsson, 1961). Card sorting is a valid technique for ranking problems such as those outlined in Figure 3.3.

Figure 3.3   Example of Problem Ranking

	Example of Problem Ranking Constraints on Agricultural Production Respondents						Total	
Problem	A	B	C	D	E	F	Score	Ranking
Drought	5	5	3	5	4	5	27	a
Pests	4	3	5	4	5	4	25	b
Woods	3	4	4	1	3	3	18	c
Cost of inputs	2	1	2	2	2	2	11	d
Labour shortage	1	2	1	3	1	1	9	e

5 = most important, 1 = least important

After Theis and Grady, 1991: 64.

Local materials, e.g., beans, seeds, leaves, sticks, stones or whatever is at hand, are ideal as scoring devices when cards are not available.

There are other scoring techniques, such as free scoring and scoring out of a maximum.

In **pair-wise ranking**, items of interest are compared pair by pair, informants being asked: Which is the preferred or dominant of the two items? Why? What is good and bad about each? The method has been developed into the **Stated Preference** approach. The particular methodology has been developed to take into account people's priorities, e.g., for different services—water, electricity, garbage collection, etc., or service levels (COWI, 2002). In the Stated Preference approach data are obtained via a set of hypothetical choice situations about people's **willingness to pay** a specified amount for water, for example. Stated Preference can be conducted by sorting cards on which the hypothetical service delivery levels are stated, and cards with new service levels may be added in the process. Technically the Stated Preference approach also allows the researcher to work directly on a laptop into which the hypothesis—or scenarios—of water service level and tariff level are entered, and can be posed to respondents under almost any physical condition.

Scoring and ranking of options, e.g., by using **matrices**, can supply information through comparisons which help to prioritize different interventions and technical solutions that are relevant to and adoptable by the recipients. Using **local measures, judgements and materials** such as tins, seeds and sticks sometimes contributes to demystify the research process. However, there is a risk of being patronizing if the use of such materials is introduced to people who are used to paper and pencils or even laptops.

Matrix ranking (Figures 3.4, 3.5 and 3.6) helps to identify people's criteria for a certain topic. The criteria are likely to differ from group to group. Note the different criteria or 'indicators' used by the three groups: young women, old women and old men in the matrix scoring and ranking of crops. The women's groups emphasize the nutritional value of the crops. The men's indicators of useful crops mostly concern production and marketing. But the women's group, especially the younger women, also operates with a larger variety of crops and criteria for ranking. Thus, the ranking and scoring exercise illustrated here is condensed information on the **criteria** applied by **different groups** to assess the perceived **value of different crops**. By splitting into the three groups more information is obtained than would have been gained in a joint ranking exercise. Discussions about such matrices help to reveal the reason for the preferences of different groups.

Experience from the Gambia participatory training exercise, from which Figures 3.4 to 3.6 are taken, showed that among many PRA techniques, matrix scoring proved the hardest and most tiring. A lot of time went into gathering symbols. Some confusion remained around which way the scoring should take place, per criteria or per option. One benefit from the exercise was that people discovered that matrices can provide a vast amount of information produced by people themselves. In this way the exercise is a true exploratory and data collection method.

Ranking and scoring can be useful for obtaining sensitive information. Practitioners and researchers who have ever asked directly about people's income or wealth know the difficulties of obtaining reliable information, if they get a reply at all. For most purposes **trends of income** and relative wealth rankings suffice. Ranks or scores are easier to obtain than absolute measures. Informants tend to be more willing—and possibly more able—to provide *relative* values regarding their wealth than give absolute figures.

Lessons

The possible utilization of data from rankings and scoring can be summarized in a few points:

- For generating discussion and awareness among the participants on what is more and what is less important, and awareness about causal relationships between phenomena.
- For generating information on people's priorities, which compares favourably with information generated through time-consuming surveys.
- For exploratory purposes to help direct further questions leading on to planning.
- For 'before and after' comparisons, e.g., in connection with monitoring.
- Rankings can be a tool for studying power relations. Other methodologies involving people's action will be required to tackle and possibly change power relations.
- In concrete terms ranking and scoring may enable people to express their preferences and balance the characteristics of a 'wish'. For example, specify a crop they would like scientists to find or breed for them.

The process and analysis of ranking and scoring exercises can be a goal in itself, while the results may be key inputs in planning documents.

Figure 3.4 Matrix Scoring and Ranking of Vegetables Grown (Young Women)

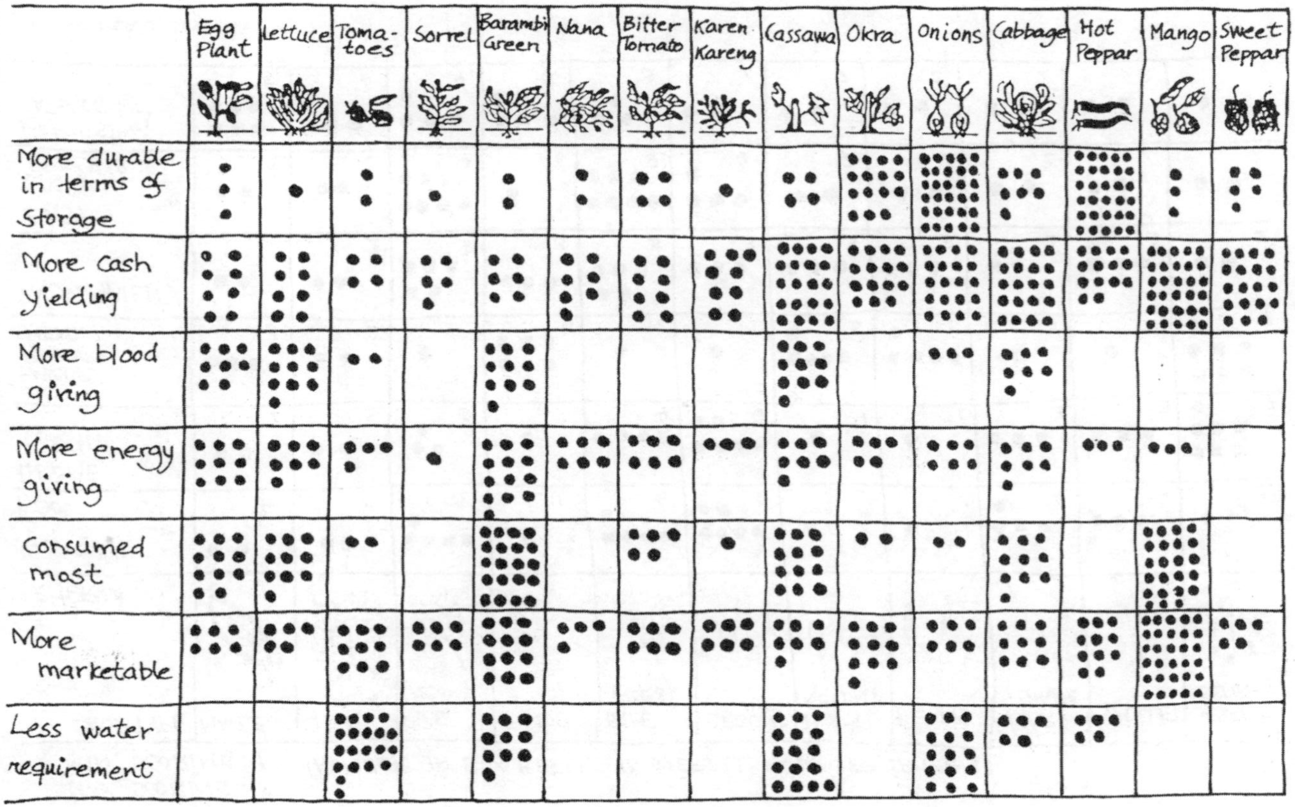

Column headings (vegetables): Egg Plant, Lettuce, Tomatoes, Sorrel, Baranbi Green, Nbuna, Bitter Tomato, Karen Kareng, Cassava, Okra, Onions, Cabbage, Hot Pepper, Mango, Sweet Pepper

Row labels (criteria):
- More durable in terms of storage
- More cash yielding
- More blood giving
- More energy giving
- Consumed most
- More marketable
- Less water requirement

After ActionAid, 1992: 56.

Figure 3.5 Matrix Scoring and Ranking of Crops Grown (Old Women)

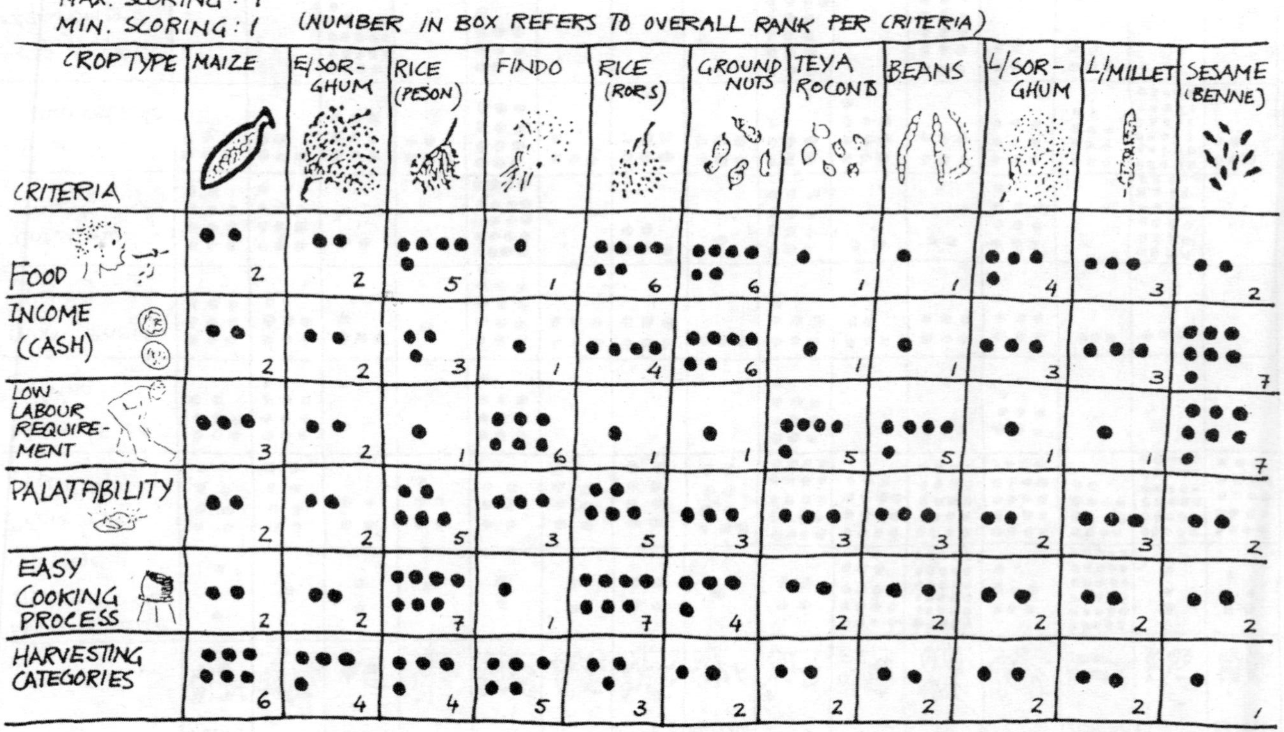

MAX. SCORING: 7 MIN. SCORING: 1

(NUMBER IN BOX REFERS TO OVERALL RANK PER CRITERIA)

CROP TYPE

CRITERIA	MAIZE	E/SORGHUM	RICE (PESON)	FINDO	RICE (RORS)	GROUND NUTS	TEYA ROCONTS	BEANS	L/SORGHUM	L/MILLET	SESAME (BENNE)
FOOD	2	2	5	1	6	6			4	3	2
INCOME (CASH)	2	2	3	1	4	6	1	1	3	3	7
LOW LABOUR REQUIREMENT	3	2	1	6	1	1	5	5		1	7
PALATABILITY	2		5	3	5	3	3	3			2
EASY COOKING PROCESS	2	2	7	1	7	4	2	2	2	2	2
HARVESTING CATEGORIES	6	4	4	5	3	2	2	2	2	2	1

After ActionAid, 1992: 43.

Figure 3.6   Matrix Scoring and Ranking of Crops Grown (Old Men)

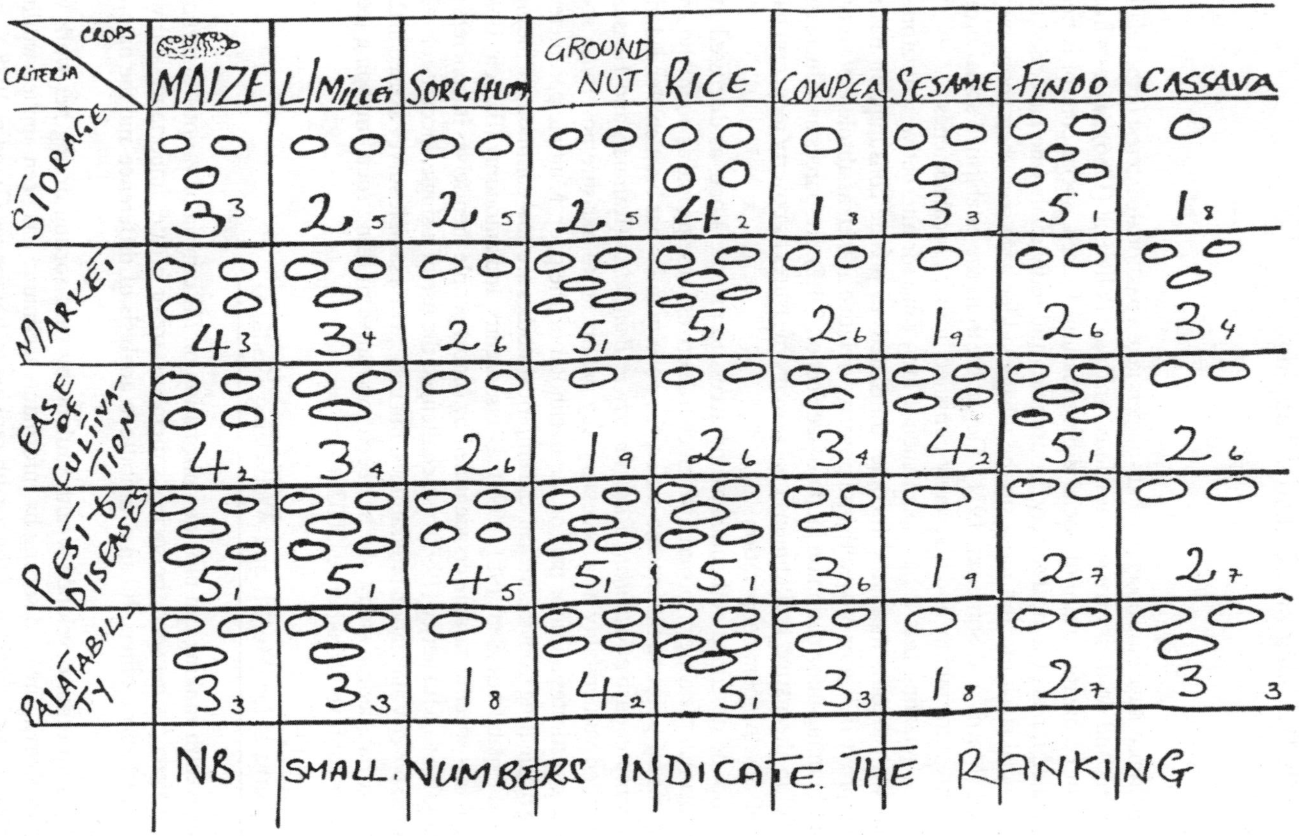

CRITERIA \ CROPS	MAIZE	MILLET	SORGHUM	GROUND NUT	RICE	COWPEA	SESAME	FINDO	CASSAVA
STORAGE	3^3	2^5	2^5	2^5	4^2	1^3	3^3	5^1	1^3
MARKET	4^3	3^4	2^6	5^1	5^1	2^6	1^9	2^6	3^4
EASE OF CULTIVATION	4^2	3^4	2^6	1^9	2^6	3^4	4^2	5^1	2^6
PEST & DISEASE	5^1	5^1	4^5	5^1	5^1	3^6	1^9	2^7	2^7
RELIABILITY	3^3	3^3	1^8	4^2	5^1	3^3	1^8	2^7	3^3

NB SMALL NUMBERS INDICATE THE RANKING

After ActionAid, 1992: 44.

3.1.3 Wealth Ranking and Social Mapping

Background

Social anthropologists have long observed that villagers take a passionate interest in the relative household standard of living and do their own subconscious rankings. Polly Hill (1986) suggests from her studies that villagers can be overtly aware of social differentiation. Indeed, social control is tied in with the socially established ranks of a local society. Households and individuals who have tried to escape from the prevailing social structure and move up the village ladder have seen their shops burnt down and crops destroyed (Marris and Somerset, 1971). Deviation from the established social order, from caste and class, is a threat to stability and is severely punished in many local societies.

It is somewhat puzzling that it has taken such a long time for alternative indicators of wealth to appear on par with income measures. Income 'translated' to private consumption has remained the most common proxy indicator of wealth and poverty—relative as well as absolute poverty—despite the difficulties of obtaining information on income (see Section 3.1.2). Resources have increasingly been allocated to develop alternative, multidimensional poverty measures as poverty reduction has become the explicit goal of development cooperation.

Poverty cannot be described and combated by access to income alone, as discussed in Section 6.2. The one-dimensional measure of poverty which characterizes those people as poor who are to be found below a fixed cut-off point on the income scale—the poverty line—has been challenged in a number of studies. The comprehensive *Rethinking Rural Poverty in Bangladesh* (Rahman and Hossain, 1995), for example, identified vulnerability as a necessary key parameter to measure poverty in societies where money income constitutes a minor part of the livelihood of the poor. Multiple parameters on poverty and well-being originating from theoretical and empirical studies are now common, including for example entitlement and capabilities (Sen, 1981, 1999), assets, dignity and autonomy (Baulch, 1996), as well as a variety of context-specific parameters identified by (poor) people themselves in concrete participatory poverty studies. Neela Mukherjee (1992) also challenged the use of a single, income-related indicator to target the poor in poverty alleviation programmes. But instead of a sample survey as used in the Rethinking Rural Poverty in Bangladesh study, she has been innovative in using social mapping techniques (see below) in similar contexts (Mukherjee, 2002).

Relational Methods for Wealth and Well-being Ranking

Well-being or wealth ranking can provide information on the criteria of various 'stakeholders' for defining which differences between the society's members are of greater importance and which characteristics are valued above others. It can contribute to **analysis of difference** and the nature of unequal social relations.

Since Barbara Grandin developed wealth ranking by card sorting during her work with pastoral communities in Kenya, the card sorting by informants technique has been applied worldwide. (For a detailed description and checklist of the wealth ranking technique see Grandin, 1988.)

The term 'wealth' ranking implies a materialistic focus on assets. It has been questioned for having a Eurocentric bias. Referring instead to 'well-being' encourages a reorientation towards 'quality of life'. Being poor in material terms does not necessarily indicate an absence of well-being. Well-being is culture-specific and difficult to quantify. Hence, wealth rankings as they are frequently practised in connection with participatory assessments make a compromise between the two poles.

Wealth or well-being ranking are typically rankings of households (e.g., Figure 3.7). The rankings are relative comparisons of wealth, or an agreed concept of well-being, and do not require discussion of absolute income and other assets. Profound experience with wealth ranking was recorded in RRA Notes No. 15.

Wealth ranking methods have led to use in:

- Targeting poorer groups for specific activities.
- Monitoring the impact of aid distribution.
- Identification of questions for focused research on specific constraints of different groups (exploratory purpose).
- Understanding local criteria of wealth and well-being and of changes in wealth.

It is important to be alert to the limitations and (un)ethical implications wealth ranking can have. For example, in communities where everybody is subject to considerable stress such as is the case with refugees, wealth ranking seems to provide irrelevant details. There, the differences in well-being would seem to be increasingly marginal and wealth ranking less suitable. Its use for people in distress should probably be avoided. Beyond a certain limit, attempting to pick out variations in stress, malnourishment and misery would appear to be irrelevant, and unethical. Be aware also that wealth or well-being rankings of households disguise what may be unbalanced intra-household relations.

Wealth Ranking in a Study on Privatization

A concrete example is how wealth ranking was used in the early stages of the collaborative policy research and training project, Policy Alternatives for Livestock Development. The project aims to facilitate the transition from a command to a market economy in the extensive livestock sector which dominates the Mongolian rural economy. The purpose was to produce information about the situation of herding households with the aim of preventing devastating consequences of the current privatization of the economy. While it is likely to increase production incentives to individual herdsmen, privatization is also likely to increase hardship for herding households. Until recently, the cooperatives carried much of the production risk connected with herding under extremely variable and unpredictable environmental conditions. With privatization, a lot of the burden of risk is being shifted back to individual herding households.

A central research hypothesis was whether 'wealth' differentials between households took on other forms under the new system, with some households better placed than others to gain access to valued grazing areas at key moments, for example. The wealth ranking exercise was an aid to the initial study of wealth, status and power (see Figure 3.7), and provided baseline information that could be used for later monitoring.

Figure 3.7   Wealth Ranking: Tsagan Hutul Brigade, Mongolia

Position	Household No.	Informant Ranking Scores				Average Ranking Score	
		INF 1	INF 2	INF 3	INF 4		
1	(*6)	25	17	20	34	24	Wealth
2	50	50	17	20	17	26	class 1a
3	35	50	17	20	17	26	
4	38	50	34	20	17	30	Wealth
•							class 1b
13	21	50	50	20	34	30	
14	32	50	34	20	50	30	
15	54	50	67	20	34	43	Wealth
•							class 2a
19	31	75	84	20	17	49	
20	15	75	84	20	17	49	
21	26	75	84	20	34	53	Wealth
22	56	50	84	20	67	55	class 2b
23	51	50	84	20	67	55	
24	*23	50	67	20	84	55	
•							
32	41	75	84	20	67	62	Wealth
33	44	75	84	20	67	62	class 3a
•							
42	*64	75	84	60	50	67	
43	37	75	84	60	50	67	
44	9	75	84	60	50	67	
45	63	75	84	80	34	68	
46	42	75	84	40	84	71	Wealth
47	3	75	84	40	84	71	class 3b
48	(57)	75	84	60	67	72	
•							
60	10	75	84	80	67	77	
61	*53	75	84	80	67	77	
62	59	75	84			80	Wealth
63	2	75	84	80		80	class 4a
64	61	100	100	20	100	80	
•							
70	67	75	84	100	100	90	Wealth
71	*22	75	84	100	100	90	class 4b
72	62	100	100	80	84	91	
73	12	100	84	100	84	92	
74	43	100	100		84	95	
75	25	100	84	100	100	96	

Note: *Indicated housholds for which detailed income and expenditure data and lease agreement forms are available.
Figures in brackets indicate households with known cases of children permanently absent from school.
Excerpts *after* Mearns et al., 1992: 33.

Wealth ranking by card sorting, as pioneered by Barbara Grandin, was used. It was based on individual interviews with people who were asked to rank households. The results were typically reported in tabulated form as shown in Figure 3.7. The research was carried out in a brigade, the organizational unit that best resembles a 'community' under Mongolian nomadic conditions. It is the largest permanent group within which all members know each other—an essential requirement for wealth ranking using the card sorting technique.

The research team camped with the herding families in their felt tents, which permitted interviews to be carried out well into the evening when herdsmen are less busy. The team divided into groups of two to three to conduct semi-structured interviews, participatory diagramming sessions and wealth ranking.

Two aspects of wealth ranking are of primary interest: (*i*) criteria for wealth, status and power, and (*ii*) key issues that emerge concerning production constraints. With regard to (*i*), a wide range of criteria were used by the informants. Productive assets were always the first to be mentioned, e.g., numbers and species-mix of private animals, self-sufficiency in meat and dairy products. Besides productive assets, a number of other material wealth indicators were mentioned—jewellery, utensils, saddles, bank savings, furniture, motorcycle, generator, quality of snuff!, and possession of Chinese silk. Criteria unrelated to material wealth revealed some important distinctions between households. On further probing, differences in status and power and, as a result, level of vulnerability, appeared to be very important: for example, 'the more articulate herdsmen have friends in high places, they can get help whenever they need it'. Life-cycle stage emerged as an important factor. Recently established households, for example, are generally poorer. So are large, young families. Single and elderly people with no one to inherit their herds were also regarded as poorer.

With regard to (*ii*), key issues emerged relating to production constraints. Examples are indebtedness and availability of labour, dependency burden, and school-children away from home. These were followed up by other research methods. For example, simple household income and expenditure surveys were conducted using a sample stratified according to wealth status as given in the wealth ranking table in Figure 3.7.

The wealth ranking method illustrated for the Tsagan Hutul Brigade in Mongolia is a *relational method* of scoring and ranking households by locally defined criteria. A drawback of this type of wealth ranking households is that intra-household inequalities are overlooked (see Section 6.3 and Vaa, 2001).

Social differentiation can also be analysed using *space related methods,* e.g., social mapping.

Social Mapping

A number of innovations have been spreading in methods to identify and understand the relative position and wealth of social groups within a community. One of them is social mapping.

Social mapping is a visual method conducted with a group. For smaller communities a map of the community is drawn, identifying each household. For larger communities, e.g., in urban areas, the ranking unit may be residential areas and neighbourhoods. A group discussion follows on what constitutes wealth and well-being and the main criteria are agreed upon. Next, each household is assessed using the well-being criteria, for which symbols are placed on the map. For example, people identify households' access to assets, to labour, to clean water sources, etc., or they may focus directly on ethnic affiliation as in the DGIS and Danida-supported water supply projects in Karnataka (DGIS, 1992).

The group 'holds the stick' to draw the map—possibly by participants taking turns and adding on to a map. Symbols are inserted and a visual map of socio-economic differences is created with group consensus (see Figure 3.8).

Figure 3.8 The Village Map with Wealth Ranking of Berapal

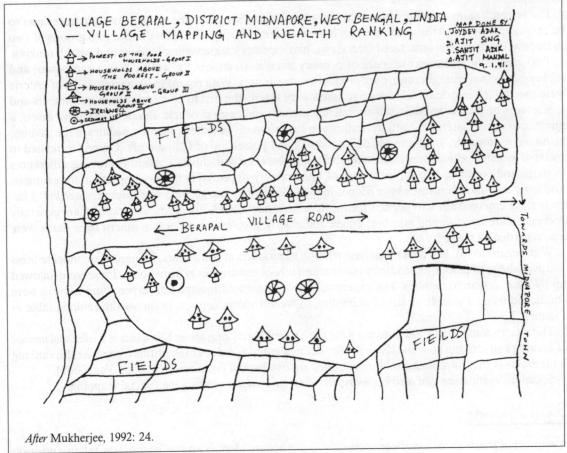

After Mukherjee, 1992: 24.

Mukherjee describes how **social mapping** was carried out in two Indian villages (Mukherjee, 1992: 23). The purpose, among others, was to identify poor households through villagers' perceptions, and to know why and how the villagers consider them to be poor.

Berapal lies in the Sadar block of Midnapore district in West Bengal, India. Well irrigation, both by private households and government agencies, has helped increase the productivity of the area. The village consists of mostly small and marginal cultivators and landless labourers. The process started by drawing the villagers together near a village school or a tea stall. The villagers were asked to map the entire village—less than 100 households—with fields, roads and houses. Then they were requested to identify the 'poorest of the poor' households in the village. This they did by marking the households with symbols. They were also asked to describe the characteristics and reasons which put the households at the bottom.

After identifying the poorest of the poor, the villagers identified the next group of poor households and explained their reasons for putting them in a group slightly better off. The villagers marked each set of households with different symbols. They identified different layers of poor households, ranking them from below, and also enumerating their characteristics until all the households in the village were marked.

The results and the map from Berapal are recorded in Figure 3.8.

The map is drawn with infrastructure and wells inserted among the ranked households. It condenses the variety of indicators of poverty used by villagers: *widow heads of households, no regular source of income, seasonal food shortage, landlessness, environmental degradation, dependency rate, etc. Level of food consumption* was seen as the absolute primary indicator of poverty in the semi-starved village. The villagers explained that poverty was accentuated by environmental degradation in the area. The forest, which provided substantial back-up during lean periods as a source of food and wood for fuel, was increasingly degraded, aggravating the hardship of the poorest of the poor who were more dependent on the forest products.

The villagers marked the group of households above the extreme poor group, distinguishing it from that group on the basis of ownership of some land. The households in the higher group would have been even better off with fewer dependants. This meant that the number of dependants was taken as an indicator of poverty—somewhat contradicting the notion that having many children is seen as a sign of wealth. This also implied that the villagers had some notion of average income per head per household.

The group of households next identified was described as having better production from land. They had more land and a better quality of life despite having large families. The production from the land helped them to meet their household consumption requirements as well as procured income from selling some produce. Many of the households in the last two groups were also beneficiaries of official income-generating projects.

Lessons

Despite the important contribution of wealth ranking applications, wealth ranking is not able to overcome all problems involved in analysing the social and economic dimensions of life in the communities concerned. Certain aspects remain difficult to understand and need to be addressed by other methods, or innovations have to be made.

Scaling up wealth ranking for use in larger communities, districts, regions, etc., has proved difficult. The strength of wealth ranking is that it is based on people's knowledge of each other. This raises the **ethical question** of privacy. Is public exposure and discussion about people's wealth and well-being not unethical? Barbara Grandin found in her Kenya studies that the need for privacy and discretion is not as important as it first seemed, being largely an apprehension in the minds of researchers rather than a taboo topic for local people. This has been confirmed in more recent studies using GIS-based mapping techniques. However, sensitivity to the local context is required and consultation with people familiar with the local societies should always precede wealth ranking and social mapping. Also, the choice of units to rank must be determined by the local context. Thus a Kitui Study found it difficult to conduct interviews about social and wealth differences. This may be attributed to the sensitive political atmosphere in Kenya at the time of the study (KIDP, 1991).

A different advantage of what Mearns et al. call the 'hidden agenda' or indirect use of wealth ranking by card sorting is the **'magic of figures':** Wealth ranking uses numbers! It gives the appearance of being the kind of 'hard' statistical method that researchers and bureaucrats have been professionally socialized to use and expect. One danger is that, having been introduced to wealth ranking, researchers may adopt only the mechanics of the technique to produce lists of average ranking scores without making use of its real potential that lies in the complexity of people's thinking beyond the numbers.

To sum up, a few general recommendations on how to conduct ranking and scoring exercises are:

- Make sure the ranking exercise is adapted to the requirements of the study and the environment.
- Discuss the relevance and decide with knowledgeable key persons which items to rank or score.
- Use people's own names for what is to be ranked and their own units of measurement.
- List the criteria. Make negative criteria positive—e.g., 'pollutes water' becomes 'prevents water pollution'.
- Ask participants to rank or score each item. For example Rank 1 = best, 2 = next best, etc., or score each out of 10, 5 or 3.
- Probe people's reasons for the order of the ranking.
- Probe for further criteria.
- Follow up on points of interest.
- Try ranking with different types of people. Be alert to the fact that inclusion and motivation of marginal groups to participate rarely happens without specific efforts.

3.2   Spreading Uses of Participatory Methods

Application of participatory methods has kept spreading, from mainly rural development projects to a wide set of issues in the South and the North. The applications include analysis, planning, implementation and evaluations in areas such as:

- natural resources and agriculture, watersheds, forestry, aquaculture, biodiversity
- technology assessments
- rural development and rural infrastructure
- programmes for equity—social inclusion/exclusion, poverty, gender, age, ethnicity, income generation
- health and nutrition, reproductive health, HIV/AIDS, water and sanitation

- education and training, development communication, consultations, facilitation, knowledge and rights
- urban development, community action, violence, street children
- policy analysis and reforms—national and sector policies, budget analysis, impact studies, decentralization, civil society
- deliberative democracy and inclusionary processes
- participatory budgeting
- human rights, women's rights, children's rights, rights-based approaches
- conflict and dispute prevention and resolution, security
- institutional and organizational change, appreciative inquiry
- participatory workshops

Since it is not possible in this book to illustrate all the wide-ranging applications of participatory methods, an attempt is made in the following pages to present a selection of areas to which the use of participatory methods has recently spread.

Illustrations of other innovative approaches are given in Section 6.4.

3.2.1 Policy Planning—Deliberative Democracy and Inclusionary Processes

The current application of participatory approaches goes beyond projects to application of participation in connection with programme strategies and policies, national policy reforms like Poverty Reduction Development Plans, and strategies for decentralization. In this context new approaches have been spreading under the common name **Deliberative Democracy** or **Deliberative Democracy and Inclusionary Processes, DIP** (PLA Notes 40, 2001).

A number of interrelated social and political factors have contributed to the recent support for, and use of Deliberative and Inclusionary Processes, DIPs, in policy making, planning, service delivery and technology assessments. Primary among them is,

> Democracy without citizen deliberation and participation is ultimately an empty and meaningless concept. This understanding of politics, and many people's desire to supplement the representation they receive via elected politicians, is often the starting point for a growing number of experiments and initiatives that create new spaces for citizens to directly influence decisions affecting their lives. These approaches aim to allow greater deliberation of policies and their practical implementation through the inclusion of a variety of social actors in consultation, planning and decision-making (Pimbert and Wakeford, 2001: 23).

Since the 1990s, deliberative and inclusionary processes have been increasingly applied to the formulation of a wide range of policies in countries in the North and the South. Several procedures, techniques and methods are used to include diverse actors in deliberative processes. They include citizen's juries, citizen's panels, committees, consensus conferences, scenario workshops and focus groups (see Section 3.1.1), deliberative polling, multi-criteria mapping, public meetings and hearings, rapid and participatory rural appraisal, RRA and PRA, and visioning exercises. These approaches and methods can differ substantially in detail and have been applied to a wide range of issues and contexts. To varying degrees they all seek to adopt the democratic criteria of deliberation and inclusion (see PLA Notes 40), for which *guiding principles* in some cases are made explicit.

In a context relating to urban management *policy reform* in Latin America—Carrión (2001), for example, shows how deepening democracy and promoting popular participation in resolving urban issues calls for clear guiding principles and methodologies (Box 3.1).

Box 3.1   Principles for Popular Participation in Community Development and Urban Management Programmes

When designing and implementing popular participation in community development (including cities) and management programmes, some criteria need to be followed:

- *Sense of totality.* Consider the city as well as the social group as a whole. Initiatives that are conceived and developed as isolated actions reproduce individualism at the community level and a divorce between policies and actions more generally.
- *Political sense.* Consider the general political scenario. Programmes or projects that are conceived and designed without a careful analysis of the political context might fail because of unanticipated external constraints.
- *Sense of autonomy.* Support efforts of the community to acquire capacities and establish conditions for making autonomous and critical decisions about what matters to them. Support training processes that transfer knowledge, which is a step towards gaining power.
- *Sense of reality.* Avoid paternalistic and/or artificial conditions when conceiving and developing programmes or projects. The likelihood that a popular housing process will succeed lies precisely in the degree of long-term self-sufficiency that can be developed by the group involved.
- *Sense of continuity.* Understand that the housing processes of the poor are 'endless' and changeable. Interventions should be based on an understanding of the notion of process that is embodied in the development of popular neighbourhoods.
- *Sense of respect.* Be extremely respectful of people's commitments and behaviour. External agents, including progressive NGOs, are involved only temporarily; the people living in the community are permanent. If external agents are to work in a community they should respect the nature and the dynamics of the people, their organizations, and their leaders.

After Carrión, 2001.

These principles for 'people's participation' in community development and democratic urban governance build on an understanding that democratization is a process of building up social dynamics, starting from the base of society—the community—and ascending to the national level. An indicator of success in democratizing local governance would be civil society organizations' participation in defining urban policy priorities. The principles can be generalized to many other situations where participatory approaches are applied to policy reforms, e.g., to **Linked Local Learning** (Section 3.2.2).

3.2.2 Decentralization Reforms—Negotiated Partnerships

Linked Local Learning, LLL, and the Three-Way
Dynamic of Local, Central, and Civic in Decentralization Reforms

A particular participatory method has been developed to enhance local *ownership* in connection with decentralization reform; i.e., the so-called *Linked Local Learning (LLL)* approach to decentralization (Lightfoot et al., 2000). The methodology has been developed in connection with farmers' agro-ecosystem management in East Africa. The overall goal of LLL is to build the capacity of local institutions (partnerships) to provide appropriate services for small-scale producers practising sustainable management of natural resources.

Key elements in the LLL methodology are:

- *Visioning* on future agro-ecosystem management.
- *Planning* on matching farmer demands with services offered.
- *Negotiating* new partnerships.
- *Action* on projects.
- *Reflection* on actions taken and partnership performance.

LLL emphasizes ownership of the process. Ownership refers to 'owning a problem situation' (being a stakeholder in an issue) *and* 'owning the resources to address it'. This means that a coalition of stakeholders must be in control of the process from the start. It is they who invite the outside facilitator to guide the process. The latter may be able to assist the coalition to search for resources, but must be able to give up control over a project. Thus, the nature and vested interests of the outsider-facilitators *matter* and is part of the challenge.

Linked Local Learning is a learning process which aims to go a step further than other participatory approaches on a learning curve towards creating ownership by making *negotiation—negotiating partnership*—central. The LLL process offers opportunities for building capacities and helping farmers, NGOs, local and national government ministries and departments, and donors in new partnerships to deal with the massive changes being imposed on the district and village levels through policies of decentralization. But the practitioners of the learning approach also point to constraints which have to be overcome. In particular, the use of *indicators* by learning groups will require time and reflection. The realization of the value of indicators to track change in both the human dimension and in the biophysical system represents a major learning effort that does not happen overnight. Indicators become relevant as a driving force for collaborative learning. But learners need resources to meet, debate indicators and track changes. The fact that resources are limited, spread over time, and need to be available with no conditionalities attached exposes a major challenge in the relationship between donors and learning coalitions.

The LLL approach has parallels to Tendler's 'model' for analysing decentralization: 'The three-way dynamic of the local, the central and the civic' (Tendler, 1997: 146). The gist of the analysis is to counter the dominant view in much decentralization thinking which originates in the 'decentralisation and participation, D&P' perspective. Tendler challenges the three basic assumptions on which the D&P perspective rests: (*i*) That the two-way dynamic between local government and civil society is one of the best ways to improve the quality of government in general; (*ii*) That decentralization is the best way to embark on the long journey towards improved local government; and (*iii*) That central governments will give up power, or at least, that advisors should invest considerable efforts in persuading them to do so. The experience from her thorough empirical studies in Africa, Asia and Latin America does not confirm the picture of local governments and non-government providers as being inherently better at tailoring services to client needs, or as having the comparative advantages assumed by the development literature. In this sense her findings confirm the ironic 'paradox of decentralization' that 'decentralisation demands more centralization and more sophisticated political skills at the national level'. (Tendler, 1997: 143). However, the donor community has focused most of its attention on downsizing the government to the exclusion of complementary measures required to increase performance. This despite the clear evidence that without measures to reorganize work in ways that increase worker commitment, downsizing does not lead to increased productivity and often makes performance worse.

Tendler's research on governance focuses on worker dedication and how it has been supported by private and public agencies providing space for worker autonomy, and for greater cooperation between labour and management. In contrast to this perspective, the mainstream development community has shown little interest in the subject of worker dedication to the work:

Guided by an almost religious belief in self-interest as an explanation of human behaviour—what Charles Sabel so aptly calls 'the science of suspicion'—the attention of the development literature has been riveted on the *absence* of worker commitment.... The donor community starts with the assumption that civil servants are self-interested, rent-seeking, and venal unless proven otherwise (ibid.: 5).

The analysis of the three-way dynamic reveals paradoxes in the Decentralization and Participation, D&P scenario: On the one hand it has exaggerated the extent to which civil society can counteract the rent-seeking tendencies of government. On the other hand, rushing to embrace the non-government sector as a way of promoting participation and civic control over the local and central governments, the donor community has chosen to ignore the problem of self-seeking behaviour and incompetence which unfortunately also prevails in parts of the non-government sector itself.

The interdependence between the local and the national levels poses a challenge to promoting complementary dynamics in encouraging more widespread deliberative and inclusionary processes—one working from the top down and the other from the bottom up, to quote Pimbert (Pimbert and Wakeford, 2001). In a world where the interests of a minority comprising the most powerful people and organizations conflict with the well-being of the less powerful majority, this is perhaps the biggest challenge of all. This challenge of macro-micro dynamics is also faced in Poverty Reduction Strategy Processes.

3.2.3 Poverty Reduction Strategy Papers, PRSP, and Processes

Participatory approaches have been part of the poverty reduction agenda for more than a decade (e.g. UNDP, 2001). But only within the last few years have more substantive guides on how to apply Participatory Poverty Assessment, PPAs, moved the focus from the community level to the national policy level (e.g., Norton et al., 2001).

What is participation and what role can it play in the Poverty Reduction Strategy Process and formulation of Poverty Reduction Strategy Papers, PRSP (see also Section 6.2)? The question is asked in the PRSP Sourcebook, and answered as follows:

> Participation is the process by which stakeholders influence and share control over priority setting, policy-making, resource allocations, and/or program implementation. There is no blueprint for participation because it plays a role in many different contexts and for different purposes.
>
> To date, participatory processes in developing countries have tended to take place at the microeconomic or project level and have become increasingly innovative as methods become more established and sophisticated. However, to achieve participatory outcomes at the macroeconomic level, it is necessary to use participatory approaches at both the microeconomic and macroeconomic levels in a complementary manner for maximum effect. These approaches entail several elements, namely,
>
> - an outcome-oriented participation action plan,
> - a public information strategy, and
> - multi-stakeholder institutional arrangements for governance (World Bank, 2002: 237).

Conducting a participatory process on a national scale can seem overwhelming. The PRSP Sourcebook, therefore, provides guidance and breaks down the process in its constituent parts. It is explained *why* participation is desirable, *which* outcome-based approach should be taken, *who* (which stakeholders) should participate, and *how*—through a number of entry-points and steps—a participatory process can be undertaken.

Some guiding principles for participation are provided, which should lead to more equitable processes for formulating, implementing and monitoring poverty reduction country strategies. These are, in brief:

- Country ownership
- Outcome orientation
- Inclusion
- Transparency
- Sustainability
- Continuous improvement

Taking a closer look at the definitions of participation used by the World Bank in the Poverty Reduction Strategy Sourcebook, it is evident that the definitions are very wide and may be difficult to turn into commitments and clear responsibilities (Box 3.2):

Box 3.2   Definitions—Participation and Dimensions of Participation—PRSP Sourcebook

Participation is a process through which stakeholders influence and share control over development initiatives and the decisions and resources that affect them.

Participation occurs in four distinct ways:
- *Information sharing:* One-way flows of information to the public.
- *Consultations:* Two-way flow of information between the coordinators of the consultation and the public and vice versa.
- *Collaboration:* Shared control over decision-making.
- *Empowerment:* Transfer of control over decision-making and resources to all stakeholders.

Dimensions of participation:
- *Scope* of participation encompasses the diversity of government processes in which different stakeholder groups are involved.
- *Extent* of participation involves the diversity of stakeholder groups participating.
- *Level* of participation equates to the level of government operations—national or local level.
- *Quality of participation* signifies the depth and diversity of views expressed, incorporation of these into strategy formulation, consensus building, establishment of partnerships for delivery of the strategy, and information sharing amongst the stakeholder groups involved.

After World Bank, 2002: 551–52.

The very broad definitions of participation raise a number of questions regarding the PRSP planning process in which they shall be used: How, for example, can the unequal power of different stakeholder groups be dealt with? What, in a given situation, is 'optimum' participation (see Box 2.3)? Which criteria to use to assess the quality of participation? 'Participation is more than holding workshops' and 'Handing over the document does not equal ownership', to quote Robb (2002) from her status analysis of Participatory Poverty Assessments, PPAs. There are many questions to deal with in the attempt to apply participatory methods in broader policy reforms for poverty reduction. A number of initiatives have been taken to address the wide spectrum of questions in the wake of the PRSP Sourcebook. This may be the time when the World Bank and the many agencies which follow in its footsteps start to include themselves as stakeholders and agents to better understand both opportunities and why participation has the limits it seems to have (see Sections 2.4 and 6.2).

It is increasingly recognized that policy areas as those described—policy reform, decentralization, natural resource management, poverty alleviation—move in areas of open or disguised conflict. Key actors in development, governments and development agencies, have started to use participatory methods to prevent and solve developmental conflicts (see Box 3.3).

Box 3.3   Alternative Dispute Resolution—Using Participatory Methods to Prevent and Solve Development Conflicts

An important, yet often overlooked, use of participatory methods is their role in preventing or solving conflicts between development stakeholders. Conflicts, or potential conflicts, are often characterized by lack of understanding, communication and trust, or even suspicion and open hostility, between parties.

An example of a conflict-prone environment is found in Khon Kaen Province, located in the Northeast Region of Thailand. The Northeast Region is emerging from a long period characterized by sometimes violent conflict between central and regional governments, NGOs, farmers and various political factions. Studies have shown that many people have not been satisfied with the government's traditional approach to decision-making and want to be included in decisions that affect them.

The University of Khon Kaen, the largest university in Northeast Thailand, has established an Institute for Dispute Resolution (IDR), which does analytical work and conducts courses in conflict resolution mainly targeting public sector employees. Under the title of Alternative Dispute Resolution (ADR) methods, which were developed as an alternative to the government's traditional DAD (decide-announce-defend) approach to development planning, IDR has identified a range of actions, including information sharing, constructive communication, process design, facilitation, mediation, negotiation and participatory monitoring as a holistic approach to conflict prevention and resolution.

Methods such as public rallies, public forums, citizens' assembly, AIC, case studies, role playing, issue-based workshops, and public ceremonies and actions by Buddhist clergy were found to be useful ways to prevent or resolve development and environment-related conflicts in Khon Kaen Province, Thailand.

ADR and other new approaches to conflict prevention and resolution have been greatly aided by the new Thai Constitution (hopefully referred to by some as 'The People's Constitution') enacted in 1997:

Provisions for Public Participation in the Thai Constitution

The Thai Constitution of 1997 grants citizens the right to participate fully in planning and implementation of development projects in Thailand and enables greater public participation in enforcement of environmental and other laws, the right to information and the right to express views through public hearings on projects and activities likely to cause serious adverse environmental and social impacts.

Section 59 gives the public the right to receive information, explanations and reasons from state agencies, state enterprises or local government organizations before permission is given for the operation of any projects or activities which may affect the quality of the environment, health and sanitary conditions, quality of life, or any other material interest concerning an individual or community. The public also has to express its opinions on such matters in accordance with the public hearing process as provided by law.

For a more complete description of the provisions for public participation of the Thai Constitution and links to the Constitution itself, see the following website: http://www.seacsn.net/publications/bulletin/oct-dec2002/focus.htm

Source: Dr Charles J. Pendley, Senior Sociologist, COWI.

To facilitate participation of the public in the planning and implementation of development projects, the participatory Appreciation-Influence-Control, AIC, approach is widely applied by the Thai government. The empowering features of the AIC approach are expressed by Dr Wasi, on receipt of the Magsaysay Award:

> I recognize that this [AIC] process is very important. It gives power to people, power of imagination, creative imagination. And by doing that together, they create power, collective power (Wasi, quoted in Taguchi, 1996).

It is a unique situation when a participatory method becomes more or less a national policy like the case of the AIC in Thailand.

3.3   Topical Applications of Participatory Methods

The spread of participatory methods means that they have been applied to most areas of development cooperation, in background research and baseline studies, during planning, design and implementation, and in evaluations. More recent applications concern topics relating to policies as described in section 3.2, and to economic analysis and technology assessments as illustrated in the next sections.

3.3.1 Participatory Budgeting and Budget Analysis

Participatory budgeting has been an important institutional innovation for deliberative forms of democracy and citizen empowerment in both urban and rural contexts. Participation in budgeting and public expenditure management is recognized as a measure to ensure accountability and transparency. It is now part of the PRSP approach. Civic initiatives have addressed budget formulation and analysis, distribution of resources, expenditure monitoring and tracking, and evaluation of public service delivery. Although no ready formula exists for how to mobilize collective action to influence budget formulation, there are a range of options—for *understanding the budget,* for *building ownership of budget analysis and advocacy,* for *organizing social collations to support budget related action,* for *creating space to actively engage in budget formulation*—from which stakeholder groups can draw. As an example, participatory budgeting pioneered by several municipalities in Brazil offers a model of how citizens can influence municipal spending more directly—funds for whom, on what and where (PLA Notes 40, 2001).

Box 3.4 describes a case from India where groups have developed skills for demystifying the technical nature of the budget.

Participants in the Gujarati budget analysis and advocacy work (Box 3.4) were able to do the budget analysis by following standard guidelines set out by the auditor general on budget coding, which made it easier to compute alternative figures and contest official statistics. This notwithstanding, participation requires the skills, specialist knowledge of budgeting, as well as particular communication skills. These requirements tend to reduce the potential active participation of many concerned stakeholder groups.

Box 3.4   Participatory Budget Analysis in Gujarat, India

Almost 8 million tribal people live in Gujarat. Despite official rhetoric of significant investment in tribal development projects, results on the ground were questionable. In the early 1990s, this prompted the NGO, Development
Initiatives for Social and Human Action (DISHA), to embark on budget analysis to check what actually was
happening to funds allotted in the name of the tribals. DISHA has since broadened to cover most aspects of
budget analysis. DISHA obtains budget documents, reviews and disaggregates departmental allocations for
different beneficiaries, researches the discrepancy between proposed and actual spending, and prepares briefs
on synthesized findings to inform public debates ....

DISHA followed the auditor general's standard guidelines on budget coding to compute alternative figures
and dispute and contest official statistics. Basic knowledge of accounting systems gave DISHA significant
confidence to go on to the next phase of doing the actual analysis of the contents. After obtaining the documents
on the day the budget is presented to the Bidhan Sabha (assembly), researchers at DISHA analyse the data on
revenue and expenditures, and interpret what the proposed allocations, if spent, mean for the poor. Three
questions are asked:

– Does the budget mention specific pro-poor policies?
– Are these matched by adequate funding commitments?
– Do they relate to the socio-economic reality of the Gujarati poor—the tribals, dalits, women, and agricultural
  labourers?

The day after the budget speech, DISHA briefs the press, and when discussions commence in the assembly, it
starts to feed Members of Legislative Assembly, MLAs, with information briefs on the sectors on a daily basis.

These four- to five-page briefs contain budget information and analysis in an accessible form .... Each brief
dealt either with a department or a subject, such as education, home affairs (police), energy, finance, or ...
project details. Typically, the briefs cover:

(a)   general information about the department and the amount it received for spending;
(b)   the percentage change in budget allocation to an item or sub-item as well as excess amounts, if any,
      committed relative to previous years;
(c)   examples of fiscal indiscipline and mathematical errors; and
(d)   items or expenditure proposals introduced for the first time.

Since 1996 DISHA has prepared approximately 30 briefs on such topics as forests, women, social welfare, and
so on. The budget information has also been disseminated in local languages through newspapers and fact sheets
to tribal villages and schools .... Budget data have also been used to write reports advocating policy change in
areas such as forestry. By analysing public expenditures, comparing what was promised versus what was de-
livered, especially to disadvantaged groups, DISHA is creating a strong system of information exchange that is
assisting communities to articulate demands and create pressure to establish accountability within the public
expenditure system.

After World Bank, 2002: 259.

Others have developed guidelines to assist a wider range of people to undertake economic analysis.
This is exemplified in the manual for economic analysis in context of forest management, presented in
Section 3.3.2.

3.3.2 Participatory Forest Management and Economic Analysis

Economic development studies have by tradition been 'extractive'—carried out by outsiders who extract information from local people, go away with the information, and never return the analysed results. Richards, Davies and Yaron have attempted to change the situation and prepared the manual *Stakeholder Incentives in Participatory Forest Management: A Manual for Economic Analysis* (Richards et al., 2002). The justification for the manual is:

> ... participation of a range of stakeholders improves the likelihood of success of all forms of forest management. Participatory forest management (PFM) in which local people are directly involved in the management process is widely acknowledged to be the best option from a development perspective and potentially in terms of sustainability of the forest resource. However, a limiting factor in the uptake and success of PFM is poor understanding of the costs and benefits faced by different stakeholders, especially the incentives of local forest users in PFM situations (ibid.: 3).

Based on an assumption of 'the rational forester', it is anticipated that local people will only adopt PFM methods if it makes economic sense to them. However, in many cases the economic or financial incentives to participate in PFM initiatives are weak compared with alternative livelihood options, including those resulting in forest depletion. To initiate change in these incentives, whether by communities themselves or by lobbying for a change in policy, people need to know the costs and benefits of alternative land use or livelihood options. To this should be added the development practitioners' need to know local value systems and have some knowledge of local Natural Resource Management, NRM, practices (Sillitoe et al., 2002).

The *Manual for Economic Analysis* is oriented to 'pro-poor' or rural-development forestry. It is an elaborate tool-box for undertaking economic stakeholder analysis, ESA, based on field experience in Nepal, Bolivia and Mexico where attempts were made to let local forest users collect and analyse the data with outsiders acting only as facilitators in the process.

The economic stakeholder analysis is composed of six stages in which cost-benefit analysis and valuation are central. It aims to help the economic analyst assess the incentives of local forest users in a context of multi-purpose forestry. But the manual also aims to help non-economists promoting participatory forest management to improve their understanding of the role of economics in the analysis of stakeholder incentives. Whatever the situation, it is vital that economic analysts collaborate with people who have in-depth knowledge of NRM 'strategies' adopted by the concerned people, for example social anthropologists and participatory research and development specialists.

The manual has incorporated the pragmatism which is often required when participatory methods are applied in field situations: It recommends making the data collection and analysis process as participatory and cost-effective as possible, including the cost to local people in terms of time constraint. This means carrying out simpler calculations with the community and more complex calculations in the office, and returning the data in an accessible form to the community for further discussion. The manual is firm on the principle that if an economic study claims to be participatory or to empower local forest users, strenuous efforts are needed to ensure that the latter feel at least a partial ownership of the study and results.

3.3.3 Technology Assessment

Inventions of participatory methods and adjustment of the 'generic' types are often prompted by the particular purpose and topic for which the participatory methods are being used. When participatory methods were first used in farming systems analysis (Conway, 1986), they included technology assessment of cultivation practices, crops, etc. Today participatory methods are applied in specialized technological areas such as the conservation and use of plant genetic resources (Friis-Hansen and Sthapit, 2000).

The sensitivity which surrounds many current technologies such as plant genetics, biotechnology, genetically modified foods, genetic testing on human beings, nuclear power, radioactive waste disposal, new information technology, to mention some, has prompted an increased use of deliberative democracy and inclusionary participatory processes, examples of which are given in Section 3.2.1 and more in PLA Notes 40.

Ways of using participatory methods for *technology analysis and evaluation* are illustrated in International Maize and Wheat Improvement Centre's (CIMMYT) manual for scientists working with farmers (Bellon, 2001). It respects the principle of gender sensitivity. Several of the diagnostic and evaluation methods are illustrated as used by men and by women.

How technology is defined and understood has implications for technology assessment and analysis. Jens Müller uses a composite definition of technology which embraces four inter-dependent constituents: *Technique, Knowledge, Organization,* and *Product* (Müller, 2003). The societal context has prompted Müller to drop his former concept 'technology transfer' and instead concentrate on the societal forces that influence technology change. Contrary to what is the norm in many technical and economic technology studies, conflicting interest and power relations are introduced in Müller's technology analysis. Similarly, for Bijker et al., 1987 and Bijker and Law, 1992, it is the *social construction of technology, SCOT*, which invites a possible participatory approach to technology analysis.

Innovative participatory methodologies or applications have been taken further within technology studies related to agricultural and natural resources research than in most other technology areas (e.g., Friis-Hansen and Sthapit, 2000; Buhler et al., 2002; Ribot, 2002). But often this happens under counter-productive pressures from funding agencies. These agencies expect full and active participation from all stakeholders in project planning. However, they often do not appreciate the theoretical and the time and resource implications of their demands. Implicitly, they contribute to 'compromised participation'. Compromised participation notwithstanding,

> That is not to say that participatory methods are useless or unnecessary in order to help identify the appropriate avenues for research and intervention. It is merely another approach that in some cases can help improve people's lives, and not in others. It is not a panacea (Buhler et al., 2002: 147).

Thus, critical realism suggests that participatory methods in technology assessment can be seen as 'merely another approach' and are not a panacea, nor a technical fix. What participatory approaches do contribute is the opportunity for stakeholders to get together and jointly analyse the issues at stake. The collective knowledge production is more than the sum of the individual contributions! But participatory analysis and planning also tend to bring diverging interests and conflicts to the surface. Many development interventions, whether at the policy, programme or community level as those illustrated in this chapter, are ridden with conflicting interests. Budgeting, poverty reduction interventions, environment and natural resource management, genetic technologies, etc., raise diverging interests. Hence conflict resolution is a necessary but often neglected measure (see Section 3.2.2). One of the tools which interest groups can use in pursuit of their course is Advocacy.

3.3.4 Advocacy

A relevant working definition of advocacy[2] is provided by the Advocacy Institute: *Advocacy is pursuit of influencing outcomes—including public policy and resource allocation within political, economic, and social systems and institutions—that directly affect people's lives.* The definition captures the essence of advocacy work, namely that it is a *means to an end*—to struggle for an agenda, for 'fair trade', for environmental protection, for pro-poor budgeting (see Box 3.4), for combating inequalities globally and nationally between ethnic groups, caste, gender, etc., or to struggle *against* all forms of discrimination, against pollution, against risks and harmful developments, etc. Advocacy should not be seen as a goal in itself. The ultimate goal must be related to sustainable improvements for the poor.

Advocacy is one of the key instruments in a rights-based approach (see Section 6.1). It is utilized by the rights holders and their supporters to address the responsibilities and accountability of duty bearers in relation to provision, protection and respect for human rights. It is also a theme that has high priority for many donors and NGOs as it aims at more long-term changes that often involve policy and/or institutional reforms, and equally important, the *implementation* of such reforms.

Basically, the advocacy strategies adopted by international NGOs can take one of two pathways: (*i*) Direct policy influence, where the NGO or others advocate on behalf of the poor; and/or (*ii*) Indirect support, where the poor are empowered to advocate for their own cause. The direct advocacy work may be successful in changing the policies and practices of the duty bearers, as the agencies can use their political leverage, network and institutional relations to pressurize for certain changes. There are, however, two fundamental issues related to direct advocacy: (*i*) Who will continue the advocacy work when the programme funding stops and/or the donor leaves?; and (*ii*) How does one ensure that the advocacy agent is actually a legitimate representative of the poor? Therefore, many international agents have realized the need to combine direct policy influence with the development of local capacity for advocacy.

A typical form of direct policy influence is *lobby*, which aims at influencing specific decision makers through targeted and *personal contact* that have a very clear message and request. Advocacy agents may also sometimes use the *media* and the *press* to put pressure on decision makers through this channel. Key activities under *capacity building* for advocacy include awareness raising, support to networking and local organizations, training in public relations, policy analysis, information work, etc.; and supporting people to analyse their own situations and identifying their rights as a process of *empowerment*.

In conclusion, it is evident that the use of participatory methods has spread to almost any issue in development work, for topical analysis at macro, meso and micro levels. The knowledge generated from

---

[2] The main author of Section 3.3.4 on Advocacy is Morten G. Poulsen, Senior Consultant, COWI.

participatory investigations can feed not only into development planning, but also into advocacy and 'empowerment' work. In themselves participatory methods are 'merely another approach', and can be applied on their own or in combination with other methods such as surveys in the broad spectrum of studies and investigations which development work necessarily builds on. Participatory methods are not in themselves transformative or instrumental. It is the type of study and its purpose—the topic of the following two chapters—which determine the selection and combination of methods.

There are certain approaches to development which invite a participatory perspective **and** the application of participatory methods by putting emphasis on people as opposed to resources. The *sustainable livelihoods approach* (Carney, 1998), for example, is holistic, comprises capabilities and 'agency', and starts from an analysis of people's strengths as opposed to an analysis of their needs and problems. A more recent approach, *political space*, 'seeks to deal with the politics of representation in (international) development and to propose an analytical method with which to approach it (Webster, 2004). The political space approach is critical of the tendency in mainstream development thinking to pose the question: 'If the rural poor are to bring the diversity of their situations into the pubic spheres of development on a daily basis, what institutional practices and organizations should be the basis for their participation?' A problem with such a question is that it tends to assume there are no appropriate organizations either of or for the poor. Hence the poor are politically inactive and have to be 'empowered'. The argument continues that new organizations of the poor need to be established and new institutional practices based upon participation and empowerment need to be developed. In political space, the argument has been that the poor already possess a political agency with which they avoid the descent into greater poverty or vulnerability. Hence, social agency becomes a central concept with which to address alternatives to the mainstream question above, e.g.: 'How do the rural poor organize to cooperate, negotiate and contest with others, both poor and non-poor?' (ibid.: 3). In other words, participation and empowerment comes from within and not as imposed by mainstream development agencies. The question is whether and how political space will be adopted by concerned development agencies.[3]

---

[3] Political space has recently been adopted as an approach to development cooperation in a large Danish NGO (DCA, 2004).

Different Types of Development Studies— Purpose, Methods and Design

CHAPTER

4

The purpose of a study and the questions asked are decisive when deciding on a study design.[1] The investigator must consider whether s/he is seeking exploratory, descriptive, explanatory or action-oriented answers, and then seek optimal combinations of research methods, given constraints of time and resources. It is necessary to have a tool-box from which to select appropriate qualitative and quantitative methods, techniques and tools. Chapters 2 and 3 provided a selection of participatory tools. A cross-disciplinary perspective and methodological pluralism characterize many development studies, and applied and strategic research, which aims to provide knowledge for decision-making on interventions, is common. But new issues continuously arise in the development discourse of a globalizing world, and basic research might help to bring relevant new knowledge to current issues of policy reforms, migration, conflict resolution, health-pandemics, etc. The aim of this chapter is to alert the reader to systematic considerations when planning and setting about field study, and to be aware of the internal logic during the research process. Attention is called to the philosophical meta-science underpinnings of the methods we apply. Chapter 5 goes into more detail about data generation and analysis.

4.1   Types and Forms of Development Studies

4.1.1 Characteristics of Different Types of Studies

Conceptually and theoretically, development studies cover a very wide range of issues. A common denominator in the current context is that *development studies* deal with international development cooperation from a social science perspective, and involve collection of primary data and field studies in different cultural settings.

The issues may differ, but are always complex, normally encompassing social, economic, technical, institutional and cultural aspects, and a historical dimension. The range of types, topics and forms seems unlimited, and a variety of methods are being used to collect and analyse data. *Field studies* imply that studies are set amongst the people, who are the subjects of a study or intervention, be this in the South or in the North. Hence, interviews only with officials and bureaucrats do not satisfy the definition, however necessary these may be as elements in field studies. In this book the emphasis is on qualitative research methods, but the demarcation line between the former and quantitative methods is fluid.

---

[1] This chapter has been updated with inputs from Merete Watt Boolsen.

Today practitioners from many disciplines—geographers, economists, sociologists, etc.—are involved in development studies, but the influence of ethnography is evident. This is not surprising as *ethnography* literally means a description of peoples or cultures, and ethnography generally prefers a *holistic approach* which stresses processes, relationships, connections and inter-dependency among the component parts (Denscombe, 2003: 84).

In the area of development cooperation, there are a set of concerns which prompt the need for development studies and research: (*i*) the nature and *causes of global and local inequity*, and *conditions* and *contexts* which influence mitigation development interventions (external factors); (*ii*) pre-*conditions pertaining to development cooperation and interventions*, for example technical, institutional and management aspects (internal factors); and (*iii*) The *consequences, effects and impact* of development cooperation. To do qualified development work, there is a need for knowledge in each of these areas which can be derived from different types of studies, e.g., policy studies, studies relating to sectors and to cross-cutting issues such as poverty, gender and governance, baseline studies, reviews, monitoring and evaluation studies.

Development work is first and foremost concerned with *applied research*, i.e., studies aimed at producing knowledge on which decisions can be made, for example, to initiate change through development interventions at the national (macro) level, at the regional or sector (meso) level, and/or at the community (micro) level. Need for information about the conditions and contexts in which interventions take place, about the modalities and processes of implementation, and the consequences and impact of interventions prompt most development studies.

A common breakdown of social science studies, which also capture different types of development studies, is: *descriptive studies, exploratory studies, explanatory studies, interpretative studies, applied and action oriented studies.* Each type may again be sub-divided into more specific types of studies with a different topical focus. Box 4.1 summarizes the major characteristics of four common types of studies: Descriptive, Explanatory, Interpretative and Action-Oriented Studies.

Box 4.1	Characteristics of Different Types of Studies			
Types of Studies	**Descriptive Studies**	**Explanatory Studies**	**Interpretative Studies**	**Action-oriented Studies**
Key Questions	How does X vary with Y?	Which X causes Y? Or which Y are caused by X?	What is X? Or How does Y interpret the phenomenon X in a given context Z?	How do people act in accordance with knowledge accumulated/ disseminated in the course of the research process?
Typical Design	Survey Enumeration	Experimental	Case-study	ı Action research ı Formative evaluation

(Box 4.1 contd)

(Box 4.1 contd)

Types of Studies	Descriptive Studies	Explanatory Studies	Interpretative Studies	Action-oriented Studies
Criteria of Data Quality	• Reliability • Validity • Precision • Generalizable	• Reliability • Validity • Precision • Generalizable • Prediction	• Validity • Totality • Mirror • Conceptual reinterpretation or knowledge production	• Validity • Does learning and change take place? • Does change take the desired directions?
Dominant perspective	Researcher's	Researcher's	The study subjects'	The study object is in dialogue with the researcher
Typical result presentation	Figures and tables and analysis	Figures and tables and analysis	Narrative, quotes, pictures and interpretation	Combinations
Researcher– Researched Relationship	Characterized by • Distance • Value-neutrality • External relationship	Characterized by • Closeness • Multiple values • External relationship	Characterized by • Closeness • Multiple values • Internal relationship	Characterized by shifting closeness and distance
Primary target group/users	• Public/private agencies • Research community	• Public/private agencies • Research community	• Users outside the research community • Sections of the public • Research community	Integrated into single organizations and groups
Application of results	• Application detached from the study's internal methods • Data-base, simulation • Instrumental	Application detached from the study's internal methods • Data-base, simulation • Instrumental	Application detached from the study's internal methods • Conceptual	• Application integrated into the study methods • Instrumental/ conceptual
Form of rationality	Goal rationality	Goal rationality	• Hermeneutic • Communicative rationality	• Emancipating rationality • Empowerment

After Launsø and Rieper, 2000: 36 (Author's translation).

The intention here is to alert the development researcher and practitioner to be conscious of and critical about which types of studies they engage in or commission others to do, because the type of study in which we engage, its purpose, focus and intended results have clear ramifications for *how* we go about collecting relevant information and for the study design in general. In the words of Guba and Lincoln:

No inquirer ought to go about the business of inquiry without being clear about just what paradigm informs and guides his or her approach (1994: 116).

'Paradigm' they define as 'the basic belief system or worldview that guides the investigator, not only in choices of method but in ontologically and epistemologically fundamental ways' (ibid.: 105). In other words, behind any study and process of inquiry are meta-science questions:

- *The ontological question*—What exists? What is the form and nature of reality and, therefore, what is there that can be known about it?
- *The epistemological question*—What is (or should be) regarded as acceptable knowledge about what exists—'what can be known'?
- *The methodological question*—How can the inquirer (would-be knower) go about finding out whatever he or she believes can be known?

In this book we prefer to talk about **types** and **forms** of studies and **meta-science** considerations, since the concept 'paradigm' has a strong symbolic connotation in some science circles and require more explanation than can be given here. But the discussions in this chapter implicitly refer to research 'paradigms' as defined by Guba and Lincoln.

4.1.2 Different Objectives, Normative Aspects and Hidden Assumptions

Study objectives can be differently formulated. For example, a *description* of particular features in a society can be formulated as,

- An *empirical* question: How *is* power distributed in society, how can the distribution of power be *explained* and *understood?* It can also be formulated as
- A *normative* question: How *should* power be distributed in society, and how can the desired distribution be *justified?* Or, it may be formulated as,
- A *constructionist* question: How *can* power be distributed in society in a more equitable way, and how can the possible situation be reached? (Lundquist, 1993: 60).

The normative and sometimes implicitly political perspective—'What should the situation be like?'—is basic in development cooperation and hence in development studies. This is a common question, not least of many participatory development studies, in which the participants are encouraged to express their interests and opinions. Often the desired reply to the question is already in the minds of the agencies which commission the research. However, the 'hidden agenda' is not revealed to the participants. Assumptions about what constitutes good practice in development cooperation exert considerable influence on the types of studies carried out in a given time period.

In development cooperation the normative assumptions—for example, about what constitutes 'best practice' for *alleviating poverty*—have had a considerable influence on which questions are asked in poverty focused development studies (see Section 6.2). These assumptions have changed considerably from one era to another with emphasis shifting from:

- economic growth or social redistribution,
- investments in physical capital or in human and social capital,
- investments in productive, private sectors or in the social sectors,
- public safety nets or community-led participatory self-help activities, to the current
- holistic Poverty Reduction Strategy Papers and devolution of responsibility to borrowers and partner countries.

Assumptions have consequences—whether they are implicit or explicit. Assumptions have consequences in terms of choice of design, choice of informants, decisions on selection of data, data-analysis, etc. Assumptions also matter with regard to choice of theory because in many cases assumptions are the building blocks of theory—i.e., theory consists of assumptions. This is discussed in Chapter 5.

4.1.3 Forms of Studies and Typical Research Questions

Forms of studies vary as much as types of studies. Forms of studies may be:

- Short- or long-term, the latter sometimes meaning longitudinal
- Longitudinal, inter-generational studies, ranging from single to multidisciplinary and multidimensional studies
- Hypothetical deductive studies
- Analytical inductive studies
- Comparative studies
- Forward-oriented, projective studies
- Baseline and impact studies
- Backward-oriented tracer studies
- Experiments
- Case studies
- Life histories
- Pilot studies

In terms of **methods** the applied development studies encompass a multitude of approaches. To mention some, there are:

- Documentary studies
- Qualitative studies, participant observation and participatory studies, semi-structured interviews
- Quantitative studies, sample surveys, empirical, statistical studies
- The comparative method—moving beyond qualitative and quantitative strategies[2]
- Culturally-adapted development market research,

each applying a variety of techniques and tools and benefiting from the inclusion of a historical dimension (see Box 4.5).

A rough rule of thumb is that *project* related studies make use of qualitative, and often participatory, methods. They relate to people at the *micro-level*, e.g., community groups and households, while *policy* related studies tend to make use of quantitative research methods, expert interviews and statistical methods. Examples in Chapter 3 did show that this division is not inevitable.

A break-down of **studies applied in the different project cycle stages** took prominence with the streamlining and phasing of development aid projects from the 1980s. Requested by donors or development authorities, project cycle-related studies are still common, and studies relating to sector programmes follow a similar cycle, that is:

- Identification studies
- Design and pre-appraisal studies
- Feasibility studies
- Appraisal studies
- Review studies
- Monitoring studies
- Evaluation and impact studies

Topical studies may be added as the need arises at different stages in this cycle. And *baseline studies* will in many cases be carried out at the start of the project and programme. The most significant recent shift in emphasis is towards *macro-economic policy and sector specific studies* with explicit focus on *context*.

Participatory development studies (see Chapters 2 and 3) emphasize the types of methods used and encompass, for example:

- Participatory and rapid assessments (PRA and RRA)
- Participatory learning and action research (PLA)
- Dialogue research
- Self-assessments—by people themselves

---

[2] See C.C. Ragin, 1987.

'Advocacy' studies—a type of action-oriented study—put the researcher in a focal role as an intermediary between community and authorities or aid organization to pledge for a particular, often conflict-ridden, issue, ideally with active local participants up front (Cranshaw, 2003).

A research strategy best suited to the complexity of real life situations typically combines a selection of the categories.

The type of studies we carry out as development researchers and practitioners should be designed to answer the questions we set out to answer. But it is often forgotten that posing questions in a certain way opens the way to particular types of studies. It is useful to recall the characteristics and typical questions which belong to different types of studies (Box 4.1).

Typical questions for the different study types could be:

Descriptive Studies
1. How does malnutrition vary with age and sex?
2. How are gender relations reflected in reproductive health and rights and in specific practices in urban and rural areas in country x?

Explanatory Studies
1. Which dietary practices, diseases and other possible factors cause malnutrition in different age groups?
2. Can reproductive health practices explain the different maternal death rates in urban and rural areas in country x?

Interpretative Studies
1. How do different groups—by age and sex—characterize malnutrition, and what are people's perceptions of causes and remedies?
2. What characterizes the maternal health situation in urban and rural areas in country x according to the perceptions of local people, and how do different groups perceive the causes of maternal death rates?

Action-oriented Studies
1. By what means do people in settlement (A) best incorporate knowledge about malnutrition? What are their current coping strategies and how do they prioritize to work with external development partners to combat malnutrition?
2. Can maternal health be improved by involving local women and men in raising awareness about the HIV/AIDS pandemic and reproductive health practices? Who will be involved? What shall the messages be? And which methods of communication will be effective?

The **types and number** of questions which can be posed and investigated are asked under constraints of time and resources which often requires the researcher and practitioner to stretch her/his imagination to come up with an acceptable study design (see Preface to the First Edition, p. 22).

In principle all studies should be determined by the purpose and type of key questions to be addressed. In reality there is no strict separation between the different research and study types as Box 4.1 may suggest. An explanatory study, for example, will normally also contain features of interpretation. Overall, good research and good studies do in fact often combine study types, hence different combinations of data quality criteria, relations between researched-researcher, etc.

4.2 Research Purpose, Goals and Focus

4.2.1 Research Purpose and Application

The objective of academic research, whether by sociologists, political scientists, or anthropologists, is to try to find answers to theoretical questions within their respective fields. In contrast, the objective of applied social research is to use data so that decisions can be made (Rubin, 1983: 6).

Characteristics of applied development studies are:

1. Research is part of a job and is judged by sponsors who are often outside the discipline of the social science researcher.
2. Research problems are 'narrowly confined' to the demands of employers or sponsors.
3. The rigour and standards of scholarship depend on the uses of results. Development studies can be 'quick and dirty' or may match high scientific standards.
4. The primary concern is with the ability to generalize findings to areas of interest to sponsors.
5. The driving goal is to have practical payoffs or uses for results.
6. Success comes when results are used by sponsors in decision-making.

Many practitioners, e.g., evaluators of development cooperation, will see these as ideal criteria, knowing very well that sponsors or policy makers and implementers in aid organizations are not always particularly keen to apply the results which have come out of evaluation studies. Why is this? Perhaps because people have opposing interests in the possible consequences of a project or programme?

A large share of development studies and much development research belong in the category 'applied research'. Hence, the modalities of applied research lies behind much of what is discussed in this book, whether explicitly stated or not. This should not be mistaken as indicating that applied research is 'better' than basic research. *Basic research* is necessary to develop and question concepts and theories and to bring new perspectives into the development discourse. With escalating globalization, the need for new insights through basic research, perhaps with more cross-disciplinary perspectives on migration, environmental protection, conflict resolution, crisis prevention, health pandemics, etc., seems greater than ever. Basic research findings can subsequently be used to enrich applied or strategic research. On their own, applied development studies seem not to have had a high success rate in critical development areas of poverty reduction, unemployment, environmental degradation, unhealthy housing, etc., perhaps because they are locked in counterproductive axioms and assumptions about causal relations and detached from the wider development discourse?

Applied and strategic development research aims to provide knowledge on which the best decisions can be made. The target may be to solve specific policy problems or help practitioners accomplish tasks. Development practitioners use several types of strategic and applied research, for example studies of structural and policy issues, social impact and evaluation studies, cost-benefit analysis and action research. Such studies are an integral part of the dominant logical framework-based 'aid models'[3] which Wilson (2004) associates with serious risks: 'Technical solutions to complex problems easily spell disaster'.

Action research is applied research that treats knowledge as a form of power and abolishes the line between research and social action. Common characteristics of different types of action research are: Those who are being studied participate in the research process; research incorporates ordinary or popular knowledge; research seeks to raise consciousness or increase awareness; and research is tied directly to political action (Neuman, 2000 and 2003). These criteria correspond well with development work.

Patton is helpful in guiding the selection of a research strategy by explaining the centrality of **purpose,** and a number of considerations concerning techniques and tools. Box 4.2 adopted from Patton (1990, 2002) summarizes a typology of research purposes for different types of research: *basic research, applied* and *action research*. Patton also includes evaluation research: summative and formative evaluation research. We retain these as important 'proto-type' development research—i.e., one is retrospective, summing up the experience of certain interventions, the other is 'formative' in suggesting how to improve interventions. Both summative and formative studies are illustrative of studies accompanying development work and are not narrowly used for evaluations.

Box 4.2 A Typology of Research Types, Purposes, Focus and Desired Results			
Types of Research	**Purpose**	**Focus of Research**	**Desired Results**
1. Basic research	Knowledge as an end in itself; discover truth	Questions deemed important by one's discipline or personal intellectual interest	Contribution to the theory
2. Applied research	Understand the nature and sources of human and social problems	Questions deemed important by society	Contributions to theories that can be used to formulate problem solving programmes and interventions

(Box 4.2 contd)

[3] Wilson problematizes the dominant aid models as blueprints whose direct purpose is to close the gap between policy and practice (i.e., 'implementation'). Based on empirical evidence from a development programme in Wollo, Ethiopia, Wilson questions the assumption that there is a correct policy and that this should and will be carried out as precisely as possible in the process of implementation.

(Box 4.2 contd)

Types of Research	Purpose	Focus of Research	Desired Results
3. Summative evaluation	Determine effectiveness of human interventions and actions (programmes, policies, personnel, products)	Goals of the intervention	Judgements and generalizations about effective types of interventions, and the conditions under which those efforts are effective
4. Formative evaluation	Improving an intervention: a programme, policy, organization, or product	Strengths and weaknesses of the specific programme, policy, product, or personnel being studied	Recommendations for improvements
5. Action research	Solve problems in a programme, organization, or community	Organization and community problems	Immediate action: solving problems as quickly as possible

Desired Level of Generalization	Key Assumptions	Publication Mode	Standard for Judging
Across time and space (ideal)	The world is patterned: those patterns are knowable and explainable	Major refereed scholarly journals in one's discipline: scholarly books	Rigour of research, universality and verifiability of theory
Within as general a time and space as possible, but clearly limited application context	Human and societal problems can be understood and solved with knowledge	Specialized academic journals, applied research journals within disciplines, inter-disciplinary problem-focused journals	Rigour and theoretical insight into the problem
All interventions with similar goals	What works at one place under specified conditions should work elsewhere	Evaluation reports for programme funders and policy-makers, specialized journals	Generalizability to future efforts and to other programmes and policy issues
Limited to specific setting studied	People can and will use information to improve what they are doing	Oral briefings: conferences; internal report; limited circulation to similar programmes, other evaluators	Usefulness to and actual use by intended users in the setting studied
Here and now	People in a setting can solve problems by studying themselves	Interpersonal interactions among research participants; informal, unpublished	Feelings about the process among research participants, feasibility of the solution generated

After Patton, 1990: 160–61 (in *Qualitative Evaluation Methods*). Reprinted by permission of Sage Publications, Inc.

It may be helpful to look at a particular topic, for example 'community groups', and see how the different types and purposes in Patton's classification make one ask research questions differently (Box 4.3).

Box 4.3 Purpose and Types of Research Questions, Illustrated with Research on Community Groups and Small Enterprises	
Basic Research	What are the variations in types of community groups and what functions do the variations serve?
Applied Research	What is the participation rate among different kinds of community groups in non-agricultural income generating activities? What explains the different rates of participation among the different groups? Can women's participation be enhanced?
Summative Research (Effectiveness)	What is the effectiveness of a national- or donor-aided training programme on small enterprise management for different community groups?
Formative Research (Performance)	How can the training programme on small enterprise management be improved and adjusted to the benefit of different community groups? What are the programme's strengths and weaknesses? How may the results be used?
Action Research	To determine how community groups can start and organize themselves around small enterprise activities, a process involving the start-up of concrete activities would be studied. Implementation or testing of activities is part of the action research process. What are the programme's strengths and weaknesses? The study can be organized as a community self-study, or a joint community and aid organization/NGO study.

Source: The author.

There are no sharp divisions between the different research types. All of the examples in Box 4.3 focus on community groups, but the purpose of each type of research and the questions asked are quite different. The types of questions asked depends on what the study is trying to accomplish, for example, to explore a new topic or new aspects, to describe a social phenomenon, a situation or a conflict, or to explain why something occurs or could be brought about to occur.

The study goal will influence whether the complementary perspectives of combining different questions will be chosen in a given situation. Are we looking for averages (using statistical methods), i.e., for the predominant reality, or are we looking for heterogeneity of many realities, in which case ethnographic methods are more relevant.

4.2.2 Research Goals and Focus

Meta-science Positions—Positivism, Interpretivism, Critical Realism and Constructivism

From the practitioner's viewpoint the academic 'position' or point of departure for a study is crucial for the focus of the study, for the questions asked, for decisions on data to be collected, and for intended results of the analysis. The most common academic 'positions' in the social sciences—referred to as 'meta-science positions' or 'science of science points of departure'—are *positivism, interpretivism* and *critical realism*, defined as follows:

1. *Positivism* is an epistemological position that advocates the application of the methods of the natural sciences to the study of social reality and beyond (Bryman, 2001: 506). Positivism is based on the assumption that there are patterns and regularities, causes and consequences in the social world just like there are in the natural world (Denscombe, 2003: 299).
2. *Interpretivism* is an epistemological position that requires the social scientist to grasp the subjective meaning of social action (Bryman, 2001: 504). Interpretivism is closely linked with *phenomenology*, which is particularly interested in how social life is constructed by those who participate in it. It regards people as creative interpreters of events, and through their actions and interpretations they are 'agents' who actively create an order to their existence (see Denscombe, 2003: 96).
3. *Critical realism* is a *realist* epistemology which asserts that the study of the social world should be concerned with the identification of the structures that generate that world. Critical realism is critical because its practitioners aim to identify structures in order to change them, so that inequalities and injustices may be counteracted. Unlike a positivist epistemology, critical realism accepts that the structures that are identified may not be amenable to the senses. Thus, whereas positivism is empiricist, critical realism is not (Bryman, 2001: 502), though in reality it often builds on empirical evidence.

A simple overview of the three positions in relation to the focus of a study, necessary data and outcome of analysis is given in Box 4.4.

In the *positivist* position, the focus is on describing a situation (in the above case 'hard' facts from school life). Consequently the data-collection will centre on 'hard' data—and when you analyse the material, the result is a description of the situation, which creates a foundation for knowledge. But mere knowledge about facts rarely constitutes a sufficient foundation for action (ref. to the case in Box 4.9 Section 4.4.2).

In the *interpretivist* position the practitioner is in a more advantageous situation with regard to applying research results. The focus is on processes, processual changes and understanding. Data is collected with that in mind, and the resulting analysis might lead to interventions in the situation.

With the *critical realism* position the focus of the study contains a normative aspect. The research questions are critical of the existing situation, power-structure, etc. The data collected deal with power

Box 4.4   Meta-science positions: Positivism, Interpretivism and Critical Realism in Relation to Focus of Study, Data-collection, and Result of Analysis—in a Study of 'Problems in Schools'

Meta-science point of departure	Focus of study	Data-collection	Result of analysis
Positivism	How many students are in the school? How many in my class? What are the functions of a teacher? What do teachers do?	Number of students Overview of functions Information from other teachers as to the above	Description of the situation but no information to 'act on'
Interpretivism	Why do the students (in my class) behave the way they do towards each other? What is the pattern of friendship—and rejection amongst the students? What is the reaction to this from their parents?	Data that will provide information and at the same time understanding— interviews and observation—about activities, priorities and (possible?) support from parents	Description and understanding of the situation. Data *might* lead to possible conflict-reducing interventions
Critical realism	How can equality between the boys and the girls in the classroom be promoted?	Data about power-relationships and their development	Analysis of the situation will direct possible interventions

After Boolsen, 1997.

structures, power relationships, and their development. The analysis of data will suggest interventions and intervention strategies. From the practitioner's point of view, application of results follows more or less directly from the analysis.

Bridging the interpretivist and the critical realism positions is the meta-theory position *critical theory*. Critical theory guides much development research. It provides an ontological and epistemological perspective, which provides an emancipatory interest in generation of knowledge, pointing to the limitations of positivist philosophies and the idea of an objective, neutral research. Critical theory is characterized as an interpretative theory with an understanding of social phenomena as being historically constructed and strongly defined by power-asymmetries and conflicting interests. Changing these power-asymmetries is perceived by adherents of critical theory as the purpose of social change. The aim of the scientific work is to generate knowledge of the political character of social phenomena and to critically reflect on the 'taken for granted' realities. A crucial element in the critical theory position is to develop knowledge with which it is possible to counteract irrational and repressive social structures and processes (Alvesson and Skjöldberg, 1994).

An alternative meta-science position, *human constructivism,* has challenged the dominant meta-science position's 'basic beliefs' within the recent decades. Constructivism (often also referred to as constructionism) is an ontological position which asserts that social phenomena and their meanings are continually being 'created' and accomplished by social actors. Further, proponents of constructivism argue that the sets of answers given are in *all* cases *human constructions*; that is, they are all inventions of the human mind and hence subject to human error (Guba and Lincoln, 1994). The implication of this view is that the advocates of any particular explanation must rely on *persuasiveness* and *utility* rather than *proof* in arguing their position.

4.2.3 Is There a Development Research–Development Work Continuum?

Social science researchers, including development researchers and practitioners, differ in orientation when it comes to using research results. One wing seeks to understand the fundamental nature of social reality. They are mainly engaged in basic research. Applied researchers, on the other hand, primarily want to apply and tailor knowledge to address specific practical issues—to contribute to change. They want to answer a policy question or solve a pressing social problem.

At this stage some reflection on differences and similarities between development research and development work is warranted. A number of development researchers and practitioners move between the different positions, from applied to basic studies and back, at different stages of their career. But suspicion and dilemmas prevail, as illustrated by Wilson, quoting Qualres van Ufford and Roth (2003),

> ... who usefully distinguish between the openness of aid organisations towards consultants and their general distrust of researchers. The consultant is seen to play a constructive role in framing development policy, assembling techniques, signs and representations, and establishing a single project logic. In contrast to this technical, orderly world, the 'de(cons)structive' vantage point of the researcher is considered threatening to aid organisations' interests. The job of the researcher investigating aid models is to bring conceptual, methodological and analytical tools of social science to bear on a problematic and bring the 'politics' back onto central stage ... (Wilson, 2004: 11).

It may be maintained that the dilemmas which Wilson sees for researchers as 'professional strangers' involved in analysis of 'aid models'[4] are similarly experienced by many practitioners (consultants):

> ... not only must they act ethically, they need to gain the confidence of people with whom they work, for research has to be a collaborative endeavour if it is to instigate exchange and learning' (ibid.).

Divergence between development researchers and practitioners may manifest itself in their different positions as described by Wilson, as well as in formal differences between short and long studies, between single-disciplinary and cross-disciplinary studies, between the principles and quality criteria. That is,

---

[4] Wilson's reference is the joint Ethio-Danish Development Programme in North Wollo, Ethiopia; various reports, Pernille Sørensen et al., Danish Institute for International Studies 2000–4.

when dealing with interventions in real life situations, development work is still often based on 'quick and dirty' studies rather than on longer-term research. At the other end of the spectrum is the never ending, the never fully analysed, the always outdated and never applied development research. It may fulfil scientific principles of sampling, representativeness, acceptable levels of accuracy, reliability, validity, etc., but its relevance is limited if the research remains unfinished and results are shelved.

Studies related to development work have to choose their methods from the same 'menu' as development research, however different the combinations, depending on purpose, time and resources. *Methods* for doing the required field studies, i.e., documentary studies, observation and interviewing in all their different degrees of formality and structure, and techniques for activating the people concerned—through the variety of participatory methods (see Chapters 2 and 3)—are used across the board.

It makes sense to talk about a continuum between development research and development work despite the multiplicity of issues and approaches if it is limited to the actors and to the field study methods. With regard to the *actors,* the escalating demand from aid organizations for people with knowledge and experience from developing countries absorbs a majority of development researchers in practical development work at one time or the other. For the indigenous researcher, the temptation to take the step into well-remunerated development work financed by foreign donor agencies is great, to the detriment of building research capacity in the South. The overall trend is that the distribution between development work and research is blurred, and applied development studies predominate.

Administrators—between Development Work and Research

Between development work and research is the manager of administrative routines whose job it is, amongst others, to commission targeted studies. It is the administrator's task to identify better practices and conditions for the acceptance and adoption of research results. With the devolution of responsibilities for development cooperation to recipient partner agencies, the 'aid manager' is increasingly a staff member of a national sector ministry or of a local government.

The modern 'administrative manager', whether in the North or in the South, has to play an increasingly flexible role, because yesterday's strategies might not apply to tomorrow's actions, or alternatively, the strategies for area A may not be applicable for area B. An example of this is an overall shift in development cooperation away from service delivery and project support towards Sector Programme Support (SPS), Sector Wide Approaches, SWAPs, and budget, policy and institutional capacity support. These areas require different studies from project interventions. However, not infrequently, complex political and ideological concepts make an entry into the development arena without being properly explained, for example through research. An example from the last decade are the mushrooming 'capacity building' initiatives, which require critical analysis (MFA, 2002–ongoing).

The escalating demand that administrators commission targeted studies prompts the need for enhanced research capacity to cope with significant changes in development policies and priorities. However, the research capacity of indigenous researchers and 'administrative managers' is not being honoured at the same rate.

4.3   Research Methods and Possible Combinations

4.3.1   Research Methods

Research is about knowledge production, seeking answers to questions through inquiry. But how does one determine the appropriate research strategy to focus a particular study? It is somewhat comforting to quote Patton, who says:

> There is no rule of thumb that tells a researcher precisely how to focus a study. The extent to which a research question is broad or narrow depends on purpose, the resources available, the time available, and the interests of those involved. In brief, these are not choices between good and bad, but choices among alternatives, all of which have merit (Patton, 2002: 224).

In development studies the 'choice' is often between establishing trends or averages from which generalizations can be drawn—with whatever caveats on generalizability that may be required—or a focus on differences, heterogeneity, imbalances, unequal relationships, etc., which may best be investigated through in-depth, interpretative case studies. Besides the methodological considerations discussed above, a research strategy combines different methods.

Research methods have been defined as tools to be used for answering specific questions and for solving different scientific or practical problems (Enderud, 1984). It is the substance of the matter—the questions to be answered—that must guide the selection of methods, not vice versa. Methods should not become straitjackets.

In Chapters 2 and 3 on *participatory methods,* we have used a definition of *methods* implying 'tools' for inquiry/investigation and analysis. A distinction can, however, be made between *methods, techniques* and *tools. Research methods*, if defined as a comprehensive set of approaches to gather evidence and analyse specific problems, encompasses techniques and tools. We use the concept *technique* to designate a practical way of collecting data and for analysing the information obtained in the research process. *Tools* are the instruments that are used in the process. Methodology encompasses theory and is not directly operational like method.

The following levels accrue:

Science of science
Methodology
Method
Investigation technique
Investigation tool/instrument

A selection of social science research methods, techniques and tools are set out in Box 4.5. Compared with the catalogue of participatory methods presented in Chapter 2, Box 2.5 and Chapter 3, it appears that there are several overlaps. Participatory methods, techniques and tools are complements to long-established social science methods.

Box 4.5   Selected Social Science Research Methods, Techniques and Tools

Methods:
Quantitative: Empirical, statistical
Qualitative: Documentary, cases, local and life histories, participatory
Experiments, pilot studies, scenarios

Techniques for Collecting Information:
Examining historical and other records, literature and proverbs
Observing behaviour, participant observation
Sample surveys
Listening to or interrogating informants:
  • Structured
  • Semi-structured
  • Open interviews
Visual aids

Tools
Diaries
Questionnaires
Checklists
Maps
Pictures, photos, drawing

Techniques for Analysis:
Computer-based data processing
Statistical methods
Distributions, variances, correlations
Transforming qualitative information into quantitative data
Graphical methods, pies, histograms, etc.
Geographical Information System, GIS
Photos, picture analysis

A number of sub-categories could be added under most of the headings mentioned in Box 4.5. Those listed are the commonly practised methods which show a high degree of stability despite adjustments over time.

4.3.2 Quantitative and Qualitative Style Research

The complexity and the purpose of specific development studies generally warrant tailor-made research designs that cannot be defined a priori even for studies on similar themes. Yet we need indications of what constitutes useful methodological approaches and study methods.[5]

Controversies have raged over appropriate research methods—for example, over the justification for using qualitative methods in social science research, and more recently, over the application of participatory methods, as discussed in Chapter 2. At the risk of over-generalization, qualitative methods are identified with interpretative and critical research and quantitative methods with positivism. The quantitative–qualitative divide should not make us forget that moving beyond qualitative and quantitative strategies is the focus of the comparative method (Ragin, 1987). At the same time, many scholars have identified synergies between quantitative and qualitative methods, e.g., for understanding and measuring poverty (Baulch, 1996; White, 2002).

It has been argued that qualitative research has expanded greatly and is rapidly displacing quantitative-style research in the social sciences (Denzin and Lincoln, 1994, 2000). Qualitative research spans a wide spectrum, of which nine major categories are summarized in Box 4.6.

There is much overlap between data types and what Neuman calls the *style* of quantitative and qualitative research (Box 4.7).

Both the quantitative and qualitative styles share basic principles of science, but the two approaches also differ in significant ways as Box 4.7 illustrates. Each has its strengths and limitations, topics or issues, but the styles also complement each other:

> The key features common to all qualitative methods can be seen when they are contrasted with quantitative methods. Most quantitative data techniques are data condensers. They condense data in order to see the big picture …. Qualitative methods, by contrast, are best understood as data enhancers. When data are enhanced, it is possible to see key aspects of cases more clearly (Ragin, 1994 in Neuman, 2003: 17).

Qualitative style research dominates in development studies, but this may be as much a reflection of the many conditionalities of time and resources which guard development cooperation in general as a reflection of priorities and 'best practice'. The best development research often combines features of each. This is particularly so when productive synergy may be established both between methods and between disciplines, as White found, using examples from studies of labour in rural Africa, of the relationships of household size and poverty, and of child survival (White, 2002).

---

[5] The reader will find detailed advice on research design, methodological considerations and methods for data collection, analysis, reporting and application of individual techniques and tools in a variety of sources referred to in this book (Bauer and Gaskell, 2000; Bryman, 2001; Denscombe, 2003; Denzin and Lincoln, 1994; Neuman, 2003; Patton, 2002; R. Kumar, 1999). For a pedagogical introduction to the Philosophy of Social Science rich in illustration of varieties of social explanation, see Little, 1991. See also Chapter 5.

Box 4.6 Examples of Qualitative Research	
Discourse Analysis	Focus on '... many dimensions of text, talk, and their cognitive, social and cultural contexts', e.g., by use of linguistic or other methods.
Ethno-methodology	Focus on social—in particular linguistic—interaction: 'By producing confusion, anxiety, bewilderment, and disorganized interaction [the ethno-methodologist] attempts to discover what is otherwise hidden: the common sense everyday rules of social interaction'.
Phenomenology	With partial interpretation, focus on '... the way people experience their world, what it is like for them, how best to understand them'.
Grounded theory	Through empirical coding, continuous comparisons and theoretical sampling, concepts and conceptual linkages which match data are generated during the research process.
Hermeneutic research	Focus on the meaning of texts/actions through analysis of relations between parts and totality/totality and parts: '... a singular event is understood by reference to whatever it is a part of'.
Content analysis	Focus on qualitative and quantitative analysis of text. The multiplicity of words in texts is classified into fewer categories.
Life history studies	Focus on 'biographical ethnography', which incorporate chronological events.
Structural ethnography	Focus on the 'meaning systems' of cultural groups and sub-groups and on 'shared systems of meaning'.
Symbolic interactionism	Focus on the fact that people '... live in a symbolic environment as well as a physical environment, and they act in response to symbols as well as physical stimuli'.

After Tesch, 1990 in H. Olsen, 2002, author's translation.

Box 4.7 Quantitative Style versus Qualitative Style Research	
Quantitative Style	**Qualitative Style**
Measure objective facts	Construct social reality, cultural meaning
Focus on variables	Focus on interactive processes, event
Reliability is key	Authenticity is key
Value free	Values are present and explicit
Independent of context	Situationally constrained
Many cases, subjects	Few cases, subjects
Statistical analysis	Thematic analysis
Researcher is detached	Researcher is involved

After Neuman, 2003: 16.

But integrating or combining qualitative and quantitative approaches also faces constraints as illustrated forthwith.

Methodological Constraints When Combining Quantitative and Qualitative Research Styles

A closer scrutiny shows that combining participatory—which often means qualitative—methods with statistical, survey methods is not always straightforward. Many practitioners have experienced development agencies requesting them to follow rigid blueprint statistical survey research and planning methods with little consideration for optimal methods. As a consequence they have proposed to add participatory and qualitative study elements, not always with success.

Case 1: An example of this was a Rural Finance Study in Uganda (Thomsen, 2002), where the researchers on their own initiative *added* a participatory element to the study.

Case 2: At a completely different scale is the World Bank's initiative to complement the National Household and Living Standard Surveys conducted as massive questionnaire-based surveys with Qualitative Poverty and Exclusion Studies, QPES, e.g. Guatemala (World Bank, 2002).

Common to the two examples seems to be the fact that **the quantitative and qualitative studies are being carried out in parallel**. They were not integrated in the planning phase, and the intended synergies between traditional quantitative survey results and participatory poverty studies were not being optimized.

The perspectives for such integration of quantitative and qualitative poverty assessments and policy studies are obvious in terms of multi-facets and triangulation. However, the constraints have to be seriously addressed if the benefits are to accrue. These constraints include time and resources to plan, sequencing of data collection, and analysis of statistical and participatory studies. In the case of projects, it is very likely that the project management is more concerned with compliance to short-term goal-fulfilment than with enhancing the understanding of complex poverty issues through integration of quantitative statistical data and qualitative participatory studies and actions, as pointed out by Thomsen for the Rural Finance Study in Uganda. The conclusion is that integrating statistical surveys with participatory research methods requires very careful consideration of the key concepts and epistemological issues involved if the two sets of information are to enhance the outcome.

Case 3: A recent attempt to integrate poverty surveys with participatory social and poverty assessments in the Danida-supported Urban Poverty Study in Bhutan (Pendley et al., 2002) has been a fruitful experience, but not without initial scepticism from the Bhutanese authorities who took the conventional view that quantitative methods are superior.

While the 'mix of quantitative and qualitative methods' is becoming the norm rather than the exception in development studies, there are still many challenges to getting the methods right. Some of these are constraints to participation at the country level, other constraints are within agencies, and yet others accrue to different meta-science points of departure.

Methodological Pluralism

This book adheres to the methodological pluralism discussed above. The statement may sound simplistic and requires justification. Little argues convincingly for *methodological pluralism* from the perspective of meta-science and pragmatic considerations. Neither *naturalism*—the view that the social sciences are methodologically similar to the natural sciences with causal explanations—nor *antinaturalism*, which argues that social sciences provide meaningful interpretations, are wholly persuasive (Little, 1991: Chapter 11). Against these two positions, Little argues that 'methodological pluralism views the sciences more as a fabric of related enterprises than as a single unitary activity defined by the 'scientific method' (ibid.: 237), and concludes:

> … we will best understand the logic of the social sciences if we pay close attention to the details of research in a variety of areas and remain sensitive to the important strands of diversity that exist in methods of inquiry, forms of empirical reasoning, and models of explanation (ibid.: 238).

Personal experience from a variety of development research and practice studies, of shorter or longer duration, supports the view that a combination of methods normally brings about better results. There are arguments for combining quantitative and qualitative methods to obtain:

- A more critical attitude to the mechanistic use of quantitative methods and a more relaxed attitude to the use of qualitative methods,
- room for combinations of quantitative and qualitative methods from different disciplines, e.g., ethnography and sociology, communication, health sciences, organizational and management studies, economics, geography, history, literature, etc., and for
- flexibility and improvisations in choice of practical methods, i.e., iteration between data and partial results, and
- the people researched are seen as subjects rather than objects and are often involved in the research process.

Interesting results have been gained from the application of information on a given subject which is embedded in oral traditions, historical records and local histories, fiction and proverbs, etc. The 'Dig Where You Stand' tradition in Scandinavia (Lindqvist, 1978; Lindqvist et al., 1982) has likewise explored a number of locally available source materials, e.g., newspapers, historical records of organizations, letters, etc., and has made history come alive for people who would normally not read research reports, least of all engage in research-like investigations themselves. This tradition is reflected in much action research, spanning a wide range of topics from democracy and sustainability (Olsén et al., 2003) to private–public partnerships (Kjaer, 2003) in the North and the South.

Possible Method Mixes—Considering Time and Cost Constraints

A brief example can illustrate a *possible choice of methods and techniques in a study on rural employment.*

Suppose we need information on employment—a central part of the simplest social assessment or socio-economic profile. Let's assume that, in a rural area, we are looking at patterns of employment in a farming community. Some of the main factors are:

- The use of labour (paid or unpaid) of different age groups, including women, men and children.
- How labour is organized, including hired labour and work groups.
- Production at both village and household levels.
- Home consumption, trading and sale of produce.

To get a general picture, we could organize periods of participant observation and interviews with key informants. This initial—exploratory—research is important, particularly in collecting meaningful data on informal work. For more detailed information we can design in-depth case-studies to draw personal profiles of particular types of informal workers. More exact data may need a carefully-timed, single survey to interview farmers and other village workers. With extra resources and time, we can arrange regular, repeated surveys, probably with a panel in several villages (a panel is a small sample for repeat visits). Alternatively, a well-resourced research project can organize observation surveys, recording the activities of all workers on a sample of farms over the study period. This method is accurate, but time-consuming and expensive (Nichols, 1991).

The example illustrates how different techniques may be applied to the same study. In fact, several aspects of the illustrated research topic could be investigated by using participatory methods and self-survey techniques. The opportunity is to optimize synergies between methods and disciplines as White emphasizes (White, 2002 and Section 5.1.2, this book).

The research strategy and concrete research plan depends on the purpose of the study, and the methods must be chosen according to the information needed. Usually this will involve a mixture of methods as suggested earlier, the exact combination being influenced not only by the researcher's optimal choice, but very much also by resources and time available.

A large number of development studies are undertaken as requested studies by a donor or other agent. Often their requests for research results are bound by very narrow time limits and may lead to counterproductive results, since studies become superficial given the short time allowed. A 'normal' appraisal study of a sector programme, for example, may require some two to three months or more for a multidisciplinary team of three to four people. Participation of indigenous team members should be self-evident, but in reality this is far from always the case.

Nevertheless, study teams of multidimensional and complex development issues are likely to experience time as a serious constraint. Often study teams are placed under pressure by the requesting agency to produce quick—hence sometimes implicitly 'dirty' and premature—results. Time should in fact always be a negotiable factor in studies related to development work in order to avoid ritualized studies, which follow the standard formulas at the risk of being depleted of substantial findings and critical considerations. The consultants or researchers who will be responsible for the results must be prepared to argue for an expedient mix of methods and a reasonable time frame which matches the requested tasks from the client.

What, then, about longer-term, independent, development research? A mixture of methods and techniques determined by time and resources is still required, but the researcher's freedom to be more flexible and adjust the methods and produce evidence as data come in is enhanced with more time available. The flexible research process is encouraged by the grounded theory approach in particular (ref. Strauss and Corbin, 1990; see also Chapter 5), but must not be mistaken for totally arbitrary choices. A timetable, e.g., a gant diagram (activity/time flow chart) indicating the major activities to be accomplished in the different phases of a study is a useful tool for allocating available time whether in research or in 'practice'. However, only if the timetable is flexible and amenable to an adjustment of activities within the overall time-frame does a time schedule make sense.

4.3.3 Interdisciplinary Perspectives

Specific disciplines are associated with different degrees of rigour:

> Economics is commonly associated with the use of quantitative methods, and because of this, supposedly, the discipline is more 'rigorous' than other social sciences, which are in turn associated with the application of qualitative methods, presumed to be less rigorous (White, 2002: 511).

These assumptions are challenged by White, who argues that the more serious distinction, which applies both to quantitative and qualitative research, is between data analysis and data mining (see Section 5.1.2).

Development concerns have given rise to a variety of demands for interdisciplinary perspectives. The purpose of addressing development problems in their complexity and addressing different layers of causal relationships (Eide, 1992) has determined the need for holistic or interdisciplinary perspectives in research and development work. For instance, provision of water and sanitation, roads, telecommunication, environmental protection, are no longer tasks for technical staff only. Nevertheless, methods to integrate cross-disciplinary understanding are not well developed. Social Assessments and Poverty and Social Impact Assessment (World Bank website and www.iaia.org/siaguide/) studies have improved the situation, but all too often team members from different disciplines are busy on their particular issues and work in parallel rather than as an integrated team, as illustrated by Rasmussen from a Reforestation Project in Sudan (Box 4.8).

McNeill makes a distinction between multidisciplinarity, by which he means working together in parallel, and cross-disciplinarity, which means working in concert (McNeill, 1992). The former is what is required in planning and policy making, for example, a team planning a district development programme, while the internal and external team dialogue across disciplines must be maintained. The latter—cross-disciplinarity—is necessary for good research in McNeill's view. It is on the borderline— or through a confrontation—between different disciplines that new ideas tend to develop and basic methodological issues are confronted. But true cross-disciplinary research is not easy, McNeill admits. Hence development research is still undertaken primarily by single individuals and limited to specific disciplines in contrast to development work, which is increasingly interdisciplinary in approach.

The cross-disciplinary perspective and skill in development work and research will have to come from altered curricula within the disciplines. But the special strengths and contents of single disciplines should not be jeopardized by turning everyone into generalists. The road engineer is not to fill the function of a sociologist or gender specialist or vice versa. But all of them must be sensitized to the approaches and perspectives of the other's work, if working together on a roads programme and on the required studies is to succeed (e.g., COWI, 2000–ongoing). Universities and other places of learning are slowly taking up the interdisciplinary challenge, but inertia prevails.

Box 4.8   The Risk of Missing the Interdisciplinary Dialogue

It is clear in the case of the 'Afforestation and Reforestation Project of the Northern Region, Sudan', that the focus through all project phases and especially during the planning phase has been more on participation than on the people. The project has tended to think that if only people participated in their work, the project was going to succeed. The imminent danger in that approach lies first of all in a perception of people's work relations as more important than their social relations. Certain indications are given as to why the project in general and the anthropologist in particular have made this crucial mistake.

During project planning the anthropologist is involved in a sort of baseline study. For the anthropologist, this is often conducted using participant observation and with the intention of focusing on social relations and social structure. Usually the anthropologist surveys the project area through a selection of households, community leaders, etc. The anthropologist feels he is on safe ground, as the methods and the baseline study required do not differ much from classical anthropological field work, apart from the time spent on doing it (much shorter for the baseline study as a consultant).

The baseline study is frequently considered a separate exercise to be undertaken by the anthropologist. He tends to believe that his independence from the planning of more technical issues of the project is an advantage. This is a misconception.

In the 'Afforestation and Reforestation Project of the Northern Region, Sudan', the anthropologist has collected and analysed a considerable amount of basic socio-economic information both from individual households and from the community in general. But where is the link between the comprehensive baseline study and the planning of the project?

From the beginning the planners were interested in implementing a project by using people's participation, more than understanding the social relations and structure. The anthropologist did not consider himself part of the actual planning. Therefore, he was not in a position to stress and make visible the importance of social structure. The lack of mutual exchange of findings and ideas made planners and the anthropologist confuse the concepts of social relations and work relations, thinking they were planning and implementing a project in correspondence with the prevailing social structure for the community as a whole.

The project has now realized the mistake of taking work relations to represent the social relations and the social structure, and to associate people's participation with work relations in particular and not with the social structure in general.

Corrective measures are taken.

After S.S. Rasmussen, 1992: 18–19.

Research Process and Research Plan

4.4.1 Basic Elements in the Research Process

The research process is basically a contribution to knowledge production. It may be argued that research results become knowledge only when they are applied. The element of application is not always seen as an outcome of research, e.g., basic research may contribute to knowledge production by feeding into other researchers' work. Figure 4.1 is a graphical illustration of the elements in the research process. The figure does not include the element of application, which would be an addition to the box 'conclusions/answers'.

Figure 4.1   Main Elements in the Research Process

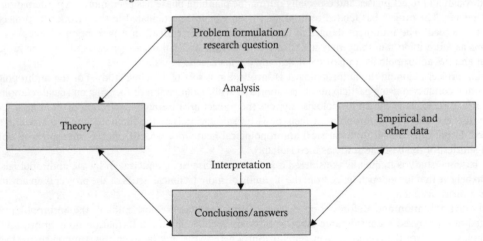

After Enderud (in I. Andersen, 2002).

The arrows in the illustrated research process indicate that the links between the elements are various analyses, interpretations and synthesis. Research purposes and foci differ, but in general the figure captures the basic elements in the research process. Development studies, however, pose a special challenge as they often require the participation of professionals from different disciplines—i.e., interdisciplinary or cross-disciplinary perspectives.

4.4.2 Methodological and Logic Considerations in the Research Process

Methodological Considerations

A variety of considerations enter into the process of doing social research and development studies. Our choices when carrying out a project or study are expressions of values and 'codes of conduct', first and foremost as professionals, but also as persons.

The choices affect

- how we work inductively, deductively or both (see Chapter 5);
- how we think scientifically, epistemologically and ontologically;
- what kind of data we are using, quantitative and/or qualitative data/information;
- what our values are; what we think about other people; and
- how we deal with ethical and practical problems and the context as a whole.

(*After* Boolsen, 2004).

The claim for methodological pluralism does not mean that research methodologies, designs, research methods, etc., can be combined in all ways. There should be an internal logic in any study. The message is that development studies should avoid the signal that 'anything goes'. Unfortunately this is not always the case and may lead to strategies being proposed that do not follow from the study questions—or worse, the implication may be that time and money have been wasted on examining and pursuing questions that do not lead to acceptable or usable solutions.

Internal project logic is what research strives for, but lessons gained in the research process may deem changes in the focus of the study necessary as the next two sections illustrate.

Internal Logic

Internal logic in a study is a key criteria to ensure higher quality not only in terms of standard criteria for good research practice, but also with regard to the relevance and use of the research results. The participatory research process described in Box 4.9 illustrates the point.

Changes in Research Focus and Purpose

A very important point in the research process is when you start to ask the basic questions: What am I going to do? What is the purpose of the study, and how exactly am I going to do it? This may sound self-evident, but to the practitioner, the project-manager or the researcher, these questions are very fundamental, because when they are answered many other questions fall into place. To answer them adequately requires a fair amount of knowledge about the topic of the study, but not least about its

---

Box 4.9   Internal Logic in a Participatory Study of School Environment

Hard-core data do not suffice to explore complex issues

A group of teachers had experienced growing frustrations in their schools for some time. All of them wanted changes to take place in their institutions. But what exactly the problems were was not clear. The teachers knew that a 'convincing study' of the problems would be important evidence to present to the authorities in an appeal for their support for change. They decided to undertake a study of the situation, but just didn't know how to produce material or evidence that would make it clear what the fundamental issue was, and how it could be addressed. In other words, it was realized from the beginning that an inquiry—(an exploratory, inter-pretative or explanatory study)—might produce evidence that could be used for initiating changes. This was a great motivating factor. Each teacher would produce a study plan from his or her perspective.

When their initial study plans and designs were produced, none of them could deliver information and/or analysis that eventually could support changes; they all dealt with *descriptions* of their schools and institutions. A common situation was that they would provide hard quantitative information in the form of 'number of students', 'number of teachers', 'number of class-rooms', 'type of facilities', 'size of location', 'number of sub-jects offered', etc. Considering that some teachers wanted to change the educational practice in the classroom, introduce experiments with delinquents, consider other ways of using the teachers' meetings, stimulate youngsters' interest in sports, and the like, it was obvious there was a huge distance between the goal and the suggested research activities.

When this picture became clear—that most of the 'would-be knowers' had proposed collection of 'hard' data—they argued as a kind of 'defence' that they (as inquirers) had left the ordinary teacher's role and were still *developing* the new role—that of the observing and critical practitioner/researcher. In the latter role, they had learned that 'How you ask questions determines the answers', 'Questions produce answers'—and other similar well-known statements in the methodology classes.[6] However, it takes knowledge, empathy and practice to formulate interesting and relevant questions and problems. To collect hard-core quantitative data is tempting, but is not sufficient to explore complex issues.

A new round of research questions had to be formulated to identify what the problems were in the schools. The initial experience was useful for preparing a better research strategy.

After Boolsen, 1997—unpublished material.

---

context, i.e., the conditions, related problems, practical possibilities, power relationships, and so on. Experience shows that the micro-level conditions for a development project or programme—e.g., intra- and inter-household power relations, aging, etc., and the macro-level conditions of sector policies, decentralization, etc., are constantly changing.

Precisely because we cannot know everything from the beginning and since we are working in an ever changing environment, it is often necessary to work with an iterative process between basic purposes, issues, aims, etc., and methodology, research strategies, choice of data, and analysis.

---

[6] This is also the title of a Scandinavian methodology book, Bengt-Erik Andersson, 1992: Som man frågar får man svar—en introduction i intervju- og enkätteknik. Raben & Sjögren. Tema Nova.

It is not uncommon to reflect on and change the research purpose throughout the whole process. In a study Boolsen finds that social science researchers modify, change and re-formulate their problem under investigation almost all the way through the research process. In most cases the reason is that the necessary data-material is not available, and they end up researching a problem which is different from the one they set out to study (see examples below).

Basically this means that knowledge is increased, differentiation is introduced, etc.—but to the practitioner the ultimate need is for data, analysis and information that can be *applied*. Consequently, increased opportunities for applying knowledge are not necessarily the same as increased knowledge (Boolsen, 1977).

Example 1
The Non-existent Research Problem Prompts a Necessary Change of Focus

Changes in focus may have different reasons, one being that getting into a field often means that new angles and perspectives are identified. Sometimes the original problem turns out to be a non-problem as illustrated in the following case:

> A research institution in Copenhagen was asked to identify *advantages and disadvantages* of foster homes compared to other institutional settings that are used when children are taken away from their biological parents who do not manage to cope with the role as parents. The empirical foundation was institutionalisation patterns of children during a 5-year period followed by qualitative interviews with some of these children. When the data was analysed, it turned out that the institutionalisation models which were expected to be investigated, compared and analysed in the study were not represented in the data (Boolsen et al., 1986).

Example 2
Non-representative Sample may Require Change of Focus

The Evaluation of Swedish support for the Promotion of Gender Equality was based on a pre-selected sample of interventions representing four different sectors. It was anticipated that each intervention represented a considerable change in gender equality due to the gender mainstreaming strategy supposedly pursued in the interventions. When the evaluation team had inquired into the changes in gender equality, it appeared that only a few of the interventions had pursued a clear gender equality goal and main-streaming strategy. Consequently, the focus of the evaluation study turned more towards reasons as to why the gender equality goal had not been pursued to the degree anticipated, and towards a focus on conditions and opportunities for strengthening a gender equality perspective in the evaluated interventions and in new interventions (Mikkelsen et al., 2002).

Designing a research plan needs to incorporate considerations on the research process and possible adjustments like the above.

4.4.3 Designing a Research Plan

Which research design is best? Which methods of investigation and data collection will provide the most useful information—and for whom? For the decision maker? For the people concerned and affected?

There is no simple, immediate and universal answer to these questions, but this does not preclude discussion and debate regarding the relative usefulness of different methods for the study of specific problems or types of problems. The answer in each case will depend on what intended users want to know, the purpose of the study, the funds available, the political context, and the intentions of the researchers. This precludes the assertion of the general superiority of one method over another.

Box 4.10 lists a number of issues that are typically necessary to address in designing a study and from which the most appropriate mix of methods can be achieved.

Box 4.10 Design Issues and Methodological Considerations for a Research Plan	
Issues	**Sample Options and Considerations**
1. What is the primary purpose of the study?	Basic research, applied research, summative evaluation, formative evaluation, action research
2. What is the focus of study?	Breadth versus depth trade-offs
3. What are the units of analysis?	Individuals, groups, programme components, whole programmes, organizations, communities, critical incidents, time periods, and so on
4. What will be the sampling strategy or strategies?	Purposeful sampling; probability sampling; variations in sample size from a single case study to a generalizable sample
5. What types of data will be collected?	Qualitative, quantitative, or both
6. What controls will be exercised?	Naturalistic inquiry, experimental design, quasi-experimental options
7. What analytical approach or approaches will be used?	Inductive, deductive, content analysis, statistical analysis, combinations
8. How will validity of and confidence in the findings be addressed?	Triangulation options, multiple data sources, multiple methods, multiple perspectives, and multiple investigators
9. Time issues: When will the study occur? How will the study be sequenced or phased?	Long-term field work, rapid reconnaissance, exploratory phase to confirmatory phase, fixed times versus open time lines
10. How will logistics and practicalities be handled?	Gaining entry to the setting, access to people and records, contracts, training, endurance, and so on
11. How will ethical issues and matters of confidentiality be handled?	Informed consent, protection of human subjects, reactivity, presentation of self, and so on
12. What resources will be available? What will the study cost?	Personnel, supplies, data collection, materials, analysis time and costs, reporting/publishing costs

After Patton, 1990: 197 (in *Qualitative Evaluation Methods*). Reprinted by permission of Sage Publications, Inc.

While there are no strict rules for the choice of research strategy and methods, there are nevertheless a number of general steps to be taken in designing a research plan (cf. Box 4.11).

These steps and the broad approach to a research inquiry are similar for many disciplines, which is the premise of Kumar's useful step-by-step guide (Kumar, 1999). Amongst the steps, field work may be a longer step in development studies.

Box 4.11   Steps in Designing a Research Plan

S
H
A   Identify and define the research problem
R   ↓
E   Review theory and undertake initial documentary studies
                                          ↓
T   Clarify goals, objectives and expectations of the study
A   in consultation with others
S   ↓
K   Choose main topics
S   ↓
                    Prepare list of sub-topics, indicators, and key questions
                                          ↓
A   Identify sources of information for each sub-topic
N   ↓
D   Select tools to collect and analyse information
                                          ↓
F   Design research tools
I   ↓
N   Outline field work tasks
D   ↓
I   Obtain research permission
N   ↓
G   Test and adjust research tools
S   ↓
                                 Collect field data
                                          ↓
T   Start analysing data in the field
H   ↓
R   Adjust objectives and reschedule
O   data collection if required
U   ↓
G   Complete data analysis and reporting
H   ↓
O   Disseminate results
U
T

An illustrative model of the 'research cycle' appears in Figure 4.2.

Figure 4.2   Illustrative Model of the 'Research Cycle'

The model of the research cycle presented in the figure serves to illustrate how the researcher determines whether the question being pursued is significant or not. Reviewing formal theory and literature may demonstrate that the curiosity or problem has already been satisfied or solved; in this case, no knowledge is needed. Research is worth doing only if it explores some part of the research cycle that is still unknown, that has not been explained well before. The researcher may test hypotheses, develop better descriptions and indicators or concepts, expand generalizations, or challenge extant theory; whatever the focus, the researcher must demonstrate that the research contributes new information. The research proposal is a written demonstration of the means by which the research will add to knowledge. The proposal tells the reader just how the research fits into the model of the research cycle.

A research proposal demonstrates a link with the research model in general, but it must also answer the following questions:

- Who might care about this research? To whom will it be significant?
- How will the researcher conduct this research?
- Is the researcher capable of doing his/her research?

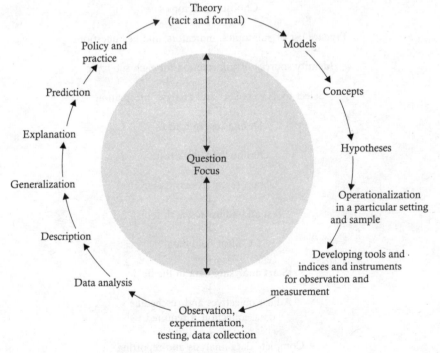

After Marshall and Rossman, 1989: 22–23 (in *Designing Qualitative Research*). Reprinted by permission of Sage Publications, Inc.

There is no rule on the weight to be given to each phase in the process of a study. However, the time required for preparation of a study, for processing, analysis and write-up of data must not be underestimated. Overlaps between the phases will also occur. Today, when portable computers are available, many researchers find it convenient to start entering data while in the field, if possible do the preliminary analysis in the field. However, all too often research proposals tilt towards home-based studies. The convenience of doing field research during holidays only, as seen in some research proposals, cannot match more ambitious plans for researching complex issues. A reasonable balance between tasks and time requirements ought to have equal relevance for practitioners who become involved in field studies.

Summary Guidelines for Field Work

Let us close this section with a few guides on field work. The message is as clear as this: 'What you do in the field—it all depends—but don't lose direction!' (Patton, 1990). Field studies are a continuous learning process. It may assist the bewildered analyst to be reminded: 'When theory is silent, concentrate on methods', and 'When in doubt, collect facts'.

Below are some **guidelines for field work** inspired by Patton:

1. Be descriptive in taking field notes—write field notes as early as possible after observations, interviews, other encounters. Keep a diary.
2. Gather a variety of information from different perspectives.
3. Cross-validate and triangulate by gathering different kinds of data—observations, interviews, programme documentation, recordings and photographs—and using multiple methods.
4. Use quotations; represent programme participants in their own terms. Capture participants' views of their experiences in their own words.
5. Select key informants wisely and use them carefully. Draw on the wisdom of their informed perspectives, but keep in mind that their perspectives are limited.
6. Be aware of and sensitive to the different stages of field work.

    (a) Build trust and rapport at the entry stage. Remember that the researcher-evaluator-observer is also being observed and evaluated.
    (b) Stay alert and disciplined during the more routine, middle phase of field work.
    (c) Focus on pulling together a useful synthesis as field work draws to a close.
    (d) Be disciplined and conscientious in taking detailed field notes at all stages of field work.

7. Be as involved as possible in experiencing the programme as fully as possible while maintaining an analytical perspective grounded in the purpose of the field work.
8. Clearly separate description from interpretation and judgement.
9. Provide informative feedback as part of the verification process of field work. Time that feedback carefully. Observe its impact.
10. Include in your field notes and research/evaluation report your own experiences, thoughts and feelings. These are also field data.

Beyond these prescriptions, the point remains that what one does depends on the situation, the nature of the subject, the nature of the programme or intervention under study, and the skills, interests, needs and point of view of the investigator (*after* Patton, 1990, 2002).

Data can originate from many sources and take many forms. In development studies interviews and documents are key sources. Theory helps us to pose relevant questions in a coherent way and select or construct data. Indicators, both qualitative and quantitative, are increasingly used to construct and analyse data. Attention is called to the common mistake of presenting plain data as if data themselves are the same as analysis. Interpretation of data requires other quality criteria for qualitative research than conventional validity and reliability criteria.

5.1   Theory Based Data Generation and Analysis

5.1.1 Theoretical Frameworks

'Theory'—or assumptions—frames how we think about and approach the study of a topic, whether we are conscious of this or not. Theory gives us concepts, provides basic assumptions, directs us to the important questions, and suggests ways for us to make sense of data. Using social theory makes us think through research (Pryke et al., 2003). Theory increases our awareness of interconnections and of the broader significance of data. Only the naïve newcomer believes that theory is irrelevant to development work and research, or that a researcher just collects the data. Without making theory explicit,[2] it is easy to fall into the trap of hazy thinking, faulty logic and imprecise concepts. Theory enables us to connect a single study to the immense base of knowledge to which other researchers contribute, for example with experience from a variety of development cooperation activities. To use an analogy, theory helps the analyst to see the forest instead of just a single tree. However, the very word 'theory' sometimes seems to scare people. They do not feel at home with theory nor use it in a productive way (Neuman, 2000).

The Deadly Paradox of Social Theory

An explanation of the 'fear of theory' may derive from *'the deadly paradox of social theory'* (Flyvbjerg, 2001). This paradox originates in the fact that *in social science the object is a subject,* i.e., self-reflecting

---

[1] The main author of Sections 5.1.1 and 5.1.2 and main contributor to 5.2 is Merete Watt Boolsen.
[2] Consultants who conduct development studies in response to Terms of Reference, TOR, commissioned by a development agency, usually make explicit their 'theory' and assumption in 'Comments to TOR' before engaging in a study.

humans and ever changing individuals, groups and relations between them, whereas the natural sciences study physical objects. Natural science aspires to the principles of 'ideal theory' established over the centuries: The ideal theory must be (*i*) explicit; (*ii*) universal; (*iii*) abstract; (*iv*) discrete; (*v*) systematic; (*vi*) complete, and applicable for prediction. Social science also aspires to work with theories, but the principles differ in significant ways. Vibeke Ankersborg (2002) suggests how the principles are interpreted from the perspective of the social science practitioner as *requirements for the social scientist's empirical work* (differences highlighted): (*i*) The researcher's *prior assumptions* and interpretations must be explicit; (*ii*) Social science theory is historically *time bound*—i.e., valid for a certain time and place; (*iii*) *Concrete,* referring to concrete situations and cases; (*iv*) *Context specific;* (*v*) *Complex,* i.e., the elements are interrelated *without* reference to a universal logic; and (*vi*) It is *interpretative,* i.e., the researcher is searching for meaningful interpretation of the relations between the elements of the 'theory', but is not seeking exact prediction. Social life is a conglomerate of interrelated elements, facts, phenomena, etc., which are not independent of each other and has to be analysed in that complexity (ibid.: 134).

There is a necessary and important link between theory and empirical investigation. Thus, researchers who proceed without theory may find themselves adrift as they attempt to design or conduct empirical studies. Likewise, theorists who proceed without anchoring their work to empirical reality risk floating off into incomprehensible speculation. It is the interlinkage between theory and empirical investigations which influences how we go about collecting data and draw conclusions from analysis.

Major Theoretical Frameworks and Substantive Theory

Social science has several major theoretical frameworks. The frameworks are orientations or ways of looking at the social world, at a level less abstract than the 'meta-science positions' referred to in Chapter 4. The theoretical frameworks provide collections of assumptions, concepts and forms of explanation (Box 5.1).

In the 'hierarchy' of theory terminology, the *theoretical frameworks* include many *formal theories* and *middle range substantive theories* (for example, theories of poverty alleviation, theories of governance, theories of urban development, theories of conflict, theories of the family, of household economics, of labour exchange, of gender equality and child survival, etc.). Thus one can apply a structural functional theory, an exchange theory, and a conflict theory to a study of 'poverty alleviation' of 'the family', etc. The theoretical framework, initial assumptions and the choice of concepts have implications for the planning and design of a study or project, the selection of data, the construction of data, and for the analysis.

Theory has many meanings, but most social scientists will agree that we can define *social theory* as a system of interconnected abstractions or ideas that condenses and organizes knowledge about the social world. It is a compact way to think of the social world. People are always creating new theories about how the world works (Neuman, 2003). Competing and changing development theories, for example, keep influencing the development discourse and the strategies and priorities in international development cooperation.

Thus, from the 1990s neo-liberal development theory has set its dominant mark on the approach to international development cooperation, pushing aside the influence of critical post-colonial dependency

---

Box 5.1   Four Major Theoretical Frameworks in Social Science

Structural Functionalism
Major concepts: system, equilibrium, dysfunction, division of labour.
Key Assumptions: Society is a system of inter-dependent parts that is in equilibrium or balance. Over time, society has evolved from a simple to a complex type, which has highly specialized parts. The parts of society fulfil different needs or functions of the social system. A basic consensus on values or a value system holds society together.

Symbolic Interactionism
Major concepts: self, reference group, role-playing, perception.
Key Assumptions: People transmit and receive symbolic communication when they socially interact. People create perceptions of each other and social settings. People largely act on their perceptions. How people think about themselves and others is based on their interactions.

Exchange Theory (also Rational Choice)
Major concepts: opportunities, rewards, approval, balance, credit.
Key Assumptions: Human interactions are similar to economic transactions. People give and receive resources (symbolic, social approval, or material) and try to maximize their rewards while avoiding pain, expense and embarrassment. Exchange relations tend to be balanced. If they are unbalanced, persons with credit can dominate others.

Conflict Theory
Major concepts: power, exploitation, struggle, inequality, alienation.
Key Assumptions: Society is made up of groups that have opposing interests. Coercion and attempts to gain power are ever-present aspects of human relations. Those in power attempt to hold onto their power by spreading myths or by using violence if necessary.

After Neuman, 2000: 60.

---

theory. The dominance of one set of theories does not in itself indicate that it is more correct than other theories. Theories can complement or contradict each other. Our choice of theories as researcher and practitioner is a matter of conviction that the chosen theoretical point of departure better helps to explain and interpret our research questions than other theories do.

Concepts are the building blocks of theory. A concept is an idea expressed as a symbol or in words. Some concepts take on a range of measurable values, quantities, or amounts. Examples of this kind of concept are *amount of income, population density* and *years of schooling*. These are *variables*. Other concepts express types of non-variable phenomena like landlessness, or phenomena which are not straightforward to measure, for example, institutions such as *bureaucracy* and *family*.

Concepts contain built-in *assumptions*, statements about the nature of things that are not observable or testable. We accept them as a necessary starting point.

For theories to help guide social research in general and development studies in particular, they need to be 'operationalized' into research questions or hypothesis. The inquiry process, however, often starts in reverse order. In development work the practitioner is, for example, often presented with a set of questions and problems for which 'solutions' are requested. *Hence the challenge is to link the research questions to theory and design an adequate research strategy.* In some cases, the exercise of linking research questions to theory reveals contradictions and gaps, and additional questions must be formulated or questions be revised. Whatever the case, decisions have to be taken about which information to collect to provide answers to research questions. In other words, information—or *data*—has to be collected.

5.1.2 Data Selection, Construction and Analysis

Data can Originate from Many Sources—and Take Many Forms

Data can, for example, take the form of:

Numbers—from unsystematic or stochastic presentation of material to very structured, easily 'read' tables, tests, etc.

Text—from conversation, interviews, newspapers, magazines, radio programmes, etc.

Images—from children's drawings, maps, photographs, posters, etc.

Sounds—from spontaneous singing and soundscapes to musical scripts and sound rituals.

Context—other sensory data such as temperature, smells, observations, and a variety of contextual impressions which influence the investigator's sentiments, feelings, etc. (Bauer and Gaskell, 2002).

Data is seldom readily present in the 'form' that is suited for further analysis and interpretation; in most cases we must 'construct' data: i.e., categorize observations, re-categorize, make summaries of interviews, of pictures, of medical files, of notes from organizations' board meetings, of everyday life scenes, etc. The research question determines what data is relevant.

Data Selection and Construction

The socially situated researcher creates, through interaction, the realities that constitute the places where empirical materials are collected and analysed. We use methods and techniques such as interviews, observational and visual methods, text and documentary analysis for producing empirical materials from which data are constructed, analysed and interpreted.

The important part of the data-construction process is the step from 'looking' or simply observing the world to the step where (part of) it is systematically examined and investigated. When this takes place, information is selected—for instance from people (interviews, observation, experimentation), from certain events, from documents about events, from communication of information, from eliciting people's attitudes, etc.

Primary data, which is collected and analysed by the researcher him or herself, differs from *secondary data* (which originate from others) in terms of the researcher's possibility to better control the relevance and quality of primary data. Yet, as discussed in Chapter 3, secondary data—quantitative statistical data in particular—are often taken to be more robust than qualitative and primary data. This despite the fact that empirical evidence is hardly unanimous in support of a particular view as demonstrated by Kenny and Williams (2001) in their analysis of cross-country econometric studies of growth.

In the research process *data is being constructed,* typically in three steps: (*i*) first, when information is selected; (*ii*) second, when data is categorized, re-categorized, summarized, etc.; and (*iii*) third, when data is subjected to systematic investigation and analysis. The outcome of analysis is also data, but in a more condensed form than raw data.

The *purpose* of a project or study determines what is *appropriate and relevant data.* The criteria of whether something can be used as data is the internal logic between data and the formulated research question, regardless of whether the data is text, image or numbers. For example, to investigate livelihood and coping strategies of landless people, you will obtain information (data) from landless people. That data relates to the research question is necessary, but not sufficient. The good sources of information (data) can be characterized as follows: (*i*) First hand; (*ii*) simultaneous; (*iii*) centrally placed; (*iv*) informs about the topic in questions; or (*v*) relates to the incidence, the phenomenon, the organization; (*vi*) the origin is clear; (*vii*) biases and tendencies—if any—are transparent; and (*viii*) relevant to the research question (Ankersborg, 2002: 129).

Sometimes the optimal data is difficult to obtain, and therefore *access to data* also determines the construction of data. *Selection of data* presupposes *handling of data,* which may require that the investigator have knowledge about statistical methods and statistical computer programmes, or knowledge about content analysis or other analytical methods. *Analytical orientation* towards qualitative data and qualitative methodology, or quantitative data and quantitative methodology, or combined methodologies also influence data construction (Boolsen, 2004).

Data construction shows that throughout the process, not only objective considerations but also *subjective, individual,* and *ethical* considerations are at play. The more serious distinction according to White is between *data analysis* and *data mining.* Data is the basis for analysis, for providing interpretations and meaning in research, but the approach may differ considerably:

> The data analyst is looking for the interpretation most consistent with the data, i.e., letting the data tell the story. The data miner knows what she is looking for and keeps digging until she finds it. Then she stops and that is the story she tells. Data miners are equally at home using either quantitative or qualitative data (White, 2002: 513).

It is not the quanti–qualitative data divide which matters, but *how* the analyst uses or 'mines' her data— roughly speaking, whether the analyst works deductively or inductively (see Section 5.2.1).

Data and Social Facts

Development studies rest on empirical data—data about the social world. There has been some reluctance to use the concept 'data' in the social sciences, since it provides associations with the natural and technical sciences. Emile Durkheim had already in the 1930s suggested that social scientists should rather apply the concept 'social facts'—

> Our definition will then include the whole relevant range of facts if we say:
> *A social fact is every way of acting, fixed or not, capable of exercising on the individual an external constraint*; or again, *every way of acting which is general throughout a given society, while at the same time existing in its own right independent of its individual manifestation* (Durkheim, 1964: 13).

When, in this book, the word 'data' is used, it then includes 'ways of acting, thinking, and feeling, external to the individual, and endowed with a power of coercion, by reason of which they control him' (ibid.: 3). The quote indicates that social facts are 'endowed with power', meaning that in any society there are ways of doing things which we as individuals adopt, knowingly or unknowingly.

This description of 'social facts'—the smallest building blocks of the social sciences—indicates that 'soft' data are in vogue. Nevertheless the social sciences, including qualitative development studies, also aim to work with data that come closer to the 'hard data' of the natural sciences, which can be quantified, measured and compared. The concept *indicators* captures the current trend in the development discourse.

5.1.3 Using Indicators

Indicators are Data—Different Uses

The demand for quick and operational measures in development work—if not always entirely accurate—has prompted the frequent use of indicators. Indicators are, as the name says, indications of something else. Indicators are used to simplify the real world—they are proxies for complex social phenomena—human development, poverty reduction, gender equality, etc. 'An indicator is a measure that is employed to refer to a concept when no direct measure is available' (Bryman, 2001: 504).

The models researchers and planners develop to depict real life situations are constructed from data: i.e., 'parameters', 'variables', 'units of analysis', 'factors', 'components', etc., and of the relationships between these. When the 'real life situations' under study are projects or other forms of intervention (projects are also 'real' although they are results of interventions), a common denominator for the units of analysis is often 'indicators'.

Sumner calls our attention to the process that creates indicators. 'Indicators are the end product of a (lengthy) social process, which at every stage is shaped by the bias of agents involved' (Sumner, 2004: 2). Indicators are identified or developed by people, regardless of whether they are quantitative, statistical or qualitative measures. Sumner points to a number of salient questions for reflection when utilizing poverty statistics:

> How are these social indicators created? Who collects them and for what purpose? How is the sample frame created? Who is omitted? What definitions are used? How are these indicators used? What are they used for? (Sumner, 2004: 2).

Whilst these points are important, Sumner continues, they are also somewhat academic when data availability is limited and the choice of indicators may simply be dictated by what is in existence (ibid.: 3).

Development studies, perhaps more than most other social science disciplines, are faced with the problem of data quality and availability. A way around these difficulties is to complement what is available with indicators constructed through a participatory process by people who possess the relevant context-specific knowledge (see Sections 3.1.1 and 3.1.2). In development studies, indicators are used for two main purposes: (*i*) to differentiate central concepts—e.g., quality of life, livelihood, prosperity, poverty, equality, etc., in order to classify or rank societies and social groups along the indicators; and (*ii*) to measure progress relating to interventions for social and economic change at the project and programme level. So indicators are used for *comparative* measures and *process* measures at the macro level (national), meso level (sector, programme, regional) and micro level (community, household, individual) (see Section 7.3.5 on Monitoring and Evaluation indicators).

Many indicators consist of measurements expressed in numbers, e.g., (*i*) as a percentage or share, (*ii*) as a rate, for example, infant mortality rate, or (*iii*) as a ratio, e.g., student/teacher ratio. Quantitative indicators can be misleading in giving the impression of greater objectivity than qualitative descriptions of real life situations. A composite measure of indicators can be combined into an index, like the Human Development Index, HDI (see UNDP's Annual Human Development Reports). The HDI is a composite measure of *life expectancy*, *education and income*. As a composite measure, it is stronger than a single indicator for ranking nations according to 'human development'. Earlier Gross National Product was used on its own as a national development indicator. However, as discussed in Section 6.2, poverty and well-being is much more than a measure of income and consumption.

Measures by means of quantitative indicators may look objective, but as Sklair has pointed out, there is a theory of development and economic growth behind indicators that are used to measure, for example, 'standard of living' (Sklair, 1991: 10).

The poverty reduction agenda of the recent decades has accelerated the attempts to cope with the meaning and measurement of poverty (see Section 6.2). Sumner analyses a variety of sources and identifies three groupings of indicators that are being used to measure poverty and well-being: (*i*) those measures based primarily on economic well-being; (*ii*) those based on non-economic well-being; and (*iii*) composite indicators. His analysis makes him argue that the choice of indicator should reflect its purpose:

> economic measures are best when quick, rough-and-ready, short run, aggregate inferences are required. In contrast, non-economic measures are better when greater depth on medium- or longer-term trends and/or dis-aggregation are required (Sumner, 2004: 1).

The utilization of indicators as proxies for people's real lives has become a science of its own. Yet, there are no standard procedures for how to identify relevant indicators. On the one hand it is easier to work with quantitative indicators such as the human development indicators. However, for specific interventions, say to investigate preferences and later measure progress, performance and impact of a nutrition programme, the human development indicators may be rather limited. Context-sensitive indicators for analysis are warranted, but they are not always easy to get hold of and can be expensive to construct and measure. Local people's judgement is important, and participatory techniques can make identification of indicators a joint exercise between different stakeholders. The analyst, coming from outside, can gain very useful knowledge of what is important to different people. This is illustrated in Section 3.1.2, which shows a marked difference in the selection of vital crops identified by three different groups: young women, old women and old men, and between the indicators each of the three groups use to rank the crops. It is an example of a participatory ranking exercise being used as an exploratory tool for identification of indicators, and as a data generation technique at one and the same time.

Some of the more innovative forms of identifying indicators rely on direct observation. Events, processes or relationships which are easily observed or measured can be used as indicators of some other variable that is more difficult to observe. Box 5.2 shows such indicators, used for measuring prosperity levels in rural Java.

Box 5.2 Measures of Prosperity in Rural Java			
Indicator	**Prosperity Level**		
	Low	**Medium**	**High**
House	Bamboo	Combination	Brick and plaster, teak
Rooms	1 to 2, small	–	Many, large
Floor	Dirt	Bricks covered with cement; limestone blocks	Polished cement blocks
Roof	Straw; fronds	–	Tiles
Windows	None	Wooden with slats	Wooden frames with glass panels
Bedding	Mats on floor	Bamboo slat beds with mats	Wooden or iron beds with mattresses and mosquito nets
Lighting	Small oil lamps	Hanging kerosene lamps	Home generator
Water source	Neighbour's well; river, spring	–	Own well
Toilet	Outdoor, not enclosed	Outdoor enclosed	Indoor
Transportation	None	Bicycle, draught cart	Motorcycle; scooter; truck; mini-van
Entertainment equipment	None	Radio, tape recorder	Battery TV
Refreshment served to interviewer	None; tea without sugar	Tea with sugar; other sweet drink	Tea or coffee with sugar plus snacks

After Honadle, 1979, in McCracken et al., 1988.

The ratings on the indicators which are used to measure prosperity in rural Java are of course context specific, and could not be transferred directly to an African setting, for example. They also contain an element of subjectivity. Yet it may be easy for people with local knowledge anywhere in the world to come up with similar indicators for their particular area. In many cases, what we need in development studies are rough indications of conditions and change. Rough indications may be a useful supplement (see Section 7.4.3 for well-being monitoring indicators), but sometimes more exact measures are warranted.

What are Good Indicators?

Planning by objectives, which took off in the 1980s, accelerated the use of indicators in connection with the logical framework approach, LFA (Sections 1.2.2 and 1.2.3). The current Poverty Reduction Strategy Process, PRSP, and implementation of the Millennium Development Goals, MDGs, retains the focus on indicators as an analytical tool, but the focus has moved away from the micro/project level to the policy and country strategy level (see below). In the process of making indicators a central analytical tool, criteria have been established for judging whether an indicator is 'SMART' and optimal for measuring an objective (see Section 7.3.4). To be 'SMART', the indicator should be:

Specific
Measurable
Attainable/Realistic
Relevant
Time-bound

In the context of the Logical Framework Analysis, indicators should also specify:

- Target group (for whom)
- Quantity (how much)
- Quality (how well)
- Time (by when)
- Location (where)

Combining these criteria, the indicator for an objective, for example **'increased agricultural production'**, might be:

500 male and female smallholders in Umbia district (cultivating 3 acres or less) increase their rice yield by 50 per cent between October 1990 and October 1991, maintaining the same quality of harvest as 1989 crops (NORAD, 1990 and 1999: 55).

In some cases the information necessary to measure the indicators (means of verification) is available from existing sources. In other cases the information must be generated by the project, programme or other intervention itself, e.g., through baseline studies.

A lot of the work undertaken to develop an expedient format for the Poverty Reduction Strategy Papers and the process involves identification and use of indicators. In a discussion on 'Where do we want to go?' in the World Bank's Sourcebook for Poverty Reduction Strategies it is emphasized how *goals*, *indicators* and *targets* are vital in the poverty diagnostics process for countries engaged in the PRS Process. The following definitions are used:

- **Goals.** The objectives national authorities want to achieve; they are often expressed in non-technical, qualitative terms—for example, 'to reduce inflation', 'to eliminate poverty', 'to foster job growth', or 'to eradicate illiteracy'.
- **Indicators.** The variables used to measure the goals—for example, 'poverty', measured by a level of consumption insufficient to fulfil minimum food and other basic needs (the 'poverty line'), data on completion of the final year of basic schooling, and so forth.
- **Targets.** The levels of the indicators that a country wants to achieve by a given time—for example, 'to reduce income poverty by 10 per cent by 2004'. These could be point estimates or a target range (e.g., by 10–15 per cent) (World Bank, 2002: 13).

Examples are then given of what are called *intermediate indicators* (of inputs and outputs) and *final outcome indicators* (of outcomes and impact):

Box 5.3 Examples of Poverty Reduction Indicators and Targets			
	Intermediate indicator (inputs and outputs)	Final outcome indicators (outcomes and impact)	Millennium development goals
Poverty and inequality	Percentage of roads in good and fair condition Productive asset ownership (land, cattle, or other physical capital)	Poverty head-count Poverty gap Average income Gini coefficient Quintile ratio	Reduce extreme poverty by one-half by 2015 Implement a national strategy for sustainable development by 2005 Reverse trends in the loss of environmental resources by 2015
Macro-economic stability	Inflation Exchange rate fluctuations Unemployment Fiscal deficit	Per capita economic growth rate Unemployment	
Security	Unemployment rate Variability in production of chief staples	Food consumption variability Income variability Malnutrition prevalence Death rate due to violence	

(Box 5.3 contd)

(Box 5.3 contd)

Health	Treatment of diarrhoea in children Delivery attendance (%) (doctor, nurse, trained midwife) Use of modern contraception (%) Vitamin A supplement Cooking fuel used	Infant mortality rate Malnutrition prevalence Adolescent fertility rate Prevalence of anaemia Total fertility rate Sexually transmitted disease infection rates Adult HIV prevalence Tuberculosis prevalence	Reduce infant and child mortality by two-thirds by 2015 Reduce maternal mortality by three-fourths by 2015 Universal access to reproductive health services by 2015
Education	Expenditure on primary education as a share of gross domestic product Percentage of schools in good physical condition Pupil-teacher ratio Teacher absenteeism rates	Third-grade math and science scores Adult illiteracy rate Female illiteracy rate Net enrolment ratio (primary, secondary, and tertiary levels and by gender) Repetition rates (by level of schooling and gender)	Universal primary education by 2015 Eliminate gender disparity in education by 2005
Empowerment	Access to media and the Internet Number of parties participating in last parliamentary elections Number of daily newspapers Female literacy rate Female control over earnings Number of TV and radio stations	Number of women in parliament and government Percentage of population voting in parliamentary elections (by gender) Prevalence of domestic violence Share of incarcerated population being held without charge	

After World Bank, 2002: 15.

Selectivity in the choice of monitorable indicators and targets, in line with priority public actions and capacity, is important. At the same time, the indicators and targets should appropriately capture disparities by social group, gender and region. In both the long-term and the shorter-term targets there is a need for selectivity so that the number and type of indicators chosen are consistent with the national capacity to monitor.

Limitations of Indicator Use in the LFA

Though the main focus of development cooperation has moved from the community and project level to sector programmes, country programmes and policies, it is still necessary to address the local level where the affected people live if the objectives for international development cooperation with the prominent goal of poverty reduction are to be fulfilled. Hence, the need to be able to measure change at community level among poor people themselves prompts the continued relevance of a tool such as the LFA with objectives and indicators (see Section 1.2).

The identification of indicators and follow-up by means of verification at the level of project/programme interventions can be a very time-consuming and cumbersome exercise. In many cases it is not even possible to find direct indicators, but only indirect ones or proxies. The classic example is when the tin roof of a house is used as an indirect indicator of wealth or increased income. A direct indicator such as crop sales may be unobtainable. The validity of the indirect indicators may in many cases be questioned, because the causal relationships between indicators and events cannot be isolated and controlled. Thus the LFA planning and monitoring tool, which works by means of indicators, is questioned on several grounds. Some of the critical points are:

- The process of formulating project/intervention goals and objectives and identifying 'objectively verifiable indicators' is in itself an educative exercise. It should be done by a multidisciplinary team and in a cross-cultural setting, i.e., with a large input of cultural knowledge of the project or programme context. However, time and other constraints rarely permit the optimal combination of people to formulate the LFA.
- The LFA is becoming an 'auditing tool' for aid organizations where its justification should be as a management tool in the hands of the indigenous organizations and people involved in the 'project'— i.e., a tool to create local 'ownership'.
- The local motivation for using the LFA as a monitoring tool is nil if the formulation of the LFA from goal formulation to identification of indicators is done by external planners, as very often happens.
- Even as an 'auditing tool' the shortcomings of the LFA are obvious:

  - Indicators are often difficult to define and costly to measure.
  - The capacity to measure and monitor indicators is limited.
  - The responsibility for using the LFA tool is sometimes not clearly allocated.

Together, the shortcomings of the LFA can turn it into a straitjacket which, contrary to the intention, may create greater distance between the planners and the implementers among whom the affected people also belong. There is a danger of planning tools like the LFA turning into rituals.

Several development agencies have relaxed the use of the logical framework after a short period of application. However, even if used with less rigour, it is necessary to have tools to simplify the study of complex interventions. Indicators are such necessary tools in development studies, whether applied in LFAs, in studies at different points in the project or programme cycle, or in studies which focus on the process of development.

Work is ongoing in many circles to simplify working with indicators. The problem is that it is much easier to come up with proposals for far too many indicators than what a study or an intervention can manage. The challenge is to identify a set of core indicators—e.g., for a certain sector or specific issue (poverty reduction for instance), and then to complement these with additional context-specific indicators. An attempt in that direction is illustrated for the evaluation of poverty reduction in development assistance (see Section 7.4.3, Figures 7.7, 7.8 and 7.9).

5.2   Analysis of Qualitative Data

5.2.1 Data and Data Analysis

Data and data analysis are separate dimensions but are often treated as one—for instance when quotations from interviews (which are 'data') pretend to be the analysis.
Bryman puts it in the following way:

> Regardless of which analytical strategy you employ; what you must not do is simply say—'this is what my subjects said and did—isn't that incredibly interesting'. It may be reasonably interesting, but your work can acquire significance only when you theorize in relation to it. Many researchers are wary of this—they worry that, in the process of interpretation and theorizing, they may fail to do justice to what they have seen and heard; that they may contaminate their subjects' words and behaviour. This is a risk, but it has to be balanced against the fact that your findings acquire signifi-cance in our intellectual community only when you have reflected on, interpreted, and theorized your data. You are not there as a mere mouthpiece (Bryman, 2001: 402).

The equivalent situation with regard to quantitative data and data analysis is found when a mere description of the figures is presented as if it was analysis.

We usually talk about two main approaches to inquiry and analysis:

- The *inductive approach* in which one begins with concrete *empirical* details and then works towards abstract ideas or general principles. There is often a 'bottom-up' perspective—seen from the point of view of the subjects—in the empirical analysis.
- The *deductive approach* in which one begins with *abstract ideas* (e.g., hypothesis) and then collects concrete, *empirical* details to test the ideas. One's point of departure in theory or hypothesis is made explicit.

The inductive and deductive approaches to inquiry and analysis can be used in any of the *qualitative analysis strategies* that are typically being used in social research, including development studies (see Chapter 4). In development studies, particularly when we work in multidisciplinary teams, we tend to *use both inductive and deductive* analysis, sometimes in alternating steps. For example, we begin with an explorative analysis of empirical data from a number of interviews with different stakeholders (induction). The preliminary analysis facilitates the formulation of hypothesis and further research questions which may then be subjected to deductive analysis. This is a useful approach for exploring issues in un-familiar contexts, and is used in the *grounded theory* approach (e.g., Pryke et al., 2003; Strauss and Corbin, 1996).

The reverse order is also possible, starting for example with a survey of questions derived from the hypothesis we want to test. The preliminary analysis of patterns in our data may reveal unexpected issues, which we want to pursue in more detail, e.g., by collecting more information on that particular issue.

A particular feature of development studies is that they are very often carried out in multidisciplinary teams. *Cross-disciplinary perspectives* may bring a richness to data analysis which single disciplines cannot reveal. *How* the preference for analytical methods of the different disciplines[3] can be optimized and integrated in analysis so as to avoid 'parallel' and maybe contradictory results needs to be carefully considered.

In order to make analysis possible, a 'qualitative researcher' analyses data by organizing it into categories on the basis of themes, concepts, or similar features. Conceptualization helps the researcher to organize and make sense of data, and is an integral part of data condensation and analysis, which begins during data collection.

Concepts (and variables)[4] may be defined by nominal or operational definitions (Box 5.4).

Definitions of concepts as those included in Box 5.4 should be generally applicable. It is evident that measures will show different results depending on the social and cultural context.

5.2.2 Interviews—A Key Source of Data

Qualitative and Semi-structured Interviews

Interviewing is the practitioner's method 'par excellence' in development studies—qualitative interviews in particular. Interviews generate information (data) (COWI, May 2004). Participatory methods have contributed to adjust the interview to make it more conversational, while still controlled and structured. In qualitative interviews only some of the questions and topics are predetermined. Many questions will be formulated during the interview. Questions may be asked according to a flexible checklist or guide, and not from a formal questionnaire. This is the semi-structured interview. The qualitative, semi-structured interview has in particular been widely used in social research, not least due to Kvale's (1996) thorough treatment of both the theoretical underpinnings and practical aspects of the interview process.

---

[3] Roughly speaking, technicians, natural scientists and economists prefer statistical, quantitative surveys, sociologists typically use a combination of quantitative and qualitative studies, and anthropologists prefer observation and other qualitative analysis.
[4] Quantitative research tends to categorize data into 'variables'. Since the quantitative–qualitative divide is breaking down, qualitative researches may also talk about variables.

Box 5.4   Nominal and Operational Definitions of Concepts

Nominal definitions are like dictionary definitions—you describe the phenomena in words.
Operational definitions describe how the phenomena can be measured.
Below are examples of operational definitions:

Example 1: **POLITICAL PARTY AFFILIATION** has been measured in different ways—among others

- What would you vote for, if there were an election tomorrow?
- What did you vote for at the previous election?
- Are you a member of a political party? If YES: which one?

Example 2: **MARITAL HAPPINESS** has been measured as:

- *Absence of divorce*—indicating that if you are (still) married, you are happy!
- *Comradeship*—measured by asking what people get from their marriage. Comradeship is often mentioned on the positive side
- *The degree of happiness*—measured on a scale from 1 to 10
- *Mutual interests*—measured by counting how many mutual interests a couple share; the more the better.
- *Time spent together*—measured by how much time a couple spends together; the more the better.

(*After* Burgess, Locke and Locke, 1963 in Boolsen, 2004).

Example 3: **POVERTY REDUCTION** is measured by many quantitative as well as qualitative *indicators*. Operational measures can relate to:

- *A poverty line below which people are defined as 'the absolute poor'*. The poverty line has been defined in different ways. Three arbitrary (nominal) definitions of the poverty line are:

  1. 'income needed to supply minimum calorie requirements',
  2. 'living on one dollar or less a day', and
  3. 'food expenditure absorbs 70% or more of a person's total expenditure'.

A change in the proportion of a population from below to above the poverty line is one measure of poverty reduction (operational definition).

Another operational measure of poverty reduction combines a measure of changes/improvements for specified groups of poor women and men in the following four 'core indicators' (see Section 7.4.3):

- *Access to* **resources** and services—measured in contrast to *exclusion*
- *Improvement* in **livelihoods**—measured in contrast to *impoverishment*
- *Expansion* of **knowledge**—measured in contrast to loss of knowledge or *reduction* of chances to improve knowledge
- *Rights enhanced,* e.g., **rights** to participate in decisions—in contrast to *alienation*.

(*After* MFA, 1996) .

An interview is not just an interview. There are questions on experience and behaviour, on opinions and values, on feelings, on needs, knowledge and background data, there are presupposition questions and neutral questions, simulation questions, etc., and questions may address the past, present or future (see Denscombe, 2003; Patton, 2002). A typology of interviews is suggested by Patton (Box 5.5):

Box 5.5 Variations in Interview Instrumentation			
Type of Interview	**Characteristics**	**Strengths**	**Weaknesses**
1. Informal conversational interview	Questions emerge from the immediate context and are asked in the natural course of things; there is no predetermination of question topics or wording.	Increases the salience and relevance of questions; interviews are built on and emerge from observations; the interview can be matched to individuals and circumstances.	Different information collected from different people with different questions. Less systematic and comprehensive if certain questions don't arise 'naturally'. Data organization and analysis can be quite difficult. Requires maximum attention by interviewer. Difficult to leave interview to assistant.
2. Interview guide approach	Topics and issues to be covered are specified in advance, in outline form; interviewer decides sequence and wording of questions in the course of the interview.	The outline increases the comprehensiveness of the data and makes data collection somewhat systematic for each respondent. Logical gaps in data can be anticipated and closed. Interviews remain fairly conversational and situational.	Important and salient topics may be inadvertently omitted. Interviewer flexibility in sequencing and wording questions can result in substantially different responses from different perspectives, thus reducing the comparability of responses.
3. Standardized open-ended interview	The exact wording and sequence of questions are determined in advance. All interviewees are asked the same basic questions in the same order. Questions are worded in a completely open-ended format.	Respondents answer the same questions, thus increasing comparability of responses; data are complete for each person on topics addressed in the interview. Reduces interviewer effects and bias when several interviewers	Little flexibility in relating the interview to particular individuals and circumstances; standardized wording of questions may constrain and limit naturalness and relevance of questions and answers.

(Box 5.5 contd)

(Box 5.5 contd)

			are used. Permits decision-makers to see and review the instrumentation used. Facilitates organization and analysis of the data.
4. Closed quantitative interviews	Questions and response categories are determined in advance. Responses are fixed; respondent chooses from among these fixed responses.	Data analysis is simple; responses can be directly compared and easily aggregated; many questions can be asked in a short time.	Respondents must fit their experience and feelings into the researcher's categories; may be perceived as impersonal, irrelevant and mechanistic. Can distort what respondents really mean or experienced by so completely limiting their response choices.

After Patton, 1990: 288–89 (in *Qualitative Evaluation Methods*).
Copyright 1990, Reprinted by permission of Sage Publications, Inc.

Interviews are undertaken with individuals or groups and can be characterized as follows:

1. **Individual interviews** are undertaken with a sample of purposely selected respondents to obtain representative information. If the interviews are part of an exploratory process, the sample should be as differentiated as possible. Interviewing a number of different people on the same topic will quickly reveal a range of opinions, attitudes and 'strategies'. Men and women tend to have different experiences—hence opinions. Resource-rich and poor people, people belonging to different ethnic or religious groups, and people of different ages represent different experiences. The bias of asking only one group must be avoided. Asking men only is the classic mistake.

2. **Key informant interviews** aim to obtain special knowledge. Key informants have special knowledge on a given topic. They are not necessarily the 'leaders'. A farmer who has experimented with different crops is as much a key informant as an extension officer; their information is complementary. And a woman worker in a rural roads labour gang is a key informant on labour relations, for example. Outsiders with inside knowledge are often valuable key informants who are able to answer questions about other people's knowledge, attitudes and practices besides their own. There is a risk of being misled by key informants' sometimes biased information.

3. **Group interviews** provide access to a larger body of knowledge, e.g., of general community information. The members may be invited—thus sampled—or those who happen to be around at the time of the interview. An interview with more than 20 to 25 people is difficult to manage. The dynamics of group interviews tend to pave the way for unexpected questions and provide additional information, i.e., 'the sum is more than an addition of individual replies'. Kumar distinguishes

focus group interviews from community meetings. Focus groups are the most widely used form of group interview in development projects and programmes (Kumar, 1987).

4. **Focus group interview or discussion** addresses a specific topic (see also Section 3.1.1). Focus groups are typically six to eight people who, under the minimum guidance of a facilitator, discuss a particular topic in detail. Patton (2002) makes a clear distinction between discussion and interview: the focus group interview is, indeed, an interview, not a problem solving session.

Box 5.5 captures common types of interviews. More detailed descriptions can be found in Laws (2003) and Denscombe (2003).

Steinar Kvale has worked for many years with the collection of data through qualitative interviews. He is very focused on the different stages around the qualitative interview: The *preparation*, the *process*, and the *practical* as well as *analytic work* following the interview. It requires knowledge, interviewing skills, empathy and understanding on the part of the interviewer, who at the same time must pursue the collection of data in a systematic, valid and reliable way.

Kvale has formulated 12 aspects of the mode of understanding in the qualitative research interview. These are condensed in Box 5.6.

The quality of an interview and the data it generates not only relate to the 'principles' for qualitative interviews, but also to how questions are asked.

Good and Bad Questions

The wording of questions, their clarity and avoiding boring the respondent with lengthy interviews for the sake of assembling 'nice to know' information—all these aspects and many more have undergone critical scrutiny (e.g., Casley and Lury, 1981; Gaskell, 2000). Good guidance is available in plenty. Improved practices leave more to be said!

In a straightforward manner, Feuerstein (1988) gives examples of good and bad questions (Box 5.7). Plain talk further facilitates communication. But nothing can fully substitute conducting an interview in the indigenous language. This is the basic advice to all development workers and researchers: learn the language of the people with whom you work! If you already know the language, use PLAIN TALK.

Questions that start with Who? Why? What? Where? When? How? help to establish the basic situation. The 'six helpers' need not all be asked. 'Why' questions should be asked sparingly because they may put the informant on the defensive. Questions should be phrased in such a way as to require explanation (open-ended questions), rather than allowing the interviewee to answer 'yes' or 'no'. Yet, as Box 5.7 shows, the more specific an open question is to the respondent's situation, the 'better' the information that can be expected. Probing questions (cross-checks) are important. This can be done by challenging answers and asking for back-up information—not by cross-examination.

A brief guideline for semi-structured interviews and common mistakes is set out in Box 5.8.

Although the first point, if interpreted to mean two to four interviewers to conduct an interview, is rarely realistic, using several interviewers should be attempted in cases where a multidisciplinary team works together for a prolonged period. The joint event is optimal for internal team dialogue and for reaching a common understanding. Using shifting pairs of team members to interview is a good way of

Box 5.6   Aspects of Qualitative Research Interviews

The purpose of the qualitative research interview treated here is to obtain descriptions of the lived world of the interviewees with respect to interpretations of the meaning of the described phenomena.

1. *Life World*. The topic of qualitative interview is the everyday lived world of the interviewee and his or her relation to it.
2. *Meaning*. The interview seeks to interpret the meaning of central themes in the life world of the subject. The interviewer registers and interprets the meaning of what is said as well as how it is said.
3. *Qualitative*. The interview seeks qualitative knowledge expressed in normal language, it does not aim at quantification.
4. *Descriptive*. The interview attempts to obtain open nuanced descriptions of different aspects of the subjects' life worlds.
5. *Specificity*. Descriptions of specific situations and action sequences are elicited, not general opinions.
6. *Deliberate Naïveté*. The interviewer exhibits an openness to new and unexpected phenomena, rather than having ready-made categories and schemes of interpretation.
7. *Focused*. The interview is focused on particular themes; it is neither strictly structured with standardized questions, nor entirely 'non-directive'.
8. *Ambiguity*. Interviewee statements can sometimes be ambiguous, reflecting contradictions in the world the subject lives in.
9. *Change*. The process of being interviewed may produce new insights and awareness, and the subject may in the course of the interview come to change his or her descriptions or meanings about a theme.
10. *Sensitivity*. Different interviewers produce different statements on the same themes, depending on their sensitivity to and knowledge of the interview topic.
11. *Interpersonal Situation*. The knowledge obtained is produced through the interpersonal interaction in the interview.
12. *Positive Experience*. A well carried out research interview can be a rare and enriching experience for the interviewee, who may obtain new insights into his or her life situation.

After Kvale, 1996: 30–31.

triangulation, for cross-checking data, and minimizing interviewer bias. The semi-structured interview requires substantial judgement by the interviewer. In all circumstances the analyst must be present, or jointly conduct interviews at the first interviews conducted by assistants, if assistants are used. Testing of the assistant's qualifications as an interviewer is vital.

Feuerstein provides a useful guideline for asking questions in general:

General Guideline for Asking Questions

1. **Do not begin with difficult/sensitive questions.** Put these near the end so that if the respondent decides not to answer these, you do not lose his/her willingness to answer earlier questions.
2. **Do not make respondents feel they ought to know the answers.** Help them by saying, 'Perhaps you have not had time to give this matter much thought?' Maybe they can find the answer later.

3. **Respondents may not have the answer.** Even though they would like to cooperate, respondents may not have the answer. Perhaps they just do not know, cannot remember, cannot express the answer well in words, have no strong opinion, or are unfamiliar with answering questions. Also, they may even be unreliable or untruthful.

4. **Decide carefully whether you should avoid emotional or sensitive words.** Using words like 'greedy', 'oppressed' or 'immoral' may seem to imply a judgement. Such words can cause bias in the answers. Respondents may be reluctant or nervous to give answers. However, if you are looking for truthful answers you may need to use such words.

5. **Avoid making assumptions.** Do not ask questions like 'How many grades did you complete in primary school?' Perhaps the respondent had no chance to go to school.

6. **Do not use confusing questions.** Avoid asking questions like 'Would you prefer your child not to be vaccinated?' Keep it simple and positive.
   Ask, 'Do you wish your child to be vaccinated?'

7. **Different ways of asking the same question.** These may be needed by the interviewer in order to be able to adapt the questions to different respondents.

8. **Use both direct and indirect questioning.** For example, asking a parent about an older child's health is not the same as asking the child about his/her own health. Older children can often provide important answers, but it is necessary to get their parent's or guardian's permission first before questioning them.

Box 5.7 Examples of Good and Bad Questions	
These are Bad Questions:	**These are Good Questions:**
Do people raise small animals?	How many chickens does your family have this year? How many goats? How many rabbits?
What foods are usually given to small children?	What foods do you give your child?
At what age do children stop getting your milk?	At what age did your child stop getting their mother's milk? (If she doesn't know, ask more questions). Did the child have any teeth then? Could he walk then?
What does your family usually eat?	What did you eat since this hour yesterday? What did your husband eat? What did your little children eat? What did your older children eat?

After Feuerstein, 1988: 82.

Box 5.8   Semi-structured Interviews, SSI, Guidelines and Common Mistakes

SSI Guidelines

- The interviewing team consists of 2 to 4 people from different disciplines
- Begin with the traditional greeting and state that the interview team is here to learn
- Begin the questioning by referring to someone or something visible
- Conduct the interview informally and mix questions with discussion
- Be open-minded and objective
- Let each team member finish his/her line of questioning (don't interrupt)
- Carefully lead up to sensitive questions
- Assign one note-taker (but rotate)
- Be aware of non-verbal signals
- Avoid leading questions and value judgements
- Avoid questions which can be answered with 'yes' or 'no'
- Individual interviews should be no longer than 45 minutes
- Group interviews should be no longer than two hours
- Each Interviewer should have a list of topics and key questions written down in her notebook

SSI Common Mistakes

- Failure to listen closely
- Repeating questions
- Helping the interviewee to give an answer
- Asking vague questions
- Asking insensitive questions
- Failure to judge answers (believing everything)
- Asking leading questions
- Allowing the interview to go on too long
- Over-generalization of findings
- Relying too much on what the well-off, the better educated, the old, and the men have to say
- Ignoring anything that does not fit the ideas and preconceptions of the interviewer
- Giving too much weight to answers that contain 'quantitative data' (for example, 'How many goats do you own?')
- Incomplete note-taking

After Theis and Grady, 1991: 55.

The care with which you plan and design your questionnaire will influence the quality of the information you obtain (*After* Feuerstein, 1988: 83; Denscombe, 2003, Chapters 9 and 10).

Box 5.9 shows the course of an interview investigation through seven stages, from the original ideas to the final report, as suggested by Kvale:

Note that in actual research these steps are not in a linear sequence. The process of research is circular and reflexive. For example, after a few interviews both the topic guide and the selection of respondents may change. Equally, analysis is part of the ongoing process of research (Gaskell, 2000).

Box 5.9   Seven Stages of an Interview Investigation

1. *Thematizing*. Formulate the purpose of an investigation and describe the concept of the topic to be investigated before the interviews start. The *why* and *what* of the investigation should be clarified before the question of *how*—method—is posed.
2. *Designing*. Plan the design of the study, taking in consideration all seven stages of the investigation, before the interviewing starts. Designing the study is undertaken with regard to obtaining the intended *knowledge* and taking into account the moral implications of the study.
3. *Interviewing*. Conduct the interviews based on an interview guide, and with a reflective approach to the knowledge sought and the interpersonal relation of the interview situation.
4. *Transcribing*. Prepare the interview material for analysis, which commonly includes a transcription from oral speech to written text.
5. *Analysing*. Decide, on the basis of the purpose and topic of the investigation, and on the nature of the interview material, which methods of analysis are appropriate for the interviews.
6. *Verifying*. Ascertain the generalizability, reliability, and validity of the interview findings. Reliability refers to how consistent the results are, and validity means whether an interview study investigates what is intended to be investigated.
7. *Reporting*. Communicate the findings of the study and the methods applied in a form that lives up to scientific criteria, takes the ethical aspects of the investigation into consideration, and that results in a readable product.

After Kvale, 1996: 88.

Interviewer Qualifications

It goes without saying that in qualitative interviewing the interviewer is very important, and his/her role, attitude, knowledge, etc., can always be questioned, criticized, or improved. It is well known that people respond differently depending on how they perceive the person asking the questions. In particular, the *sex, age* and *ethnic origins* of the interviewer have a bearing on the amount of information people are willing to divulge and their honesty about what they reveal (Denscombe, 2003: 169). In other words, there is an interviewer effect.

Denscombe has the following advice on tactics for the good interviewer:

Tactics for interviews: Prompts, probes and checks:

Remain silent	(prompt)
Repeat the question	(prompt)
Repeat the last few words spoken by the informant	(prompt)
Offer some examples	(prompt)
Ask for an example	(probe)
Ask for clarification	(probe)
Ask for more details	(probe)
Summarize their thoughts	(check)

('So if I understand you correctly …. What this means, then, is that …')
After Denscombe, 2003: 179.

Kvale has presented a useful list of qualification criteria for the interviewer—see Box 5.10.

Box 5.10   Qualification Criteria for the Interviewer

1. *Knowledgeable:* Has an extensive knowledge of the interview theme, can conduct an informed conversation about the topic; being familiar with its main aspects the interviewer will know what issues are important to pursue, without attempting to shine with his or her extensive knowledge.
2. *Structuring:* Introduces a purpose for the interview, outlines the procedure in passing, and rounds off the interview by, for example, briefly telling what was learned in the course of the conversation and asking whether the interviewee has any question concerning the situation.
3. *Clear:* Poses clear, simple, easy and short questions; speaks distinctly and in a manner that is easy to understand, does not use academic language or professional jargon. The exception is in a stress interview: then the questions can be complex and ambiguous, with the subjects' answers revealing their reactions to stress.
4. *Gentle:* Allows subjects to finish what they are saying, lets them proceed at their own rate of thinking and speaking. Is easy-going, tolerates pauses, indicates that it is acceptable to put forward unconventional and provocative opinions and to treat emotional issues.
5. *Sensitive:* Listens actively to the content that is said, hears the many nuances of meaning in an answer, and seeks to get the nuances of meaning described more fully. The interviewer is empathic, listens to the emotional message in what is said, not only hearing what is said but also how it is said, and notices as well what is not said. The interviewer feels when a topic is too emotional to pursue in the interview.
6. *Open:* Hears which aspects of the interview topic are important for the interviewee. Listens with an evenly hovering attention, is open to new aspects that can be introduced by the interviewee, and follows them up.
7. *Steering:* Knows what he or she wants to find out: is familiar with the purpose of the interview, what it is important to acquire knowledge about. The interviewer controls the course of the interview and is not afraid of interrupting digressions from the interviewee.
8. *Critical:* Does not take everything that is said at face value, but questions critically to test the reliability and validity of what the interviewees tell. This critical checking can pertain to the observational evidence of the interviewee's statements, as well as to their logical consistency.
9. *Remembering:* Retains what a subject has said during the interview, can recall earlier statements and ask to have them elaborated, and can relate what has been said during different parts of the interview to each other.
10. *Interpreting:* Manages throughout the interview to clarify and extend the meanings of the interviewee's statements; provides interpretations of what is said, which may then be refuted or confirmed by the interviewee.

After Kvale, 1996: 148–49.

In semi-structured and conversational interviews, which do not make use of questionnaires, the control and guidance of the interview requires other techniques. These are first of all checklists of questions, issues or themes.

Checklists and Note-taking

Checklists can be more or less formalized and prepared in advance. A minimum is a 'mental' checklist of questions. You memorize the questions and issues to be covered. It is an advantage to write down a list of key questions and key probes in advance to sharpen the focus of an interview. This may do more to help the investigator's memory than result in a very detailed checklist for the interview session itself. Box 5.11 gives examples of short, topical checklists of interview themes suggested for 'beneficiary' assessment in the areas of health, education and energy (Salmen's terminology).

Box 5.11 Interview Themes for 'Beneficiary' Assessment—Education, Health and Population, and Energy	
Education	**Topics for Discussion**

(a) Expectations from education
(b) Schooling for girls (obstacles to attendance)
(c) Role of religion
(d) Quality of education received
   • degree of learning
   • utility of what is learned
	(e) Distance from home to school
	(f) Physical aspects, maintenance, furniture, general appearance
	(g) Language (for example, French, Arabic, national)
	(h) Economic situation: is school seen as an aid or a hindrance to productivity

Health and Population
(a) Health problems affecting family
(b) Perception of health service provided by
   • government
   • NGOs
   • traditional healers
(c) Degree and reason for attendance at health centre
(d) Problems of village (agricultural production, water, education, etc.)
	(e) Family size
	(f) Use of family planning methods and meaning of the same
	(g) Suggestions for improving well-being of family

Energy (a) Process involved in obtaining utility service (b) Cost of acquiring connection and how it is paid for (c) Users of electricity in the household, business, institution and how often it is used (d) Location where meters are installed and how often and accurately they are read	**Topics for Discussion with Electricity Users:** (e) Problems encountered paying utility bill; perceived fairness of bills (f) Quality and efficiency of repair service (g) Level of satisfaction with service (h) Handling of complaints filed with the utility (i) Attitude towards utility company; how service can be improved
Topics for Discussion with Potential Electricity Users: (a) Interest in acquiring electricity service and how it would be used; perceived advantages and disadvantages (b) Cost of being connected and how it compares with the cost of other energy sources (c) Perceived problems with paying bills, suggestions for improvements	(d) Existence of user cooperatives, for example farmers' clubs or women's clubs—potential as vehicle for credit for electricity (e) Occurrence of illegal connections and how users feel about it (f) View of utility company and services it provides
After Salmen, 1992: 25.	

Using sequences or chains of interviews, alternating between group interviews, individual and key informant interviews contributes both to expanding the scope and validation of information. Different checklists must be considered for different target populations.

Note-taking

The output of semi-structured interviews is, in the first instance, **notes**. Good, detailed and comprehensive recording is essential. Sometimes this is easier said than done if, for example, the interview is conducted by one person only. Helpful points are:

- Number questions and mark answers.
- Assign one member of the interview team to take notes, but rotate the task.
- Design recording tools which facilitate later analysis of the collected information.
- Pre-coding of answers to more standardized and observable information is recommended, e.g., sex, approximate age, type of house.
- Interview notes—and field notes in general—may be arranged under headings for naming items.
- Loose-leaf notes on paper prepared for entering a file permit a more sophisticated filing system than a solid note-book.
- Brief field notes can be made during the interview itself and transcribed in more detail afterwards, preferably immediately after when memory is fresh.
- Audio tape recording is a standard method of capturing interview data. The interviewee's acceptance of recording is important.

Remember, your notes are your raw material.

5.2.3 Analysis and Interpretation of Interview-based Data

There are many ways of analysing data generated by qualitative methods.[5] The most adequate analytical approach depends on the purpose of the analysis. A few guiding principles for how to analyse qualitative data are nevertheless relevant:

1. Be conscious of how qualitative data (e.g., from interviews) can be interpreted differently.
2. Select an adequate method for analysis or combination of methods at an early stage in the research process.
3. Be explicit about the chosen method of analysis in reporting.
4. Recall that interviews will always contain an element of interpretation.

---

[5] In this section 'qualitative research' refers mainly to research which generates data from qualitative research interviews.

The analysis is not a purely mechanical process. It hinges on creative insights, which may well occur when the researcher is talking to a colleague, or as Gaskell says, 'in those moments of contemplation when driving, walking or taking a bath'. The point is well taken for all research but is unfortunately violated in much development work and research: Allow time for contemplation and reflection!

The broad aim of the analysis is to look for meanings and understanding. What is actually said in the interview is the 'data', but condensation is required in order to analyse the information. Analysis should go beyond accepting data at face value. Collection of data is linked to the analysis, interpretation and presentation of findings. The process of data collection—e.g., from qualitative and semi-structured interviews—is not an end in itself. Yet there are no strict formulas for analysing qualitative data as there are for the analysis of quantitative data originating from structured interviews. The procedures are neither 'scientific' nor 'mechanistic'. In Wright Mills's phrase, qualitative analysis is 'intellectual craftsmanship' (Mills, 1959).

There is typically no precise point at which data collection ends and analysis begins, either. In the course of gathering data, ideas emerge about analysis, and interpretation appears. These ideas become part of the record of field notes. This overlapping of data collection and analysis improves both the quality of data collected and the quality of the analysis, so long as the analyst is careful not to allow these initial interpretations to distort additional data collection (Patton, 1990: 378).

This does not mean that there are no guidelines to assist in analysing qualitative data. The focus on process and iteration, holistic perspectives and people's knowledge, has fostered a great deal of constructive advice (e.g., Miles and Huberman, 1994; Patton, 2002). Kvale devises methods that can be used to organize the interview texts, to condense the meanings into forms that can be presented in a relatively short space, and to work out implicit meanings of what was said, which make the interview analysis more amenable. Similar methods are used to analyse text and talk (see Section 5.2.4).

Coding Qualitative Data

A useful way of organizing qualitative data for analysis is coding. A researcher organizes the raw data into conceptual categories and creates themes or concepts, which are then used to analyse data. A good thematic code is one that captures the qualitative richness of the phenomenon. It is usable in the analysis, the interpretation, and the presentation of research. To code data into themes, a researcher first needs to learn how 'to see' or recognize themes in the data. Seeing themes rests on four abilities:

1. recognizing patterns in the data;
2. thinking in terms of systems and concepts;
3. having tacit knowledge or in-depth background knowledge (e.g., it helps to have historical insight into the process of colonization and de-colonization to understand the current power relationships in an African society); and
4. possessing relevant information (e.g., one needs to have considerable information about gender [in]equality in order to analyse—or formulate—a gender mainstreaming strategy) (see Neuman, 2000: 420–25).

Coding is used to different degrees in qualitative research, but is particularly associated with the *grounded theory* approach to condense data into categories. In the research process the researcher reviews the data on several occasions and uses different or successive coding (see Box 5.12). Coding is guided by the research questions and may lead to additional themes, as illustrated in the example in Box 5.12.

Box 5.12   Different Coding Procedures in Qualitative Research

Coding procedures

- **Open coding:** the analytic process through which concepts are identified and their properties and dimensions are discovered in data. Open coding is performed during a first pass through recently collected data to locate themes and assign initial codes.
  - In brief: identify/disclose *concepts, categories* (groupings of concepts), *characteristics and dimensions.*

- **Axial coding:** the process of relating categories to their sub-categories, termed 'axial' because coding occurs around the axis of a category, linking categories at the level of properties and dimensions. Axial coding is a second pass through the data. Additional codes or new ideas may emerge and the initial codes be adjusted.
  - In brief: identify/disclose a *phenomenon or key event, causal conditions and relations, contexts of the phenomenon/ event, intervening (structural) conditions influencing the phenomenon/event,* identify *action and consequences of action that influence the phenomenon/event.*

- **Selective coding:** the process of integrating and refining the theory. During selective coding the researchers look selectively for cases that illustrate themes. Comparisons and contrasts are done after most or all data collection is complete.
  - In brief: identify a *story line* using the concepts and analytical relations already disclosed, identify a *core category, its characteristics and dimensions, relate categories to each other, reorganize categories and identify categories to fill gaps.*

After Neuman, 2003; Olsen, 2002; Strauss and Corbin, 1996.

Example:
Selective Coding of Gender Relations in Coping Strategies during Drought
By the time of selective coding the researcher has well-developed concepts and has organized the overall analysis around several core ideas. For example, a researcher studying people's coping strategies during a dry season in an African village decides to make *gender relations* a major theme of the study of *coping strategies*. In selective coding, the researcher goes through his or her field notes, looking for differences in how men and women approach securing food for themselves, their children and the aged, how they talk and act about the drought situation, how men and women prioritize spending of the limited resources available, etc. The researcher then compares male and female attitudes on each part of the theme of *gender relations and coping strategies*.

The coding techniques described above are generic and can be used in most types of analyses. There are also more specific data condensation and analysis methods for which the reader may consult more elaborate sources (e.g., Bauer and Gaskell, 2000; Neuman, 2003). One such method is analysis by matrix displays.

Matrix Displays—Data Condensation and Analysis

A useful procedure for analysing qualitative interview data is to construct a matrix with the research questions set out as the column headings, and what each respondent or group said as the rows. In a final column notes and preliminary interpretations can be added.

It is common to use both graphical overviews and tables, in which one can enter text rather than numbers, to help the process of analysis. Miles and Huberman (1994) talk about these analytical tools as 'displays' and 'matrix displays' and use them to describe context, to analyse historical trends, causal networks and relations, sequencing, causal models, etc. Analysis by matrix displays is highly applicable for qualitative interviews, but has wider coverage for analysis of qualitative data. The advice for the person who faces the task of analysing large amounts of qualitative data using matrix displays is summarized in nine points:

1. Look at your research question(s) and key variables, and think of the data that are or will be available. Sketch the matrix roughly.
2. Get a colleague to look at your format to help you detect the assumptions you are making, and to suggest alternative ways to display your data.
3. Set up the revised matrix by using your word processor if possible. Aim for a display that will go on one large sheet, even if that sheet covers a wall. You have to be able to see it all at once.
4. Don't try to include more than a dozen or so variables in rows or columns; five or six is more like it. If you are drawn to a design with larger numbers of variables, plan to cluster or partition them. In effect, regroup the matrix into 'streams' or adjacent 'families'.
5. Expect that your preliminary format(s) will be iterated several times during early data entry—and often later on as well. You'll always get better ideas about how the matrix should be set up.
6. If the matrix is an ordered one, expect to transpose rows and columns for a while until you have a satisfactory version. Most work processors can do this quite easily.
7. Always stay open to the idea of adding new rows or columns, even late in your analysis operations.
8. Keep rows and columns fine-grained enough to accommodate meaningful differentiations in the data, but not so fine as to bury you under indiscriminate detail.
9. Keep in mind that any particular research question may require a *series* of matrices; for example, an initial partially ordered descriptive matrix, leading to a small summary table, then to variously ordered, more boiled-down matrices. Think ahead to this possibility but allow new matrix forms to emerge as the analysis proceeds. Trust us: they invariably do (Miles and Huberman, 1994: 241).

When we talk about qualitative data, the cell entries in the matrix are typically text. For example:

- direct quote, extracts from written-up field notes
- summaries, paraphrases, or abstracts
- researcher explanations
- ratings or summarized judgements
- combinations of the above

However, **working with qualitative data does not preclude** *counting.* In qualitative research numbers tend to get ignored. After all, the hallmark of qualitative research is that it goes beyond *how much* there is of something to tell us about its essential qualities, says Miles and Huberman, and continue:

> However, a lot of counting goes on in the background when judgements of qualities are being made. When we identify a theme or a pattern, we're isolating something that (a) happens a number of times and (b) consistently happens in a specific way. The 'number of times' and 'consistency' judgements are based on counting. When we make a generalization, we amass a swarm of particulars and decide, almost unconsciously, which particulars are there *more often, matter more* than others, *go together,* and so on. When we say something is 'important' or 'significant' or 'recurrent' we have come to that estimate, in part, by making counts, comparisons, and weights.
>
> So it is important in qualitative research to know (a) that we are sometimes counting and (b) when it is a good idea to work self-consciously with frequencies, and when it's not (ibid., 1994: 253).

With this qualification of types of valid data condensations into text and figures, interpretation and drawing conclusions can continue.

Steps in Interpretation and Drawing Conclusions

Analysis and interpretation of data can continue after the matrix, and possibly graphical displays, have been made. Box 5.13 summarizes how the analysis and interpretation can continue. The 13 steps, which Miles and Huberman call *tactics,* are arranged roughly from the descriptive to the explanatory and from the concrete to the more conceptual and abstract.

Investigating by the use of semi-structured interviews, and analysing and interpreting the data involve many challenges. There are no formulas for determining significance. There are no straightforward tests for reliability and validity. 'There are no absolute rules except to do the very best with your full intellect to fairly represent the data and communicate what the data reveal given the purpose of the study' (Patton, 1990: 372). Despite the modesty, Patton gives guidance on qualitative analysis and interpretation and shows how the quality and credibility of qualitative analysis can be enhanced. These include reminders on:

- Focusing the analysis according to purpose.
- Strategies for analysing interviews, observations and content analysis.
- Finding patterns and developing category systems in inductive analysis.
- Recognizing processes and linkages in data and analysing causes, consequences and relationships.

In short, qualitative research based on interviews as well as on other types of data presented in the following sections demands that the analysts be closely involved in the process from conceptualization to presentation of results.

Box 5.13   Steps in Interpretation and Drawing Conclusions

1. Noting patterns, themes
2. Seeing plausibility
3. Clustering

1–3 help the analyst see 'what goes with what'

4. Making metaphors—like 1–3 is a way to achieve more integration among diverse pieces of data
5. Counting—a familiar way to see 'what's there'
6. Making contrasts/comparisons—a pervasive tactic that sharpens understanding. Differentiation sometimes is needed too, as in 7
7. Partitioning variables

We also need tactics for seeing things and their relationships more abstractly. These include

8. Subsuming particulars into the general
9. Factoring—an analogue of a familiar quantitative technique
10. Noting relations between variables
11. Finding intervening variables

Finally, how can we systematically assemble a coherent understanding of data? The tactics are

12. Building a logical chain of evidence
13. Making conceptual/theoretical coherence

After Miles and Huberman, 1994: 345–46.

5.2.4 Other Sources of Qualitative Data—Text Analysis and IT Tools

Text Analysis

After interviews, the other broad source of data in development research is text, i.e., text of many sorts, from official documents, archives, historical records, newspapers, to web-based texts and folkloristic narratives, with or without illustrations, pictures and images.[6] The text may also be derived from transcribed interviews.

Documentary analysis is used in most studies relating to development planning and evaluation, but the depth and transparency of the required *content analysis* varies significantly. For those who get involved with *negotiation* for example, knowledge of *argumentation analysis* is useful (see below). An extraordinarily rapid growth of interest has happened in recent years in a particular form of content analysis, namely *discourse analysis*. Because there has been such a fast expansion of discourse analysis as

---

[6] For the latter see the magazine *Visual Anthropology*, e.g., Vol. 12, Nos 2–3 (1999), K.G. Tomaselli, *Encounters in the Kalahari*.

an alternative qualitative analytical approach, even in the field of development studies, it requires a brief presentation here.

Discourse Analysis

Strictly speaking, there is no single 'discourse analysis', but many different styles of analysis that all lay claim to the name. What these perspectives share is a rejection of the realist notion that language is simply a neutral means of reflecting or describing the world, and a conviction in the central importance of discourse in constructing social life. Discourse analysis is the name given to a variety of different approaches to the study of texts, which have developed from different theoretical traditions and diverse disciplinary locations. This is how Gill (2000) introduces discourse analysis and records that there are probably at least 57 varieties of this analysis.

A quote from Vivian Burr helps to clarify 'discourse analysis' and its relations to 'social constructionist' thinking:

> The origins of discourse analysis in critiques of traditional social science mean that it has a rather different epistemological basis from some other methodologies. This is sometimes called social constructionism, constructivism or simply constructionism. There is no single agreed definition of these terms, but the key features of these perspectives include:
>
> 1. A critical stance towards taken-for-granted knowledge, and a scepticism towards the views that our observations of the world unproblematically yield its true nature to us.
> 2. Recognition that the ways in which we commonly understand the world are historically and culturally specific and relative.
> 3. A conviction that knowledge is socially constructed—that is, that our current ways of understanding the world are determined not by the nature of the world itself, but by social processes.
> 4. A commitment to exploring the ways that knowledge—the social construction of people, phenomena or problems—are linked to actions/practices (Burr, 1995).

The essence of discourse analysis is hermeneutic, i.e., it is concerned with interpretation of human action, but based primarily on text and talk analysis. 'Discourse' refers to all forms of talk and texts. Discourse analysts see all discourse as *social practice.* They are interested in texts in their own right, rather than seeing them as a means of disclosing a reality which is deemed to lie behind the discourse. Language is seen as a practice in its own right. People use discourse to *do* things—to offer blame, to make excuses, to present themselves in a positive light, etc. To highlight this is to underline the fact that discourse does not occur in a social vacuum. To take an example: We know that respondents orient themselves to the 'interpretive context'. They are apt to express themselves differently about their views on a development intervention—for example about access to potable water and hygiene practices—whether this is to a fellow villager, to a family member, to a local government official, or to a representative of an international development cooperation agency. Discourse analysts argue that all discourse is occasioned and situated.

One outcome of this epistemological position is that discourse analysis cannot be used to address the same sorts of questions as traditional approaches. Instead, it suggests new questions or ways of reformulating old ones (Gill, 2000: 173). Rather than asking *why* so and so happened, discourse analysis helps to answer *how* so and so is happening.

Like other 'qualitative researchers', discourse analysts have to immerse themselves in the material being studied. Coding is one analytical device to search for pattern in the data and form a tentative hypothesis. Prescriptions are few, but steps of how to go about discourse analysis are suggested (Box 5.14).

Box 5.14   Steps in Discourse Analysis

1. Formulate your initial research questions.
2. Choose the texts to be analysed.
3. Transcribe the texts in detail. Some texts, such as archive material, newspaper articles, or parliamentary records, will not require transcription.
4. Sceptically read and interrogate the text.
5. Code—as inclusively as possible. You may want to revise your research questions as patterns in the text emerge.
6. Analyse (a) examining regularity and variability in the data, and (b) forming tentative hypotheses.
7. Check reliability and validity through: (a) deviant case analysis; (b) participants' understanding (when appropriate); and (c) analysis of coherence.
8. Write up.

After Bauer and Gaskell, 2000: 188–89.

Gill attempts, but admits that it is difficult to explain how actually to go about analysing texts:

> Pleasant as it would be to be able to offer a cookbook style recipe for readers to follow methodically, this is just not possible. Somewhere between 'transcription' and 'writing up', the essence of doing discourse analysis seems to slip away: ever elusive, it is never quite captured by descriptions of coding schemes, hypothesis and analytical schemata. However, just because the skills of discourse analysis do not lend themselves to procedural description, there is no need for them to be deliberately mystified and placed beyond reach .... There really is no substitute for learning by doing (Gill, 2000: 177).

Few new approaches to qualitative social research have aroused as much criticism from other social scientists as discourse analysis (e.g., Bredsdorff, 2002), perhaps because of the risks of relativist interpretations and emission in speculation embedded in the discourse analysis approach.

A few reflections and guiding principles on the wider category of content analysis follow, with an example of the more rigorous Argumentation Analysis.

Content Analysis

Research methods go through cycles of fashion, says Martin Bauer (2000), with reference to *text as data*. A window of opportunity for text as data has been created with the World Wide Web and online archives for newspapers, radio and television programmes. This can be an important complement to analysis based on interviewing, which predominates in social research. There is a renewed interest in content analysis and in its techniques, in particular in computer-aided techniques.

Bauer counts six Content Analysis designs. The simplest and least interesting is the purely descriptive study that counts the frequency of all the coded features of the text. The most ambitious designs are parallel designs, involving longitudinal analysis in combination with other longitudinal data, such as from repeated waves of unstructured interviewing (ibid.).

Conducting a content analysis, whether manually or by computer-aided techniques, involves a number of steps: *sampling of text, categorizing and coding, analysis and validation* (see also Box 5.15).

Box 5.15   Content Analysis—General Approach

STEPS IN CONTENT ANALYSIS
1. Theory and circumstances suggest the selection of particular texts.
2. Sample texts if there are too many to analyse completely.
3. Construct a coding frame that fits both the theoretical considerations and the materials.
4. Pilot and revise the coding frame and explicitly define the coding rules.
5. Test the reliability of the codes, and sensitize coders to ambiguities.
6. Code all materials in the sample, and establish the overall reliability of the process.
7. Set up a data file for the purpose of statistical analysis.
8. Write a codebook including (a) the rationale of the coding frame; (b) the frequency distributions of all codes; and (c) the reliability of the coding process.

After Bauer, 2000: 149.

Content analysis is a good example of the importance of theory-based analysis. As reflected in step one, methods are no substitutes for good theory and a substantive research problem. To make a good content analysis, the researcher's theory and the research questions shall inform the selection and categorization of the text materials, either implicitly or explicitly.

It is useful to be reminded that being explicit is a methodical virtue. That is, coherence and transparency are particularly important merits of the quality of the content analysis.

Argumentation Analysis

Argumentation analysis is a form of content analysis. It is an analysis of how a line of argumentation is built. The line of argumentation can be sought in texts depicting speech. The discipline of argumentation is very old. Going back to Aristotle, who referred to three main qualities in a speech:

- logos (reason, logic),
- ethos (morality, moral code), and
- pathos (emotion, affection)

Each argument structure gives special weight to one of the three principles according to the target audience it tries to influence. For example, Aristotle believed that public speaking is bound to contain more pathos, as the emotional component has a strong influence on lay people. Transposing this idea to modern-day analysis, we could pursue an argument structure comparison based on these three characteristics. Each argument can be assigned a numerical value on three scales (logos, ethos, pathos) which, provided they prove reliable, can be used for descriptive comparisons (*After* Liakopoulos, 2000: 169).

Argumentation analysis is relevant in social research, e.g., for analysis of transcriptions of focus groups discussions. Liakopoulos gives advice on how to work with argumentation analysis, e.g., by following five steps (Box 5.16).

Box 5.16   Steps in Argumentation Analysis

1. Collect a representative sample that incorporates the views of all interested parties in the debate.
2. Summarize the main points in a paragraph with minimum paraphrasing.
3. Identify the parts using the definitions provided and test them for reliability.
4. Collate all argument parts in a schematic presentation in order that they may be read relative to each other.
5. Offer interpretation in terms of the general context and the merit of the completeness of the argument.

After Liakopoulos, 2000: 170.

In the book The Uses of Arguments (1958), Toulmin presents a theory of argumentation. Liakopoulos explains the approach and provides a graphic representation of the argument structure (see Figure 5.1). An argument is judged according to the function of its interrelating parts. The simplest argument takes the form of a 'claim' or conclusion preceded by facts (data) to support it. But often a qualifier of the data is required: in other words, a premise that we use to assert that the data are legitimately used to support the claim. The premise is termed a 'warrant'. Warrants are crucial in determining the validity of the argument because they explicitly justify the step from data to claim, and describe the process in terms of why this step can be made.

Figure 5.1   Argumentation Structure

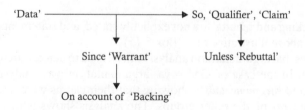

After Liakopoulos, 2000: 153–54.

Liakopoulos illustrates the argumentation analysis with a case study concerning genetically modified (GM) soya beans. The unit of analysis is written texts (newspaper articles) that refer explicitly to the views, beliefs and convictions of actors in the soya-bean debate. These are representatives of *industry, science* and *environmentalists*. There may be numerous examples of arguments, but the interest lies in the central statements.

Examples of each of the argument parts **Claims, Data** and **Warrant** are given in Box 5.17.

Sometimes data can be claims which have been validated in previous arguments, e.g., in arguments that are generated from a scientific source (see column 2 bullet 4).

Box 5.17 Argument Structure Concerning Genetically Modified Soya Beans		
Claim: A statement that contains structure and is presented as the outcome of the argument supported by facts	**Data: Facts or evidence that are at the disposal of the proponent of an argument**	**Warrant: A premise consisting of reasons, guarantees or rules used to assert that the data are legitimately utilized to support the claim**
• 'Biotechnology is the solution to world hunger' • 'Genetically engineered foods have unpredictable long-term effects on health' • 'The risk assessment of the genetically engineered soya is not appropriate'	• 'Population growth is rapid and there is lack of food' • 'Regulators in the EC have already approved of GM crops' • '93% of the public say "yes" to the question: "Do you believe that foods that contain GM foods should be labelled?"' • 'Foreing genes can pass into the intestinal cells (data), so GM foods can alter the DNA of those who eat them (claim)'	• 'Risk assessment of genetically engineered foods does not include full environmental impact assessment' • 'Our society has the ability to work out the costs and benefits of new technology and decide about it'
After Liakopoulos, 2000: Chapter 9.		

In addition to **Claim, Data** and **Warrant** the argumentation model above includes

Backing: A premise that supports the warrant in the argument, and
Rebuttal: A premise that limits the generality of the warrant with further conditions, for example with 'unless'.

It is common that backing and rebuttal are not explicitly stated, and statements of backing and rebuttal are not included in the above illustrative case (Box 5.17).

Liakopoulos illustrates that argumentation analysis can be used to detect different claims from different actors (interest groups). In the case of GM soya, argumentation was analysed from the three actor groups *industry, science* and *environmentalists*, showing that their claims were internally consistent but at variance with the arguments of the other groups. The analysis shows which lines of arguments are consistent. But which lines of argument are stronger or 'correct' is a matter of subjective judgement.

Computer-assisted qualitative data analysis does not help in drawing the 'right' conclusion. But it does help with the management of large masses of qualitative data!

Computer-assisted Qualitative Data Analysis

Several programmes have been developed in recent years with the purpose of making analysis easier. Basically what they do is to substitute a pair of scissors and glue. Electronically, huge amounts of data can be 'handled', re-arranged, and looked at from different perspectives. Categorization (which means 'isolation' of certain factors) may also take place; 'isolation' of certain text fragments can be done; intersection of factors may be looked at, etc. Commonly available functions include:

- *Memoing*—adding commentary to the process of analysis
- *Coding, tagging, labelling*—identifying similar text units
- *Retrieving*—finding units in the same category
- *Linking*—text-text, code-text, memo-text, memo-code, code-code
- *Boolean searching*—finding specified combinations of codes such as 'and', 'or' and 'not' relations
- *Graphical interface*—representing the relations between codes and texts
- *Comparisons between texts of different origins*—social categories, time series
  (Gaskell, 2000: 54).

The purpose is to be able to find patterns, explanations, formulate hypotheses, theories, or fragments of theories, and so on. Along with all the new possibilities, a critical debate questioning the potential methodological merits and dangers is going on (see below).

Until the early 1990s, there were few computer-assisted programmes for qualitative data analysis, with rather limited use. The 'Ethnograph' was probably the best known programme for text-based qualitative data analysis. Later came NUD*IST (Non-numerical Unstructured Data Indexing Searching and Theorizing). Today the market is full of programmes aimed at different types of qualitative data and at different purposes.

If you are unsure about which software is likely to meet your needs, demonstration copies of many of the main packages (e.g., the Ethnograph, NUD*IST, NVivo, winMax, and ATLAS/it) can be downloaded from several sites on the Internet, e.g., http://www.scolari.co.uk and http://www.scolari.com.

Many practitioners who work primarily with qualitative and semi-structured interviews will occasionally need to undertake smaller questionnaire-based surveys. For them, it is useful to have access to relevant but simple software. A web-based survey and data collection software, easy to use for questionnaire-based closed and open-ended questions, is Ultimate Survey. The programme can convert data to excel, and the software makes it easy to prepare a questionnaire for electronic response from respondents who are provided with a link, facilitating continuous statistical operations and analysis. Ultimate Survey was used in the study on Returned Development Workers (Hartoft, 2003). A demonstration version of Ultimate Survey is available at http://www.razza.com/products/ultimatesurvey/.

Since the advent of the first computer programmes that support qualitative research, there has been a lively debate about their potential methodological merits and dangers, with discussants expressing both great optimism and concern. Kelle (2000) summarizes methodological benefits and problems:

Concerning the benefits—and risks—of software for qualitative research, the following aspects are frequently mentioned:

First by mechanizing tedious and cumbersome tasks of data organization, such as searching and copying text segments, a computer can lead to greater efficiency. Thus, *software helps to save time*, and *assist the management of larger samples*.

Second, the use of software packages can make the *research process more systematic and explicit*, and therefore more transparent and rigorous, while systematizing procedures that previously had been unsystematic and enabling researchers to codify exactly how they analyse their data. Thus *computers could add trustworthiness to a methodology that has always suffered from the reputation of seducing the researcher into unsystematic, subjective or journalistic styles of inquiry*.

Third, by releasing the researcher from boring and cumbersome mechanical tasks, software for textual data management can *free up time that can be spent on more creative and analytic tasks*. Thus, computer programs can enhance the researcher's creativity, by allowing them to experiment and to 'play' with the data, and to explore the relationship between different categories more thoroughly.

Warnings about the potential methodological dangers of using computers often relate to the possibility that the computer could alienate the researchers from their data, and enforce analytical strategies that go against the methodological and theoretical orientations that qualitative researchers see as the hallmark of their work.

According to most researchers, there are more benefits than problems in using computers and computer-based analytical programmes, and many of the so-called problems are misconceptions of what the machines can do—among other things replace the researcher's own line of thinking, own creativity or own theoretical process.

The field of computer-assisted qualitative data analysis can be seen as the most rapidly developing in the domain of qualitative methodology, with its own networking projects, conferences and list on the Internet. The literature describing software packages in detail is always in danger of becoming rapidly outdated, and the concerned scholar does best in consulting with other scholars and libraries which will be updated on the current developments.

5.3   Standards of Quality for Qualitative Research

5.3.1 Sampling, Biases, Reliability and Validation

How is it possible to ensure the quality of qualitative research results? Some analysts adapt the quality indicators of quantitative social research, i.e., *validity* and *reliability* (Kvale, 1996). In addition, Kvale talks about quality criteria such as analytical and practical *skill*—e.g., the ability to falsify and to 'theorise'; *communicative validity*—i.e., validations of results in such a way that others are convinced about the validity; and *pragmatic validity*—i.e., the criteria that the results of the analysis are relevant and useful.

In the qualitative tradition there is much less clarity of what the criteria for good quality research are. Yet, 'if qualitative research is to compete on the wider stage it must justify its methods and claims and meet the demands of *public accountability, confidence* and *relevance*', say Gaskell and Bauer (2000: 349, emphasis added).

Sampling

One of the critical and controversial areas in the sound use of qualitative and participatory methods is selection of respondents and sampling. It does not pose the same problem in conventional survey methodology, since a range of sampling techniques and principles has been developed to suit different research purposes.

Sampling procedures include the following main categories:

- Simple random sampling
- Systematic sampling
- Stratified sampling
- Purposive sampling

To these may be added more detailed sampling techniques, e.g.,

- Cluster sampling
- Quota sampling
- Stage-wise sampling
- Snowball or chain sampling
- Sampling from maps
- The random walk

A wide selection of literature addresses research principles in relation to qualitative research, including sampling procedures (e.g., Guba and Lincoln, 1989; Kumar, 1999; Laws, 2003; Neuman, 2003; Patton, 2002; Scheyvens and Storey, 2003). It is becoming normal practice in qualitative research in development to let sample selection be determined by informational considerations. If the purpose is to maximize information, the sampling is terminated when no new information is forthcoming from additional sampled units. This strategy leaves the question of sample size open, yet requires some guiding criteria to determine what is enough once the sampling unit or elements are established—e.g., individual, household, gender-specific group, organization, or text-items, etc. FAO has taken a concern in sampling in relation to application of participatory methods (see Box 5.18):

PRA methods originate in rural settings characterized by high stability. Stability of populations to be sampled also facilitate the sampling exercise. Stability, however, does not always characterize real life

Box 5.18 Sampling Considerations in the Participatory Rural Appraisal, PRA 'Tool Kit'	
Problem	**Possible Solutions**
1. How to ensure that the views of less visible target groups are not under-represented in interviews	• Stratify the sample of interviews that will be carried out during field visits to include specific proportions of various groups (resource-rich/resource-poor, men and women, old/young, landless/landed, different ethnic groups).
2. How to combat the common problem that more remote agroecological zones are poorly represented in RRA field visits	• Pre-select sites that include these zones when the team plans their programme.
3. How to include some random sampling that is not too time-consuming to compose a sample and find people in a limited time period to generate information that is convincing to planners who require more statistical or quantitative evidence of a team's findings	• Use the Null Hypothesis (interview a limited number [4 to 8] of individuals) to <u>disprove</u> rather than <u>prove</u> something which has been a working assumption or finding of earlier monitoring surveys. If most of your 'sample' does not conform to the rule, you can be sure your working hypothesis is questionable, since the statistical likelihood of encountering so many exceptions to the rule is very low. • (a) Use the <u>quick and dirty</u> sampling programme developed by Ronald Ng (see Annex 2 in this FAO source) to obtain a sample for a complementary, sample survey to the RRA itself. • (b) Use existing lists to draw a quick sample (health registers, nursery registers, voting lists) with a random numbers' table in the field. • (c) Interview a small sub-sample from a previous, formal survey sample (such as one conducted by the M&E unit of the project earlier on, or from a baseline survey if such exists).
4. What to do to test hypotheses that are only formulated halfway through the RRA exercise	• Try a random sample halfway through the field visits to test emerging hypotheses. Plan a second visit and make the RRA an interactive process.

5. What to do when households are reluctant to give accurate information on sensitive issues	• Combine individual interviews with:
	    Group interviews
	    Participant observation
	    Direct measurement
	    Secondary data review
	    Unstructured, casual conversations
	    Ranking or planning games
	    Key informants
	    Change of households

After FAO/SIDA, 1989: 33–34.

situations. Some sections of the population are more mobile than the sampling theory seems to account for. The result may be 'sample gone' when you need it (see Box 5.19):

Box 5.19   Help—The Sample is Gone! Moving Targets in Refugee Studies

The image of the rural community is almost paradigmatically present in the way we perceive sampling in development studies. In the village we can walk from house to house with our carefully prepared questionnaires; we can design pilot studies, studies and follow-up studies because the villagers seem to be ever-present; history is easily grasped because several generations have lived close together in the same place for ages; informants have time to chat with foreigners, and they are very knowledgeable about the deeply-rooted local culture; local institutions integrate villagers into tight networks, everybody knows the whereabouts and opinions of the others, and segments and factions have systematically divided and segregated villagers since Adam and Eve.

Doing refugee studies represents a challenge to this image. Due to the volatile and delicate nature of refugee situations, things can change extremely rapidly. As refugees are subject to changeable and arbitrary government decisions, you may well find yourself with a well-prepared plan for sampling in a refugee site discovering that the sample has been relocated, dispersed or repatriated. Here, imagination and improvisation are key words. Discontinuity and heterogeneity is the rule rather than the exception. Families have been split (or have split up for strategic reasons) and networks have been mutilated; in fact you may have to sample in multiple field sites if you want to do something like a 'community study', Guatemalan refugees in settlements in Mexico, for example, have developed a spider's web of relations between family and household members in Guatemala, at the Mexican border, in large Mexican cities, in Los Angeles, in Florida, and in Canada.

Migration studies in general have shown that we have to be cautious about sampling on the basis of images of rooted, stable and homogeneous communities. Modern society is complex and nomadic.

After Stepputat, 1992.

Biases, Reliability and Validity

The biases—or errors—associated with sampling and poor interviewing techniques are but a few of the possible biases in development studies. The biases associated with development studies, accentuated by different cultural norms and interpretations, language differences, filtering of information through assistants and interpreters, may overshadow sampling errors.

The attitude to biases has been relaxed with the shift towards qualitative and participatory methods. 'Lay open your values and your methodology' may be a better principle than to aim for unobtainable objectivity.

Many topics chosen for study and development intervention touch very profound dimensions of personal experience, to such a degree that the reliability and validity of the study results must be questioned. Thus Hastrup illustrates the fundamental difference between hunger as an experienced phenomenon or as a neutral subject of study (see Box 5.20). The Hunger Experienced case illustrates that *reliability* (repeated observations using the same instrument under identical conditions produce similar results) and *validity* (what is measured is accurate and reflect the 'truth' or 'reality'), are not symmetrical. Measures of hunger may be reliable in the sense of replicable measures. The validity of the measure touches people's subjective experience of hunger. Thus, perfect validity is not even theoretically attainable. The parallel to other current development issues, e.g., poverty, is striking.

Box 5.20   Hunger Experienced

Where hunger is still a collective experience, it is well known that suffering cannot be measured. To claim that a standard definition of hunger is required before science can proceed with the issue is grotesque. In a recent study it is regretted that 'famine, as a descriptive term ... has emotional overtones'. That is to regret the very point: there is no reliable way of separating the material aspects of famine from the emotional aspects. The horror and confusion created by hunger is an important part of its character. It is part of the definition of famine.

When hunger is turned into famine, quantity has already turned into 'quality'. The usual disguise of hunger as demographic disaster and economic instability blurs this fact. No matter what the immediate causes of the disaster are, it has multiple consequences. Hunger cannot be subjected to any simple measure. Malthus must be done away with; the convenience of making suffering anonymous is alarming.

The alternative is to undertake detailed studies of people's actual feelings and their own interpretations of hunger. An example is found in Megan Vaughan's analysis of a hunger disaster in Malawi. The hunger meant not only physical misery, but also social anomy of a sort not recorded in figures but in the songs of the women. They sing for example:

'We have suffered this year,
Our husbands want to divorce.
Oh, what can we do against the hunger'.

A mass of cultural and social information is hidden in this small verse, sung by the women while grinding. A closer study of the particular famine shows that women and children in particular suffered during the famine. Men left their homes as usual to find food, but in the year of the famine they did not return. They settled in other areas with other women where food was sufficient.

Hunger is a window on the social structure, and in Malawi also on the loose marriage fabric. From such studies it is revealed that the experience of hunger, and for that matter of war and plague, are connected to common social experience. It is not a phenomenon outside in the demographic/economic sphere, where figures only count. It is an obvious theme of anthropological interest.

After Hastrup, 1992: 60–61 (in *Det antropologiske projekt*). Reprinted with permission from Gyldendal Publishers.

5.3.2 Criteria for Good Practice

In addition to the classical quality concepts of validity and reliability—and representative sampling—the quality concepts of qualitative research are captured in the following vocabulary: *trustworthiness, refutability, neutrality, authenticity, transferability, applicability, credibility, consistency.*

It is commonly agreed that it is possible to propose criteria for improving quality, if this is done in a relatively open and permissive way that preserves the enterprise of qualitative research as a creative and exploratory enterprise that cannot be contained by the strict imposition of methodological rules.

The interpretation of validity remains rather general as expressed by Maxwell: 'I use validity in a fairly straightforward, commonsense way to refer to the correctness or credibility of a description, conclusion, explanation, interpretation, or other sort of account' (Maxwell quoted in Olsen, 2002: 144). Quality is embedded in convincing other researchers—and concerned stakeholders—about the validity of one's own research.

The practitioner working with qualitative data can get guidance on how to ensure quality from the six criteria summarized in Box 5.21:

Box 5.21 Six Criteria of Good Practice to Guide Qualitative Research	
Criteria of good practice	**Characteristic**
Triangulation and reflexivity of perspectives	**Triangulation**—A criterion of good practice in qualitative research using several methods or conceptualizations on the same problem. This often leads to contradictory evidence which reflects back on the research process. The resolution of these contradictions needs to be documented. **Reflexivity**—The ways in which researchers should reflect upon their own practices.
Transparent documentation of procedures	**Transparency**—A criterion of good practice in qualitative research. The selection of the data, the time and location of the collection, and the procedures of analysis should be sufficiently documented so that they can be imitated. It fosters public confidence in the data.
Details of corpus construction	**Corpus construction**—The process of collecting materials in qualitative research. It is not based on random principles, but is nevertheless systematic, considering relevance, homogeneity, synchronicity and saturation. It involves extending functions and strata (external variables) until the range of focal representations (internal variables) of an issue are saturated.
Thick description of results	**Thick description**—A marker of good practice of qualitative research. Research is often reported with detailed descriptions of situation, events and experiences as revealed in interviews, observations or documents making extensive use of verbatim citations. This increases the relevance of the evidence, and fosters the confidence of the audience in the data.
Evidence of local surprise	**Surprise**—A criterion of quality in qualitative research. To avoid the fallacy of selective evidence, qualitative researchers may want to document their own surprises during a research project. New evidence in the sense of novel insights may only be credible if they are based on local surprises experienced by the researcher.
Communicative validation	A quality criterion that may sometimes apply for qualitative research. The results are fed back to the respondents who provided the information and they are asked to agree or disagree with it, to ensure that their situation is not misrepresented. However, in investigative research of powerful actors, the invitation to 'censor' the researcher's account may not be appropriate.

After Bauer and Gaskell, (2000: 349–50).

The criteria in Box 5.21 may act as a set of guidelines to inform the design, analysis and reporting of qualitative inquiry, and a reminder to the researcher to check that appropriate steps have been taken. A much longer list on 'Some quality standards for research in development' can be found in Laws (2003: 73–76). The criteria are helpful in an ongoing debate about what is good qualitative research rather than a definitive solution to what is essentially a problem of practice.

CHAPTER

6

*Chapter six is the place for updating central issues and approaches which are given new attention or are relatively new on the development cooperation agenda: **A rights-based approach, RBA** (Section 6.1) currently substitutes the conventional needs based approach in several agencies. An appetizer is given of what RBA is and how it can be approached. **Poverty measures and analysis** (Section 6.2) are set in the context of the evolving agenda for addressing the overarching goal of **poverty reduction** in the framework of the Poverty Reduction Strategy Papers (PRSP) and Millennium Development Goals. Lessons on implementation of the **mainstreaming strategy for promotion of gender equality** (Section 6.3) highlight implications in terms of **gender analysis,** including identification of gender indicators. The PRSP offers a framework for integrating gender into poverty diagnostics, while gender mainstreaming is being contested in the name of **empowerment of women.** Innovative approaches in development cooperation incorporate participatory methods in various ways (Section 6.4): **Appreciative Inquiry, AI** adds a constructive alternative perspective to the predominant problem focus of much development work. The **Social Capital Analysis Tool (SOCAT)** illustrates a combined tool where participatory methods have been incorporated to assess the role of social capital in relation to poverty reduction. Lastly, **Geomatics** illustrates a **spatial method** combining high-tech GIS with anthropological methods and integration of indigenous knowledge. This genuinely cross-disciplinary tool illustrates potentials in the hands of development planners as well as indigenous groups, and is currently gaining momentum.*

6.1   A Rights-based Approach to Development[1]

A rights-based approach to development is a conceptual framework for the process of human development that is normatively based on international human rights standards and operationally directed to promoting and protecting human rights. Essentially, a rights-based approach integrates the norms, standards and principles of the international human rights system into the plans, policies and processes of development. The norms and standards are those contained in the wealth of international treaties and declarations. —*OHCHR Website, 2004.*

A rights-based approach to development describes situations not simply in terms of human needs, or of development requirements, but in terms of society's obligations to respond to the inalienable

---

[1] The main author of this section on A Rights-based Approach to Development is Cecilia M. Ljungman, COWI, in cooperation with Sarah Forti and Britha Mikkelsen.

rights of individuals, empowers people to demand justice as a right, not a charity, and gives communities a moral basis from which to claim international assistance when needed. —*UN Secretary General Kofi Annan, 1998.*

(A rights-based approach) means having the courage to build local, national, and global movements that argue for specific duties to be met by governments, corporations, and individuals that will enable all people to enjoy their rights. Above all, it involves abolishing the development enterprise as a neo-colonial programme of correction administered from rich to poor and replacing it with a common political project that recognises everyone's equal rights and judges the behaviour of all on the basis of how they realise or violate these rights. —*Hugo Slim, 2002.*

In the last decade, human rights-based approaches have gained more attention in the development discourse. Although a consensus on the basic constituent elements of this approach appears to be slowly emerging, there is no single, universally agreed rights-based approach. The above statements on human rights approaches illustrate compatible but different perspectives on rights-based approaches that range from incorporating the norms, standards and principles of the international human rights system into development work, to a complete paradigm shift that involves replacing the development effort. This section aims to provide an introduction to the concepts of a rights-based approach, its strengths and challenges.

'Development' and the Human Rights Agenda

Regarding socio-economic development as part of the human rights agenda is not new. It dates back to when the authors of the Universal Declaration of Human Rights (1948) articulated economic, social, cultural, civil and political human rights in a single document with the aim of preventing the horrors of mass war from ever happening again. However, the effort to translate this document into legally binding obligations was thwarted by the ideological divisions between the western liberal democracies (which championed civil and political rights) and the East Bloc (which prioritized economic, social and cultural rights). One effect of this was the separation of the UN's development activities from its human rights efforts.

The end of the bipolar era gave rise to new opportunities for the development community. The emergence or resurgence of democracies, civil conflicts, war, acts of genocide and the rise of an 'international civil society' in the post-Cold War period brought human rights to the forefront. Discourse on the relationship between human rights and international development cooperation gradually regained prominence and became a feature of the host of world summits held from the 1990s onwards.[2] When the UN launched its reform process in the late 1990s, the Secretary General saw an opportune occasion for the UN to reassert itself in its mandate to '(assist) in the realisation of human rights and fundamental freedoms'

---

[2] For instance the World Conference of Human Rights in Vienna (1993); the World Conference on Women in Beijing (1995); the Social Summit in Copenhagen (1996); the World Food Summit in Rome (1997); the World Summit on Sustainable Development in Johannesburg (2002).

(art. 13(1)b, UN Charter). The Secretary General has since taken the significant step of calling for the mainstreaming of human rights in *all* of the UN's development work.

Meanwhile, several organizations such as CARE, Save the Children and UNICEF started to develop rights-based approaches.[3] Likewise, some bilateral donor agencies, e.g., Sida and DFID, began promoting rights perspectives in their assistance. Rights and development gained further impetus in 2000 when UNDP's *Human Development Report* focused on human rights and human development. It presented a compelling argument for an integrated approach to development, drawing upon the principles of international human rights and the strategies of human development to advance dignity and well-being. In 2002, the UN in collaboration with the Bretton Woods institutions prepared draft *Guidelines for a Human Rights Approach to Poverty Reduction Strategies.*

6.1.1 The Principles and Concepts of Human Rights

Human rights are moral and legal entitlements. They are fundamental for peoples' well-being, dignity, and the pursuit of their full potential. They can also be described as the 'social and political guarantees necessary to protect individuals from the standard threats to human dignity posed by the modern state and modern markets' (Donnelly, 1989). Human rights may be formulated concretely as: 'the right to vote' and 'freedom from torture', or in more abstract terms, such as the 'right to food'. The latter constitutes the entitlement to the social arrangements needed to facilitate access to food.

Human rights take departure in the *International Bill of Rights* which comprises the *Universal Declaration of Human Rights*, and the consequent *International Covenant on Economic, Social and Cultural Rights* (ICESCR) and the *International Covenant on Civil and Political Rights* (ICCPR) which came into force in 1976. These treaties, which have been drafted, debated and adopted by the member states of the United Nations, contain a broad range of guarantees that address virtually every aspect of human life and human development. Other central human rights documents are the *Convention on the Rights of the Child* (CRC), *Convention on the Elimination of All Forms of Discrimination Against Women* (CEDAW), and the *International Convention on the Elimination of All Forms of Racial Discrimination* (CERD). In addition, norms, standards and principles have been developed by legitimate international processes and fora.

On paper there is ample evidence of a wide international consensus of the human rights framework. The 160 world leaders who endorsed the United Nations Millennium Declaration in 2000 resolved 'to respect fully and uphold the Universal Declaration of Human Rights' and 'to spare no effort to promote democracy and strengthen the rule of law, as well as respect for all internationally recognised human rights and fundamental freedoms, including the right to development'.[4]

---

[3] It is noteworthy that the International Labour Organization was actually applying a rights-based approach to labour standards even before the UN was established.

[4] Despite the official international consensus on the human rights regime, human rights remain a contested subject area. Some developing countries regard human rights as another aspect of Western hegemony serving Western interests, and associated with donor-imposed conditionalities.

Rights-holders and Duty-bearers

Human rights law recognizes three groups of agents: (*i*) rights-holders; (*ii*) duty-bearers; and (*iii*) 'other actors'. All people belong to the first group—we have human rights simply because we are human beings—these rights are held *equally* and *inalienably*.

To have a particular right implies having a claim on other people or institutions that they should help in ensuring access to this freedom. By signing the human rights treaties, States[5] are the *principal duty bearers* in their respective countries. It obliges the State to *respect*, *protect* and *fulfil* all human rights for all citizens (see Box 6.1). The duties of the State are sometimes misinterpreted as requiring it to meet all needs of all people, which would imply an immense burden of public budgets. Rather, fulfilling human rights requires the State to facilitate, provide and/or promote rights. Thus, if it can be justified from an effectiveness and sustainability standpoint, states can meet their obligations by acting as a regulator or facilitator of other actors who provide services, such as the market and civil society (Moser and Norton, 2001). However, rights-holders are not passive recipients but active subjects who are expected, whenever possible, through his or her actions, to ensure the satisfaction of human needs, individually or in association with others.

Realizing human rights often implies some public expenditure.[6] In recognition of the resource constraints that poor countries face, international law allows for *progressive realization* of some rights over a period of time as long as the State takes deliberate, concrete and targeted steps in the direction of realizing human rights—although core obligations, including for instance non-discriminatory practices, must always be respected.[7] In addition, the *International Covenant on Economic, Social and Cultural Rights* (1976) comprises measures to assist poorer States in realizing human rights by obligating other States to international cooperation.[8]

While governments have a *legal* obligation to protect and realize human rights, 'other actors' such as organizations and individuals also have *moral* obligations under the *Universal Declaration of Human Rights* to respect and promote human rights (see Box 6.2). They can therefore be described as *moral duty-bearers*.

Moral duty-bearers exist not only at the local levels; NGOs, aid agencies, private sector organizations, trans-national corporations, regional organizations and the United Nations are all moral duty-bearers. As the world becomes increasingly globalized, moral duty-bearers at the international and trans-national levels may be expected to assume a greater responsibility in the promotion and protection of human rights.

---

[5] Over 140 states have committed to realizing human rights for their citizens by respecting, protecting and fulfilling human rights.

[6] It is often held that realizing economic, social and cultural rights are more costly than realizing civil and political rights. However, this is not necessarily the case. For instance, fulfilling a citizen's right to vote (right to political participation ICCPR, art. 25) is likely to have greater implications on public expenditure than respecting a citizen's right from being unlawfully evicted from his/her home (right to housing art. 11 ICESCR).

[7] The non-fulfilment of human rights does not necessarily mean that a State is in non-compliance with its obligations, as long as it has taken all measures within its power to ensure an expeditious progressive realization.

[8] *International Covenant of Economic, Social and Cultural Rights*, Part II, article 2.1.

Box 6.1   Obligations of State Parties to International Human Rights Law

The obligation to respect requires the State and all its organs and agents to abstain from carrying out, sponsoring or tolerating any practice, policy or legal measure violating the integrity of individuals or impinging on their freedom to access resources to satisfy their needs. It also requires that legislative and administrative codes take account of guaranteed rights.

The obligation to protect obliges the State and its agents to prevent the violation of rights by other individuals or non-state actors. Where violations do occur the State must guarantee access to legal remedies.

The obligation to fulfil involves issues of advocacy, public expenditure, governmental regulation of the economy, the provision of basic services and related infrastructure and redistributive measures. The duty of fulfilment comprises those active measures necessary for guaranteeing opportunities to access entitlements.

Source: UNDP, 2001.

Box 6.2   Obligations of Other Parties

'*The General Assembly* proclaims *This Universal Declaration of Human Rights* as a common standard of achievement for all peoples and all nations, to the end that every *individual* and *every organ* of society, keeping this Declaration constantly in mind, shall strive by teaching and education to promote respect for these rights and freedoms and by progressive measures, national and international, to secure their universal and effective recognition and observance, both among the peoples of Member States themselves and among the peoples of territories under their jurisdiction' (Preamble of *The Universal Declaration on Human Rights*, our emphasis).

The moral duty bearers implied by the preamble can be divided into the following groups:

- Primary duty-bearers—e.g., parents for children, teachers for students, police for crime suspects, doctors/nurses for patients, employers for employees.
- Secondary duty bearers—e.g., institutions and organizations with immediate jurisdiction over the primary duty-bearers, e.g., school principals, community organizations, hospital administrations, etc.
- Tertiary duty bearers—e.g., institutions and organizations at a higher level/more remote jurisdiction (NGOs, aid agencies, private sector organizations).
- External duty-bearers—e.g., countries, institutions, organizations with no direct involvement, e.g., WTO, UN, INGOs, Security Council, African Union.

6.1.2 Towards Operationalization of a Human Rights Approach

A growing number of development cooperation organizations claim to be applying a rights-based *approach*. The majority, however, are actually applying a human rights *perspective* to development assistance and poverty reduction. A rights-based perspective may, however, be a first step in the direction of a rights-based approach, until an organization's capacities and methodologies have been adequately developed to allow for a full-scale right-based approach.

A human rights perspective typically recognizes that there is an intrinsic link between poverty and human rights at the policy and strategy level. It may be contributing to the realization of human rights and may also embrace the human rights principles listed below. At best, however, a human rights perspective *mainstreams* human rights by applying them consistently throughout the development cooperation process; but it is not guided by the realization of *all* human rights for *all* people as the first and foremost goal. Moreover, a human rights perspective does not shift to a paradigm where the concept of rights-holders and duty-bearers permeate every aspect of development cooperation (this is further discussed below), and where the process of development becomes a sub-set of the realization of human rights (see Box 6.3).

Box 6.3   Poverty and Development in a Rights-based Approach

A rights-based approach holds that someone, for whom a number of human rights remain unfulfilled, such as the right to food, health, education, information, participation, etc., is a poor person. Poverty is thus more than lack of resources—it is the manifestation of exclusion and powerlessness. In this context the realization of human rights and the process of development are not distinct. On the contrary, development becomes a sub-set of the process of fulfilling human rights. In fact, development itself is recognized as a human right.[9]

The distinction between a human rights *perspective* and a human rights *approach* is a reminder to organizations that a rights-based approach can be a gradual process. The following sections focus specifically on the scope of a rights based approach to development cooperation, and on the challenges involved.

The human rights-based approach has many elements in common with other approaches currently used by development practitioners: For example, the emphasis on participation in development work resonates with the right of individuals to take part in the conduct of public affairs and the related rights of association, assembly and expression; the focus on transparent budgetary processes in the effort to promote good governance within the framework of development support corresponds with the right to information; aid interventions that aim at providing social safety nets relate to the right to a reasonable standard of well-being, food, shelter, health, education and social security. Likewise, many of the techniques and management practices used in development work remain valid and important tools for a rights-based approach. Box 6.4 illustrates differences between the commonly applied needs-based approach to poverty reduction and human development, and the rights-based approach.

There are three basic features that distinguish the rights-based approach from other approaches. These are (*i*) the legal basis; (*ii*) the normative framework; and (*iii*) the process of realizing the overall goal (the process is a goal in itself):

---

[9] The World Conference on Human Rights, held in Vienna in 1993, reaffirmed by consensus the right to development as a universal and inalienable right and an integral part of fundamental human rights.

> **Box 6.4   Illustration of the Differences between a Needs Approach and a Rights Approach**
>
> | Needs Approach | Human Rights Approach |
> |---|---|
> | Works toward outcome goals | Works towards outcome and process goals |
> | Recognizes needs as valid claims | Recognizes that rights always imply obligations of the state |
> | Empowerment is not necessary to meet all needs | Recognizes that rights can only be realized with empowerment |
> | Accepts charity as the driving motivation for meeting needs | States that charity is insufficient motivation for meeting needs |
> | Focuses on manifestations of problems and immediate causes of problems | Focuses on structural causes of problems, as well as manifestations and immediate causes of problems |
> | Focuses on the social context with little emphasis on policy | Focuses on social, economic, cultural, civil and political context and is policy-oriented |
>
> *After* Collins, Pearson and Delany, 2002.

(i) Legal Basis

Fundamentally, a rights-based approach differs from poverty reduction/human development approaches to development by claiming that others have duties to facilitate the fulfilment of people's rights and fundamental freedoms, which thereby necessitates action. This claim is backed by international law that specifies **obligations that are legally binding under international law**.[10] By ratifying or acceding to the international human rights treaties, States have agreed to these binding international legal obligations that require them to take necessary legislative, administrative or policy measures, and to provide appropriate remedies in case of violations. A State also commits to report on its practices and performances relating to implementation.[11]

The departure in international law establishes a legitimate conceptual framework that consists of duty-bearers and rights-holders. Thus at the core of a rights-based approach is a 'two-pronged' strategy of aiming to realize human rights by:

strengthening duty-bearers to fulfil their obligations; and
empowering rights-holders to claim their rights.

---

[10] In comparison, the establishment of goals and motivation for action of other approaches can appear arbitrary or 'lawless' (Human Rights Council of Australia, 2001).

[11] Ratification of international treaties also creates relations between States by making respect for human rights a matter of legitimate international observation—and action—of individual States' performance or violations.

While an exclusive focus on either rights-holders or duty-bearers may be necessary and useful in the short term, a long-term one-sided strategy is unlikely to bring about the accountability dynamic that is at the core of the approach as illustrated in Figure 6.1.

Figure 6.1   Rights-based Approach

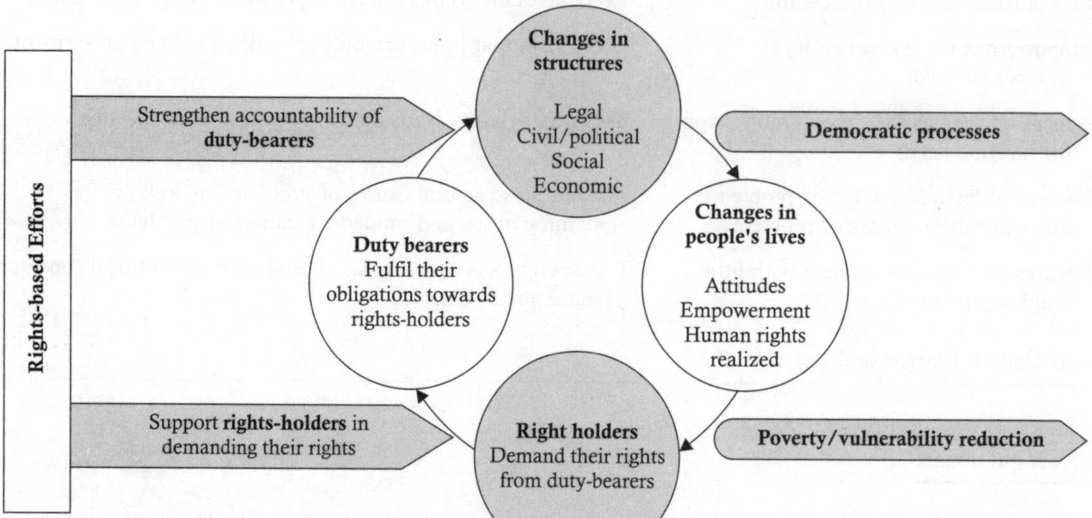

In a dynamic world there will be feedback from democratic processes and poverty reduction to continuous rights-based efforts.

An internationally recognized normative framework sets specified levels of human rights.

(ii) Normative Framework

The international instruments and the authoritative interpretations of the human rights treaty bodies offer normative clarity and a road map for development to policy makers and practitioners. There are **six key principles** that are derived from the human rights instruments. These are:

1. Universalism and inalienability;
2. Equality and non-discrimination;
3. Indivisibility and inter-dependence of human rights;
4. Participation and inclusion;
5. Accountability; and
6. Rule of law.

These principles are constituent components of a rights-based approach. The implications of these principles in the effort to operationalize a rights-based approach are discussed in the following paragraphs.

Re. 1. Human rights and their **universality and inalienability** are often insufficiently understood by many rights-holders and duty-bearers. The principle of universality of human rights means that every woman, man, and child is entitled to enjoy his or her rights simply by virtue of being human.[12] Universality is what distinguishes human rights from other rights—such as citizenship or contractual rights. The rights are inalienable in that they cannot be taken away from someone or voluntarily given up.

Both claiming and realizing a right requires prior understanding of human rights, their universality and inalienability. Efforts are therefore required to raise awareness among individuals and communities with the aim of empowering them to claim their rights. Civic education (both as an effort on its own and as an integral part of specific development initiatives), which consists of providing information and enhancing knowledge about rights and duties, is an essential activity to operationalize a rights-based approach (Goonesekere, 2003). In parallel, raising awareness among principal duty-bearers as well as the range of local, national and international moral duty-bearers through dialogue and advocacy becomes an important endeavour. In this effort, the international human rights law offers an authoritative basis for *advocacy* (see Section 6.1.4).

Re. 2. The principle of **equality** and **non-discrimination** requires that all persons within a society enjoy equal access to the available goods and services that are necessary to fulfil basic human needs. Equality before the law prohibits discrimination in law or in practice in any field regulated and protected by public authorities. The principle applies to all state policies and practices, including those concerning health care, education, access to services, travel regulations, entry requirements and immigration.

For a rights-based approach the principle of **equality and non-discrimination** implies that the development effort should target excluded groups that may, for instance, have inadequate access to social services. These groups may be discriminated against by state policies and practices and/or cultural practices, or in other ways enjoy less economic, social, cultural, political and civil rights than others. A rights-based analysis (see Box 6.5) assists in the identification of prevailing discriminatory patterns. The two-pronged approach with focus on rights-holders and duty-bearers implies that efforts should be focused on empowering these groups, while at the same time strengthening the State actors' capacity to realize the rights of these groups. Depending on the causes for the exclusion, the latter may entail legal and administrative measures to remove explicit legal inequalities in status and entitlements, and revise policies that imply indirect discrimination. It could also include public sector reform and capacity-building, decentralization and democratization of local government, and/or infrastructure development.

---

[12] Some argue that human rights are not universal but a product of western Judeo-Christian traditions. The supposed 'cultural relativism' of human rights is a hotly debated topic, but there are strong arguments against this position. See for instance Chapter 10 in Amartya Sen's *Development as Freedom* (1999) that illustrates how enlightened societies across the globe and in different eras have shared the same common values. Jody Kollapen (2003), Chairperson of the South African Human Rights Commission, points to how human rights existed in pre-colonial Africa. Another area of contestation is the right of the individual versus collective rights.

Box 6.5   Rights-based Analysis

- Rights-based analysis takes departure in the principles of equality and non-discrimination to identify patterns of poverty, powerlessness, social exclusion and discrimination, which are usually sustained by socio-cultural and political-legal institutions.
- The **analytical framework** of a rights-based approach goes beyond socio-economics to also encompass aspects of a society's social, cultural, legal *and* political dynamism. It aims to capture the root causes of the perpetuation of poverty, exclusion, discrimination and power relations that sustain inequity (Moser and Norton, 2001). With this multi-faceted approach, a more complete analysis of a country's development situation, which potentially captures social and political processes, can be achieved. The problem analysis takes departure in whose rights and what rights are *not* being realized. This crucially requires disaggregating data according to gender, citizenship, social status, ethnicity, etc., in order to indicate the extent to which different categories of people are affected or increasingly enjoying their human rights.
- The analysis aims to determine what immediate, underlying and structural obstacles there are to realizing rights. This includes examining social, cultural, legal and administrative frameworks. This requires studying how people's claims are processed by authorities in the different arenas of negotiation (e.g., customary law, religious law, statutory law, constitutional law, etc.) (Moser and Norton, 2001; The Human Rights Council of Australia, 2001).
- A rights-based analysis must necessarily identify responsible duty-bearers (UN, 2003). Not only does this include the state at different levels, it also comprises the identification of other duty bearers in society, including the family, the community, corporate actors, etc. The capacities and resources of the duty-bearers to fulfil their duties should be assessed.

Re. 3. The principle of **indivisibility** and **inter-dependence of rights** recognizes that the enjoyment of one right is indivisibly interrelated to the enjoyment of other rights because all rights are inter-dependent. The inter-dependence of rights is a reflection of the multidimensional character of well-being (see Box 6.6). While all human rights—civic, political, economic, social and cultural, should be treated with the same importance,[13] depending on the specific context certain rights will take priority. However, the principle of **non-retrogression** states that the prioritization of some rights must not deliberately be at the expense of the level of realization of other rights. Thus care must be taken to ensure that other rights maintain at least their initial level of realization.

The principles of **indivisibility and inter-dependence** imply a holistic scope. This does not, however, mean that all rights must be addressed at once. The rights that are least realized, or which can be considered contextually strategic by having the most potential to assist in the realization of other rights, could constitute the focus of the assistance.

---

[13] Although it has been reaffirmed that rights are indivisible in innumerable resolutions since the drafting of the Universal Declaration on Human Rights, this is sometimes contested. In western democracies it is sometimes argued that economic, social and cultural rights are not rights at all but political objectives. This is usually based on the misconception that they are necessarily costly to implement and that implementation can only be done progressively. On the other hand, some governments have shown reticence to accept the equal importance of civil and political rights, arguing that what good is the right to vote or freedom of expression if you are starving and illiterate?

> **Box 6.6   The Multi-faceted Dimensions of Well-being**
>
> Child mortality among poor people can offer an example of the inter-dependence of rights. The high mortality figures among children in developing counties are not simply an effect of disease or a dysfunctional health system. A number of underlying factors contribute to mortality in early childhood. These include the mother's access to education, information, health care, food, work, credit, participation in public life, and power over resources.

Re. 4. The principle of **participation**—which is recognized as a right in itself[14]—means that every person and all peoples are entitled to participate in, contribute to, and enjoy civil, economic, social and political development in which all human rights and fundamental freedoms can be fully realized. It also means that all people are entitled to participate in society using their maximum potential. This in turn necessitates taking steps to facilitate participation, including the provision of a supportive environment to enable people to develop and express their full potential and creativity.

Participation is an imperative in the rights framework since it is an entitlement guaranteed by international law. In effect, as much importance is attached to the processes of achieving goals as it is to the goals themselves. A rights-based strategy, therefore, must aim for *free, active* and *meaningful* participation of targeted communities. 'Free' means participation that is not imposed. A community could therefore in theory come to a decision to have their views *represented* by someone, or could decide to entrust technicians to make specific technical choices for a project. 'Active' requires that the participation process is going somewhere; and 'meaningful' participation entails that it is consequential for goals achieved (Human Rights Coucil of Australia, 2001: 58). A rights-based strategy views participation from a rights-holder and duty-bearer perspective: On the one hand the aim is to enhance rights-holders' capabilities to advocate for their entitlements so that they can define for themselves their own entry points for change. On the other hand, the strategy must address the duty-bearers' capacity to recognize, respect and fulfil the right to participation. It should deliberate the question: 'How can existing procedures, structures and processes be reformed or supplemented to secure free, active and meaningful participation of rights-holders?' Box 6.7 illustrates how an evaluation team recommends participation as a means to apply a human rights perspective to de-mining.

Re. 5. The principle of accountability is derived from the fact that rights imply duties and duties demand **accountability**. To demand accountability from policy makers and other actors whose actions impact on the rights of people contributes to moving development from the realm of charity to that of obligation, making it easier to monitor progress. This is arguably the most important value added of a rights-based approach. Accountability requires that the government, as the legal and principle duty bearer:

1. Accepts responsibility for the impact it has on people's lives;
2. Cooperates by providing information, undertaking transparent processes and hearing people's views; and
3. Responds adequately to those views (UNDP, 2000).

---

[14] *Declaration on the Right to Development*, General Assembly Resolution 41/128, article 1, 1986; and the right to take part in the conduct of public affairs (article 25, ICCPR).

Box 6.7   Human Rights Perspectives and Mine Action

The evaluation of Danish support to mine action found that the prioritization of mine clearance was in the emergency phase, at least in theory, a function of the number accidents. As mine-affected countries began to normalize after the conflict and mine casualties began to stabilize (due to, for instance, increased knowledge of the location of mine fields), mine action agencies began to emphasize socio-economic reasons for mine action. Roads, electricity pylons, irrigation systems, schools, agricultural land, etc., were prioritized as a function of their potential socio-economic benefit. However, this approach overlooked the weakest and most marginalized groups affected.

The evaluation team became aware of the fact that the presence or mere suspicion of mines had a considerable impact on human rights. The rights of mine-affected communities that were typically affected were, for instance, the right to life and physical integrity, adequate food, education, work, association, and a standard of living adequate for mental and physical health and well-being. The evaluation therefore concluded that regarding mine action as first and foremost a response aimed at ensuring the fundamental human rights of mine-affected populations could help prioritize efforts and could ensure a more comprehensive poverty focus. Furthermore, manifestly linking human rights and mine action could strengthen the underlying mine action concept that mine action is about *people* and mines, not least by improving the participation of mine-affected communities. Moreover, a rights approach could help solve the conceptual, institutional and funding gap caused by the split between humanitarian and development assistance since both forms of assistance are compatible with an overall aim of realizing human rights.

After Ministry of Foreign Affairs/Danida, 2003.

Accountability requires conditions for transparency and avenues for challenging and seeking redressal for decisions or actions negatively affecting rights. While duty-holders must themselves determine the appropriate mechanisms of accountability, all mechanisms must be accessible, transparent and effective (OHCHR, 2002). Other duty-bearers that assist the government in fulfilling its obligations, such as donors, aid organizations, NGOs and development practitioners, are accountable in the same way.

Rights-based development cooperation aims to strengthen a government's accountability to ensure open, transparent, effective, efficient and responsive systems ('good governance'). Bearing in mind the two-pronged strategy, a rights-based approach fundamentally seeks to empower rights-holders to demand accountability and, if necessary, seek redress. This could include establishing an independent monitoring and inspection panel with the function of arbitrating disputes or grievances within the framework of a development effort.

Re. 6. Human rights must be protected by law. **Rule of law** entails that disputes should be solved through adjudication by competent, impartial and independent processes. Aggrieved rights-holders require access to the judicial machinery to invoke their rights to institute legal proceedings for appropriate redress. However, the legal apparatus in many poor countries is weak, under-developed, under-resourced, and often undermined by the ruling elites. For human rights to become a development tool, the judicial system needs to function and be accessible to all. A rights-based strategy therefore needs to take into account the state of the judicial system, the prosecution, police, and other institutions for upholding rights. In addition, religious, customary and living law and their respective corresponding mechanisms need to be considered in terms of their relationship to marginalized groups and their conformity with human rights.

(iii) Process Goals

The process of realizing human rights is central to a rights-based approach (see Box 6.8). A person is a subject of his or her rights and an active participant in his or her development. Human rights are thus by necessity:

- Active—dependent on the participation of individuals and groups; and
- Practical—they must be applicable in the daily lives of people.

Therefore, rights should not only be *promoted* and *protected* by duty-bearers, but *practised* and *experienced* by rights-holders. The rights and freedoms which are of particular importance to ensure practicality and active enjoyment of human rights are the right to information, freedom of expression, the right to take part in the conduct of public affairs, and the right to participation in the development process.

Box 6.8   Formulating Rights-based Objectives

The so-called 'development' or long-term **goals** of a rights-based aid initiative should be formulated in rights language. (Human Rights Council of Australia, 2001) For instance, the goal of a health sector reform programme would refer to the right of everyone to enjoy the highest attainable standard of physical and mental health (Article 12, ICESCR). While some practitioners argue that the essence of a rights-based approach can be achieved without specifically using rights language (OHCHR, 2002), this runs contrary to the concepts of transparency and dialogue, which are essential in a rights-based approach. As important as the outcome of an initiative is the process of getting there—since a rights-based implementation process is underpinned by participation, which is a right.

By consistently applying the rights-based principles discussed above to all activities and processes, a rights-based approach to development cooperation aims to contribute to the practicality and active enjoyment of human rights. As a result, the approach regards the realization of human rights as both an outcome goal and a process goal, which implies that the *means* of achieving human rights is itself of great importance.

When the *legal basis*, *normative framework* and *process goals* that distinguish a rights-based approach are put into practice in a development cooperation project between a bilateral donor and a recipient government, it may have the components described in Box 6.9.

(iv) Tools for Operationalizing a Rights-based Approach

There are still relatively few tools to assist organizations in operationalizing a rights-based approach. Some of those worth mentioning include the draft guidelines for a rights-based approach to poverty

---

Box 6.9   Components of a Rights-based Project

- People involved in the project have a thorough knowledge of the international human rights framework;
- Initial negotiations with the agency of the receiving government make it clear which right(s) is at issue;
- The feasibility study involves communities themselves in the design of the project, and not only in its implementation;
- Communities are provided choices and they are given undertakings regarding the project;
- Information is provided, including the communities' entitlements and their decision-making powers;
- The timetable of outcomes includes the provision of penalty clauses;
- Access is provided to the project decision makers and to grievance procedures;
- Guarantees are given in case of project failures to ensure the provision of services;
- Explicit provisions for relevant information and skills regarding entitlements would be a standard part of the project package, which may include, for example, financial provision for communities to provide their own advisors;
- At the feasibility study stage, project designers analyse the other rights that are breached (through omission or commission) in the area and consideration is given to whether the project can address these or how else they can be addressed;
- Negotiations with provincial and local government authorities make it clear which right(s) is at issue;
- The responsibility for project evaluation and monitoring includes the participation of communities, who are also encouraged to advise the donor agency of problems even after the project is terminated. The donor agency is in turn responsible for advising the recipient government at the local and national levels of these problems.

After Human Rights Council of Australia, 2001.

---

reduction (OHCHR, 2002), which the World Bank and the UN collaborated on. UNDP and OHCHR have also developed a simple checklist for programme staff (UNDP/OHCHR, 2003). Furthermore, the Human Rights Council of Australia (2001) has put together a manual that, although geared towards government-to-government assistance, has been a source of inspiration to NGOs developing a rights-based approach.

In addition, NORAD (2001) has developed a handbook in 'human rights assessment'. The handbook assists practitioners in asking the relevant questions concerning human rights, implementing and monitoring them. It is particularly suitable when trying to apply a human rights *perspective* to a project. It includes a simple scoring tool for assessing how a programme affects human rights, people's *awareness* about their rights, and whether or not it *empowers* people to claim their rights. A simplified version appears in Box 6.10. The scores used in the checklist are suggestive only. Their main function is to rouse attention and awareness to trends and tendencies as regards human rights impact.

The scores represent a non-metric ordinal scale with increasing orders, but with no exact ranking. Human rights enhancement often requires institutional reform, or a change of attitudes, traditions or customs. Therefore, measuring human rights advancement often implies that economic, social, cultural and political processes are being reviewed. In some cases this may require follow-up research, additional information gathering, and/or targeted studies.

Box 6.10 Human Rights Impact Analysis Tool		
Human rights issue	**Score**	**Follow up**
AWARENESS		
1. What is the programme's assumed/actual impact on equality and non-discrimination?		
2. Has the population directly affected been informed about the programme?		
3. Does the programme respect/has it respected everyone's right to seek, and impart information relevant to its implementation?		
EMPOWERMENT		
4. Does the programme respect/has it respected the right to express views freely in the preparation and implementation?		
5. Does the programme promote/has the programme promoted participation in decision-making of groups affected?		
6. Does the programme uphold/has the programme upheld the right to organize?		
7. Does the programme respect/has it respected the right to just and favourable conditions of work?		
8. Does the programme affect/has it affected the fulfilment of the right to an adequate standard of living for target groups and other people affected?		
9. Does the programme affect/has it affected the opportunity of people for self provision in terms of income generating activities?		
10. Does the programme address the right to compensation for those negatively affected?		

Legend for scoring:
PI—Positive Impact   **NC**—No Change   **NI**—Negative Impact   **NA**— No Information Available

After NORAD, 2001.

6.1.3 Challenges of Implementing a Rights-based Approach

There are considerable challenges to effectively implementing a rights-based approach to development. (*i*) *The first set of challenges* relate to the inadequacy of state legal apparatuses, inconsistencies between law and practice, and poor awareness of human rights among state actors and citizens:

- Although a majority of States have ratified the human rights treaties, many States have not codified the treaties into the domestic legal framework, which may contain laws that are contradictory to human rights;
- Even when there is a formal coherence between domestic law and international human rights law, the policies and practices in a country may be applied in ways that are contrary to human rights principles;
- Many poor countries often suffer from under-developed legal and judicial systems that debilitate the rule of law;
- Citizens may be unaware of their rights, which makes it impossible for them to claim them; and
- Poor people are often deterred from approaching the formal legal system by the cost of engaging a lawyer, the opportunity cost of time spent in court, and the general education and level of skills necessary to engage in litigation.

To address these challenges, a rights-based development effort needs to undertake *advocacy* and be prepared to provide technical assistance to ensure that a state's formal laws comply with the human rights regime. As discussed in the previous section, building the capacity of the justice and law sector and raising awareness of human rights among duty-bearers and rights-holders are of central importance. An effective rights-based approach would thus include initiatives ranging from promoting the inclusion of civic education in national curricula, to providing targeted human rights training and supporting a free, independent and pluralistic media sector. Most organizations cannot tackle all these issues, but the composite development effort can make headway in these areas.

(*ii*) *A second set of challenges* concern the cadre of development workers:

- The international development community has inadequate knowledge of the human rights regime; and
- There is comparatively little experience of applying rights-based approaches and insufficient practical guidance available.

The fact that the majority of development practitioners have, at best, limited knowledge of the human rights and associated instruments[15] requires a systematic educational effort within the development community (United Nations, 2003). A rights-based approach to development is, however, still at a pioneering stage, which means that *practical guidelines will need to be elaborated* in step with the development, application and experience of the approach. In this respect, sharing and documenting lessons learnt will be very valuable. To enhance its human rights proficiency at both the conceptual and practical levels, some organizations may adopt a strategy of introducing and developing a rights perspective in the short term while gearing up for a full-fledged rights-based approach.

(*iii*) *A third set of challenges* points to the limitations of the international human rights framework. Compliance with international law primarily relies on a state's own legal system, courts and other official

---

[15] Among the exceptions are those NGOs who have conceived of development as a popular movement for social justice and thereby concur with the political philosophy of human rights.

bodies. When the legal system in a country is under-developed with regard to human rights and/or the governing regime violates the rights of its citizens, the international human rights system can play a role.[16] However,

- The international system for responding to violations of human rights is often accused of being ambiguous and sluggish and can be undermined by political agendas of UN member states; and
- There is no independent international judiciary to assist in enforcing human rights in member states.

The human rights framework may have shortcomings, but it is the best system created so far.[17] In any case, using an internationally recognized legal regime as a basis for development cooperation is preferable to development efforts taking place without a legal foundation. Furthermore, it is not a static regime, but can and has developed in line with changes in international relations and the demands of international civil society. A high proportion of the most significant initiatives to draft new international instruments and to establish new procedures and machinery have come about as a result of concerted NGO campaigns designed to mobilize public opinion and lobby government support (Steiner and Alston, 2000: 940). This suggests that the application of a *rights-based approach to poverty reduction* can potentially lead to an organic development of the international rights regime so that it better serves the world's poor and the development community that aims to assist it. As Philip Allott holds, there is cause for optimism:

1. The idea of human rights having been thought, it cannot be un-thought. It will not be replaced, unless by some idea which contains and surpasses it.
2. There are tenacious individuals and non-statal organisations whose activity on behalf of human rights is not part of international relations but is part of a new process of international reality forming (Allott, 1990: 703).

6.1.4 Human Rights, Freedom and Poverty Reduction

The cost of providing shelter, education, health care and social services to the world's poor has been estimated at US$ 4.5 billion per annum. It is a massive sum, but roughly the same figure that the world spends on arms in just two weeks. The obscenity denies one-fifth of the world's population their fundamental right to survive and live in human dignity (Häusermann, 1992).

International development cooperation has not been able to reach the results aimed for. The persistence of deprivation and lack of very basic needs among the majority of the world's people has led to an

---

[16] The Americas, Europe and Africa each have regional arrangements for addressing human rights. The European and Inter-American systems, in particular, have innovative institutions and processes. See the relevant documents in *Basic Documents on Human Rights* edited by I. Brownlie (2002).

[17] In a similar vein, *democracy* is considered the best system of government we have managed to create, yet it is not without its problems.

increased questioning of development policies and practices. There has been a growing recognition in the post-Cold War era that development and prosperity are closely linked with non-economic concerns that are considered to belong to the social and political realm. Amartya Sen has, for instance, shown that famine has never afflicted any country that is independent, goes to elections regularly, that has opposition parties to voice criticisms, and that has a free and independent media (Sen, 1999). Poverty has thus come to be redefined as going beyond the lack of material resources and including lack of power and choice. In the same vein, as argued by Sen, the quality of life and well-being should be measured not by people's wealth, but by their freedom. Freedom, or human rights, is both the primary aim as well as the principal means of development (ibid.). Without the effective realization of human rights, it is hard to foresee any sustainable development.

As both a strategy and a tool, a rights-based approach to development is in a much better position to ensure that development efforts address the broad concepts of poverty and poverty reduction—lack of material resources, power, influence, choice and freedom. Moreover, it provides the poor with an internationally recognized legal basis for their free, active and meaningful participation in the development process. Furthermore, rights-based development assistance has a considerably larger scope for preventing violent conflict, a phenomenon that has contributed to both deepening and widening poverty in several parts of the world.

The way human rights are being bandied about in the development rhetoric today can pose a threat to the approach. It is not uncommon to find donor agencies today claiming that all development assistance contributes to social and economic rights. Misuse of this kind contributes to watering down the human rights concepts, leaving us with little more than a buzzword. As a consequence, the key elements that make the approach fundamentally different from the service-based approaches that have dominated development assistance for several decades need to be steadfastly safeguarded by the proponents of rights-based approaches.

The full implications of a global rights-based approach to development in the world order would be nothing short of a paradigm shift in the effort to reduce poverty. The consequences would, however, not be limited to countries of the South and the development community. Equality, participation, rule of law and accountability have implications for the relationship between the rich and poor countries. Both parts would be placed on an equal footing and be judged on how they realize or violate human rights. In our globalized world, corporations, civil society organizations, and the multilateral system would be expected to play their part in pursuing the realization of human rights in line with equality, participation, rule of law and accountability. Poverty alleviation is not only a question of combating the deprivation of material needs, but as much a question of poor people's deprived rights and freedoms.

6.2   Poverty Reduction—Evolving Agenda and Poverty Analysis

6.2.1 Evolving Approaches—Rights-based, Millennium Goals and PRSPs

The last decades have witnessed an international consensus on the fact that poverty reduction is the overarching goal for international development cooperation. International banks, multilateral and bilateral aid agencies, and NGOs unanimously agree on the objective, though they differ substantially in approach. And networks for the dissemination of poverty research information have appeared (CROP recurrent). Fundamental processes of change have taken place over the last decades as a result of globalization and technological advances. This, together with new insights from experience with different types of development cooperation, have continuously prompted a reassessment of and adjustment to poverty reduction strategies.

In the 1980s, the NGO community and UNICEF laid the foundation for the re-emergence of poverty reduction as the primary objective, insisting that economic management must have a 'human face'. Bilateral development agencies increased the poverty focus of their bilateral cooperation programmes and used their influence in multilateral organizations to press for greater attention to poverty reduction. At the start of the 1990s the World Bank reinvigorated its poverty focus, returning to some of the themes which had characterized World Bank strategy in the 1970s, e.g., 'redistribution with growth' and 'basic needs'. The resulting three-tiered strategy—discussed in the development community under the name of *The New Poverty Agenda* (Lipton and Maxwell, 1992)—focused on:

- The promotion of economic opportunities for the poor;
- Investment in human capital;
- Provision of safety nets to protect livelihoods.

The contribution of the UN system has been no less significant for the promotion of national poverty reduction strategies (Grinspun, 2001), recognizing explicitly that the formulation of poverty reduction is indeed a political undertaking.

Both agencies, the World Bank Group and the United Nations, continue to play a dominant role in the poverty reduction discourse as the following sections will show. Few poverty reduction strategies represent strictly one perspective—the economic, the social or the political. But 'structure' and 'agency or actors' are differently weighted.

It is useful to be reminded that much of today's 'poverty reduction' discourse has precedents in 'development' and 'well-being' discourse. The interest is not new either. It drove the 'pioneers' of political economy—Marx, Smith, Ricardo, Malthus and Mill—a list to which Sumner adds 'the likes of Arthur Lewis and contemporary economists who have focused primarily on poverty and well-being such as Paul Streeten, Amartya Sen, Martin Ravallion and Ravi Kanbur, to name but a few'. In a brief historical overview from the 1950s till today, Sumner convincingly argues that the meaning and measurement of poverty and well-being is closely entwined with the evolution of development economics and its relationship with (or within) development studies (Sumner, 2004). It is not least the tension between economics' tendency to dominate the discourse versus the non-economic aspects of social phenomena and multidisciplinarity that has shaped the meaning and measurement, according to Sumner. The most important characteristics of poverty and well-being and how they are measured are characterized as follows:

> Over the last 50 years, the debate on this subject has moved from well-being as economically deter-mined to broader conceptualizations of poverty, from considering the 'means' of well-being to analysing the 'ends', from identifying 'needs' to identifying 'rights', from no or few indicators to many, and from (at best) an afterthought to a central focus of the development discourse. In each decade since the Second World War, the dominant meaning and measurement of well-being have been shaped by the prevailing context and practice of development (ibid.: 3).

Evolution of the Dominant Meaning and Measurement of Well-being, 1950s–2000s

Period	Meaning of well-being	Measurement of well-being
1950s	Economic well-being	GDP growth
1960s	Economic well-being	GDP per capita growth
1970s	Basic needs	GDP per capita growth + basic goods
1980s	Economic well-being	GDP per capita but rise of non-monetary factors
1990s	Human development/capabilities	Human development and sustainability
2000s	Universal rights, livelihoods, freedom	The MDGs and 'new' areas: risk and empowerment

After Sumner, 2004: 3.

The struggle between economic well-being and non-economic well-being has manifested itself in different ways throughout, for example, in the 1990s between universal measures of poverty and those measurements which sought to capture the local experiences of well-being. Without going through the phases chronologically, for which Sumner's analysis is recommended, reflections on particular aspects of the poverty/well-being discourse and measures follow.

Poverty, Power and Politics—Political Space and the Rights-based Approach

Political Space

Conceptually, one crucial aspect of poverty has to do with structural inequalities and the power struggles these give rise to. In many situations particular groups of people are politically excluded and economically exploited by others who are seeking to maintain a relation of dependence. Such relations range from those within the household through to inter-sectoral relations involving substantial populations. Examples range from gender relations or those between landowner and sharecropper to the impersonal relations based upon prices between urban consumers and rural producers. These are relational dimensions of poverty, concerned with the processes by which poverty emerges, says Webster and Engberg-Pedersen (2002) in their introduction to the Political Space approach to the analysis of poverty. Poverty is manifested in a lack of resources and opportunities compared to others, reflecting a condition of *relative deprivation*. Here, poverty is seen as the comparative lack of a good livelihood, assets, information and knowledge, rights, and so forth (see also Section 7.4.3). In situations where deprivation involves a lack of the necessities required to maintain a basic standard of living, one approaches the condition of *absolute poverty*. Society's role in setting standards and expectations and *context* remain central issues in the discussion of poverty.

The other side of the political space approach emphasizes marginalized people as social actors seeking to cope with their conditions and develop strategies to exploit emergent opportunities. Vulnerable and excluded people tend not to be passive victims of an unjust world. Their action and strategies provide a rich source of material for understanding poverty and for working towards poverty reduction. The failure to recognize the importance of these activities and the motivations and constraints faced by the poor are central reasons as to why poverty reduction policies and programmes are often of little use or serve simply to reinforce the problems of poverty (ibid.: 4–5). Methodologically there is no excuse, since 'developments in qualitative methodologies enable us to identify and research poverty dynamics and dimensions that sustain marginalisation and exclusion in ways previously unknown or ignored' (ibid.: 2), which has facilitated a major reassessment of existing and alternative approaches towards poverty reduction (Baulch, 1996; Chambers, 1995).

The authors of the political space approach are careful to add that to place emphasis upon the *agency* (and structural relations of power) of the deprived does not have to imply that, given the opportunity, they can pull themselves up by their own bootstraps and overcome impoverishments. Indeed, the focus of the empirical studies they have collected is on the central role of *local organizations*. The political space approach also shares complementary features with the rights-based approach.

Rights-based Approach

In the *Rights-based Approach, RBA* to development and poverty reduction, which was the topic of Section 6.1, a key objective in development work is to enhance the freedom of choice of poor women and men by supporting their empowerment; an objective which can only be accomplished through the active participation and representation of poor people in processes of political, social and economic change. A rights-based approach puts the inclusion of deprived, excluded and marginalized groups on the development agenda, and asserts that governments and other 'duty-bearers' are accountable to the people with regard to commitments to development goals. It indicates that a broad-based democratic system is needed to fulfil human rights and promote opportunities for poor people to participate—directly or indirectly—in decisions that concern their lives.

Development of effective poverty reduction strategies and interventions requires a good understanding of existing power structures, including gender-based power structures, and involves identification of the primary stakeholders, poor women and men, and ways to support their empowerment and active participation. That means that both the agency of the poor and their representatives, and the political dimensions of development are emphasized.

The democratic and human rights approach to development and poverty reduction thinking, strongly inspired by Sen (1984, 1999), has gained momentum over the last decade in multilateral organizations (e.g., UNICEF), bilateral organizations (e.g., DFID, Sida) and in NGOs (e.g., CARE, DanChurchAid). The fact that the approach rests on the international and regional conventions on human rights (see Section 6.1), which form a common value reference point in the dialogue with partner countries and agencies, adds to its strength. Adherence to the international conventions reinforces the legitimacy of supporting poor people in their demands for a better life, and provides a foundation for agencies to address these issues (see Sida, 2002). The human rights frameworks provide a normative base for poverty reduction, while democracy organizes political and social life to this end. However, the rights-based approach also demands a thorough understanding of the relationship between poverty reduction, democracy and fulfilment of human rights, which is not easy to establish and measure. These, and the claim that the *process* is as important, if not more, than the results and outcome of the rights-based approach, may be reasons why competing strategies—some would say complementary strategies—emphasizing macro-economic policies, measurable results and monitoring by use of indicators, prevail.

Millennium Development Goals and Poverty Reduction Strategies

At the turn of the century, international conventions and declarations increasingly set the parameters for the poverty reduction agenda. Along with the *human rights conventions* (see Section 6.1) backing the rights-based approach to development and poverty reduction, the *Millennium Development Goals* and the *Poverty Reduction Strategies* set the international agenda for poverty reduction strategies. And as a guide to operationalization, the *OECD/DAC Guidelines for Poverty Reduction* (2001) provide a common platform for understanding and cooperation for all the signatories. The common guiding principles are the *promotion of holistic development, national ownership, country-led partnership* and *policy coherence.*

In 2001, the international commitment to reduce poverty resulted in the adoption of the Millennium Goals as the road map for the implementation of the UN Millennium Declaration. The first of the eight **Millennium Development Goals (MDGs)** is to halve the share of the world's population living in extreme poverty and hunger between 1990 and 2015 (see Box 6.11). The other seven goals and the 18 targets associated with the millennium goals aim towards poverty reduction in various ways.

In parallel with the process initially led by the UN of formulating the MDGs, the World Bank and International Monetary Fund (IMF) have taken the lead on a new approach to cooperation for poverty reduction. **Poverty Reduction Strategy Papers (PRSPs),** to be prepared by lending countries, are at the heart of the anti-poverty framework announced in 1999. They are intended to ensure that debt relief provided under the enhanced Highly Indebted Poor Countries (HIPC) Initiative and loans from the international finance institutions help reduce poverty in the poorest and most indebted countries in the South. Approximately 70 heavily indebted countries are expected to prepare Poverty Reduction Strategy Papers, initially for a three-year period. A number have already done so or are in the process of preparing an Interim PRSP.

Box 6.11   The Millennium Development Goals, MDGs

1. Eradicate extreme poverty and hunger[18]
   - halve the proportion of people living in extreme poverty on less than $1 a day between 1990 and 2015
   - halve the proportion of people who suffer from hunger between 1990 and 2015
2. Achieve universal primary education
3. Promote gender equality and empower women
4. Reduce child mortality
5. Improve maternal health
6. Combat HIV/Aids, malaria and other diseases
7. Ensure environmental sustainability
8. Build a global partnership for development

After UNDP/HDR, 2003.

The focus of the PRSPs, according to the World Bank, is on

identifying in a *participatory* manner the poverty reduction outcomes a country wishes to achieve and the key public actions—*policy changes, institutional reforms, programs, and projects* ... which are needed to achieve the desired outcomes (www.worldbank.org/poverty/strategies) (emphasis added).

There are **five core principles** underlying the development and implementation of poverty reduction strategies. The intention is that the strategies should be:

- **Country-driven:** with governments leading the process and broad-based participation by civil society and the private sector in all operational steps;
- **Results-oriented:** focusing on outcomes that would benefit the poor;
- **Comprehensive:** taking account of the multidimensional nature of poverty;
- **Long-term in approach:** recognizing the depth and complexity of some of the changes needed;
- **Based on partnership:** involving coordinated participation between governments and other actors in civil society, the private sector and the donor community.

There are several new features of the PRSP approach. Countries are, for example, being asked to draw on inputs from all sections of society—a practice which was already common in some countries much earlier, e.g., in Uganda (ACPDT, 1995), but is now being promoted globally. Participation is a key feature of the PRSP process, but *on request* from the external partners.[19]

---

[18] Each of the eight goals has targets attached. Only targets for goal number one are included in the box.

[19] A comparative study of the participatory aspects of the policy-making process that led to the formulation of Malawi and Zambia PRSPs by Arne Tostensen et al. showed that civil society organizations played an active role in both countries. Robb's analysis of a cross-section of countries gives a more mixed picture of the level of participation.

Participation can happen at the various stages in the Poverty Reduction Strategy Process (see Section 3.2.3). It can range from simple information sharing to more extensive consultations and joint decision making, to situations where the relevant stakeholders take on responsibility for monitoring the process and evaluating its success (see Section 2.1.4). It must be acknowledged that all stakeholders cannot participate at all times, but room must be made to make policy processes more responsive to the needs of poor people. The PRSP Sourcebook, Chapter 7 (World Bank, 2002), provides substantial guidance on the participatory process.

Millennium Development Goals and Poverty Reduction Strategy Linkages

The Millennium Development Goals and the concept of Poverty Reduction Strategy Papers have had an unprecedented influence on international development cooperation and the overarching poverty reduction agenda. But which of the two processes is dominant? And what are the linkages or possible linkages? These questions are subject to many studies (e.g. COWI, April 2004).

The Millennium Development Goals and the Poverty Reduction Strategy Processes are results of two different processes, initially led by the UN and the World Bank/IMF respectively. Today, the World Bank/IMF have taken upon themselves to monitor the progress towards the Millennium Goals and to discuss the PRSP concept in view of the MDGs, while the UN recognizes the importance of the PRSPs in reaching the MDGs at the country level and invites to a two-way process of information sharing. Many development agencies and their partner agencies ask whether the two processes should and could be better linked to ensure coordination to reduce transaction costs at the country level. However, before doing so it is important to recognize the key difference between the MDG and PRSP concepts. They are not easy to reconcile in all aspects. Briefly stated, the MDGs are global goals that are handed down to the national level from the international level. Contrary to this, the PRSP process takes national ownership, the national policy process, and the national context as its starting point, however much the process may still be facilitated from outside. And the time-perspective varies considerably between a few years for the PRSP and the longer-term 2015 goals of the MDGs. For development agencies to align both the MDGs and the PRSPs and reduce national transaction costs a suggestion has been made to actively promote a closer institutional linkage between the processes, though the modalities have still to be worked out.

Benefits, Risks and Limitations

The new approach embedded in the PRSPs is in many respects a triumph for those NGOs and others who have campaigned for debt relief. It offers an unprecedented opportunity for development efforts to refocus on poverty reduction, and for civil society organizations to influence anti-poverty policy. But it also raises many critical questions as pointed out by McGee (2000), not least:

- Will it be seen by poor countries as yet another imposition from abroad—just the latest form of aid conditionality to be accommodated?
- How to ensure that the rushed timetable and conflicting interests do not undermine the proposed participatory approach.

- How to avoid excessive emphasis on the Paper, as opposed to the underlying Strategy—which is, after all, the point of the exercise.

There are many who doubt whether the good intensions enshrined in the PRSP principles can be achieved in practice, especially given the tight time-frame. One thing is clear, however: If the PRSP approach is to succeed in its ambitious objectives, building effective participation into the process will be essential. But participatory initiatives often suffer from weaknesses that can jeopardize the process and reduce their impact, and IDS (2000) and World Bank (2001) point to the following problems which may affect the participatory process envisioned for the preparation of the PRSPs:

- **Unrealistic or un-stated expectations**—which can create frustration and cynicism among participants;
- **Insufficient time** allowed for proper participation or consultation;
- **Inadequate dissemination** of information, or providing it in an inaccessible style or language;
- **Representation**—lack of transparency over the criteria for selecting participants, and failure to represent the poorest, most marginalized groups;
- **Lack of follow-up and feedback**—and failure to follow the process through to its conclusions.

The World Bank has been suspected of holding the minimal view of what participation means:

As long as people are allowed to speak … about their hardships, this is considered participation in the eyes of the Bank … what the Bank has yet to figure out is that genuine participation is a deeply political process of representation and negotiation (The Bangkok-based NGO Focus on the Global South, quoted in PANOS 2002).

To date, participatory processes in developing countries have tended to take place at the micro-economic or project level, and have become increasingly innovative as methods become more established and sophisticated. However, to achieve participatory outcomes at the macro-economic level, it is necessary to use participatory approaches at both the micro-economic and macro-economic levels in a complementary manner for maximum effect. Methodologies are being developed, e.g., for participatory budget analysis (see Section 3.3.1), but linking macro and micro level analysis has proved to cause considerable headaches.

Despite many critical questions, the new approach offers an unprecedented opportunity for development efforts to address poverty reduction in its many dimensions. However, nothing can substitute the political will of those in power to combat poverty. Expedient approaches can be decisive, but can never be the technical fix that eliminates poverty. There is a risk that advice on tools and procedures and developing 'Papers' substitutes for the *implementation* of the strategies for poverty reduction. Considerable advocacy work goes into supporting poverty reduction strategies effectively. However, not many agencies are well prepared to engage in advocacy. The international development community, with the UN at the lead, has launched a campaign to spread knowledge and awareness about the intentions of the Millennium Development Goals. It remains to be seen if effective advocacy approaches will be included.

In the meantime, the greatest challenges remain in terms of stronger advocacy for fair and equal relations and opportunities and in translating the good intentions of the current PRSP approach into substantive poverty reduction strategies and outcomes. Challenges *do* also relate to the concept, the measurement and analysis of poverty, and its antecedent prosperity and well-being.[20] To do successful advocacy work and undertake successful interventions, development agencies, groups and individuals need awareness and some knowledge about how poverty analysis can be undertaken. Considerable advances have been made in developing analytical tools over the last decade, the gist of which should be captured in the following and other sections in this book (e.g., Sections 3.1.3, 5.1.3, and 7.4.3, 7.4.4 and 7.4.5).

6.2.2 Poverty Measures and Analysis

Poverty Manifestations and Poverty Analysis

Poverty manifests itself in many different ways: hunger, ill health and premature death, ignorance, vulnerability, discrimination and insecurity, denial of dignity, and other expressions of deprivation. Poverty varies between places, over time and in depth. To use development cooperation to combat poverty therefore requires well-grounded poverty analyses. These should be sensitive to the particular context and rest on an understanding of the basic characteristics of poverty:

- *Poverty is complex:* It comprises a wide range of aspects and situations that together constitute the livelihood of poor people—men, women and children.
- *Poverty is context specific:* The features of poverty are derived from the particular environmental, socio-cultural, economic and political characteristics of the situation in a given area.
- *Poverty is relative:* Deprivation is defined by those concerned in relation to their notions of what is judged to be a decent life in terms of economic resources, security, adequate health and education, opportunities to participate in social life and fulfil important cultural functions, etc.
- *Poverty is dynamic:* The manifestations of deprivation will change over time. Individuals and groups may move in and out of poverty depending on the local situation as well as on external forces, e.g., natural or human disasters, economic crises and armed conflict.

Analysing poverty is essential for decision-making, for public debate, for planners—and not least for those for whom a specific intervention is designed. Over the last decade livelihoods and poverty analysis has increasingly included 'voices of the poor' (ACPDT, 1995; Adesida and Oteh, 2004; Epstein et al., 1998; Narayan et al., 2000 and 2002). This has contributed to a significant shift in the interpretation away from a mainly materialistic to a multi-faceted interpretation of poverty. The inclusion of perspectives

---

[20] Carol Graham has set her research 'political sustainability of market-oriented growth in countries where markets are newly emerging' in the context of *Happiness* and *Hardship* (2002).

on poverty of poor people themselves has been scaled up in the proposed participatory approach of the Poverty Reduction Strategies as discussed above.

There is no blueprint for how poverty analysis should be undertaken and the subsequent strategy formulated. Nevertheless, there are some established *practices, perspectives* and *methods* to consider:

1. *Poverty mapping and diagnostics* should map the *causes* and *dynamics* of poverty and not just describe the symptoms (Minot and Baulch, 2003). Geographical poverty mapping for identification of poverty 'pockets' and vulnerable areas may be included, e.g., based on GIS (see Section 6.4).

2. *Macro, meso and micro level analysis*, which will normally require that both *qualitative and quantitative methods* are applied.

3. *A plurality of perspectives.* In some cases differences in *access* to material or productive resources is important. In other contexts relevant perspectives include *regional* or ethnic divisions or *ideological* perspectives, based on religious and political identities. Differences coupled with *age* and *gender* are important.

4. *Consulting the poor about poverty* (see Box 6.12) considering the ethical dimensions involved (see Chapter 8).

5. *Methods recognizing the multidimensional nature of poverty.* For example, (*i*) the assets-vulnerability framework of the Sustainable Livelihoods Analysis (DFID, 1999); identifies strategic assets for people's livelihoods; focuses on people's capabilities and not only on problems and obstacles. (*ii*) Participatory Poverty Assessments, PPAs (Norton et al., 2001) capture dimensions of poverty such as vulnerability, risk and seasonality, and intra-household differences based on age and gender; includes analysis of *access* to common public goods and to dimensions of *social capital* (see Section 6.4) such as inter-household linkages based on kinship and ethnicity and poor people's coping strategies.

6. *Specific Critical Aspects* can relate mainly to structure or agency or blends of these:

   (*i*) *Structural aspects:* social, political and economic structures in a given context, institutional aspects, sustainability, cost effectiveness and implementation capacity, relations between poverty and armed conflict.

   (*ii*) *Agency aspects:* Factors, e.g., power relations prompting exclusion and creating inequality relating to gender, age and disabilities, gender norms and stereotypes, ethnic affiliation and cultural distinctiveness, stigmatizing conditions, e.g., HIV/AIDS.

7. *Basis for action.* Poverty analysis provides entry points and opportunities for effective development interventions grounded in people's own realities and efforts. The poor themselves, striving day-by-day towards a better and fuller life and coping with atrocities, are the main actors in poverty reduction. Which interventions support their empowerment?

Poverty Analysis for Pro-poor Interventions

Some critical aspects in poverty analysis for development interventions particularly concern the complexity of poverty. Poverty analysis is done at different levels and relates to different processes. In the

Box 6.12   Consulting the Poor about Poverty: Summary Checklist

The following fundamental tasks need to be addressed in designing a Participatory Poverty Assessment, PPA, process:

- Identifying the central institutional location for the PPA (seeking commitment, access to policy information, and influence)
- Finding technical assistance (seeking experience, flexibility, capacity to deal with different areas and functions—training, analysis, and so on)
- Identifying implementation partners for different functions (financing, policy influence, design and analysis, training, dissemination, logistics, field management, and so on)
- Agreeing on objectives and research agenda (seeking shared commitment among key partners, clarity, manageable scope)
- Identifying members for field teams (according to agreed-on criteria, which may include openness to change in values/attitudes, flexible availability for follow-up, expertise and experience, understanding of and access to policy debates, area/linguistic/cultural familiarity)
- Identifying sources of financial support (seeking flexibility, long-term commitment)
- Selecting field research sites and participants—geared to represent the social and livelihood conditions in poor communities in the country/state/province (seeking credibility for results, a manageable scale for field work, appropriate dis-aggregation to investigate causal links, enhanced value for policy analysis)
- Developing an integrated methodology for field research, synthesis of findings and policy analysis using results (seeking an appropriate balance between standardization and flexibility for the goals of the PPA; a guiding conceptual approach; methods that allow for comparison, aggregation, and synthesis of diverse materials)
- An implementation plan for field work (which allows space for reflection, sharing of experiences, recording, reporting, and analysis)

The following are key lessons from the experience and practice of PPAs:

- Gear the timing of the design process to building ownership and commitment in key partners
- Set clear objectives and establish a flexible structure for support
- Work with key stakeholders to establish the thematic focus for the PPA
- Establish space for a process with integrity at the community level—respect, follow-up and feedback for participants

Finally, the following potential pitfalls should be borne in mind during consultations with the poor:

- When facilitated by outsiders, participatory approaches can raise expectations of local people for future involvement
- The outcome depends on the attitude and vision of the persons facilitating the process
- If carried out too quickly, consultations can lead to incorrect conclusions
- The choice and sequence of methods needs to be adapted to fit each situation
- In most cases, consultation with the poor will not lead to quantifiable results

After Norton et al., 2001: 31 and World Bank, 2002: 546.

context of programmes and projects, factors such as sustainability, cost-effectiveness and implementing capacity are critical. In sector work, institutional aspects may come to the fore (Sida, 2002). The dynamics of the social, political and economic structures in each specific context need to be understood. To understand the processes that can lead a country into or out of poverty, it is also important to consider aspects such as ethnicity, gender, age and disability.

Causes and expressions of poverty, as well as strategies to overcome poverty, may vary between women and men. It is therefore important to include the perspectives of women as well as those of men in a poverty analysis. Gender inequalities usually have roots far removed from the immediate life situations of poor people and beyond their control. Therefore, measures directly targeting poor women and/or men are not enough. Measures that affect both direct and indirect gender-poverty linkages are required. This includes supporting gender equality in political participation, representation and decision-making (Sida, 2002: 43).

The issues to be covered in poverty analysis vary and depend on the size and complexity of the proposed intervention and support. Poverty analysis is undertaken prior to an intervention to justify the likely impact on poverty reduction and thus to guide decisions.[21] There are many types of interventions to combat poverty. Based on OECD/DAC (2001) suggestions, three major types of interventions have been identified:

- Support to general structural changes—e.g., for a strong public sector reform agenda and budget support to counter inequalities and support growth. The focus of the analysis is on issues such as: What is the potential for pro-poor development? What are the bottlenecks or obstacles to achieving this?
- Indirect or inclusive actions for broad groups of people focusing on sectors of special importance to the poor, e.g., basic education or small-scale enterprise. Poverty analysis both for these and programmes that are not directly pro-poor need to address gender-biases in the poverty analysis.
- Interventions directly and predominantly focusing on poor people, e.g., targeted community based organizations among the poor. Issues of relevance and efficiency come into focus. Poor people live in social contexts with power relations, gender discrimination and resources that could be increased or lost through outside interventions.

For a comprehensive country strategy programme, combinations of the three types will most often be relevant, even when emphasis is placed more on one category than another (Rasmussen et al., 2001). Exact guidelines cannot be given on the extent to which issues and interrelated issues like gender relations and equality, environmental sustainability, children's rights, etc., need to be covered. A choice must be made case-by-case in consultation with the partners involved. The choice will also include which analytical

---

[21] Due to the complex interconnections between poverty and other factors, it is not always easy to establish the causal relationships. Thus, it is for example easier to document that environmental problems contribute to increased poverty than the reverse (see Sørbø et al., 2002).

approach to use or combine, i.e., the income/consumption and/or the participatory approach, or combinations of these (Box 6.13).

Box 6.13 Methodology of Two Analytical Approaches to the Study of Poverty/Well-being		
Methodology	**Income/consumption approach**	**Participatory approach**
1. *Determination of well-being*	External a priori determination by third party	Internal/external—interactive group determination. Time and context specific
2. *Measurement of well-being*	Quantitative: Income/consumption expenditure levels	Qualitative/quantitative: Multiple criteria
3. *Sources of Data*	Questionnaire survey	Participatory Poverty Assessment
4. *Objectives*	Description	Critical Understanding/Empowerment

Within each of the two analytical approaches, a lot has been done to develop appropriate methodologies. Concrete studies have contributed to elaborating the two approaches and the linkages between them (Pendley et al., 2002). In both approaches *indicators* are central.

6.2.3 Indicators of Poverty and Prosperity—Monitoring and Evaluation

From the historical studies of meaning and measurement of poverty and well-being undertaken by Sumner (2004), three clusters of indicators can be identified and categorized: (*i*) those that measure poverty as primarily economic well-being; (*ii*) those that measure poverty as primarily non-economic well-being; and (*iii*) those that measure poverty as composites (see also Section 5.1.3). There is little disagreement on the characteristics of a 'good' indicator, regardless of whether it belongs in any of the three categories, says Sumner:

> The measure should have an underlying conceptualisation of well-being (we know human beings need food for example), be policy-relevant (i.e., meaningful to policy-makers), a direct and unambiguous measure of progress, specific to the phenomena, valid, reliable, consistent, measurable, user friendly, not easily manipulated, cost effective and up-to-date .... Fine in theory, but what commonly used poverty indicators could jump through all these hoops? (Sumner, 2004: 2).

Choice of indicators may simply be dictated by what is in existence (ibid.: 3).

The income/consumption approach to poverty analysis relies on quantitative measures. For the average development practitioner, indicators captured in the Human Development Index, HDI, and in the measures of Human and Income Poverty, captured in the Human Poverty Index, HPI, are a good starting point when national level information and comparisons are required (UNDP/HDR, 2003, Tables 2 and 3). While the HDI measures average achievement, the HPI measures *deprivations* in the three basic dimensions of human development captured in the HDI:

- *A long and healthy life*—vulnerability to death at a relatively early age, as measured by the probability at birth of not surviving to age 40.
- *Knowledge*—exclusion from the world of reading and communications, as measured by the adult illiteracy rate.
- *A decent standard of living*—lack of access to overall economic provisioning, as measured by the unweighted average of two indicators, the percentage of the population without sustainable access to an improved water source, and the percentage of children underweight for age.

Originally the measure of deprivation in a decent standard of living also included an indicator of access to health services. But because up-to-date reliable data on access to health services are lacking in many countries, this indicator was left out in the 2003 Human Poverty Index and deprivation in a decent standard of living was measured on the two indicators: percentage of the population without sustainable access to an improved water source and the percentage of children under weight for age (ibid.: 342).

It is worth noting that how poverty and well-being are measured depend on what indicators are available. But it also depends on the definition accepted. To quote Sumner:

If poverty is defined as basic needs or material standard of living, then economic or money-metric measures might seem more appropriate. However, if poverty is defined as capabilities or rights, then non-economic or non money-metric measures would seem more insightful. One implication of accepting a multi-faceted definition of well-being is that it is quite feasible for a person to be poor in one aspect but non-poor in another—i.e., the concept of 'poor' is actually fragmented—thus having a very strong post-modernity resonance regarding the loss of meaning in long held concepts (Sumner, 2004: 7).

Economic or money-metric indicators have continued to dominate poverty and well-being measures. The three large groups are (*i*) income per capita; (*ii*) those utilizing the income-poverty line; and (*iii*) those assessing income inequality. Why are economic measures so popular (with policy makers in particular), asks Sumner. It is because they are useful when quick, rough-and-ready, short run, aggregate inferences are required to make an assessment. They are more responsive, changing much faster than non-economic social data. They are likely to be more readily available than non-economic measures. However, there are also disadvantages, such as omissions of non-market activity, of unrecorded informal sector work, of subsistence activity, environmental degradation, etc. Second, they are static measures and do not capture the dynamics of poverty—that households may move in and out of poverty over the course of a given period. And finally, the measures take limited account of differential experience (e.g., intra-household, as they are typically based on the household head). Using poverty estimates based on a *poverty line*—e.g., population living on one dollar a day—is also risky, since there are different ways to define and construct a poverty line. With these and several other limitations of economic indicators, are there then comparative advantages of measuring poverty and well-being in non-economic terms? Yes, says Sumner, non-economic measures of well-being, e.g., empowerment and participation indicators, are more useful when a medium or longer-run assessment is required, because they address more directly the *ends* or outcomes of policy (being educated and healthy) rather than the inputs or *means* (greater income). Although they are slower and more expensive to collect, often requiring their own tailored surveys and/or combined methods, they have the additional benefit of being amenable to dis-aggregation, making them instructive for distributional impacts of policy changes. These advantages have to be weighed against what may be limited data availability and quality (ibid.: 7–11).

Donor agencies are supporting partner countries to strengthen their capacity for providing and handling statistical data. But for many reasons discussed throughout this book, quantitative statistical data often cannot stand alone in the analysis of complex issues like poverty and need to be complemented by qualitative information provided by people themselves. Box 6.12 gives some advice on consultations with people about poverty. Participatory poverty assessments, which are best conducted at the community level, capture information in social and poverty maps, in causality diagrams, in rankings and scorings, in drawings and drama, with the advantage of reflecting local interpretations. Participatory methods have opened up a way for the poor to be heard. People are normally willing to talk about wealth—and poverty—in relative terms and readily give information about other people's situation.

People, including poor women and men, do have ideas of what causes poverty and in many cases also of how poverty can best be alleviated. Before engaging in poverty-oriented interventions, it is vital to listen. The explanations are also apt to vary considerably from one area to another, and may look like the points shared by a group of Nepalese for an evaluation of Poverty Reduction in Danish Bilateral development assistance (MFA, 1996) (Box 6.14):

Box 6.14   Examples of Perceived Causes of Poverty, Nepal

- Lack of access to natural resources—water, land—for raising productivity
- Exploitation by local leaders—loans, labour
- Large family size—fragmentation of limited property and land inherited, betrayal
- Labour shortage when girls and boys are in school
- Poor education
- Laziness
- Costly cultural and ceremonial practices

After Ministry of Foreign Affairs, 1996.

Observation by the researcher or practitioner can provide easy and 'cost-effective' information, as shown by Honadle (McCracken et al., 1988) in the 'inverted' poverty index (see Section 5.1.3 and Box 5.2). McCracken suggests a number of easily observable *indicators of prosperity*, roughly distributed on *low, medium* and *high prosperity*. For example, for each of three prosperity levels, *roofs* on houses typically fall in the categories of straw roof, corrugated iron, and tiles. Such indicators can be identified by the experienced researcher with considerable local knowledge, or local people can help to identify the indicators. Rough indications are sometimes sufficient to indicate differences and trends.

Indicators are important for Monitoring and Evaluation (see Chapter 7), which will constitute a vital link in the learning process of the PRSPs. The World Bank has dedicated a chapter in the PRSP

Sourcebook for guidance on how to monitor and evaluate PRSPs with suggestions on what to do and what to avoid. However, the treatment of monitoring and evaluation in PRSPs has generally focused more on improvements in data availability and quality than on other sensitive areas such as institutional arrangements (COWI, 2004). In practice, monitoring has run into various problems related to overlapping areas of responsibilities, lack of coordination among actors, and delays in the flow of information. There has been least progress in the more technically difficult areas of evaluation of the impact of key actions. A good monitoring system comprises not only data and tools such as household surveys, but establishment of the responsibilities and relations of government and non-government institutions that collect, analyse and use the data. A more widespread use of different types of participatory approaches to monitoring, involving civil society organizations, may help solve the problem of building good quality monitoring and evaluation systems.

A concluding point could be that the choice of indicator should reflect its purpose. Economic measures are best when quick, short-run, aggregate inferences are required, while the non-economic measures are better when medium or longer-term trends on well-being and/or dis-aggregation are needed. The purpose of indicators, as well as availability and the quality of what is available all need to play a role in choosing them. The alternative, Sumner argues (2004: 15), would be a *well-being profile*—a range of measures and/or a *hierarchy of indicators*—where some indicators are judged to be more important than others. It is a sound argument that if poverty and well-being are multi-faceted, then it would seem appropriate that the selection of indicators should reflect this.

6.3   Women in Development and Gender Perspectives

6.3.1 From WID to Gender—Mainstreaming Gender Equality

The changing approaches to 'women in development' illustrate the inter-dependence between theories and methods (Chapter 5). Moser's now classic texts on women's triple roles and their practical and strategic needs and interests[22] (1989 and 1993), for example, have impinged on how development agencies formulate policies on gender equality and develop tools to analyse and address 'women in development' and 'gender and development' issues. Many other gender analysts from the South and the North have influenced the gender discourse and how the policy-setting UN system has promoted gender issues through global summits, in gender polices, gender training materials, etc. Gender analysts and feminist researchers, e.g., Naila Kabeer (1994, 2002), March, et al. (1999), Ghita Sen (1985), M. Molyneux (1985), Mary B. Anderson (1991, 1998) and Carolyn Hannan (2003) have contributed in a large measure to the way the dominant concepts 'gender mainstreaming' and 'women's empowerment' are adopted in international development cooperation by multilaterals, bilateral agencies and NGOs. At the same time

---

[22] The ideas about practical and strategic gender interests were developed by Molyneux (1985) and later adopted by Moser.

they contribute ideas on how to go about gender analysis while keeping the continuous critique of the concepts and approaches alive.

Theoretical frameworks are dynamic and continually evolve and change. Like Moser, Connelly et al. (2000) provide a useful overview of the different phases of the dominant development and feminist theoretical frameworks, since 1930 till the turn of the century. They emphasize that theories should be criticized and redefined for a number of reasons, not least because most feminist and development theories have their roots in the West and need to be tested and redefined in other contexts. Thus the dominant gender analysis frameworks, a few of which are touched upon below, have reflected empirical evidence from development cooperation in different societies over the years. In brief, the gender discourse has moved through various phases from women in development, WID, to gender and development (GAD), gender implying a focus on the relations between women and men and a need for awareness on the part of women, but before that of all men (Bilgi, 1992). The recent cutting edge thinking about development and feminism reflects globalization.

The theoretical perspectives on women in development have changed in a number of ways, and influenced development cooperation (see Box 6.15) with methodological implications for how women in development and gender relations are addressed in development studies. For example:

- from an undifferentiated population of women to the relationship between men and women, i.e., from 'women in development' to 'gender perspectives' which incorporate social relations and differentiation between women and men, and between women—not all women, nor all men, are equal;
- from the single role of women as reproducers to the triple role of women, i.e., with roles of reproductive, productive and community managing work;
- from practical gender needs to practical and strategic gender needs (see definition after Box 6.15);
- from women seen as victims to women seen as actors and agents;
- from a top-down to a bottom-up perspective; and
- the unit of analysis has changed from an emphasis on the individual woman and the household to socially and ethnically distinct groups of women and men and the relations between them.

The frequent changes in perspective suggest that gender analysis has not found a final form, but is recognized as being a mandatory element in development work. Global United Nations summits during the last three to four decades have consolidated the centrality of gender and development. *Equality* between women and men is now firmly placed on the international agenda after the United Nations Fourth World Conference on Women in Beijing in 1995. The *Beijing Platform for Action, PfA*, adopted at the Conference, clearly recognizes that *gender equality* and *women's empowerment* are essential for addressing the central development concerns of poverty and insecurity, and for achieving sustainable, people-centred development. The global agreement reached at the PfA was that *gender equality is the goal, mainstreaming gender equality is the strategy.*

The focus on equality between women and men is based on two important premises: (*i*) First, that equality is a matter of human rights; (*ii*) second, that equality is a pre-condition for effective and sustainable people-centred development.

Gender equality can be defined as *equal rights, opportunities and obligations* of women and men, and an increased potential for both women and men to *influence, participate in and benefit from* development

Box 6.15 Different Policy Approaches to Third World Women				
Issues	**Welfare**	**Equity**	**Anti-poverty**	**Efficiency**	**Empowerment**
Origins	Earliest approach: – Residual model of social welfare under colonial administration – Modernization/ accelerated growth: economic development model	Original WID approach: – Failure of modernization – Influence of Boserup and First World feminists on Percy Amendment – Declaration of UN Decade for Women	Second WID approach: – Toned-down equity because of criticism – Linked to Redistribution with Growth and Basic Needs	Third and now predominant WID approach: – Deterioration in world economy – Policies of economic stabilization and adjustment rely on women's economic contribution to development	Most recent approach: – Arose out of failure of equity approach – Third World women's feminist writing and grassroots organizations
Period most popular	1950–70: but still widely used	1975–85: attempts to adopt it during and since Women's Decade	1970s onwards: still limited popularity	Post 1980s: now most popular approach	1975 onwards: accelerated during 1980s still limited popularly
Purpose	To bring women into development as better mothers: this is seen as their most important role in development	To gain equity for women in the development process: women seen as active participants in development	To ensure that poor women increase their productivity: women's poverty seen as problem of underdevelopment not of subordination	To ensure development is more efficient and more effective: women's economic participation seen as associated with equity	To empower women through greater self-reliance: women's subordination seen not only as problem of men but also of colonial and neocolonial oppression
Needs of women met and roles recognized	To meet PGN* in reproductive role, relating particularly to food aid, malnutrition and family planning	To meet SGN** in terms of triple role—directly through state top-down intervention, giving political and economic autonomy by reducing inequality with men	To meet PGN in productive role, to earn an income, particularly in small-scale income generating projects	To meet PGN in context of declining social services by relying on all three roles of women and elasticity of women's time	To reach SGN in terms of triple role—indirectly through bottom up mobilization around PGN as means to confront oppression

After Moser, 1989: 1808.
Note: MDGs point to the most current approach to Gender and Development.

* **PGN**—Practical Gender Needs are needs identified by women and men which arise out of the customary gender division of labour.
** **SGN**—Strategic Gender Needs reflect a challenge to the customary gender relations and imply changes in relationships of power and control between women and men.

processes. The *mainstreaming* strategy aims to situate gender equality issues at the centre of broad policy decisions, institutional structures, and resource allocations with respect to development goals and processes. Mainstreaming implies that attention to the conditions and relative situations of different categories of women and men, boys and girls should pervade all development policies, strategies and interventions. *Analysis* of their respective roles, responsibilities, access to and control over resources and decision-making processes, needs and potentials, are the first important steps in a mainstreaming approach.

In line with the Platform for Action, most development agencies have developed gender mainstreaming strategies for all their work, for sector programmes or projects. The strategies often reflect two perspectives, (*i*) 'mainstreaming' strategies, i.e., incorporating gender policies into conventional project and programme work, and/or as (*ii*) 'agenda setting' strategies or specific interventions which aim to create the conditions under which women and men can challenge conventional patterns and structural inequalities and start to redefine gender initiatives (e.g., Anderson, 1991; Danida, 2004).

More recent gender mainstreaming strategies retain a double focus, that is (*i*) to get the gender perspective on women and men 'mainstreamed' into all their activities, policies, strategies, interventions, etc., and (*ii*) targeted interventions or 'affirmative action' to support women- or men-focused activities where the situation deems this necessary, e.g., to combat violence against women, severe discrimination, trafficking, etc. (e.g., EC, 2003; UN, 2002).

Experience shows that the distinction between practical and strategic gender needs is a useful conceptual tool. It has limitations in assisting analysis since practical and strategic needs are not discrete entities. It is not always clear what a practical, and what a strategic need is. Different contexts and cultures influence the interpretation. At the same time, they are interrelated in such a way that satisfaction of practical gender needs, for example education, may lead to fulfilment of strategic needs, to participation in decision-making (see Mikkelsen et al., 2002).

6.3.2 Gender Analysis and Approaches to Gender Mainstreaming

The purpose of gender analysis is to understand the mechanism underlying both dominant development problems and policy, programme and project interventions in terms of their implications for women and men, girls and boys, and for the relationship between them. Again, **whose** interpretation counts is vital:

> Gender analysis aims to break the **MAMU syndrome**, i.e., interpretations of society monopolized by **M**iddle **A**ged **M**en with **U**niversity training!

Recognition of the important role that women play in development has contributed to the conceptual and methodological evolution in gender analysis. The recognition that women and men play different roles in society and therefore often have different needs and interests provides both the conceptual framework and inspires the methodological tools for incorporating gender into planning.

Development agencies have been influential in setting the agenda for gender analysis on the assumption that gender sensitivity enhances the aims of development aid: effectiveness, relevance, sustainability and equity. Despite the inventions of gender planning tools already made, there are still many questions as to how to translate gender analysis into planning practice. A few methods and techniques are described in what follows.

Gender Mainstreaming Elements

What exactly is gender mainstreaming—and how does one go about it? The question is continuously asked, and the concept contested, despite a wide range of tools which have been developed to help the process by agencies such as OECD/DAC, UNIFEM, Oxfam, Asian Development Bank, World Bank, and many others. However, there is no straight answer to how gender equality is pursued through mainstreaming. Pursuing gender equality is not a technical fix. It resembles the question how best to combat poverty, as poverty reduction, like gender equality, aims to diminish social inequalities (see Section 6.2). Neither conventions and declarations nor analytical approaches to eradicate inequalities are sufficient, however necessary legal regulations, policies and 'better practices' are for combating inequalities.

Although a *mainstreaming strategy towards gender equality* has no standard definition, it is generally interpreted to include the following elements and dimensions, which should be reflected in *gender analysis*:

- *Clear policies and priorities of goals*—at national and intervention levels. Gender equality is a goal in itself, but optimizing synergies between the gender equality goal and other prioritized goals such as poverty reduction is important.

- *Gender mainstreaming strategies and gender analysis methods* should include:
  - a reasonable level of *gender analysis* specific to an intervention. It includes an assessment of gender needs and interests, women's and men's roles and responsibilities, access to and control over resources and decision processes, potentials and opportunities. Gender analysis should go beyond a simple 'head count' of the number of women and men participating;
  - one or more *clear goals* relating to changes in gender equality;
  - some means of *monitoring and reporting* on the changes in gender equality (diminishing *inequalities*) with identifiable link to the intervention (attribution);
  - *Dialogue* between a development agency and its partners, civil society organizations, etc. Some agencies (e.g., Sida) have started to work on how to qualify dialogue and give guidance to stakeholders on how to operationalize and use dialogue as a tool to promote the gender agenda;

- *Resources and Capacity:*
  - *Human resources*—internal or external to an organization, making optimal use of national/local gender expertise, often needs strengthening to enhance capacity and is part of gender analysis;

- *Gender equality training* for own and partner agency staff takes many forms—general issues on gender, including new topics such as 'masculinities' and 'femininities',[23] sector or intervention specific, on-the-job, institutionalized, for men and women or separate;
- *Gender analysis tools*—gender analytical frameworks (see section below), checklists, handbooks, sector and topic specific prompt-sheets,[24] training packages,[25] are rich and available from many sources. Local availability should be sought rather than 're-inventing the wheel';

- *Stakeholder analysis* and identification of *actors,* e.g., 'beneficiaries', partner agencies, coordination offices, consultants—international and national—cooperating donor/funding agencies, are included in gender analysis to determine possible roles and responsibilities;
- *Institutional arrangements; mechanisms for promoting gender equality*—from the national to the local programme/project level, e.g., gender units, gender focal points, technical assistants, civil society and advocacy groups, etc., are necessary but not necessarily sufficient unless their roles and responsibilities are recognized and implemented;
- *Sex dis-aggregated data and information* is paramount to assess change in gender equality. Publicly available sex dis-aggregated information should be sought, e.g., in National Human Development Reports and in local gender-profiles.[26]

Gender Analytical Frameworks

A variety of frameworks to analyse gender relations are used in development work. They can be helpful tools in planning gender-sensitive research projects, or in designing development interventions which address gender inequalities. Drawing on the experience of trainers and practitioners, March et al. (1999) provide a very useful overview and step-by-step instructions for using different gender-analysis frameworks, and summarize their advantages and disadvantages in particular situations.

The 'framework' is literally illustrated as a matrix containing the main variables which characterize each analytical framework. Briefly stated, these are:

- **Harvard Analytical Framework**—focuses on resource allocations for women and men. It makes use of the following tools. Tool 1: Activity Profile—productive and reproductive activities for women/girls and men/boys. Tool 2: Access and control profile to resources and benefits for women and men. Tool 3: Influencing factors—constraints and opportunities. Tool 4: Checklist of questions for the main stages in the project cycle.
- **People-Oriented Planning**—is an adaptation of the Harvard Analytical Framework for use in refugee situations in particular. The main tools are: Tool 1: Refugee Population Profile and Context Analysis. Tool 2: Activities Analysis. Tool 3: Use of resources analysis and an adaptation of Harvard Tool 2—Women's socio-political profile compared to men's.

---

[23] See, for example, BRIDGE: Gender and Participation, Cutting edge pack. August 2001.
[24] Available, for example, from DAC/OECD, World Bank and Sida.
[25] OECD-DAC/DCC Gender Training Programme (1998) and Skutsch: Gender in Energy Training Pack (1997).
[26] See, for example, Sally Baden et al., Country Gender Profile: South Africa (1998).

- **Moser Framework**—At the heart of the Moser Framework are three concepts: women's triple role (reproductive work, productive work and community work). Tool 1: Gender roles identification/ triple role. Tool 2: Gender needs assessment—Practical and Strategic Gender Needs. Tool 3: Dis-aggregating control of resources and decision-making within the household. Tool 4: Planning for balancing the triple role. Tool 5: Distinguishing between different aims in interventions: the WID/ GAD Policy Matrix (see Box 6.15).
- **Gender Analysis Matrix (GAM)**—aims to help communities determine the different impact development interventions have on women and men. Tool 1: Analysis of four 'levels' of society— women, men, household, community. Tool 2: Analysis of four kinds of impact—labour, time, resources, socio-cultural factors.
- **Capacities and Vulnerabilities Analysis Framework**—to help outside agencies plan aid in emergencies, to meet immediate needs and build on the efforts of people to achieve long-term development. Tool 1: Categories of capacities and vulnerabilities—physical and material, social or organizational, motivational and attitudinal. Tool 2: Additional dimensions of 'complex reality'— dis-aggregation of communities and other social relations by gender.
- **Women's Empowerment (Longwe) Framework**—analyses equality by sectors but concentrates on separate areas of social life. Tool 1: Measures Levels of Equality—Negative, Neutral or Positive— from Welfare, Access, Conscientization, Participation, to Control. Tool 2: Women's Empower-ment—level of recognition of 'women's issues'—using the same scale as Tool 1.
- **Social Relations Approach**—a method of analysing existing gender inequalities in the distribution of resources, responsibilities and power and for designing policies and programmes which enable women to be agents of their own development. The framework uses concepts rather than tools to concentrate on the relationships between people and their relations to resources and activities— and how these are re-worked through 'institutions' such as the state or the market. The framework, developed by Naila Kabeer (1994), has later been complemented by Kabeer's framework for conceptualizing, studying and implementing Empowerment. The Sen-inspired idea of the framework hinges on the 'ability to exercise choice'—including 'choosing not to choose'. The three key interrelated concepts are resources (pre-conditions), agency (process) and achievements (outcomes) (Kabeer, 1999, 2002).

The frameworks discussed in more detail by March et al. (1999) do not pre-empt what exists. A recent framework is presented in connection with the preparation of Poverty Reduction Strategy Papers, PRSPs. The key concepts are Opportunity, Capability, Security and Empowerment. All of these frameworks may inspire the researcher and practitioner, who will be able to adjust or design context-sensitive frameworks.

Other aspects pertaining to gender analysis relate to gender stereotypes.

Challenging Gender Stereotypes

Stereotypical assumptions about women's position in society and in the household are prevalent in development cooperation. Box 6.16 illustrates the challenge to empirical studies when the assumptions of the nuclear family, with the man as breadwinner and the woman as housewife, are torn to pieces.

Analysis by gender frameworks as the ones above challenge concepts like 'the household' and frequently reveal unequal access to and control over resources in favour of male household members.

Box 6.16 Challenging Stereotype Assumptions Made by Planners about the Household		
Household	**Assumptions**	**Empirical and Methodological Challenge**
The structure of low-income households	**Nuclear**	High proportion of other household structures, e.g., extended families, women-headed households
The organization of tasks in the household	**The man is the breadwinner**	Women and men involved in different roles depending on the gender division of labour in the context
	The woman is a housewife	Women's multiple roles: reproductive, productive, community managing and community politics roles
The control of resources and decision-making in the household	**Equal access to resources**	Often there is unequal access to resources for different household members
	Harmonious gender relations in the household	Gender relations are conflicting
	Household is therefore treated as a unit	Need for dis-aggregation of the household

After Levy, 1990.

In a study of gender relations and the environment of urban poverty in Bamako by Mariken Vaa, the gender perspective avoids gender stereotypes. Vaa notes,

One obvious advantage of a gender perspective is that it includes men, and questions the assumption embedded in established institutions and procedures. In instances of planned change, rather than focusing solely on women-specific problems and what leeway their ascribed roles give them, it may be more fruitful to look at how the society or community in question is gendered, in order to come to grips with how interventions can involve both men and women in their various social roles (Vaa, 1995).

Gender stereotypes must be avoided when indicators are formulated. This may be difficult if, at the same time, a participatory approach is used to have local people define indicators. Alternative approaches are likely to show different results, e.g., having women and men separately identify relevant gender indicators is likely to differ from identification in mixed groups. Both situations provide for 'negotiation' over the most relevant indicators. On a global level, considerable efforts have gone into the identification of gender-sensitive indicators from the macro to the micro level.

6.3.3 Gender-sensitive Indicators, Poverty and Power

Gender-sensitive indicators provide an important basis for gender analysis. After 25 years of good intentions, some progress has been made in dis-aggregating core human development indicators by sex and composing various gender-related indices, e.g., the *gender-related development index, GDI*. At the project and sector programme level the response to gender dis-aggregate data is still lagging behind. The Human Development Report (e.g., UNDP, 2003 and annual) includes the following gender indices country by country:

- Gender-related development index
- Gender empowerment measure
- Gender inequality in education
- Gender inequality in economic activity
- Gender, work burden and time allocation
- Women's political participation

There are other important sources providing statistics on The World's Women (UNIFEM, recurrent). The ongoing work to monitor the Millennium Development Goals and develop Poverty Reduction Strategy Papers has prompted work on a gender-informed poverty analysis. In some countries PRSPs are prepared for regions. A test for integrating gender and poverty in diagnostic studies is included in Chapter 10 of the Sourcebook for Poverty Reduction Strategies, PRS (World Bank, 2001). Along a critical path to integrate gender into the poverty diagnostic stage of the PRS is a step to generate data on the four dimensions of poverty (opportunity, capabilities, security and empowerment). This analysis will often require the use of different data collection methods to produce key indicators on the four dimensions. The indicators and data collection methods are proposed and described in Box 6.17:

It is to be hoped that a realistic sample of the proposed studies in Box 6.17 will be undertaken. The results would help to inform an ongoing non-conclusive debate on the relationship between poverty and gender inequality. Part of the discourse is phrased as 'Feminization of Poverty' (i.e., whether there are more poor women than poor men, and whether women's poverty differs from and is more extreme than that of men's). Studies quoted in Engendering Development (World Bank, 2001) show several correlations between gender equality, economic and social development, and poverty reduction. An often quoted relation is between mothers' education and improved child/family health (micro and macro level). Another indication of a positive relationship at the macro level is between extreme gender inequality and poor economic growth.

In a review of literature on 'Feminization of Poverty', Wennerholm (2002) is careful not to draw unsubstantiated assumptions about the degree of poverty that has a feminine face. The required studies—both at the macro and micro level—are difficult to undertake as access to documentation of gender dis-aggregated contexts is rather limited. The shifting policy approaches to women in development—from welfare, to equity, to anti-poverty, efficiency and empowerment (Box 6.15)—signal not only a vivid discourse, but also theoretical and methodological uncertainties. These are reflected in contesting perspectives of what are relevant gender-sensitive or women-specific interventions.

Box 6.17 Indicators of the Gender Dimensions of Poverty and their Measurement

Dimension of Poverty	Indicators	Measurement
Opportunities	• Time budget and time poverty • Employment and labour force participation • Capital and assets	• Household surveys, focus groups, and direct observation • Household and labour market surveys, household surveys, records of credit and finance institutions
Capabilities	• Demographic indicators (infant mortality, life expectancy, etc) • Education • Health and nutrition • Qualitative indicators of capabilities (culture, freedom and autonomy)	• Household and health surveys, clinic records, anthropometric studies, national and sectoral statistical records • Household surveys, school records • Household surveys, clinic records, participant observation, focus groups • Focus groups, participant observations, national quality of life surveys
Security	• Economic vulnerability • Exposure to violence • Social capital	• Household surveys, focus groups, Participatory Rural Appraisal (PRA) techniques such as timelines, and periods of stress, diaries • Focus groups, participant observation, case studies • Household surveys, inter-household transfer studies
Empowerment	• Political empowerment • Control over household resources	• Voting records, key informants, participant observation • Household surveys, case studies, participant observation, key informants, focus groups

After Bamberger et al., 2001: 347.

Provision of micro-credit to women, for example, has been questioned by Lairap-Fonderson (2000) for 'enabling more to be extracted from women'. Her argument follows Foucault's conception of disciplinary power (Foucault, 1978), though without coercion. The more influential analysts when it comes to understanding power and power relations between women and men are Naila Kabeer and Jo Rowlands. In order to understand the process of empowerment, Rowlands (1997, 1999) calls attention to different forms of power:

• **power over:** controlling power, which may be responded to with compliance, resistance (which weakens processes of victimization) or manipulation

- **power to:** generative or productive power (sometimes incorporating or manifesting as forms of resistance or manipulation) which creates new possibilities and actions without domination
- **power with:** a sense of the whole being greater than the sum of the individuals, especially when a group tackles problems together
- **power from within:** the spiritual strength and uniqueness that resides in each one of us and makes us truly human. Its basis is self-acceptance and self-respect which extend, in turn, to respect for and acceptance of others as equals (Rowlands, 1997: 13).

Having considered some of the different manifestations of power, Rowlands explores empowerment on three dimensions: *personal, relational* and *collective.*

Documentation on changes in gender equality as a result of gender mainstreaming has proved to be difficult. The mainstreaming strategy is under increasing attack, e.g., from the empowerment perspective, which itself is an element in mainstreaming!

6.3.4 Contesting Perspectives—Mainstreaming and Women's Empowerment

Reviews and evaluations of recent development cooperation interventions, which should have revealed clear traits of gender mainstreaming, have shown a gap between policies and practice (e.g., EC, 2003; EC/Sida, 2003; Sida, 2002). Repeated observations on 'the evaporation of policies for women's advancement' (Longwe, 1995, 1999) have prompted questions such as: Is the strategy wrong? Is implementation the problem? Are the implementers incapable? Is lack of commitment the problem?, etc.

The proponents of the gender mainstreaming strategy refer to the global mandates for gender mainstreaming. It is not enough to be 'in line with' international goals and recommendations on gender equality, says Carolyn Hannan (2003). It is critical to effectively use these global goals and recommendations for action in development cooperation, as an integral part of the policy frameworks developed in agencies and in policy dialogue with partners. It is thus also important to improve the focus on legally binding commitments that governments have made through international conventions, in particular the Convention on All Forms of Discrimination against Women, CEDAW. Hannan points out that gender specialists need to be aware of the risk of inadvertently hindering the implementation of gender mainstreaming by portraying it as too complex. It is important to distinguish between general problems relating to development cooperation which affect all areas of work, and problems and challenges which are specific to the promotion of gender equality. Thus, in organizations where the promotion of gender mainstreaming is popularly perceived as extremely difficult and minimal efforts are made to implement it, the question should legitimately be raised: Is the promotion of gender equality so intrinsically more difficult than poverty eradication, promotion of human rights, and achievement of effective participatory governance? It is important to expose the values and attitudes underlying perceptions of gender mainstreaming, particularly if they lead to inaction on gender equality within an organization, says Hannan. She points to a number of areas where change would be most needed. They include: *Gender equality policies* are to be regularly updated; *the country strategy process* is a critical entry point for integrating gender into country level analysis and sharpen *policy dialogue and sector approaches. Institutional arrangements* must reassess the role of *gender specialists; management* to have adequate levels of awareness, commitment and capacity for the promotion of gender equality; *competence development* of all professional staff in an organization, i.e., awareness, knowledge and commitment to know *why* promotion of gender equality is important and *what* to do, and fostering the capacity to ask the right questions in relation to a particular piece of work and know where to go to find the relevant information (particularly developing the understanding that there is a lot of analyses and information available at local levels). *Methodologies and tools* are under-utilized—a failing due to the lack of attention to incorporating gender perspectives into existing processes and tools, such as existing sector guidelines, manuals and handbooks.

Somewhat in contrast to the *mainstreaming approach* is a discussion on how to *understand* women's situation, rather than how to intervene and aim to change it, as implied in development cooperation. Women's empowerment is central in this discourse, one fostered by academic women in particular. In Discussing Women's Empowerment—Theory and Practice (Sida, 2002), Arnfred, for example, contends that 'Gender mainstreaming is a policy adopted—if at all—from above .... progress in the matter will depend entirely on committed individuals, i.e., on the chance existence of feminists, male or female, in the departments' (2002: 81–82). The DAWN group of feminist researchers from the South is, for example, quoted for listing a series of structural barriers to gender mainstreaming: 'Conspicuous neglect, wilful misconceptions, low position of "national women's machineries" in government hierarchies, stubborn male resistance within bureaucracies and a generally hostile environment' (DAWN, 2000: 105–6).

That the gender agenda is often sidelined is explained by Lisa Richey as a result of ambiguous strategies. Thus, in the post-Cairo and post-Beijing environment, 'women's reproductive health' emerged as a crucial site for negotiation between *development, demographic* and *feminist* agendas. Because these strategies are often ambiguous and may even conflict, struggles over interpretation arise in implementation, with particular implications for women's empowerment. Richey's (2000) analysis of a Tanzanian family planning project shows that a demographic agenda of fertility reduction leads to a narrow focus on the family planning component of the project. When these two agendas compete with feminist goals to improve women's health and increase women's empowerment, the feminist goals are often ignored.

The 'mainstreaming' versus 'empowerment' discourse represents different theoretical and political points of departure. In this context it is interesting to look at the methodological implications. Structure and agency play an important role. Kabeer's conceptualization of *empowerment* suggests that it can reflect change at a number of different possible levels (Box 6.18).

Box 6.18 Levels of Empowerment	
'Deeper' levels:	Structural relations of class/caste/gender
Intermediate levels:	Institutional rules and resources
Immediate levels:	Individual resources, agency and achievement

Kabeer (2002) quotes an Egyptian researcher, Kishor, who has used national data to explore the effects of direct and indirect measures of women's empowerment on two valued functioning achievements: infant survival rates and infant immunization. Since women bore primary responsibility for children's health, she hypothesized that their empowerment would be associated with positive achievement in terms of the health and survival of their children. Her analysis relied on three categories of composite indicators to measure empowerment: 'direct evidence of empowerment'; 'sources of empowerment'; and 'the setting for empowerment'. These are summarized below, together with the variables which had greatest weight in each indicator of empowerment:

1. **Direct evidence of empowerment**
   (*i*) Devaluation of women:
   reports of domestic violence; dowry paid at marriage
   (*ii*) Women's emancipation:
   belief in daughters' education; freedom of movement
   (*iii*) Reported sharing of roles and decision-making:
   egalitarian gender roles; egalitarian decision-making
   (*iv*) Equality in marriage:
   fewer grounds reported for justified divorce by husbands; equality of grounds reported for divorce by husband or wife
   (*v*) Financial autonomy:
   currently controls her earnings; her earnings as share of household income

2. **Sources of empowerment**
   (*i*) Participation in the modern sector:
   index of assets owned; female education
   (*ii*) Lifetime exposure to employment:
   worked before marriage; controlled earnings before marriage

3. **Setting indicators**
   (*i*) Family structure amenable to empowerment:
   does not now or previously live with in-laws
   (*ii*) Marital advantage:
   small age difference between spouses; chose husband
   (*iii*) Traditional marriage:
   large educational difference with husband; did not choose husband

After Kabeer, 2002: 35–36.

The results of a multivariate analysis found that the indirect source/setting indicators of women's empowerment had far more influence in determining the value of her achievement variables than the direct measures. There may be several explanations which are beyond the scope of this presentation. The aim here is to illustrate the importance of context-specific indicators—e.g., within some analytical categories as the three levels chosen in the particular study of women's empowerment.

To conclude, there are important perspectives on women in development and gender relations which have not been addressed in this section. The rights-based perspective and approach to development (Section 6.1) is prompting a focus on women's rights in all three spheres: reproductive, productive and decision-making spheres. The rights perspective carries prospects for women and men at the micro level in particular, while other approaches focus on macro-level policies, e.g., the relatively recent Gender Budget Initiatives. 'If you want to see which way a country is headed, look at the country's budget and how it allocates resources for women and children' (UNIFEM, 2001).

Imagination brings us furthest when we work with concepts as non-exact as 'mainstreaming', 'empowerment' and 'poverty reduction', for that matter. This is not the same as 'anything goes', but the advice is to be open about one's own approaches and to search for dialogue and exchange about these with other development practitioners and researchers, and the rich networks involving development practitioners as well as academics and feminist researchers, e.g., OECD/DAC gender network and BRIDGE. Do not wait for the exact definitions and 'correct' approaches to be developed by others and presented to you as a recipe for gender analysis! To be transparent about how inspiration has been taken from others and shared with those the research concerns helps to keep the discourse alive.

6.4   Innovative Approaches—Appreciative Inquiry; Social Capital Assessment; Geomatics

Development work is about change—in people's ways of doing things, in their attitudes, behaviour and practices. People organize their lives in formal and informal relations and networks. The impact of rapid change on all human systems—families, schools, organizations, communities, governments—has become a focus of concern.

Development professionals try to understand conditions that foster change and the consequences of development interventions on people's lives. Development interventions are increasingly used proactively to induce change in organizations, e.g., to 'build capacity' in the organizations through which people participate in political and social affairs.

The increased attention to organizations and social networks has prompted changes in the way organizations[27] are looked at as fora for people's participation. On the one hand new methods for practising organizational analysis based on 'Appreciative Inquiry' of positive experiences are spreading, indeed in contrast to the dominant analytical approaches which depart from organizations' problems. From another entry point new perspectives on organizations focus on the informal and less tangible networks which shape people's lives, i.e., the 'social capital' in human communities. The potential of social capital in combating poverty has prompted the World Bank to develop the Social Capital Assessment Tool, SOCAT, which combines participatory and survey methods. Prospects for comparative, space-related analysis are on the other hand embedded in Geomatics, i.e., in the current innovations of methods undertaken jointly between anthropologists and specialists practising high-tech remote sensing and Geographical Information Systems, GIS.

---

[27] 'Organization' is used in its broadest sense to indicate formal as well as non-formal organization, e.g., development interventions. See also Hornstrup and Loehr-Petersen, 2003.

6.4.1 Appreciative Inquiry

Appreciative Inquiry, AI, is a strategy for purposeful change that identifies the best of 'what is' to pursue dreams, visions and possibilities of 'what could be'. AI is recognized as a participatory approach to organizational analysis and development, and appears in more recent introductions to participation (IFAD, 2001). It is a cooperative search for the strengths, passions and life-giving forces that are found in all human relations, in organizations and institutions. Appreciative Inquiry turns the problem-solving approach around and focuses on a community's or organization's achievements and potentials rather than its problems. The contrast to the Logical Framework Approach, LFA, which departs from problem analysis, is obvious. But rather than seeing the two approaches as contradictory, it is possible to see the Appreciative Inquiry approach as complementary to the LFA.

The rationale for an Appreciate Inquiry approach rests on the observation that many interventions, even those which include participatory techniques, learning and action, often fail to sustain community participation when the implementing organization withdraws. Could this be related to the fact that local people are left with the impression that their community is full of problems? That the focus on needs fosters a sense of dependency, which reduces the motivation of people to initiate their own development activities? (Elliott, 1999).

It is unintended consequences of this kind which has prompted a shift away from problem-oriented methods toward processes that build on local strengths and achievements—a perspective that is strongly professed by Appreciative Inquiry practitioners. But what is in the name Appreciative Inquiry?

> Appreciative Inquiry ... is an inquiry process that tries to apprehend the factors that give life to a living system and seeks to articulate those possibilities that can lead to a better future. More than a method or technique, the appreciative mode of inquiry is a means of living with, being with, and directly participating in the life of human systems in a way that compels one to inquire into the deeper life-generating essentials and potentials of organisational existence (Cooperrider, 1990).

Some practitioners of Appreciative Inquiry refer to Cooperrider's ideas in the context of an emerging science paradigm (for a comparison of the current and emerging paradigms, see Watkins and Mohr, 2001: 8). Appreciative Inquiry is grounded in several paradigms. Two are of particular interest: (*i*) the impact of the *New Sciences* (quantum physics; chaos, complexity, and string theory) on human systems; and (*ii*) *social constructionism*—the idea that we create our world by the conversations we have with one another (ibid.).

Appreciative Inquiry, AI, is described by its practitioners as much as a world-view as a method and an inquiry approach which rests on **five core principles:**

1. The constructionist principle;
2. The principle of simultaneity (inquiry itself prompts change);
3. The anticipatory principle (what we anticipate, think and imagine influence change);
4. The poetic principle (valuing story telling); and
5. The positive principle.

Whitney and Trosten-Bloom (2003) have recently added three more principles:

6. The wholeness principle (the experience of wholeness brings out the best);
7. The enactment principle (acting 'as if' is self-fulfilling);
8. The free choice principle (free choice liberates power).

Along these lines—being a world-view as much as a method and resting on principles—Appreciative Inquiry has many similarities with participation and participatory approaches. The wording is different but the elements and perspectives in Appreciative Inquiry share the basic ideas of deliberative democracy and inclusionary citizen processes.

Appreciative Inquiry is fond of models through which the approach can be grasped. AI has been developed and 'consolidated' into what is now known as the Four-D Model, or the four stages in the Cycle of Appreciative Inquiry:

Figure 6.2   The Appreciative Cycle—Four-D Model

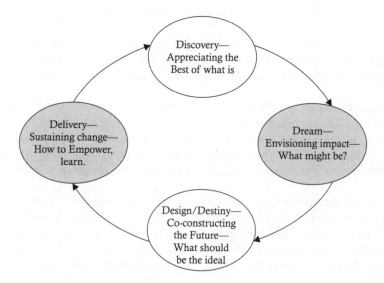

After Watkins and Mohr, 2001: 43, and IFAD, 2001: 86.

The model can also be depicted to contrast two different Paradigms of Action Research (Box 6.19).

The Four-D model was developed in a concrete context for *Building Partnerships* in Zimbabwe, involving Save the Children, and adapted for use in its partnerships with national organizations.

What exactly goes into the four stages depends on the concrete case. Thus, the objectives of promoting small-farmer groups, for which IFAD proposes the application of Appreciative Inquiry, differs from organizational development objectives of large-scale corporations for which the approach has been

---

Box 6.19   Two Different Processes for Organizational Change

Paradigm 1: Action Research Assumption:	Paradigm 2: (AI) Action Research Assumption:
Organizing is a problem to be solved	Organizing is a mystery to be embraced
'Felt Need' Identification of the Problem ↓	Appreciating 'Valuing the Best of What is' ↓
Analysis of Causes ↓	Envisioning What might be ↓
Analysis of Possible Solutions ↓	Dialoguing What should be ↓
Action Planning	Innovating What will be

After Srivastva and Cooperrider, 1990 and Watkins and Mohr, 2001: 42.

---

frequently used. One thing is common to the use of Appreciative Inquiry in different organizational contexts, i.e., the use of *provocative statements/propositions*.

To take an example from the design phase:

The design phase is intended to be *provocative* and aims to develop, through consensus, short- and long-term goals that will contribute to the organization's, the community's or group's overall vision. These goals are likely to take the form of statements such as:

- 'This group has mobilized the necessary resources and built a school within the next year.'
- 'This community has planted one thousand trees over the next two years to ensure the forest's survival for future generations.'
- 'This group has eliminated gambling and drinking in the village in the next six months.'

The criteria for formulating provocative propositions are:

- that they are based on the dream and the information generated during the discovery;
- they are desired, realistic, stretches (provokes); and
- they are voiced in the present tense (pretending that the group has already achieved its goals). The reason for this is that the 'planning mode—i.e., we are going to—can be valid forever—and is not provoking'.

In the delivery/destination stages, group members turn their imagination towards developing strategies, establishing roles and responsibilities, forging institutional relationships, and mobilizing resources to achieve their goals. To facilitate this important process of translating design into action, the Appreciative

Inquiry method has been further developed by Mohr and Jacobsgaard (forthcoming training material, 2005) around the Four I's: Initiate, Inquire, Imagine and Innovate.

With the group's goals in mind, people begin to consider how to build a social architecture for their project or programme that might, for example, redefine approaches to leadership, governance, participation, or capacity-building. As they compose strategies to achieve their 'provocative' propositions, local people incorporate the qualities of community life that they want to protect and the relationships that they want to achieve.

Experience shows that Appreciative Inquiry is also a very useful tool as an evaluation methodology, in particular for participatory evaluation, as it combines the retrospective appreciation of what has gone well, as well as the forward-directed translation of dreams into design and ideas for future delivery.

6.4.2 Social Capital Assessment Tool (SOCAT)

Social capital is assuming an increasingly important role in the development discourse. Research conducted worldwide under the World Bank's Social Capital Initiative (SCI) in the 1990s led to a prominent place for social capital in the World Bank's poverty reduction work.

The broad definition of social capital which derived from the Social Capital Initiative (Grootaert and Bastelaer, 2002: 2) is:

> Social capital is defined as the institutions, relationships, attitudes, and values that govern interactions among people and contribute to economic and social development.

There is reluctance on the part of those who attempt to de-construct social capital to impose a narrow definition on a still-evolving conceptual debate. So broad is this definition that Groetaert and Bastelaer make a disclaimer 'that the last elements of this definition can be interpreted broadly to allow for the existence of damaging or harmful social capital' (ibid.: 13). Social capital is *harmful* when social networks are used for criminal acts, for example.

But what *is* social capital and how does social capital impinge on development cooperation? These questions are thoroughly addressed in Grootaert and Bastelaer's 'Understanding and Measuring Social Capital' (2002). Box 6.20, based on World Bank SCI research, gives a taste of what Social Capital can be in real life situations:

In one form or another, the five statements demonstrate the critical role of social interaction, of trust and reciprocity in producing collective outcomes, both beneficial and harmful.

In order to approach measuring social capital and making it operational, e.g., in development cooperation, the concept 'social capital' is broken down into forms and scope (Figure 6.3). A distinction is made between two forms of social capital. The *first,* which Uphoff (1996) called *structural social capital,* refers to relatively objective and externally observable social structures such as networks, associations and institutions, and the rules and procedures they embody. Water-user committees and neighbourhood associations are examples of structural social capital. The *second* form, known as *cognitive social capital,* comprises more subjective and intangible elements such as generally accepted attitudes and norms of behaviour, shared values, reciprocity and trust.

Box 6.20   What is Social Capital?—Examples

- Particular villages on the Indonesian island of Java build and maintain complex water delivery systems that require collaboration and coordination, while other villages rely on simple individual wells.
- Residents in apparently similar Tanzanian villages enjoy very different levels of income due to differences in their abilities to engage in collective action.
- Households in Russia rely on informal networks to gain access to health services, housing, education, and income security.
- Some neighbourhoods of Dhaka organize for local trash collection, while others allow garbage to accumulate on the streets.
- Hutu militias rely on fast networks of information and high levels of mutual trust to carry out a terrifyingly efficient genocide in Rwanda.

After Grootaert and Bastelaer, 2002: 1.

A second distinction that allows isolation of the elements of social capital is based on its *scope*. Social capital can be observed at the *micro* level, as Robert Putnam's studies in particular are known for (1993), in the form of horizontal networks of individuals and households and the associated norms and values that underlie these networks, for example choral groups, bowling teams, etc. The *meso* level captures horizontal and vertical relations among groups at a level situated between individuals and society as a whole. Regional groupings of local associations, such as the Andean poor people's organizations, are examples, as described in one of the World Bank's Social Capital studies. Finally, social capital can be observed at the *macro* level, in the form of the institutional and political environment that serves as a backdrop for all economic and social activity, and the quality of the governance arrangements. Social capital, here, is put into the realm of institutional economics, which emphasizes the quality of incentives and institutions such as the rule of law, the judicial system, etc.

The discussion of the forms and scope of social capital is illustrated in Figure 6.3.

Figure 6.3   Forms and Scope of Social Capital

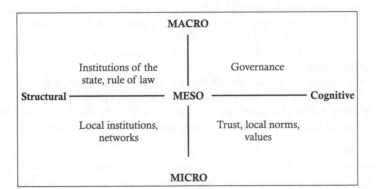

Source: Grootaert and Bastelaer, 2002: 4.

Growing empirical evidence indicates that social capital is best measured using a variety of qualitative and quantitative instruments. Despite its name, social *capital*, it cannot be comprehended strictly within the economic paradigm, using quantitative methods. Neither can it be investigated solely through anthropological or sociological case studies. As a consequence the Social Capital Assessment Tool (SOCAT), developed in connection with the World Bank's Social Capital Initiative, integrates quantitative and qualitative instruments and participatory methods (ibid.).

Ideally the measurement of social capital should capture all four quadrants of Figure 6.3, but in practice most experience has been gained with measurement at the micro and meso levels. It is not possible to go into the details of all the different tools which compose the SOCAT. A few details from the participatory interview guide for group discussions are recorded in Box 6.21.

Box 6.21   Participatory Interview Guide for Community Profile and Asset Mapping

1. *Definition of community boundaries and identification of community assets.* The group interview begins with a mapping exercise. Setting out large sheets of paper and distributing markers, the facilitator asks the group to draw the geographic boundaries of the community. The assembled group also identifies the community's principal assets, resources, and important local landmarks on the map. This mapping exercise usually generates open discussions, with participants speaking freely about items such as the location of drinking water supplies, roads, and school buildings, and residential patterns. This exercise also opens the way to discussions on other issues.

2. *Discussion of case study of community collective action.* It is useful to focus discussions of collective action and solidarity on a specific case in which the community worked collectively to resolve an issue, whether or not the outcome was positive. The facilitator probes a specific instance of collective action undertaken at some time within the past three years.

3. *Discussion of community governance and decision-making process.* The community informants identify leaders within the community and describe the processes of leadership selection and community decision-making. Facilitators probe specific instances that illustrate these features of community-level social capital.

4. *Identification of local organizations.* Both formal and informal organizations are assessed in terms of accessibility by different community members, involvement of different groups in the community, and extent of inclusion and exclusion. A brief history of each organization is recorded. For the most important organizations, this information will be supplemented later with data collected for the organizational profiles.

5. *Assessment of the relationships between organizations and the community.* This assessment is done by means of a Venn diagram exercise. Organizations are assessed in terms of their contribution to different community purposes and their accessibility by different community members. This Venn diagram exercise is simple to conduct, and has an immediate visual appeal.

6. *Institutional networks.* Another visual exercise, institutional mapping, also serves to spark animated discussions. Functional relationships between pairs of organizations are mapped using a flowchart. All sorts of organizations working within the community are considered, including local government departments, non-governmental organizations, community groups, and other civil society actors.

After Grootaert and Bastelaer, 2002: 26–28.

The following outputs, many of which are 'generic' PRA outputs, are typically obtained from the open-ended community interviews:

- Community maps indicating the location of community assets and services
- Observation notes of group process and summary of issues discussed
- List of existing (and desired) community assets and services
- List of all formal and informal community organizations
- Case study of previous collective action
- Venn diagram indicating the accessibility of different local organizations
- Institutional (web) diagram of relationships among local organizations and service providers.

Other tools of the SOCAT are:

1. Community profile and asset mapping
2. Community questionnaires
3. Household surveys
4. Organizational profile interviews and profile score-sheet.[28]

The participatory community exercises constitute a set of qualitative data about the extent and nature of social capital in the community. These data complement the quantitative information collected with the help of the structured community interviews and the household profiles.

The elaboration of the SOCAT tool may give the impression that Social Capital is an isolated area for social analysis. This may sometimes be the case when little is known about social interactions and networks in the context of a particular project or programme. Social Capital is, however, becoming an integral parameter in many studies, exemplified for example by Müller's Technology Analysis (Müller, 2003), and in assessments of the sustainable rural livelihood approach (Figure 6.4).

Figure 6.4 Assets Considered in the Sustainable Rural Livelihood Approach

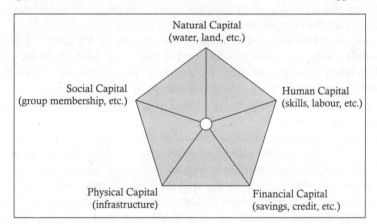

After Carney, 1998.

---

[28] For more on the related Balanced Scorecard approach which supplements financial measurements with non-financial measures in organizational assessment, see different publications by Kaplan and Norton, e.g., 2001.

Social capital captures relations between people and groups and is an obvious element in livelihood analysis. The SOCAT—itself combining several tools—is a flexible instrument which can be combined with other tools, for example with space-related methods—the topic of the next section.

6.4.3 Geomatics[29]—Space-related Information—Tools for Empowerment?

Geographical Information Systems and Indigenous Knowledge

Space-related analysis in the form of participatory mapping has become one of the more frequently applied PRA methods (see Section 2.4). Mapping—social mapping, resource mapping, poverty and well-being mapping and other sketch mapping—has the advantage of motivating many people to 'talk' about their community in a spatial language which captures indigenous, local knowledge. But sketch maps have limitations, e.g., their simplicity and limited spatial coverage detract from their relevance for analysis of more complex relations, which other space-related methods compensate for. Sketch maps also have low credibility among some hard-core development practitioners and agency staff (Campbell, 2002), and the message communicated in simple sketch maps may be lost in communication with uninterested decision makers who only appreciate sophisticated map-representations. Here, the alternative space-related methods under the name 'Geomatics' provide prospects for relevant interdisciplinary research between *natural science* and *social science*, including *participatory methods and 'indigenous knowledge'* on space-related geographical issues such as natural resources and infrastructure, control and rights over land, forests, water, poverty pockets, etc.

Geomatics is a relatively new generic term for methodologies using advanced digital technology for data recording, storing and analysing geographical imagery, which is making its way into development work. Geomatics embrace the components GIS, RS and GPS, set out in Box 6.22.

GIS is the computer-based system used to integrate and analyse the RS and GPS data in combination with other information, and to visualize the data and derived map products as maps on the screen or printed maps. This 'other information' may, for example, be indigenous knowledge about natural resources, vegetation, migration patterns, etc. When the two systems of space-related data—indigenous knowledge and high-tech GIS—are carefully integrated, it can enrich the utility of digital space-related information for development purposes.

GIS makes it possible to combine physical and social data in different 'layers' of information and provide vital knowledge for development planning on issues such as deforestation ratios, land use patterns, sacred sites, mythological places, settlement sites, migration patterns, natural resources, mineral deposits, gendered spaces, water catchment areas, fishing and hunting grounds, biodiversity hot spots, armed conflict loci, transport corridors, infrastructure, settlements, land ownership, cadastral information, population densities, poverty distribution, electoral data, health and social services, etc. More specifically,

---

[29] The section on Geomatics builds on inputs from Søren Hvalkof: GIS, Remote Sensing and Participatory Approaches, DIIS, August 2003, and from Charles Pendley, Rasmus Ødum and Dorthe K. Nordentoft, COWI.

Box 6.22   Geomatics—Components

GIS—Geographic Information Systems; computer-based programmes for organizing and analysing spatial information.

The most commonly used GIS softwares are MapInfo (www.mapinfo.com) and ArcGIS (www.esri.com). These software products are offered in different versions from low-cost (free) GIS data viewers to full fledged GIS with add-on modules for advanced users.

RS—Remote Sensing; basically any geographical information gathering from a distance without the observer coming in direct contact with the object or phenomenon observed. Aerial photography and satellite imagery are most common (Wilkie and Finn, 1996).

Satellite imagery is available in very different resolutions from the global coverage of weather satellites to high resolution imagery, e.g., of Landsat and SPOT. High solution RS imagery is typically used for mapping of features such as land use/forestry cover or infrastructure. RS data can also be used as base maps for field surveys as a better alternative to topographical maps that are sometimes unavailable or out-of-date, or as background maps for other map layers in a GIS.

Links: Overview (www.infoterra-global.com), Landsat (www.eurimage.com), SPOT (www.spotimage.fr), IKONOS (www.euspaceimaging.com), IRS (www.spaceimaging.com), QuickBird (www.eurimage.com).

GPS—the Global Positioning System; is used for geo-referencing, i.e., identifying any given point in the landscape or on a map by its geographic coordinates.

For field work, simple GIS data collection can be done using small handheld, easy-to-use GPS receivers available at a relatively low cost (USD 500–1000). The accuracy of a point measurement is typically 5–10 metres.

---

it also becomes a tool to document and support claims, for example, for the indigenous population in a given area as witnessed by many indigenous organizations, which today have a technical GIS unit (Hvalkof, 2003).

GIS is a database management system designed to acquire, manage, manipulate, visualize and display spatially referenced (geographic) forms of data. In particular, datasets take the form of layers or themes; each layer is a specific natural, cultural or derived variable that describes the environment of the study. It is possible to juxtapose or 'overlay' different datasets to produce a visual representation or map. For example, spatially referenced data from the national census on local infrastructure and on the provision of government services can be overlaid to identify the population with least access to education, etc. (Campbell, 2002). Box 6.23 illustrates how physical and social data have been overlaid in an integrated environmental planning process in Thailand.

GIS is also rapidly entering the Internet scene, mainly in the form of applications for visualization and querying of map data, but increasingly with facilities for data editing. Commercial web map providers offer low-cost standard solutions for presentation as a set of GIS map layers with facilities for zooming and panning the map section, and for locating features on the map by simple querying of attribute data such as a town by town name, or a district by district name. A service like this can be an excellent tool for

---

Box 6.23   Integrating Social, Physical and Environmental Data and GIS/Web Mapping to Support Integrated Development Planning—A Case from Thailand

The CAPEQM (a Thai-English acronym for Changwat [Provincial] Action Plans for Environmental Quality Management) Project is located in Khon Kaen Province in Northeast Region, Thailand, and has been supported by the Danish Government. This Project has developed a public access web-based mapping facility covering Khon Kaen Province which integrates physical, environmental and social data. Since the project ended in October 2003, the website is now managed by the Regional Environmental Office (REO) 10 in Khon Kaen.

A user can access the website using any common Internet browser. The user can specify the type and level of maps to be generated from a menu consisting of administrative levels (province, district, or tambon—the lowest administrative unit in Thailand) and layers, consisting of geographical features and administrative boundaries, transportation network, land use, forest cover, surface and ground water resources, soil fertility, pollution and flood risk, and social and socio-economic data. It is possible for the user to compile a map using any combination of these layers and data.

The social and socio-economic data is contained in two large nationwide databases maintained by the Community Development Department (CDD), Ministry of Interior, referred to as NRD2C and BMN (Basic Minimum Needs). At present this data is collected and updated biannually by CDD.

Among the social and socio-economic data which can be displayed on a map with any combination of the other map layers are:

- Population size, density and growth rates
- Dependency ratio
- Household size and age and gender distribution
- Average household income
- Main and secondary occupations and unemployment rates
- Employment rates by occupation, age and gender
- Education attainment rates by sex
- Land ownership and size of landholdings (proxy indicator for poverty)
- Use of animals and mechanized farm equipment in agriculture (proxy indicator for poverty)
- Housing type and quality (proxy indicator for poverty)

Presented as map layers, socio-economic indicators can be used alone or in combination with other layers showing natural resources, infrastructure and information such as:

- Existing forest type, cover and use
- Watershed classification and boundaries
- Water bodies
- Precipitation
- Irrigation facilities
- Water flow, quality and yield
- Soil groups/landforms
- Mineral resources
- Infrastructure/transportation

(Box 6.23 contd)

(Box 6.23 contd)

Developing spatial plans runs through three main work processes:

1. Baseline Data Analysis of the existing situation and problems and potentials;
2. Outlining objectives and strategies; and
3. Integration across sectors and synthesis of all aspects into a coherent balanced special framework.

These are iterative processes with feedback mechanisms connecting the various tasks and their outputs. Integrated maps are both a tool in and a result of the spatial planning process. The tasks and approaches of the main planning phases can be exemplified as:

Tasks and Approaches	Baseline Data Analysis	Objectives and Strategy Setting	Integration and Synthesis
Technical Tasks	• Data collection and reviewing • Establishing GIS and web-mapping • Analysis of data and checking validity • Analysis of problems and potentials	• Prioritize problems & potentials • Outline strategy including objectives and principles	• Define criteria for planning maps • Transform data • Draft planning maps and measures • Balance competing or conflicting interests • Identify implementers/ responsible partners
Participatory Approaches and Methods	• Consultations among planners, professionals and people with knowledge about local issues • Public forums • Opinion polls	• Stakeholder workshops • Round table discussions • Technical working group meetings • Collaboration planning & management team meeting	• Technical working group meetings • Public information • Round table discussions • Partnership initiatives • Public forums • Collaboration planning & management team meeting
Results	• GIS and web-mapping with baseline data • Description and mapping of current problems and potentials • Listing and location of main problems and potentials	• Strategy setting for the direction of the plan • Decision on planning issues	• Planning maps & measures • Stakeholder agreement on plans and measures

Developing such interactive maps provides a rich possibility for building on local and indigenous knowledge. However, it must be pointed out that developing interactive maps requires a considerable input of technical expertise from database specialists, programmers and a webmaster, supported by a number of subject area specialists.

After CAPEQM, September 2003.

the dissemination of data to a broad audience, including project stakeholders, NGOs, etc. Facilities for renting space are now available in so-called 'GIS Hotels' for organizations such as municipalities, NGOs, companies, and others who do not want to engage in developing their own GIS databases (http://standard.gis-hotel.dk).

From Technical Towards Social Interest in GIS

In the 1980s GIS and satellite images of the accelerating deforestation in the Brazilian Amazon and the spreading desertification of Sahel and adjacent regions in Africa hit the international media causing global alarm, proving the power of visualizing complex cause and effect relationships in relatively simple thematic maps. Still, the more subtle uses on a lower scale and scope were not commonly known, and socio-economic and development researchers have been slow to see the possibilities in spatial analysis.

Geographers and other earth scientists are the users *par excellence* of the new technologies for spatial analyses. Archaeology was also fast in adopting geomatic methodologies and applying it in research. From the 1980s geomatics had been applied to multiple spatial planning and control activities (both rural and urban), and soon spread into the area of nature conservation, biodiversity monitoring, degradation control, and natural resource management. In development work GIS has been successfully used for managing data on the interrelationship between land degradation, settlement, poverty and vegetation, and in designing and implementing development projects. Box 6.24 illustrates the use of GIS for Cadastre (Land Registration) Projects.

Land information data should be handled with care. Conflicting interests between development researchers and practitioners and people on the ground are apt to evolve. Social scientists in particular have felt the divergent interests, as illustrated below (Campbell, 2002).

In the social sciences it is anthropology, more particularly anthropology concerned with socio-ecological research and landscape ethnography that has taken on GIS and found it to be a useful tool for integrating micro-level ethnographies into larger regional socio-economic studies, merging and comparing information, and visualizing the results (Aldenderfer and Maschner, 1996). This notwithstanding, the powerful political potential of geomatic approaches was realized and mobilized not by the academia, but by the *indigenous movement*, who envisaged a tool for liberation and for substantiating their claims (Parellada and Hvalkof, 1998).

GIS can be an important bridge between the technical and natural science and social science interests when its potential in historical analysis is utilized. This was the lynch-pin in research supported by the Danish Council for Development Research (Box 6.25 and the Gran Pajonal maps 1958 and 1996, Figure 6.5).

Indigenous organizations and support NGOs in Peru rapidly adopted the new digital technology for spatial analysis and mapping, pragmatically using a trial and error approach to the high-tech methodologies, combining it with maps based on local knowledge and ethno-cartography, and produced new types of territorial documentation. Once adapted to the local realities, the new technology made it possible for the indigenous organizations to auto-demarcate and classify their own territories and resources, empowering them to negotiate territorial ownership and management with the governments from a much more favourable bargaining position.

Box 6.24   GIS in Cadastre (Land Registration) Projects

GIS in Land Registration Projects

Traditionally, the Cadastre information about delimitation and ownership of land parcels was represented on hand-drawn Parcel Maps and a Registry Book, respectively. Globally the trend moves towards replacement of such manual systems with computerized Land Information Systems (LIS)—special purpose GIS, in different tempi. The main objective is to (re)establish reliable cadastre data.

The demarcation of land parcels is verified by land surveying in the field. This work is based on the old land parcel maps, high resolution remote sensing data (orthophotos; georectified mosaics of aerial photography), and GPS equipment to establish the geometry of the parcels with a high level of accuracy. The land parcel demarcation data is entered into the LIS and linked via unique land parcel identifiers to the ownership data, which is also verified and entered into the database of the LIS.

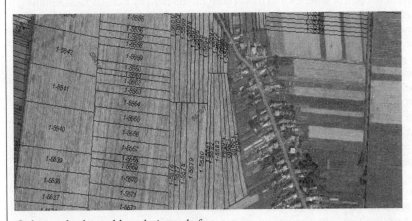

Cadastre—land parcel boundaries, orthofoto

The resulting Land Information System provides a modern tool to support the maintenance of a reliable Cadastre which has several purposes and holds potentials that are slowly being exploited. To start with the latter: The land information system is an instrument for *indigenous people* for demarcation and registration of their collective private ownership and territorial and land rights. Generally LIS is for documenting and thus ensuring land and property ownership for *entitled citizens*. For the individual, the security provided is a prerequisite for mortgage raising and for willingness to invest in, for instance, soil improvement, house building, and resource extraction.

At national level, a Cadastre is a necessary basis for efficient land administration, including land regulation and administration of rights and obligations. It is also required for *property valuation and taxation and to achieve a transparent real property market.*

In addition to constituting a major part of the project output, GIS and geographical data are also used extensively as tools in project implementation. GIS is, for instance, used for planning and monitoring the progress of field work, and map data is used extensively for navigation and parcel identification in the field.

After Dorthe Nordentoft, Cadastre and GIS International, COWI.

Box 6.25   Inter-ethnic Relationship between the Colonist Settlers and the Indigenous Population in a Peruvian Amazon Area

The case study focused on the fundamentally different production systems and underlying ideologies of two separate populations. It traced how the changes in national and international policies over a 50-year period affected the livelihoods and power relations of the two groups, and how this was reflected in changing land use patterns and in the ecology of the area.

The study was based on a combination of historical research in archives, three years of ethnographic and anthropological field work in the region, and a larger GIS-based spatial analysis. GIS data came from different aerial photo surveys with different scope and scale from the 1950s, 1960s, 1980s, and finally combined with satellite images from 1996.[30]

The comparative analysis was phased according to three significant historical periods with notably different policy parameters: (*i*) The initial period of colonization and agricultural ventures in the 1950s; (*ii*) a period in the 1980s characterized by grand development schemes and modernization followed by indigenous land titling; and finally (*iii*) monitoring the effects of these changes a decade later in the late 1990s when most landownership had changed from settlers to indigenous communities.

The combined efforts of historical studies, conventional anthropological and sociological analyses, and the GIS-supported spatial analysis generated interesting results regarding the relationships between environmental degradation, production systems, forest regeneration, ideology and international policy.

With the help of the geomatic technologies, a digital database was constructed with the different data and layers. This is relatively easy to update with remote sensing data. Its main use is thought to be for continuous monitoring of development in the area and to generate more generalized lessons about sustainability and options for future development for the indigenous as well as for the settler population.

The combined results of the anthropological and spatial socio-ecological analyses have been applied continuously in the elaboration of indigenous strategies for local development initiatives and territorial consolidation. It has been shown that the new spatial analyses and mapping technologies are useful not only for synchronic social analysis, but are able also to facilitate diachronic analyses and visualize social dynamics, in this case over a 50-year period, by mapping social and ecological processes of change.

Once the data is digitized it is relatively easy to combine it with other GIS databases both on the higher level of spatial analysis and on the ground level of participatory mapping where local people produce their own maps, e.g., of resource distribution, land use patterns, land tenure structure, hunting ground and trails, etc.

But powerful analytic tools such as GIS can also be misused. This risk is constantly discussed in the research community, but has no simple solution. Like in all other research involving human societies and individuals, involved researchers must be very conscious of risks and ethical implications when storing and disseminating information.

After, Hvalkof, 2004.

---

[30] The GIS and Remote Sensing component was developed at the University of Massachusetts, Amherst, where technical and human resources for cross-disciplinary support was available, contrary to the research environment in Denmark at the time.

During the last two decades, hundreds of millions of hectares all over the tropical zones of South and Central America have been demarcated and titled collectively to indigenous communities and organizations, radically changing the relationships of power in the local contexts. Many national and regional indigenous organizations today have a technical GIS unit. It provides prospects of integrating high-tech imagery with local knowledge and other context relevant data, collected and systematized in participatory studies by social scientists, for example. Similar processes are now taking place in Asia and Africa, where indigenous organizations and support NGOs specialized in land demarcation and titling are working hand-in-hand to secure the territorial rights of the indigenous peoples.

Competing Discourses—Promise and Problems of Space-related Analysis

Analytical and practical challenges relate to the integration of different knowledge systems and epistemologies of the involved natural and social sciences when using geomatics in development. A concern with GIS arises in overlaying datasets to create 'maps' that purport to show the way space is utilized. Such maps are essentially based on Western cultural perceptions that 'see' human activities as occupying or occurring in discrete and non-overlapping spaces. Notions of individualism and private property lie at the heart of such representations, regardless of longstanding anthropological critiques of their inappropriateness. Such ideas misrepresent and misinterpret non-Western cultures. African land tenure provides excellent examples of the interpretative problems involved, because the variety and fluidity of social arrangements negate simplistic spatial maps. Semi-nomadic or *transhumant* herders may, for example, think of routes traversing a piece of land as more important than a grazing potential of the land itself. Challenges arise when studies attempt to take into account the changing effect of state policy, of deepening rural poverty, or processes of land concentration, etc., while at the same time trying to understand the continued role played by *customary law* in regulating access to land (Freydenberger, 1998).

The challenges relating to 'integrating' high-tech GIS with indigenous knowledge—of cultivation patterns, of settlements and physical movements, etc.—in many ways resemble the challenges which the integration of modern and traditional health systems are facing. A parallel indigenous health programme implemented through cooperation between Danish and indigenous medial expertise and anthropologists, also in the Peruvian Amazon, has recently been documented and illustrate the exceptional opportunities (Hvalkof et al., 2004).

A more fundamental problem with mapping indigenous knowledge concerns the *nature of indigenous knowledge*. Indigenous knowledge can be understood as a form of local knowledge that is dynamic and context specific, and which is intimately related to the livelihoods of a people (Agrawal, 1995). Significantly, indigenous knowledge is communicated orally and is not always widely available, but 'owned' by specific individuals or social groups. It differs fundamentally from natural and technical science in its holistic character, which is linked explicitly to a culture (e.g., through symbolic meaning systems, ritual, morality, etc.) and through a sense of 'kinship' that establishes an ongoing relationship between a people and an environment. This relation is often based upon a cyclical concept of time that interconnects social, personal, environmental, and spiritual processes and events (Rundstrom, 1995). As such, indigenous knowledge represents a different epistemology from natural science.

Figure 6.5   Gran Pajonal, Settler Community Oventeni, Peru, 1958 and 1996

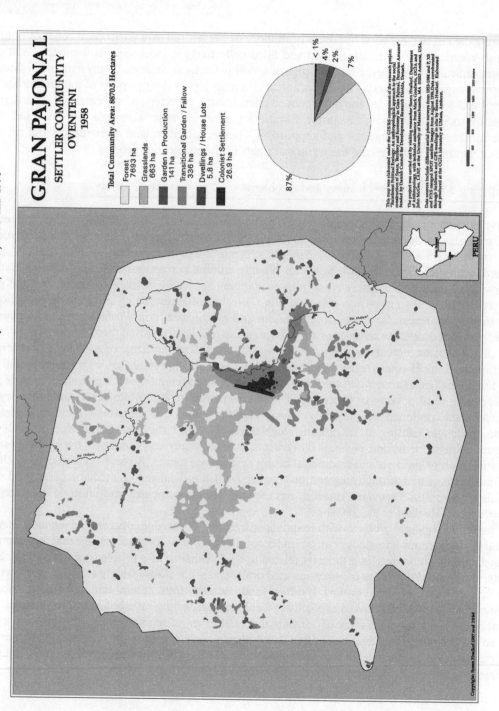

GRAN PAJONAL

SETTLER COMMUNITY
OVENTENI
1958

Total Community Area: 8870.5 Hectares

Forest
7693 ha

Grasslands
663 ha

Garden in Production
141 ha

Transitional Garden / Fallow
336 ha

Dwellings / House Lots
5.8 ha

Colonist Settlement
26.9 ha

< 1%
4%
2%
7%
87%

This map was elaborated under the GIS/RS component of the research project: "Rainforest Political Ecology: An anthropological approach to the social construction of Space, Territory and Economy in Gran Pajonal, Peruvian Amazon" funded by Danish Council for Development Research Danida, Denark.

The project was carried out by visiting researcher Søren Hvalkof, Department of Anthropology with Center for Development Research, CDR and collaboration with Mark Goodwin, Michael Dove, and John McGee, PLAZ, at the University of Massachusetts, MA. 01003 Amherst, USA.

Data sources include different aerial photo surveys from 1953-1984 and P.3X and P.XS mosgal SPOT satellite images from August 1996. Data corroborated through field surveys and GPS readings in situ by Søren Hvalkof. Elaborated and produced at the OGIA laboratory at UMass, Amherst.

0   40   800   1280   5600   3000 metres

PERU

Rio Chilthen

Rio Chilten

Copyright: Søren Hvalkof 1997 and 2004

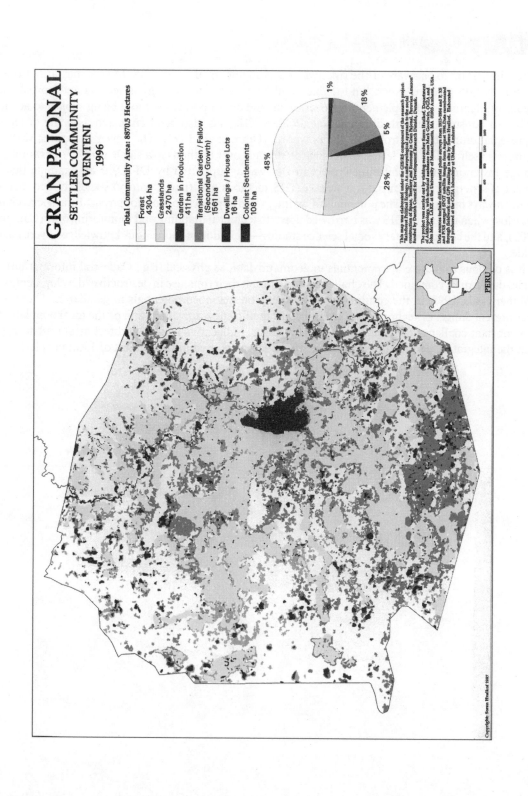

GRAN PAJONAL

SETTLER COMMUNITY
OVENTENI
1996

Total Community Area: 8870.5 Hectares

Forest
4304 ha

Grasslands
2470 ha

Garden in Production
411 ha

Transitional Garden / Fallow
(Secondary Growth)
1561 ha

Dwellings / House Lots
16 ha

Colonist Settlements
108 ha

48%

1%

18%

5%

28%

This map was elaborated under the GIS/RS component of the research project: "Rainforest Political Ecology: An anthropological approach to the social construction of Space, Territory and Economy in Gran Pajonal, Peruvian Amazon" funded by Danish Council for Development Research Danida, Denmark.

The project was carried out by visiting researcher Søren Hvalkof, Department of Anthropology, with sabbatical assistance from Mark Goodwin, CGIA and John McGee, LAEF at the University of Massachusetts, MA, 01003 Amherst, USA.

Data sources include different aerial photo surveys from 1953-1994 and P. XS and P//95 merged SPOT satellite images from August 1996. Data corroborated through historical GGPS dispating in situ by Søren Hvalkof. Elaborated and produced at the GGIA laboratory at UMass, Amherst.

PERU

0   400   800   1200   1600   2000 meters

Copyright: Søren Hvalkof 1997

It is important to be aware of the risk involved in an uncritical use of GIS. Misuse may arise from the legitimacy GIS gives to expert 'knowledge', and because the technology is seen as an unproblematic means of planning and implementing government and donor policies without being subject to account-ability or consultation with different stakeholders. GIS has also been criticized as being 'a techno-representation readily controlled by the powerful' (Dunn et al., 1997). The power associated with GIS manifests itself at different levels, including the struggle over methods in a single study. For example, the Range Inventory and Monitoring Project in Botswana, supported by DFID, is an example that the potential synergies between natural science/GIS methods and (participatory) social science methods do not always materialize. The potentials of an integrated approach to monitor physical and social change were lost when the use of GIS was narrowed down to technical mapping and monitoring only (Campbell, 2002), and the complementary social science studies—including of indigenous knowledge—were pushed aside.

It is obvious that there are potentials in geomatic data, as physical (e.g., Cadastral information) and social data can be combined. The challenge is to prevent their (mis)use in destructive 'developmentalism' (Weiner et al., 1995) in the continuous drive to exploit untapped potentials in geomatics. There is the ever-present danger of technological overkill, cost inefficiency, and alienation of the local population. It is a constant challenge to researchers, NGO activists, indigenous leaders and technical staff to ensure that the integrated, participatory geomatic methodology is used in the interest of local people.

Monitoring and Evaluation, M&E, are separate steps in the planning cycle but treated together in this chapter unless otherwise stated, since monitoring and evaluation have much in common—as management tools, a basis for learning, and methods applied. The chapter is set in the context of escalating demands for documentation of performance, accountability, results, effects and impact—some talk of an 'audit culture' and 'tyranny of evaluation'. The espistemological questions, what can be measured and what can be attributed to the ever moving target of development interventions, have prompted an interest in evaluating processes as much as outcomes. The movement seems to be from evaluation studies to streams. A variety of approaches to M&E are presented, indicator or narrative-based for example, reflecting that there are different purposes and intellectual and practical skills required to do good evaluations. Guidance is provided on participatory M&E including stakeholder and beneficiary analysis, and nine cases are included to illustrate the richness and inspire the prospective evaluator.

7.1 Monitoring and Evaluation—for Accountability and Learning

7.1.1 Definitions of Monitoring and Evaluation

Monitoring is the continuous assessment of the progress and performance of a development intervention. Evaluation is the end or ex-post assessment of an intervention, its impact and lessons learnt. Since many of the methods used for monitoring and for evaluation are similar, monitoring and evaluation, M&E, are not as sharply separated in this chapter as some would prefer, in particular practitioners who are involved in either monitoring or evaluation. A separation of monitoring and evaluation would also be conceptually justified. Monitoring is a necessary management tool for those responsible for the process of a given intervention. Evaluation is also a management tool, but more so for organizations and agencies, who need to learn from better practices and let these lessons be reflected in their future work and strategies. Apart from that, this chapter will show that monitoring and evaluation is more than a management tool. On the one hand M&E are auditing tools for funding agencies. On the other, they can be important events for sharing experience between different stakeholders affected by an intervention, particularly if the monitoring and evaluation events are organized as participatory activities.

Aid agencies are increasingly under pressure from political constituencies to document the benefits of resources spent on development cooperation. If benefits are not satisfactory, the sources may dry up. The agencies are requested to clarify the impact an intervention is expected to have for poor people, and how this will be achieved. This requires monitoring and evaluation of the intervention, regardless of whether this is a project or programme or support to a policy or strategy. Calls for accountability, efficiency and improved management performance have led to a more intense focus on the monitoring and evaluation stages of the planning/project cycle (Figure 7.1).

Figure 7.1 The Project Cycle

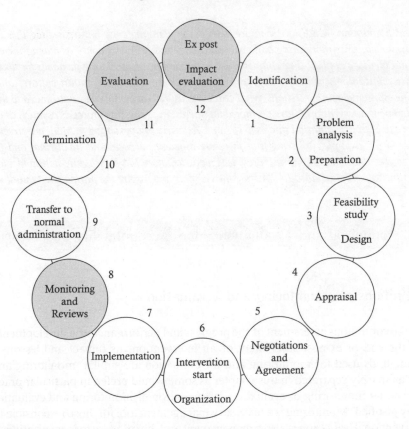

Many organizations are exploring new ways of measuring the progress, achievements and impact of their work. Results Based Management, RBM, requires monitoring and evaluation in one form or the other. Key questions are: How can changes and results be tracked continuously over time? How can we know what works and what does not? How does one distinguish effective from ineffective programmes? And who should be making these judgements? How can a learning process be established to support strategic choices for improvement? And how can evaluations be conducted in ways that lead to use of evaluation findings? (Patton, 1997: 4). Such questions, asked by public and private organizations alike, have contributed to a dramatic expansion of Monitoring and Evaluation. Conventionally, questions as those just posed have been answered through an approach that involved outside experts measuring performance against pre-set indicators, often after a project or initiative was over. More recently, funding agencies and organizations have been searching for ways, which are continuous and oriented towards *stakeholder involvement* and *organizational learning*, to monitor. RBM, which is widely practised by organizations, requires systematic monitoring and evaluation. Results Based Monitoring and Evaluation is one answer (Kusek and Rist, 2004).

M&E is about measuring change. But it is also about building people's and organizations' capacities to improve learning and self-reliance regarding their own development. The fact that M&E can help to *empower* primary stakeholders by creating opportunities for them to reflect critically on the intervention's direction and help decide on improvements is central in *participatory* M&E (see Section 7.3).

This chapter presents different monitoring and evaluation approaches and experiences, including participatory monitoring and evaluation, PM&E. The focus is on aid impact monitoring and evaluation of aid projects and programmes. But first, a few definitions and points of clarification:

The rough distinction between monitoring and evaluation is set out in Box 7.1:

Box 7.1   Definitions of Monitoring and Evaluation

Monitoring

A continuing function that uses systematic collection of data on specified indicators to provide management and the main stakeholders of an ongoing development intervention with indications of the extent of progress and achievement of objectives and progress in the use of allocated funds. DAC, 2001.

The regular collection and analysis of information to assist timely decision-making, ensure accountability and provide the basis for evaluation and learning. It is a continuing function that uses methodical collection of data to provide management and the main stakeholders of an ongoing project or programme with early indications of progress and achievement of objectives. IFAD, 2002.

Evaluation

The process of determining the worth or significance of a development activity, policy or programme ... to determine the relevance of objectives, the efficacy of design and implementation, the efficiency of resource use, and the sustainability of results. An evaluation should (enable) the incorporation of lessons learned into the decision-making process of both partner and donor. DAC, 2001.

A systematic examination and documentation of an ongoing or completed project or programme. It aims to answer specific management questions and to judge the overall value of an endeavour and supply lessons learned to improve future actions, planning and decision-making. Evaluations commonly seek to determine the efficiency, effectiveness, impact, sustainability and the relevance of the programme or organisation's objectives. An evaluation should provide information that is credible and useful, offering concrete lessons learned to help partners and funding agencies make decisions. IFAD, 2002.

Organizations emphasize the distinction between monitoring and evaluation differently, but the general use of the terms implies that monitoring embodies the *regular tracking* of inputs, activities, outputs, reach, outcomes and impacts of development activities—at the project, programme, sector and national levels—while evaluation is an *end* or *ex-post* assessment of these with more focus on outcome and impact assessment (see Figure 7.2). The distinction is epitomized in aid organizations which integrate monitoring into their day-to-day management of development assistance, while evaluations are undertaken by semi-independent evaluation units (MFA/Danida, 1999). Most organizations and writers stress that 'monitoring and evaluation are synergistic' (OED/World Bank, 2002: 28) or complementary (Cracknell, 2000: 72) (see also Box 7.2).

Figure 7.2 shows how monitoring and evaluation are integral parts of the Project Cycle Management framework.

Figure 7.2   Monitoring and Evaluation in the Framework of Project Cycle Management

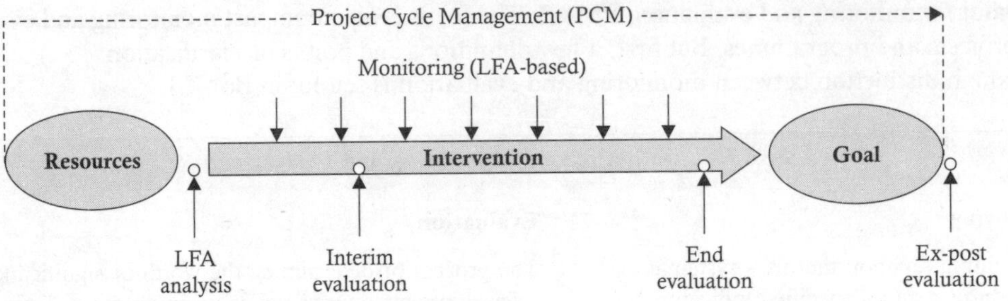

Source: COWI, 2000: 9.

Figure 7.2 illustrates how an intervention makes use of resources in order to meet specific goals and needs. The intervention is the process designed to achieve the goals. The initial request for support is analysed using logical framework analysis, LFA. LFA is also used to define the strategy, design the intervention and specify which indicators to use when monitoring progress. Finally, evaluation is the tool for providing knowledge for continued implementation. Ex-post evaluation may be used for impact assessment.

The following distinction between impact assessment, monitoring and evaluation is useful:

Timing: Monitoring occurs frequently and evaluation periodically. Impact assessment occurs infrequently, usually towards or after the end of an intervention.

Analytical level: Monitoring is mainly descriptive, recording inputs, outputs and activities. Evaluation is more analytical and examines processes, while impact assessment is mainly analytical and concerned with longer-term outcomes.

Specificity: Monitoring is very specific and compares a particular plan and its results. Evaluation does the same but also looks at processes, whereas impact assessment is less specific and, in addition, considers external influences and events (Roche, 1999: 27).

In other words, monitoring is the continuous assessment of the progress in a development intervention, while evaluation is the end or ex-post assessment of impact and lessons learnt. Monitoring contributes to the ongoing learning during programme implementation, while evaluation contributes mainly to learning for sustainability and for the improved planning of new interventions. The main target groups for learning from monitoring are managers, implementers and primary stakeholders of a given project or programme, while target groups for learning from impact assessments and evaluations are mainly development planners. There is no absolute distinction between monitoring and evaluation, as the Noakhali study referred to in Box 7.2 illustrates.

Box 7.2   Monitoring-cum-evaluation of a People-centred Rural Development Project

A very illustrative example of monitoring-cum-evaluation of a people-centred rural development project is the Greater Noakhali Rural Development Project in Bangladesh, funded by Danida from the mid-1970s for two decades. Monitoring was already established in the 1980s as an ongoing management tool, and as the basic data collection system for evaluation (Nielsen, 1990). The efforts put into the 'effect and impact monitoring' in the early days of what for many years was seen as Danida's Flag Ship project has later functioned as a basis for a unique ex-post impact evaluation of the overall project and its sub-components: Impact of Physical Infra-structure Component, of Fishpond Component, of Mass Education Programme, of Rural Poor Programme as well as Intensive Village Studies, Extensive Village Studies, and a study of Institutional Aspects.

After MFA/Folke, 2001/5.

Types and Categories of M&E and Related Activities

The monitoring and evaluation literature includes dozens of different types and categories of M&E studies (for more details, see Section 7.2.1). One explanation is that there are no unanimous definitions of what monitoring and evaluation entails, though DAC provides definitions and guidelines (e.g. DAC, 2001). A recent variant is designated *post-modern evaluation* (Krogstrup, 2001: 101). Post-modern evaluations are concerned about value-relativism, and aim to incorporate all interest groups in democratic negotiations about which evaluation-questions to include—something which in practice is close to impossible. They face the challenge of being caught in a naive consensus ideal. A somewhat similar approach which deliberately works with different 'truths' about the practices under evaluation is being developed in the name of *Deliberative Democratic Evaluation* (House and Howe, 2000) (see also Section 3.2.1).

In addition to the many different types of monitoring and evaluation, demarcations between monitoring and evaluation and other 'disciplines' are also fluid. '*Quality Assurance*', for example, which is now widely used in technical but also in organizational and social development assistance, is one such area, having much in common with the auditing aspects of monitoring and evaluation. '*Peer Reviews*' is another monitoring and evaluation device under critical scrutiny, not least in the evaluation of scientific knowledge and research quality (Hansson, 2002).

It is the tremendous acceleration of evaluation research over the last decades—in the wake of accelerated strategic planning and public regulation (Flyvbjerg, 1998)—which has contributed to what Cracknell calls 'paradigm wars' between different 'schools' of evaluation. The intention in this chapter is to present and illustrate the booming field of monitoring and evaluation, which the reader may want to investigate further. The intention is not to highlight all these evaluation 'paradigms' in any detail.

In this chapter, monitoring and evaluation are sometimes dealt with simultaneously, sometimes separately. The difference is made explicit when it is significant for the context and the cases of M&E included.

A point to remember is that the steps in the intervention/project cycle are not discrete. Monitoring and evaluation interlink with the other steps in the cycle in such a way that plans for how M&E will be designed and integrated must be considered at an early stage of planning an intervention. Thus, an evaluation design has implications for the kind of indicators and data that is to be collected and used in earlier stages as well as throughout the intervention/project cycle.

7.1.2 Learning from Change

Monitoring and evaluation are management tools (see Box 7.3). In combination, they provide the knowledge required for (*i*) effective programme management; (*ii*) reporting and accountability; and (*iii*) informing policy and strategy. In brief, the major purposes of M&E are to provide *accountability* and *learning from change*.

Box 7.3   Improving Management of Development Interventions by Strengthening M&E

Effective M&E can
- provide information needed for day-to-day decisions in the ever-changing context of projects and programmes
- provide information needed to guide the project and programme strategy towards achieving the goal and objectives
- provide early warning of problematic activities and processes that need corrective action
- help empower primary stakeholders by creating opportunities for them to reflect critically on the project's direction and help decide on improvements
- build understanding and capacity amongst those involved in the interventions
- motivate and stimulate learning amongst those committed to making the intervention a success
- assess progress and so enable accountability requirements to be met.

After IFAD, 2002, Section 1–7.

Monitoring and evaluation are being applied for *organizational strengthening and institutional learning*. This requires organizational capacity, or capacity development if capacity is not present. Organizations and institutions, including NGOs and Community Based Organizations, CBOs, use M&E to keep track of their progress and build their work on lessons about risks and success. This helps to strengthen individual and organizational capacities of self-reflection and learning, which can be used to demand greater social responsiveness and ethical responsibility, as Estrella points out and illustrates with many different cases (2000).

An element of learning from M&E is the capacity for undertaking M&E (see Box 7.4).

M&E is increasingly being used to monitor and evaluate policy. This raises questions regarding how micro-level M&E data generated at community or project/programme levels can be used to inform national and macro-level strategies and policies. The micro-macro linkage is an important challenge to monitoring global initiatives such as the PRSP initiative, which takes on conditional power to effectuate debt relief for Highly Indebted Poor Countries, HIPCs (see Sections 3.2.3 and 7.4).

Box 7.4   Evaluation Capacity Development

Monitoring and evaluation (M&E) is necessary to achieve evidence-based policy making, management and accountability—these uses make M&E invaluable for the effective management of public expenditures toward poverty reduction. Evaluation capacity development (ECD) aims to achieve sustainable M&E capacities and systems in countries so that they can conduct M&E and utilize its findings. The World Bank is increasing substantially its support for ECD activities, and is now active in 21 countries.

After OED/WB, 2002.

To help develop international evaluation capacity the World Bank in cooperation with Carleton University, Canada, has now established an annual 4 weeks training programme for 'Building Skills to Evaluate Development Interventions' (IPDET recurrent). The course 'is designed to meet the professional development needs of senior- and mid-level evaluation and audit professionals working in developed and developing country governments, as well as the needs of professional evaluators working in bilateral and multilateral development agencies and banks.'

(IPDET, 2004).

The issue of learning from monitoring and evaluation includes a paradox. For, as Picciotto points out, evaluation is the quintessential public good. But it is not in the private interest of anyone to be evaluated. Yet, collectively, everybody benefits from evaluation. Overall, the lack of responsiveness of development decision makers vis-à-vis the lessons learned through evaluation—for example, the persistence of over-optimistic appraisals and the lack of risk analysis—is widespread. So, due to open or hidden resistance to evaluation, continued vigilance is needed to overcome the obvious obstacles that evaluators face in their respective agencies (Picciotto, 1995). And organizations need to work seriously with their organizational culture to appreciate that M&E and capacity development are conditions for improved organizational performance.

7.2   Aid Evaluation, Basic Evaluation Designs and Primary Uses of Evaluation Findings

7.2.1   Types of Aid Evaluation

A useful distinction when dealing with development aid is between goal-oriented and process-oriented monitoring and evaluation, each with different degrees of stakeholder participation. Where the emphasis is on 'beneficiary' participation, the literature talks about participatory monitoring and evaluations (COWI, 2000; Cracknell, 2000; Estrella, 2000; Patton, 2002).

To illustrate by evaluation, *goal-oriented* evaluation focuses on whether the planned goals of an intervention have been achieved. Achievements are measured against standards set when the intervention was planned. The evaluation refers to the goals and objectives derived from an intervention's Logical Framework Analysis. Goal-oriented evaluation is interested in questions such as *how much* was achieved, *when* it was achieved in accordance with work plans, *how* it was achieved, and at *what costs.*

By contrast, *process-oriented* or just *process evaluation* is defined as *an evaluation aimed at setting out and understanding the internal dynamics of a project, programme or institution.* In process evaluations, evaluators are interested in contemporary processes, working relationships, institutional changes, management and implementation processes, rather than actual, measurable effects. Process evaluations focus on describing and assessing *what* happens and *why.* Process evaluation is similar to monitoring, but tends to be initiated for organizational learning rather than as routine monitoring of performance and achievements (COWI, 2000). *Appreciative Inquiry*, described in Section 6.4.1, is increasingly being used in connection with self-evaluation and process evaluations (Jacobsgaard, 2002).

When the emphasis is on people and stakeholder involvement, we talk of *participatory evaluation.*
The three types of evaluations, i.e,

- goal-oriented evaluation;
- process evaluation; and
- participatory evaluation

are not mutually exclusive, but appear in combinations of each and they all cut across different categories of evaluation. OECD/DAC member countries generally distinguish between the following categories:

- project evaluation
- programme evaluation
- country strategy evaluation
- sector evaluation
- thematic evaluation and
- evaluation of different forms of aid

The main purpose of an evaluation normally belongs to one of these categories, but in combination with elements of other categories. For example, the Sida-supported Evaluation of Mainstreaming Gender Equality (Sida, 2002), the last big evaluation in which I was involved, is primarily a thematic (gender equality) evaluation. It includes evaluation of selected projects and country strategies, but only to assess how Sida's Gender Equality Policy is reflected in country strategies and may have contributed to changes in gender equality in different types of projects—in particular changes relating to selected projects in human rights and democratization, urban development, non-formal education, and health care projects.

7.2.2 Basic Evaluation Designs and Baseline Data

Though evaluation designs differ a lot, there are some basic designs for measuring change: (*i*) the so-called 'before' and 'after' intervention comparison; (*ii*) the comparison of area 'with' and 'without' intervention; and (*iii*) comparison of 'group influenced by intervention' with 'control group not influenced by intervention'. Box 7.5 shows these ideal types and the ideal requirements for initial baseline information:

Box 7.5   Basic Evaluation Designs

- **The after-study with no control group** and limited baseline information. Assessments and judgements are based on evaluator's general experience and compared with similar evaluations (the most common—least costly approach).
- **The after-study with control group** and limited baseline information. Comparison of a target group exposed to an intervention with control group not exposed to the intervention. The design assumes that 'all other things are equal' between the two groups. The effect of the intervention is the difference between the two groups.
- **The before-and-after study** requires extensive baseline information. The effect of the intervention is the difference in the target group's situation at the time of initiation of the intervention and after a specified time—say one to two years.
- **The before-and-after study with control group** requires extensive baseline information. This is the most time-consuming and costly approach, and is hardly undertaken as aid evaluations.

In aid evaluations it is rarely possible to control the situation to such a degree that one clear-cut evaluation design can be chosen. Confounding factors external to the intervention under evaluation, such as droughts, economic crisis, epidemics, other development interventions, etc., cannot be totally controlled, nor their effect measured as compared with effects of a particular aid intervention. Each evaluation design poses its own problems of reliability and validity when trying to capture changes through causal relationships between aid interventions and effects. Evaluators cannot eliminate all of these when measuring the 'moving targets' of development assistance. But they can make sure that the limitations of evaluation design and data sources are made explicit (COWI, 2000: 28–30).

Decisions need to be taken on *measurement,* i.e., on how to measure change, which data to collect and criteria to use, in order to quantify or assess the significance of the changes. The data requirements, measures and analysis vary with the evaluation design. In the last instance, however, the determining factors for choice of evaluation design relate to *resources* and *time* as much as to the ideal design for a specific objective of an evaluation. Aid evaluations, therefore, also tend to combine elements from different evaluation designs and a variety of methods for data gathering and analysis—as much as a given context permits. This is illustrated in the M&E cases throughout the chapter. For example, the Uganda-based Gender and Poverty Impact Monitoring for Agricultural Sector Programme Support (MFA/Danida, 2000) is a long-term (three to four years) thematic (gender and poverty), sector oriented monitoring-cum-evaluation and impact study, combining baseline study, context, process and participatory evaluation, and including control groups in the design (see Case 7, Section 7.4.4).

Baseline Data

Baseline studies comprise in principle the first step of what will eventually become evaluation studies. A baseline study involves carrying out a review of the situation immediately before a development activity starts. Baselines provide useful benchmarks of the situation 'then' and suggest suitable indicators for measuring the situation 'now'. And baselines may serve to fine-tune the project design and strategy, particularly if there is a good balance between qualitative and quantitative data (Cracknell, 2000).

Aid organizations may include baseline studies in their Evaluation Guidelines. In 1994, the Swedish International Development Cooperation Authority (Sida) produced a baseline study handbook outlining the key issues and steps of baseline studies (Box 7.6):

Box 7.6   Baseline Studies

Steps in carrying out a baseline study:

1. Decide if a baseline is necessary (usual answer will be yes).
2. Draw up terms of reference. These should include:

   - Background information
   - Objectives of the study
   - Scope and focus of the study
   - Who will conduct the study
   - Methodology—generally a combination of methods will be appropriate, including interviews, public meetings, workshops, surveys, ranking techniques, and participatory rural appraisal, PRA
   - Time plan
   - Reporting procedure

3. Choose the team
4. Decide when to conduct the study
5. Review the final report—check it covers terms of reference
6. Disseminate and utilize the baseline information

Coming to the core of the task, the information collected will of course depend on the nature of the project, but it will normally include the following:

A. Socio-economic information, i.e., demographic; information about the community, its social and economic organization and infrastructure; and information about households.
B. Sector-specific information, i.e., information related to specific sectors such as natural resources, health education, environment, etc.
C. Issues of local concern, i.e., issues that local people feel strongly about. Such information can only be obtained by participatory research methods, and it should also cover suggested solutions from the 'grass roots'.

After Sida, 1994.

These ideal steps are rarely followed. Anybody who has been involved in evaluations will be aware of the problems of measuring change and impact because adequate baseline data are lacking. The classic problems with baseline data are: data overload, poor recording of data, or no baseline data collected for particular objectives. In many cases baselines need to be reconstructed with different degrees of success. The main sources for reconstruction of baseline information are (*i*) project documents and records; (*ii*) memorized baseline information from key person interviews; and (*iii*) baseline information from other organizations.

In order to overcome problems concerning baseline data, Roche suggests the following **key lessons for baseline data collection:**

- Aim to collect only those data that is seen to be particularly relevant to assessing the outcome of the project and that will be difficult to identify through recall or baseline reconstruction methods.
- Aim to collect only as much information as the organization actually has the capacity to analyse, organize and store. Don't be tempted to match the kind of data and analysis that a larger organization might collect.
- Recognize that it is impossible to predict all the information that might be needed and that any baseline will need to be updated.
- Explore the possibility of creating 'rolling baselines' by following the progress of a particular number of people or groups throughout the course of the project.
- Investigate the possibility of using new individuals, groups, or communities which become involved in a programme as a baseline for comparison with existing participants.
- Ensure that collected data is properly recorded, filed and stored. Make sure that the organization knows where these files are held and what they contain, and that there is an adequate system for retrieving the information when it is needed (Roche, 2000: 76).

The quality of baseline information spills over into the quality of subsequent monitoring and evaluation and the utilization of findings.

7.2.3 Primary Uses and Users of Evaluation Findings

If the two main purposes of evaluations are *accountability* or control and *learning* (MFA/Danida, 1999), then the primary uses of evaluation findings can be classified into three main groups: (*i*) making overall judgements; (*ii*) facilitating project or programme improvements; and/or (*iii*) generating knowledge (see Box 7.7).

All three uses of evaluation findings—to render judgement, to improve programmes, and to generate knowledge—support decision-making. The three kinds of decisions, however, are quite different:

(*i*) Rendering judgement about overall merit or worth for summative purposes supports decisions about whether a programme should be continued, enlarged, disseminated, or terminated—all major decisions.

Box 7.7 Three Primary Uses of Evaluation Findings	
Judge merit or worth	Summative evaluation Accountability Audits Quality Control Cost-benefit decisions Decide a programme's future Accreditation/licensing
Improve programmes	Formative evaluation Identify strengths and weaknesses Continuous improvement Quality enhancement Being a learning organization Manage more effectively Adapt a model locally
Generate knowledge	Generalizations about effectiveness Extrapolate principles about what works Theory building Synthesize patterns across programmes Scholarly publishing Policy making

After Patton, 1997: 76.

(*ii*) Decisions about how to improve a programme tend to be made in small, incremental steps based on specific evaluation findings aimed purposefully at instrumental use.

(*iii*) Policy decisions informed by cumulative knowledge from evaluations imply a weak and diffuse connection between specific evaluation findings and the eventual decision made—thus the term enlightenment is also used (Patton, 1997: 79).

Results of monitoring and evaluation are useful in particular if they can be turned into action. It is not always possible to take action which satisfies all groups of stakeholders, but the results must be shared by those who can make use of them. In most cases there will be several groups involved; each one with its particular needs and expectations (see Box 7.8).

Today, it is necessary to add that technology in general and the Internet in particular affects the form in which M&E data can be collated and hence also influences the use of M&E data. Rist talks about 'evaluative knowledge' and suggests 'a shift from evaluation studies to streams of evaluative knowledge' (Rist, 2002). This has implications for the powerful discussions about utilization-based evaluation, which Patton has taught the evaluation community for years (Patton, 1997), and makes Rist suggest that: Utilization paradigms are now those of knowledge management and organizational learning. Both focus on institutional uses of knowledge, not that of individual users.

Box 7.8	Who Needs to Get the Evaluation Results, Why and How?		
Audience	Role in Evaluation and Follow-up	Which Results they Need to Get and Why	How They Can Get the Results
Community not directly involved in programme	Takes a small part (e.g., answering questionnaires)	Summary of results to create interest/support for programme	Meetings. Discussions. Mass media. Newsletters. Pictures
Community directly involved in programme	Takes a part in planning and carrying out evaluation	Full results and recommendations so that they can help to put them into action	Through participation in evaluation. Meetings. Study of results. Mass media. Newsletters. Pictures
Programme staff	Responsibility for coordination, facilitating community decision-making and action	Full results and recommendations to be able to put them into action	Through participation. Meetings. Study of report
District-level departments, agencies, organizations	Receive information and/or specified active role. Disseminate lessons learnt. Support future action	Full results or summary only for analysis of lessons learnt and policy decision-making	Full report or summary (1 to 2 pages). Discussions with evaluation coordinators. Mass media
Regional level	Same as district level	Same as district level	Probably summary only. Discussions. Meetings
National level ministries, agencies, organizations	Receive information. Disseminate lessons. Support future action	Full results or summary for analysis of lessons learnt and policy making	Summary. Discussions. Meetings
External funding agency	Receive information. Disseminate lessons. Support future action	Full results or summary for analysis of lessons learnt and policy making	Full report plus summary discussions
International agencies, UN development agencies	Receive information. Disseminate lessons. Support future action	Full results or summary for analysis of lessons learnt and policy making	Probably summary only. Discussions. Meetings

After Feuerstein, 1988: 154.

However, observations that evaluation communities are lagging behind the new electronic realities need to be tempered by the risk of getting carried away with the symbolic and ritualistic functions of M&E rather than their actual use, and the risk of being absorbed in the maintenance of enormous M&E data banks for the sake of the data banks and the monitoring systems themselves. Aid monitoring and evaluation must be connected to action—to adjustment of project and programme strategies and of the institutional frameworks in which they are implemented, whether M&E takes the form of studies or streams of evaluative knowledge. Electronic and Internet realities can support the utilization process, but cannot substitute it.

7.2.4 Evaluator Roles—Professional Evaluators

A critical feature of M&E is quality. But it is in relation to *participatory* monitoring and evaluation that the question of *who* becomes essential. The critical feature in a PM&E approach is its emphasis on *who* measures change and *who* benefits from learning about changes (Estrella, 2000: 3–6). This includes a distinction between 'insiders' and 'outsiders'.

Monitoring and evaluation, and evaluation of aid interventions in particular, often require professional assistance to design data collection systems and to collate and analyse data. Collaboration between the external evaluator and project and programme staff is essential. Once an M&E system is up and running, the need for professional assistance may be reduced. The involvement of divergent stakeholders in M&E requires that the process is facilitated by someone who is familiar with optimal communication techniques and conflict resolution, and who can take on the role of a mediator. Hence, mediation has come to be a key qualification of the professional evaluator (Box 7.9).

Box 7.9   Different Evaluator Roles

The following list represents typical roles of an evaluator

- The evaluator is a neutral, problem solving *social engineer* in accordance with the instrumentalist-rational interpretation of the role of evaluations in political-administrative decision-making processes
- The evaluator is a *controller* in an attempt to hold implementing agencies responsible for their decisions and actions
- The evaluator is an *advisor* concerning initiation and adjustment of initiatives and activities
- The evaluator is a *mediator* between divergent knowledge interests
- The evaluator is a *facilitator* in support of weak groups' attempts to increase their decisions and influence over their own lives

After Albaek, 1998: 97.

It is not possible in general to determine whether one evaluator role is better than another. That depends on the knowledge interests which the evaluator attempts to satisfy. One thing is certain, however—that problems will arise if the evaluator is not conscious about the knowledge interests being pursued. There is also a great risk that the evaluator will be blamed for 'wrong' evaluation results since 'a different point of departure should have been taken'. Consequently, the evaluator should be aware of his or her role in accordance with the evaluation design used.

Even then, there are many conflicting interests in evaluations which the professional evaluator must consider. Accusations that professional evaluators try to please the authorities who hire them in order to get jobs in future, are part of the discourse on the value of evaluations. This is the subject of a recent study undertaken on behalf of the Danish Parliament to establish the independence of evaluation teams (MFA, 2003).

Participatory monitoring and evaluation may also engage outside experts, e.g., to facilitate the inclusion of a wider number of stakeholders—on the premise that this will result in a number of ideas and perspectives. Outside evaluators may play a critical role in helping to establish and design a PM&E system, and in analysing and learning from findings. The role of external evaluator in PM&E is increasingly performed by national academics or by NGOs who have the advantage of local knowledge.

Monitoring and Evaluation, but evaluation more specifically, has emerged at the interface between science and action, between knowing and doing. Evaluation as a discipline is engulfed in a multiplicity of assumptions, e.g., that M&E assessment involving multiple stakeholders can strengthen ownership, partnership and a results-based aid orientation. At the same time it is recognized that participatory monitoring and evaluation requires skills and approaches that are not traditional:

- **Capacity building** in indicator development, monitoring and negotiation for all stakeholders.
- **Joint indicator development** and designing processes for gathering and sharing data openly that are built in from the beginning, not tacked on at the end.
- **Communication skills, in particular in group facilitation, negotiation, conflict resolution and participatory methods.** Evaluation departments and project management often lack these skills and an understanding of why they are important. Reorienting donor agencies, government staff and civil society organizations means changing attitudes and behaviour, and learning new skills and approaches.
- **Support from high level champions.** Because most evaluation professionals do not fully understand participatory approaches to M&E, and because involving stakeholders empowers the stakeholders to demand transparency, insist on accountability, and raise critical questions, use of the approach may be opposed by people resistant to change. High-level champions may be needed who will support and defend the participatory approach and justify the need to address critical questions or uncomfortable findings.

In the words of Picciotto, to tell truth to power is the task of evaluators!

In the following sections a few cases will illustrate some of the issues presented above. It may be useful to clarify the distinction between *thematic evaluation of participation* and *participatory evaluation*, when these concern aid-related participation and evaluation. The distinction can be illustrated by two Danida evaluations (Cases 1 and 2).

7.2.5 Case 1: Thematic Evaluation of Participation and Empowerment

The evaluation, Danish Support to Promotion of Human Rights and Democratization (MFA, Danida 1999/11), contains a thematic evaluation on Participation and Empowerment, as participation and empowerment are indivisible aspects of human rights and democratization programmes. The study is not in itself a participatory evaluation with any significant involvement of different stakeholder groups. Based on desk and supplementary field studies, the evaluation aims at learning for future Human Rights and Democratization support. It is an interesting study since few thematic evaluations of participation and empowerment through aid interventions exist. A few salient points from the evaluation are:

- Some 460 Danida supported projects with participation and empowerment objectives were identified in 53 countries from 1990 to 1998. This sounds like a large number, which may be related to the fact that it is unclear how participation and empowerment were defined for sampling the 460 interventions.
- Two-thirds of the popular participation and empowerment projects were funded through Danish NGOs.
- A stronger explicit poverty focus can be identified in projects supported by Danish NGOs. Yet only a small number of these projects have explicitly promoted local participation.
- The rather imprecise use of concepts in the interventions studied means that 'ownership' is seen to capture key dimensions of 'participation' and 'empowerment'. Hence 'ownership' tends to be used synonymously with 'participation' and 'empowerment'.
- Subsuming participation and empowerment under ownership misses the collective dimensions of empowerment, e.g., of civil society organizations.
- Participation is commonly referred to as a *means* or as an *end* in itself in the analysed interventions, while clarifications, e.g., of instrumental and transformational participation in aid interventions, are missing. An important lesson is that more systematic strategic considerations about these aspects of participation are required to improve project and programme design.
- Little evidence was found of any systematic use of participatory approaches in evaluations of projects which had been conducted earlier. Hence feedback lessons to Danida had been limited.
- This thematic evaluation was conducted by external consultants in cooperation with national professionals using a combination of desk study and field studies where interviews were the major approach.

Lessons from the thematic evaluation on Participation and Empowerment are that Danida and its partners need to address participation and empowerment concepts, objectives and strategies much more systematically to get beyond the trap of rhetoric. This is an important lesson which is also confirmed in other donor agencies' assessments of the use of participatory approaches in bilateral development cooperation (see Sida, 2000). Whether and how the evaluation results are picked up in the aid and partner organizations and lessons applied in future interventions are important questions.

7.2.6 Case 2: Participatory Evaluation of Business Sector Support Programme, Tanzania

This evaluation is said to be Danida's first attempt at *a participatory evaluation*. The distinguishing feature of participatory monitoring and evaluation is a high degree of stakeholder involvement in defining the issues and participation in conducting the relevant studies and analysis. The Evaluation of Business Sector Support Programme, Tanzania (MFA/Danida, 2003), was planned as a participatory evaluation in which representatives of agencies and stakeholders (including beneficiaries) work together in designing, carrying out and interpreting the evaluation. The role of the external evaluation team is primarily to serve as facilitators in order to support the groups' analytical and innovative processes.

In order to guide the participatory evaluation process, an Evaluation Guide was developed. In addition to the participatory evaluation procedures the components of the programme were also subject to a more conventional evaluation, and were evaluated according to the five DAC evaluation criteria (MFA/Danida, 1999): *relevance, impact, effectiveness, efficiency* and *sustainability.*

Lessons learnt relating to the participatory evaluation approach are:

- The participatory evaluation methodology is more time-consuming than the conventional form of evaluation—but provides important instructive information.
- Lessons learnt are more appropriate for the implementing institutions than for the donor—which was intentional.
- The external evaluators functioned mainly as facilitators in the joint process of defining evaluation questions and reflecting on these by local stakeholders.
- The external facilitators often wanted to dig deeper into some issues than those prioritized by the participants, since a lengthy consensus process in some cases made the sharpness disappear.
- A shift from a passive reactive attitude by the national stakeholder participants to an active participation in the evaluation process took place. A positive side effect may be that the participating institutions will benefit from the more positive evaluation attitude in future.
- The participatory evaluation methodology has prompted cooperation between programme components to the great appreciation of the participants.
- Combining the conventional evaluation methodology around the five DAC principles with participatory evaluation methodology complicated the facilitator's tasks.

A positive overall lesson about the use of a participatory evaluation approach is that attention to the internal learning processes has widened the comprehension of the institutions and made the evaluation results more direct and appropriate for the individual institutions. The evaluators conclude that if this process had taken place earlier in the implementation phase, the results of the process would have been useful for adjustment of the programme structure and for changes in some activities.

In other words, this conclusion indicates that participatory monitoring and evaluation approaches should be thought of and be integrated in similar development interventions at an early stage.

7.3　Participatory Monitoring and Evaluation

7.3.1　Why Participatory Monitoring and Evaluation?

The widespread acknowledgement that participation by primary stakeholders improves development relevance and outcomes is evidenced when staunch proponents of traditional M&E take on board PM&E. To quote the 'grand old man' of development aid evaluation, Basil Cracknell:

> I cannot see how the participatory approach can entirely replace traditional evaluation, if only because of the accountability imperative, but there can be no doubt that only if some kind of participatory methods are used can there be any prospect of getting really useful feedback about what makes for success or failure in people-centred projects .... even if participatory methods are used there will still need to be some element of objectivity if possible .... (Cracknell, 2000: 342).

Cracknell quotes many others who, like himself, see participatory approaches as complementary to traditional aid evaluation. Cracknell also seems to agree with most others on the need for some plausible degree of 'objectivity'. Whether objectivity is more likely to result from traditional evaluations than from participatory evaluation is a matter of approach and adherence to principles such as those outlined by Chambers (see Box 2.8) and Roche (1999). However, traditional evaluations tend to make use of quantifiable indicators and produce quantified results which signal objectivity—rightly or wrongly. It is the inclusion of *primary stakeholders* (Section 7.3.2) in monitoring and evaluation which prompts the attraction of *participatory* monitoring and evaluation.

PM&E is attracting interest from many quarters. It offers ways of assessing results and learning from results that are more inclusive and more in tune with the aspirations of those directly affected, and that allow development organizations to better focus on their goal to improve poor people's lives. By broadening involvement in identifying achievements and analysing results, a clearer picture can be gained of what is happening on the ground.

The distinction between monitoring and evaluation is particularly difficult to sustain in the case of people-centred or participatory projects, for example rural development projects, because the data requirements for monitoring and evaluation are almost identical. Experience has shown that one cannot wait until these projects are 'completed' before collecting information for evaluation. People-centred projects are seldom 'completed' in the sense that a bridge is built or a power line installed—they tend to run on without any obvious end date (Cracknell, 2000: 173).

PM&E moves away from being an activity undertaken for, and by, outsiders, to one that builds on local community activity and increases its capacity to record and analyse local conditions. The information generated should contribute to improving learning and action, in addition to the regulatory, watch-dog function of many traditional monitoring programmes (Abbot and Guijt, 1998: 20).

PM&E is a tool for learning from experience—from success and from failure, and for doing better in future. Thus defined, PM&E does not differ from traditional M&E. However, PM&E serves a dual purpose: (*i*) it is a management tool which enables people to improve their efficiency and effectiveness; (*ii*) it is also an educational process in which participants increase awareness and understanding of factors which affect their situation, thereby increasing their control over the development process. Much of this is shared with traditional M&E. The participants tend to differ with outsiders dominating conventional M&E and local stakeholders dominating PM&E. Box 7.10 illustrates how the difference between conventional and participatory evaluation has been interpreted and explained by implementing agencies such as PROWWESS, Promotion of the Role of Women in Water and Environmental Sanitation Services.

Box 7.10	Differences between Conventional Evaluation and Participatory Evaluation	
	Conventional	Participatory
Who	External experts	Community people, project staff, facilitator
What	Predetermined indicators of success, principally cost and production outputs	People identify their own indicators of success which may include production outputs
How	Focus on 'scientific' objectivity; distancing of evaluators from other participants; uniform, complex procedures; delayed; limited access to results	Self-evaluation; simple methods adapted to local culture; open, immediate sharing of results through local involvement in evaluation processes
When	Usually upon completion; sometimes also mid-term	Merging of monitoring and evaluation; hence frequent small-scale evaluations
Why	Accountability, usually summative, to determine if funding continues	To empower local people to initiate, control and take corrective action

After PROWWESS, 1990: 4.

The inclusion of many representatives of diverse interest—or stakeholder—groups is the 'axis' around which the PM&E process revolves, as people together analyse existing realities and seek points of action. The inclusion of 'stakeholders' is the distinguishing feature of participatory M&E, as described by Estrella in 'Learning from Change' (2000). Stakeholders include, among others: 'beneficiaries'; project and programme staff and management; researchers; local and central government politicians and technical staff; and funding agencies. PM&E takes advantage of the fact that these diverse groups of people view, describe and act on changes through different lenses. It recognizes the importance of people's participation in analysing and interpreting changes, and learning from their own development experience.

The interest in PM&E is partly a reflection of the international development community's dissatisfaction with the commonly practised 'top-down' approaches to M&E. Traditional M&E approaches have been characterized as oriented solely to the needs of funding agencies and policy makers, while stakeholders directly involved in or affected by the development activities meant to benefit them have little or no input in the evaluation.

Other factors which influence the interest in PM&E is the trend in aid management where greater emphasis is placed on achieving results, and there is a demand for greater accountability and demonstrated impact (see Box 7.11).

Box 7.11   PM&E—Focus on Results, Accountability and Transparency

PM&E broadens participatory approaches in identifying and analysing change. It involves giving voice to the poor and their organizations in decision-making and providing civil society an opportunity to influence the governance process in the country. It focuses on results and lays a foundation for increasing accountability and transparency in decision-making around public actions, resources and services.

PM&E is a social learning process as much as a technical process. It involves trust, negotiation and dialogue. It provides a tool for dialogue between multi-stakeholders across power and other differences. Thus PM&E 'creates space' for participation. By opening up the range of stakeholders involved in the monitoring and evaluation process, PM&E also builds broader ownership and commitment.

The iterative nature of the PM&E process is essential for its success and for its sustainability. Feedback and information generated from one round of PM&E process is incorporated into future rounds of decision-making and programme implementation.

After Shah and Youssef, 2002: 29.

Participation increases the utilization of evaluations. However, there is a confining dimension in the use of PM&E projects—which are still the most commonly monitored units despite the move toward sector programme support—i.e., the persistence of the project cycle with relatively fixed procedures for the individual steps. PM&E anticipates participation at all stages of the project/programme cycle. To introduce participation only at the M&E stages may be counterproductive unless participants are selected according to *substantial knowledge* of the project. Optimal participation in monitoring and evaluation requires the participants to have been involved already during earlier stages, i.e., in decision-making and planning and in the implementation process of an intervention, and in sharing the benefits.

Despite variations, four common features are considered to contribute to good participatory monitoring and evaluation practice: (*i*) participation, (*ii*) learning, (*iii*) negotiation, and (*iv*) flexibility (Estrella and Gaventa, 1998). It strives to be an internal *learning process* that enables people to reflect on past experience, examine present realities, revisit objectives, and define future strategies, by recognizing different needs of stakeholders. Stakeholders *negotiate* their diverse claims and interests, i.e., what will be monitored and evaluated, how and when data will be collected and analysed, what the data mean, and how findings will be shared and action taken is negotiated. The PM&E process is also *flexible* and adaptive to local contexts and to constantly changing circumstances. By encouraging *stakeholder participation* beyond data gathering, PM&E can serve as a tool for *self-assessment*. It is about promoting self-reliance in decision-making and problem solving—thereby strengthening people's capacities to take action and promote change. But who actually can and do participate in monitoring and evaluation?

Who Participates on Whose Behalf?

Asking questions about who participates and who is excluded, as well as how and by whom different kinds of actors are represented, is a key to knowing something about whose interests are being nurtured. PM&E requires the involvement of people, i.e., representatives of different stakeholder groups—in different steps:

- Deciding what areas to monitor
- Selecting indicators for M&E
- Designing data collection systems
- Collating and tabulating data
- Analysing the data and information
- Using the results

Much is assumed of those who become representatives of others in various consultative bodies, for example in connection with PM&E. Yet, comparatively little work has been done in development studies on understanding who they are, on what basis they come to represent others, what motivates them, and the implications of their participation. Only very few accounts of participatory mechanisms in practice give information about who actually participates and who are excluded. We get little sense of who exactly is speaking for or about whom, and how they themselves would regard their own entitlements and identities as participants, says Cornwall (2002: 24–28).

Most aid monitoring and evaluation initiatives, including participatory M&E, represent some form of 'invited participation' rather than 'self-initiated participation' (see Box 2.3). But since monitoring is a continuous activity and evaluation is undertaken after implementation of an intervention, there is a possibility of ensuring continuity in who participates. All participants may not be equally involved in the different phases, but stakeholder involvement beyond management representatives is crucial in deciding what to monitor, in selecting indicators, and in analysing results. But who are stakeholders, and how are they identified? And do they differ from 'beneficiaries'?

7.3.2 Stakeholder Analysis and Beneficiary Assessment

Evolving approaches aim to make M&E more participatory and effective by including a wider range of stakeholders at every stage of the project or programme process. The shift 'away from externally controlled data-seeking evaluations towards recognition of locally relevant or stakeholder-based processes for gathering, analysing and using the information', which Abbot and Guijt (1998) talk about, means involving (groups of) people in stages of monitoring in which they have rarely been involved before. Evaluation is an alien culture (see Box 7.12).

Box 7.12   Evaluation—An Alien Culture

The culture of evaluation that we, as evaluators, take for granted in our own way of thinking, is quite alien to many of the people with whom we work at the programme level. Examples of the values of evaluation include: clarity, specificity, and focusing; being systematic and making assumptions explicit; operationalizing programme concepts, ideas and goals; distinguishing inputs and processes from outcomes; valuing empirical evidence; and separating statements of fact from interpretations and judgements. These values constitute ways of thinking that are not natural to people and that are quite alien to many. When we take people through a process of evaluation—at least in any kind of stakeholder involvement or participatory process—they are in fact learning things about evaluation culture and often learning how to think in these ways. Recognizing this leads to the possibility of conceptualizing some different kinds of process uses of evaluation.

After Patton, 2002.

Involvement of different stakeholders in monitoring and evaluation will inevitably require some form of capacity building, either of external people to understand local conditions for monitoring, or of local people to understand external systems, or both, as they develop a mutually acceptable M&E process.

A useful definition with qualifications of *who* are stakeholders is given by Sida:

Stakeholders are individual persons, groups and institutions with vested interests in an intervention. **Primary stakeholders** are those who will be directly or ultimately affected by an intervention, either positively (beneficiaries) or negatively. **Secondary stakeholders** are intermediaries such as implementing organisations, or other individuals, persons, groups or institutions involved in interventions including funders. **Key stakeholders** are those of the primary and secondary stakeholders who can significantly affect or influence an intervention either positively or negatively during the course, and who will share responsibility for quality and sustainability of subsequent effects and impact (Sida, 2000: 11).

Identifying the main stakeholders of an intervention can be done through a stakeholder analysis (see Box 7.13 for a checklist on how to identify stakeholders). The purpose is to ensure that the relevant parties become involved in planning the intervention, and later in evaluation. If participation was not an integral part of an intervention when it was planned, it can be difficult to adhere to a participatory approach at the evaluation stage. A framework for making the evaluation 'optimally' participatory (Cornwall, 2000) can still be established by those responsible for the evaluation, ensuring that stakeholders are involved in formulating Terms of Reference, selecting the evaluation team, analysing data, and formulating conclusions and recommendations.

A stakeholder analysis will normally show that stakeholders are not homogeneous entities. The interests of various groups and individuals may differ significantly and may even be contradictory. The challenge for the evaluation is to bring the different opinions into the open.

In other words, evaluation teams are faced with finding a balance between naïve consensus thinking and an ability to handle conflict resolution. The real ability to handle this balance may be more important for the development practitioners and partners who have the task of coping with conflicting stakeholder

---

Box 7.13   Stakeholders and Stakeholder Analysis

Checklist 1—How to identify stakeholders

Has a stakeholder analysis been undertaken and did it answer questions like:

- Who depends on the intervention?
- Who are interested in the outcome of the intervention?
- Who will influence the intervention?
- Who will be affected by the intervention?
- Who will work against the intervention?

Consider whether the following stakeholders are relevant to the evaluation exercises:

- The central government level, including normally bot the line ministry (e.g., agriculture), the ministry of finance and/or planning and ministry of foreign affairs
- Local authorities
- The intervention manager and staff
- Target groups
- Civil society including NGOs
- Possible co-sponsors

Source: COWI, 2000: 15.

---

interests which affect an intervention. The decision to make a follow-up beneficiary assessment may be part of the solution (see Section 7.3.9).

Beneficiary Assessment

Sometimes special studies are needed to track specific issues in relation to or in the wake of monitoring and evaluation studies. Beneficiary assessments may be useful to ensure that the views of beneficiary stakeholders are taken fully into account in evaluations. As a supplement to Monitoring and Evaluation of the Agricultural Knowledge and Information System programme described in Section 7.3.9, Salmen has outlined a framework for Beneficiary Assessment (see Box 7.14).

The characteristics of 'Beneficiary Assessment' are:

- Listening to the local people; talking to them in their own language; living amongst them for a period of from several weeks to several months.
- Working closely with the decision-takers to ensure that the information being collected in the field addresses their concerns.
- Ensuring that the results are credible to development planners, e.g., by using representative sampling, and by quantifying, as much as possible.
- Incorporating the values of the beneficiaries, i.e., to maximise sustainability (Salmen, 1995).

Box 7.14   Beneficiary Assessment—Getting the Stakeholders' Views

Beneficiary assessment involves a process of information gathering to assess the value of an activity as perceived by its intended beneficiaries. For Agricultural Knowledge and Information Systems programmes, it involves structured conversational interviews with farmers, extension agents, extension managers, agribusiness personnel, and researchers. Extension programme beneficiary assessment is based on interviews with a fairly large sample of farmers, stratified as needed by region, gender, ethnicity, exposure to extension services, area coverage by extension programmes, or other factors. The interview stresses listening. The purpose of the beneficiary assessment is to influence programme policy and programme management.

A review of experience in 10 African extension projects found that the structure for beneficiary assessments varied widely, but that the approach was considered quite effective as a tool for M&E. Farmers in direct contact with extension agents benefited substantially, with resulting impacts on productivity. Farmer-to-farmer technology transfer and service provision to women farmers was generally ineffective. Farmers' major criticism of extension was the narrow focus of services. Extension managers found beneficiary assessments to be a positive exercise, effective in introducing policy changes, and resulting in more participatory approaches, including better links to existing and local organizations and greater responsiveness to farmer needs.

After Salmen, 2000.

Beneficiary assessment uses some of the techniques of participatory rural appraisal. But 'admirable as they are, these beneficiary assessments still fall well short of the full participatory procedures involved in PRA. Beneficiary assessments constitute more a "snapshot" at one point in time, rather than a continuous process of impact monitoring, whilst they contain little of the element of "empowerment" which is so characteristic of the PRA approach' (Cracknell, 2000: 87).

Beneficiary assessments were first used by the World Bank, but is now spreading to other organizations. The Danish Ministry of Foreign Affairs, Danida, has undertaken several, for example a Beneficiary Assessment for participatory forestry management projects in Tanzania (MFA/Rasmussen, 2002). The consultant for the study explains that:

Beneficiary Assessment is about answering the questions of **how** and **why** a certain process and activity took place and were perceived by beneficiaries, more than the outcome of that process— the **what**. When beneficiaries (managers and users) involved in a given activity develop an understanding of the processes, this provides strong basis for process-oriented decision-making and change management. The traditional assessment of what has taken place is not superfluous. However, when an activity goes wrong or becomes successful, its duplication, expansion, and repetition depend on the understanding of why that activity was successful—or not. A beneficiary assessment can in other words improve a process and activity to become more than just based on risks and assumptions—if not mere trial and error .... As the beneficiary assessment discovers and analyses the processes involved in the planning and implementation of a given activity and recognises the perceptions, views and sentiments of beneficiaries, it simultaneously decodes and provides documentation to management on issues that have often been subject to non-substantiated speculations and rumours. And beneficiaries are given a voice both in the process of the assessment but also very much during reporting to management (MFA/Rasmussen, 2002: 9–10).

The method of Beneficiary Assessment is based on qualitative techniques, e.g., conversational interviews. However, the large number of qualitative interviews conducted prompts the necessity and provides an opportunity for simple quantification. These give management documentation, which can facilitate the prioritization of project changes. For a comprehensive update on Beneficiary Assessment—the idea, the principles, and uses of the results in environmental contexts, the reader is referred to Rasmussen (2003): *Why and how to negotiate an environment for participation.*

7.3.3 Monitoring and Evaluation Methods and Tools

Monitoring and Evaluation makes use of a variety of methods and tools for data collection and analysis, which are used for many other types of studies as well. The special tasks which go into planning, undertaking and using M&E data suggest that M&E methods can be grouped according to tasks and types of activities. In its Guide to Management for Impact, IFAD categorizes 34 different methods, including participatory methods, for project M&E as follows:

1. Sampling-related methods
2. Core M&E methods
3. Discussion methods for groups
4. Methods for spatially-distributed information
5. Methods for time-based patterns of change
6. Methods for analysing linkages and relationships
7. Methods for ranking and prioritizing

For each category three to eight methods and tools are explained in terms of purpose, steps and application tips in IFAD's Guide, which also gives useful pointers for further reading about each method and tool (2002: Annex D). Box 7.15 lists the methods in brief, many of which are synonymous with the so-called Participatory Rural Appraisal, PRA, methods for data collection and analysis (see Box 2.5).

Regardless of whether the monitoring and evaluation results are to be used immediately for adjusting a project or programme or are to be used to make better project plans in the future, in most cases the results are to be presented in a report. Today monitoring data, and sometimes also evaluation data, will be stored in databases. However, databases are not enough. Data needs to be used and analysed, and results have to be derived and digested if databases are to be justified. Tables, graphs and charts are useful visual information. But all results, of evaluation in particular, cannot be presented as quantitative information. The meaning is not always contained in numbers.

Simple monitoring charts are sometimes better at communicating the message than overloaded tables. Whether illiterate or highly educated, anybody can understand the message in the 'smiley' monitoring charts in Figures 7.3 and 7.4.

Box 7.15   Methods for Monitoring and Evaluation

1. Sampling-related methods
Random Sampling
Non-random Sampling

2. Core M&E methods
Stakeholder Analysis
Beneficiary Assessment
Documentation Review
Physical Measurements
Direct Observation
Cost-Benefit Analysis (CBA)
Questionnaires and Surveys
Semi-structured Interviews
Case Studies

3. Discussion Methods for Groups
Brainstorming
Focus Groups
Nominal Group Techniques (Simple Ranking)
Strengths, Weaknesses, Opportunities and Threats (SWOT)
Dreams Realized or Visioning
Drama and Role Plays

4. Methods for Spatially-distributed Information
(Sketch) Mapping
Transects
GIS Mapping
Photographs and Video

5. Methods for Time-based Patterns of Change
Diaries
Historical Trends and Timelines
Seasonal Calendars
Most Significant Change

6. Methods for Analysing Linkages and Relationships
Rich Pictures (or Mind Maps)
Impact Flow Diagram (or Cause-Effect Diagram)
Institutional Linkage Diagram (or Venn/Chapati Diagram)
Problem and Objectives Trees
M&E Wheel (or 'Spider Web')
Systems (or Inputs-Outputs) Diagram

7. Methods for Ranking and Prioritizing
Social Mapping or Well-being Ranking
Matrix Scoring
Relative Scales or Ladders
Ranking and Pocket Charts

After IFAD, 2002: Annex D.

Figure 7.3   Monitoring Chart—One-month Chart for Monitoring Progress in a Community Forestry Project ('Smiley' Monitoring Chart)

COMMUNITY FORESTRY MONITORING CHART Month June				NURSERY	TREE PLANTING	FERTILIZER	EXTENSION SUPPORT	GROUP MEETINGS	LOAN REPAYMENTS	FUELWOOD	FODDER	FRUITS	SOIL IMPROVEMENT	VISITORS
😃		5	☺			✓	✓	✓						
🙂		4	☺	✓										✓
😐		3	😐							✓	✓		✓	
☹		2	☹									✓		
😠		1	😠		✓				✓					

Figure 7.4 Monitoring Chart—Six-month Chart for Those More Familiar with Using a Rating Scale ('Smiley' Monitoring Chart)

COMMUNITY FORESTRY MONITORING CHART			NURSERY	TREE PLANTING	FERTILIZER	EXTENSION SUPPORT	GROUP MEETINGS	LOAN REPAYMENTS	FUELWOOD	FODDER	FRUITS	SOIL IMPROVEMENT	VISITORS
😊	5	January	3	3	4	5	4	2	2	3	4	3	1
🙂	4	February	3	4	4	4	4	3	3	3	4	4	2
😐	3	March	4	4	3	5	5	3	3	4	4	3	3
🙁	2	April											
😠		May											
😡	1	June											

After FAO, 1990: 25.

In addition to being easy to understand, almost anybody, literate or illiterate, can participate in preparing the 'smiley' monitoring charts.

In participatory monitoring and evaluation, local planners, staff and participating users all take part in the reporting of results. The format will be decided jointly, but a division of labour for making the necessary calculations and writing will of course be required. Some results may be best presented in narrative writing, others numerically, and some in spoken words and presentations. There may be survey and questionnaire results. Participation does not mean that conventional methods are done away with. For some types of standardized information, questionnaires may be the most appropriate technique. Analysis of the numerical results may be presented as percentages, as shares, graphs and tables (see Section 7.3.6, Case 3, Figure 7.6).

From concrete examples of M&E studies it is clear that methods and tools are being adapted and mixed to suit a specific situation. Which specific methods and mixes to apply must be decided when setting up the M&E system—allowing for enough flexibility to add supplementary methods and drop others if lessons during the M&E process so suggests.

7.3.4 Setting up Participatory Monitoring Systems and Evaluation Frameworks

A short description of the steps which are considered necessary to set up a participatory monitoring system is given in Box 7.16.

Box 7.16   Key Steps in Setting up a Participatory Monitoring System

1. Make the decision to start a participatory monitoring process
2. Identify possible participants
3. Identify the objectives of the monitoring from the perspective of each of the participating groups
4. Clarify (or identify) the objectives of the work being monitored
5. Identify and select indicators*
6. Select methods re. indicators—considering time, skills, technology and resources
7. Decide frequency and timing of monitoring
8. Prepare and fine-tune the methods
9. Data collection—systematic implementation of the monitoring calendar
10. Dealing with the data—collate, analyse, share
11. Documentation of the findings
12. Using the information

* A way to help clarify whether an indicator is optimal for measuring an objective is to see if the indicator is 'SMART': Specific, Measurable, Attainable/Realistic, Relevant, Time-bound (see also Section 5.1.3).

In real-life situations, each step consists of several activities. For example, there should be moments for critical reflection on how to make sense of the information gathered, and for reflection on how to use the information for improvements. Planning for the necessary conditions and capacities—i.e., what is needed to ensure that the M&E system actually works, must also be addressed. Elaboration of the steps involved in setting up and using PM&E systems can be found in, for example, Abbot and Guijt (1998).

A formalized description of the steps in monitoring as in Box 7.16 hides what is, in fact, an iterative and negotiated process to which all the monitoring partners can contribute. Experience shows, however, that in many cases local people are only involved in step 9, i.e., the actual data collection. The review of a variety of monitoring experiences makes Abbot and Guijt suggest that there are four central questions and dilemmas that need to be understood when embarking on a participatory monitoring process:

- What are the perceived benefits for different stakeholders of participating in monitoring?
- Assuming that everyone will benefit in some way, what is the degree of participation of each stakeholder group in different stages of the monitoring work?
- Given different objectives and world-views, how does one agree on indicators?
- Given the methodological compromises that any partnership demands, how can one deal with the trade-offs, particularly those between 'scientific rigour' and 'participation'?

To make M&E operational, one needs detail on many parameters. The art is to find a balance between 'nice to know' and 'need to know' information, with the weight heavily placed on 'need to know'. Everyone who has been involved in M&E studies will know that an M&E Matrix can help to steer the type and amount of information to be gathered and analysed. The M&E matrix is a useful tool for organizing and keeping track of the information gathered (Box 7.17).

Box 7.17 The Monitoring & Evaluation, M&E, Matrix					
Performance Questions	Information Needs and Indicators	Baseline Information Requirements Status and Responsibilities	Data-Gathering methods, Frequency and Responsibilities	Required Forms, Planning, Training, Data Management, Expertize, Resources and Responsibilities	Analysis, Reporting, Feedback and Change Processes, and Responsibilities
Example—Project Key Outcome 1:					
Example—Project Activity 1.1:					
Source: (IFAD, 2002: 5–13).					

The above M&E matrix is very comprehensive, and ideally to be considered for setting up an M&E system for a large aid intervention. The categories of information include,

1. the M&E (performance) questions to be assessed
2. data needs and indicators on which information is required
3. baseline information requirements
4. data gathering methods, and who is responsible for collecting data when
5. instruments for data collection and data management and required M&E skills and resources
6. desired analysis, reporting, dissemination and feedback of results for utilization and adjustments
7. for each category of information the allocation of responsibility needs to be explicit.

These categories of M&E information are required for monitoring the overall project outcome (e.g., food security for all people in region X) and related activities; and likewise for sub-components of a project if such exist (e.g., improved agricultural technologies, micro-credit scheme for poor women, water supply—for drinking and irrigation, rural infrastructure, etc.).

In project and programme evaluations a simpler version of an M&E matrix may be sufficient. For example, in the recent evaluation of Mainstreaming Gender Equality in Swedish Development Assistance in which the author was involved, the evaluation team made M&E matrices a key tool both in intervention specific and country strategy evaluations. Not only did the M&E matrix help the team to pose key evaluation questions for each intervention: (*i*) *What* are the key gender equality questions, in particular interventions? (*ii*) *How* have they been addressed by the donor and partners? (*iii*) *Which changes* have occurred in gender equality which may relate to the interventions? and (*iv*) *Why* have changes occurred or not occurred? The matrices also helped us to *compare* findings across the three countries, Nicaragua, South Africa and Bangladesh, in which the evaluation took place (Sida, 2002, 2003).

Since indicators are the most common 'tool' and type of information associated with monitoring and evaluation, they need more explanation.

7.3.5 Monitoring and Evaluation Indicators

An indicator is a proxy for describing or measuring a complex situation or phenomenon, e.g., poverty reduction or well-being (see Section 5.1.3). In development work we use indicators to **describe** projects/programmes and project contexts in order to get an overview, but the most important use of indicators in development work is to indicate **change**. Indicators are used to measure change, i.e., to **monitor and evaluate** change that relates to development interventions. Without some kind of indicators we cannot monitor the **achievements, progress** or **impact** of development programmes. As the name suggests, an indicator only indicates—indicators do not tell the full truth about the situation and change (see also Section 5.1.3).

There are several categories of indicators. Box 7.18 includes the most common indicator typology with illustrative examples from Natural Resource Management interventions.

It will be noted that the examples mentioned in Box 7.18 are both quantitative and qualitative indicators. A useful conceptual framework that attempts to represent both the quantitative and qualitative aspects of programme work in a farmer-to-farmer programme in Mexico is illustrated as a 'cone' by Estrella (see Figure 7.5).

The 'cone' focuses on three levels across a continuum of tangible and intangible impacts: individual and family, organizations and society. The purpose of this framework is to allow comparisons across a number of projects using fixed categories and variables, but also to present specific indicators reflective of stakeholders' particular priorities and contexts.

The selection of appropriate indicators is in itself part of setting up the M&E system and of the participatory M&E process. In principle the indicators should be defined in the project Logical Framework Analysis. But an LFA does not always exist, nor do indicators always suffice for M&E.

There are certain criteria which help the selection of useful indicators, for example the SMART criteria mentioned in Box 7.18. These criteria, for example the criteria of 'specific' and 'measurable', or the preference for quantitative indicators, are not always easy to meet. Other helpful criteria are suggested to identify a 'clear' indicator:

A clear indicator includes the following elements:

- specified target group to which the indicator will be applied
- specific unit(s) of measurement to be used for the indicator
- specific time-frame over which it will be monitored

	Box 7.18 Types and Characteristics of M&E Indicators	
Type of indicator	**Characteristic**	**Examples**
Input indicator	Concern resources devoted to the project/ programme	• Amount of project funding • Degree of community input to project planning, by socio-economic grouping and sex
Process indicator	Monitors achievement during implementation, to track progress towards the intended results.	• Receipt of cash or in-kind payment by socio-economic grouping of household • Relative/equal participation across socio-economic groups and by women and men in project committee
Output indicator	Identifies short-term results	• **x** specified improved cultivation practices on private land adopted by **y** men and **z** women farmers • specified institutional mechanisms established and operating satisfactorily for management of natural resources on common land
Outcome/impact indicator	Relate to the longer-term results of the project	• % men and % women land users in priority watersheds practice sustainable dry land agriculture and forestry on private and common land • Poverty reduced for 95% of participating men and women, well-being increased in terms of **livelihoods, access to resources, knowledge, and/or rights** (each to be defined with stakeholders)

- reference to a baseline/benchmark for comparison
- defined qualities—e.g., what is meant by 'adequate', 'effective', 'successful', etc., as a qualification of an indicator?

These criteria can help to distinguish a *strong indicator* from a weak one. To take an example, if the aim is to assess impact at the objective level of a project, an indicator formulated like: 'Enterprise start-ups, in particular by women' is too vague to be measurable. Instead, specifying the indicator precisely would, for example, turn the indicator into the following: 'The number of new formal and informal enterprises started each year by poor female-headed and male-headed households in province X as compared to the original number'. (IFAD, 2002: 21–22). The latter is a strong, measurable indicator.

In aid monitoring and evaluation it is often necessary to rely less on quantitative indicators than on qualitative indicators. Box 7.19 illustrates both a quantitative and a qualitative indicator, which are relevant but not sufficient towards the measure of the same objective.

The example in Box 7.19 shows that the qualitative indicator provides more information on contents—'active involvement in management and decision-making'. At the same time it shows that a qualitative indicator can also have a quantitative dimension and a time perspective—'at least 50 per cent of women participating ... by end of year 2 ... from a baseline of 10 per cent'.

Figure 7.5 The 'Cone'—Conceptual Framework of Indicators in a Farmer-to-Farmer Programme

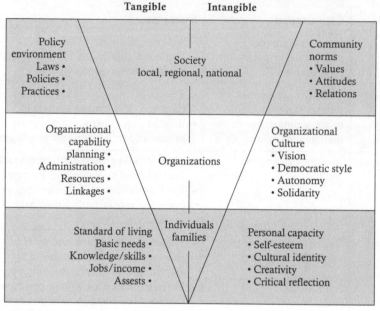

Tangible   Intangible

Policy environment Laws • Policies • Practices •	Society local, regional, national	Community norms • Values • Attitudes • Relations
Organizational capability planning • Administration • Resources • Linkages •	Organizations	Organizational Culture • Vision • Democratic style • Autonomy • Solidarity
Standard of living Basic needs • Knowledge/skills • Jobs/income • Assests •	Individuals families	Personal capacity • Self-esteem • Cultural identity • Creativity • Critical reflection

Source: Estrella, 2000: 43.

Box 7.19   Examples of Quantitative and Qualitative M&E Indicators

Objective: Men and women farmers in selected villages adopt improved cultivation practices on private land and take charge of the development and management of the natural resources on common land.
Quantitative indicator: Women form at least 33 per cent of project committee members by the end of year 2.
Qualitative indicator: At least 50 per cent of women participating in the project committees report active involvement in management and decision-making by the end of year 2 (from a baseline of 10 per cent at the start of the project).

Several other indicators than the two mentioned would be required to measure whether this particular project objective is being met. We will not go into all of them here. The point is that no matter how many indicators a project identifies, *indicators only indicate*. They do not tell the full story of change. Therefore, instead of collecting information about a large number of indicators and wasting a lot of time on gathering information that will never be used, it is worthwhile to think through which are the (few) indicators that provide enough information for a project to learn about its achievements, progress, and outcome or impact. That does not necessarily have to be many indicators. Preferably only five to six indicators for each indicator category (see Box 7.18) should be used in order to keep an M&E system manageable. The process of reaching agreement on which indicators are optimal can be quite lengthy, as the case on Gender and Poverty Impact Monitoring (Section 7.4.4) shows.

The more precise one can make each indicator, the less likely it is that misunderstanding about the indicator will occur among the people involved in collecting M&E data and analysing them. Seeking local indicators can bring about some useful results as stand alone indicators or as complements to more standard types, e.g., well-being and poverty indicators (Box 7.20):

Box 7.20   Examples of Local Well-being and Poverty Indicators

Local poverty indicators
- type and size of funerals (used in Ghana and Burkina Faso where spending on funerals is valued)
- availability of new clothes for celebrations (common indicator in many locations)
- postponement of marriages due to lack of dowry (Somalia)
- regular use of shoes (India)
- eating a third meal per day (common indicator in many locations)
- possibility of sleeping in a different room than the farm animals (India)
- women who possess cooking utensils or plates for guests in adequate size and quantity (Mali, Sudan)

Common standard poverty indicators
- household real income, consumption of staples, malnutrition among children
- access to off-farm income, access to capital, access to labour
- access to basic needs services, access to safe water, access to basic education, access to basic health services

After IFAD, 2002, Section 5: 20–24.

Most development agencies recommend 'community participation' in the identification of project objectives, indicators, and in monitoring and evaluation. But the interpretation of what this implies is diffuse, and learning *how* to undertake participatory monitoring and evaluation is still in the pilot stage, as Case 2 indicated and Case 4 will show with a different participatory approach that focuses on Most Significant Changes, MSC. The MSC is sometimes referred to as monitoring without indicators, in contrast to approaches illustrated in Cases 5 and 6. Cases 5 and 6 show in different ways how indicators normally play an important role in monitoring and evaluation. But first, Case 3 illustrates an element of how participatory M&E was applied in monitoring and evaluation of impacts of participatory research.

7.3.6 Case 3: Ranking by Farmers of Forages

Monitoring and Evaluation of Impacts of Participatory Research Projects

The following example is taken from a forage adoption impact assessment exercise carried out with smallholder farmers in M'Dak, Vietnam, by the International Centre for Tropical Agriculture, CIAT.

The case illustrates one participatory method, preference ranking, which was used as one among other methods in the impact study.

Workshops were conducted with each of six villages in the commune in community focus groups, which ranged from 30–60 farmers depending on village size.

A typical exercise in one of the focus groups started with a discussion about how planting forages led to farmers 'being happy'. As the farmers came up with a list of actual and potential immediate, inter-mediate and long-term impacts, these were written up on a large sheet of paper with arrows, linking impact that had a cause and effect. Questions such as 'How does this make you happy?' or 'What follows on from this impact?' prompted farmers to think about how each problem was related to the others. In all, the workshop participants identified 24 different impacts that forages had or were expected to have on their farming system. (The 24 indicators appear in Figure 7.6 after ranking and statistical analysis.) After the impacts had been written down, the farmers were each given a set of ranking cards and asked to rank the impacts according to importance.

Figure 7.6   Statistical Analysis of Farmers' Ranking of Forage Impacts, M'Drak, Vietnam

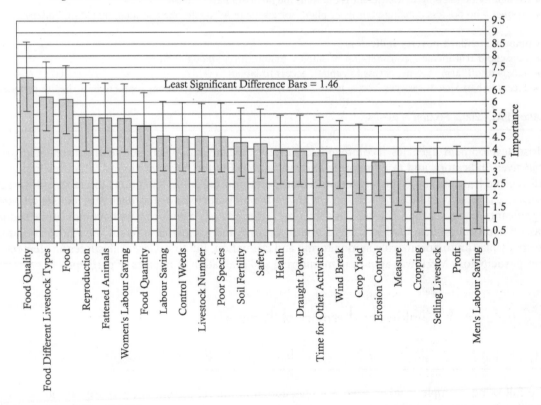

Source: Cramb and Purcell, 2001.

After the ranking exercise the cards were collated and taken away for analysis. A generalized linear model (GLM) was estimated. The results, summarized in Figure 7.6, showed that the ability of forages to provide good quality feed and fatten different types of animals were considered to be the most important impacts. At the other end of the scale, the potential of forages to increase the sale price of livestock or the reduction in adult male labour in the household were considered not important (or not achievable).

Many more methods were used in Cramb and Purcell's study on how to monitor and evaluate impacts of participatory research projects. Like Figure 7.6 above, they illustrate that participatory methods can often be subjected to statistical analysis and be presented in a comprehensive semi-structured form.

7.3.7 Case 4: 'Keep it Simple'—The Most Significant Change, MSC, Approach

The Most Significant Change, MSC, approach is a participatory tool for continuous *monitoring* and evaluation. It was initiated by Rick Davies and first tried out in 1994 as an evolutionary approach to facilitating organizational learning in the NGO CCDB in Bangladesh. Since then it has been adapted by several organizations in Asia and Africa. The Danish/International NGO, Danish Association for International Cooperation (called 'MS' in Danish), is currently introducing and testing the MSC as a monitoring tool. The description of MSC in this section is based on Peter Sigsgaard's assessment (2002).

'MS' works with a partnership-based programme in Africa, Asia and Central America, within a broad mandate of 'poverty reduction' and 'intercultural cooperation'.

The major reason for trying out an alternative monitoring approach like the MSC was the painful realization that the modified logical framework system 'MS' and its partners had struggled to put in place for *documentation* of activities and *organizational learning*, did not work. The paucity of usable documentation and knowledge gained stood out clearly against a background of everyone being extremely busy with the collection of all kinds of fragmented monitoring data. Data was rarely used in the analysis of effects and impact; neither was it stored for future use, Sigsgaard reports from 'MS'.

We also realised that we were sharing this misery with nearly all other organisations, including the big, official donor agencies. Everybody seemed to invest a lot in following the ritual (2002: 9).

The radically different MSC methodology was well in line with the values guiding 'MS''s partnership activities. Second, it was *participatory*—it does not alienate the actors—and it looked simple: With MSC you simply ask people to identify positive or negative changes observed over a period of time within a given *domain* of interest. The same people are asked which change they find the most important, and *why* they have chosen it as *the most significant change*. The outcome of the exercise will be a number of recorded 'stories' about change.

The attractions of the MSC approach to monitoring at first glance seem to be:

- It is time-saving, as one does not have to agree on pre-constructed, quantitative indicators;
- it is involving and participatory and suits a partnership-based organization well;

- it is transparent and free from pseudo-objectivity;
- it demystifies monitoring and is better in line with the epic tradition of many non-western cultures;
- it is suited to make use of information which is already generated, for example in partnership review workshops;
- it demands that the information be used at all levels—beneficiary, partner-organization and at country programme levels; and finally
- MSC serves as a supplement to already functioning parts of traditional M&E systems.

However simple and suited the MSC approach may look for an NGO like 'MS', it still involves careful planning and has its own limitations. To get started, 'MS' developed a set of guidelines to guide the story telling as dialogues around the three *domain's* of 'MS''s mandate, that is:

(*i*) poverty reduction
(*ii*) intercultural cooperation
(*iii*) organizational performance.

However, several issues remain, which a guide cannot solve. For example, the practical issue of sampling: Who is to tell their story about significant changes—regarding 'poverty reduction', 'intercultural cooperation' and 'organizational performance'? Who will facilitate the dialogue and verify the stories? How will prioritization of the most significant change stories be facilitated? Who will record the information and how will it be used and by whom? And, in addition, what *is* a story? Is a statement a story? (see example in Box 7.21). Decisions must be made on these and many other issues before starting.

Box 7.21   A Story of Most Significant Change in the Domain of Poverty Reduction—Mozambique

'During the previous years we did not complain about the lack of possibilities to sell our products—because we had nothing to sell. Today we complain.'

The above statement is a condensed story from a longer version quoting members of farming groups in Nacaroa:

'We have seen some small change towards the better in terms of production this year. This is partly due to the help (seeds and tools) we get from the District Agricultural Office and the visits of the Development Worker. People have produced a little surplus of peanuts, cashew and maize, but we have a problem in selling the products. Prices are low and we are far away from the route of the buyers. It is important to us to sell and get some income, because we want to be able to send our children to school. You could say that the change is that we now have **hope** for the future; we are expecting to advance in terms of development. It is, however, too early to say that our expectations are met.'

Justification, i.e., why did Danish development workers and their national partners choose this story from a list of 26 stories told, was: 'The story brings to life a reality, which is often hidden in the ordinary, statistically oriented "valuations". The farmers quoted know what they want to accomplish, and they are realistic about development being a gradual process. This is promising if you think in terms of sustainability. The story also expressed a paradox in development: New problems (marketing) arise when the initial ones (increased production) are solved. Some will lose, others will win.'

After MS, 2001: 8–9.

Several methodological lessons were learned from 'MS' pilot testing, e.g.: (*i*) The MSC system is only partially participatory. Domains of interest, in this case poverty reduction, intercultural cooperation and organizational performance, are centrally decided and the sorting of stories according to significance is hierarchic. (*ii*) Most participants easily fell to talking at length about activities conducted. This also applied to the interviewers, who had difficulties in grasping the idea; they did not always probe; did not ask for examples and sometimes even put the answer into the mouth of the respondents. (*iii*) Although the MSC approach follows the principle 'keep it simple', training on MSC use is obviously required.

A recognised limitation is that the MSC is not suited as a stand alone approach for ex-post, objectives based evaluation. But the data collected and insight gained through MSC can feed well into an evaluation.

7.3.8 Case 5: M&E of Agricultural Knowledge and Information

Agricultural Knowledge and Information System Projects and Programmes

With the move from project to sector programme support, the challenge to good M&E encompasses how to measure the translation of sector policies into tangible effects at the community level. Agricultural Sector Programme Support is a good case for illustrating how M&E of the sector-specific as well as cross-cutting issues have been approached. A framework and options for M&E of Agricultural Knowledge and Information System (AKIS) projects and programmes has been proposed (Alex and Byerlee, 2000). The framework for M&E Systems builds on the Logical Framework, and is basically indicator based:

Performance indicators (or 'KPI'—key performance indicators) are the basis for project or program M&E. Performance indicators derive from logframes and provide for performance measurement at two levels: process indicators that measure program inputs and outputs, and impact indicators that measure outcomes (changes related to the 'Project Development Objective') and impacts on social goals. Tracking input use and direct project accomplishments often requires multiple indicators, but these are relatively easily measured. Outcome and impact indicators are more difficult, as they are a result of project activities, but are influenced by many other factors.

Project indicators will vary depending on specific project strategies and objectives. Sound indicators must be characterized by time, quantity, and quality (TQQ). They should specify when change in the indicators is expected to be achieved, the extent of change expected, and the quality standard for the expected change. Qualitative indicators are acceptable, but must be specific enough to be unambiguous as to whether or not they are achieved (ibid.: 9–10).

Good illustrative indicators are provided (ibid.: 25–33) for possible goal and objective, outcome, output and input indicators for Extension Projects, Institutional Development, Technology Dissemination, Research Projects and Agricultural Education Projects—i.e., the sub-components of AKIS programmes. The menu of outcome indicators contains approximately 80 indicators. Measurement is typically in terms of percentage changes and values, and possible *data sources are global data base, country data base, project data base, special studies and expert reviews.* To use the proposed framework for monitoring and evaluation of a specific Agricultural Sector Programme requires careful decisions. Working with 80 indicators is rarely practical. A limited number of relevant indicators should be selected to meet the needs of specific projects and programmes, reflecting the principles for selecting key performance indicators (see Box 7.22). The level, especially for outputs vs. outcomes, at which a specific indicator is relevant, may vary depending on the specific project or programme.

Box 7.22   General Principles for Selecting Key Performance Indicators

- Relevant to the development objective of the project
- Unambiguous as to definition, valid and specific in reflecting changing conditions, and consistent and verifiable in measurement
- Meaningful and of interest to project management and stakeholders
- Significant and selective in that the monitoring system should limit the number of indicators to a manageable number
- Practical in terms of the ability to collect data on a timely and cost-effective basis and with a reasonable degree of reliability
- Provide information on impact dis-aggregated by gender, poverty status, ethnicity, or other characteristics of the client group
- Acceptable to the aid recipient partners, funding agency and other stakeholders
- Quantifiable to the extent possible, or, if qualitative, based on a common understanding of what constitutes success
- Responsive in reflecting changes due to project activities and sensitive in demonstrating change in as short a time frame as possible.

After Alex and Byerlee, 2000: 10.

The proposed M&E framework for agricultural knowledge and information projects and programmes is a good guide for designing hands-on M&E systems for concrete projects and programmes. The overall recommendations for the framework can be used in other sectors and situations. These are:

1. Describe details of the M&E system in project appraisal document;
2. Request M&E data from the early stages of a project;
3. Develop permanent M&E capacity for implementing institutions;
4. Establish a comprehensive set of key performance indicators;
5. Establish project baseline data;
6. Avoid large surveys;
7. Use a combination of data collection methods;
8. Ensure utilization of M&E data.

The following case will show how indicators are formulated and used for institutional capacity building.

7.3.9 Case 6: Indicators for Institutional Capacity Building

Institutional Capacity

Capacity development is arguably one of the central development challenges of the day, as much of the rest of social and economic progress will depend on it ... capacity development is not merely a stepping stone towards higher levels of human development; it is an end in itself. For individuals, for institutions and for societies, this demands a continuous process of learning and relearning ... (UNDP, 2002: 21).

This quote accompanies UNDP's introduction of a new paradigm for capacity development (Box 7.23):

Box 7.23 A New Paradigm for Capacity Development		
	Current paradigm	**New paradigm**
Nature of development	Improvements in economic and social conditions	Societal transformation including building of 'right capacities'
Conditions for effective development cooperation	Good policies that can be externally prescribed	Good policies that have to be home-grown
The asymmetric donor-recipient relationship	Should be countered generally through a spirit of partnership and mutual respect	Should be specifically addressed as a problem by taking countervailing measures
Capacity development	Human resource development, combined with stronger institutions	Three cross-linked layers of capacity: individual, institutional and societal
Acquisition of knowledge	Knowledge can be transferred	Knowledge has to be acquired
Most important forms of knowledge	Knowledge developed in the North for export to the South	Local knowledge combined with knowledge acquired from other countries—in the South or the North

After UNDP, 2002: 20.

Evaluating 'capacity development' faces a set of specific challenges, since agencies rarely have clear ideas about objectives, outputs, intended outcomes and ultimate impact of capacity development interventions. The challenges to develop a relevant methodology are consequently very tricky, as is currently being experienced in an ongoing 'Capacity Development Evaluation', which has developed into more of a research endeavour (MFA/Boesen, et al., 2002-ongoing).

'Capacity development'—capacity strengthening, capacity building, etc.—is one dimension in comprehensive sector programmes and in the monitoring and evaluation of these. For example, several components of the Environmental Sector Programme in Nicaragua, supported by the Danish Ministry of Foreign Affairs, Danida, have a strong element of institutional capacity building. It is an assumption that increased efficiency (improved public administration) within the institutions responsible for Natural Resource Management in Nicaragua will affect environmental quality positively. A main challenge has therefore been to define relevant indicators by which progress in institutional development and administrative capacity can be monitored.

Initially, a shared understanding of the term 'institutional capacity' and 'institutional capacity building' was built up around the operational definitions outlined in Box 7.24.

Box 7.24   Operational Definition of 'Capacity'

- *Structure of organization* (goals, mandates, legislation, obligations, management organization, etc.) which forms the foundation for operation.
- *Strategy*—an articulated methodology for an organization to achieve its goals in a programmatic sense.
- *Systems*—(operation systems and processes, such as management procedures, management information systems, financial management information systems, permitting systems, guidelines, manuals, standards, and the like) which establish the way of operation.
- *Interrelationships*—formalized and functioning network with other actors.
- *Human resources*—adequacy of human resources of the organization in terms of number, competencies (skills and knowledge), experience, attitudes, social interrelationships and confidence.
- *Incentives* in terms of adequate human resources policies and human resources management practices, sufficient financial compensation, acceptable working conditions and environments, recognition systems for well-accomplished work and the like.
- *Financial resources* to ensure the financial sustainability of the function of the organization.
- *Physical infrastructure*, such as office buildings, office equipment, communication equipment, etc.

After MFA/Ødum, 2001.

It will be seen from the capacity definition that the different elements of capacity are closely interlinked. Thus a capacity strengthening exercise should identify all major interlinkages and analyse to what extent it is necessary to address all elements, or whether some could be left out. In most organizations the interlinkages are so strong that all elements need to be addressed if major improvements are to be achieved. Addressing a few elements in isolation would produce negligible results only.

The definition also shows that the mandate and legislation as well as the formalized and functioning networks between the organization and other actors are part of an organization's capacity. No organization exists in a vacuum. All are part of a broader institutional and organizational set-up. Thus, clarifying mandates and identifying and analysing interlinkages with external actors are required as well. *Analysis and indicators reflecting external context are important elements.*

Organizational and institutional capacity building rests heavily on the commitment by top management. Accordingly, *analysis and indicators that reflect management commitment are required.* It is management who can ensure that *monitoring of indicators—internal and external—*is internalized in the organization.

Institutional Capacity Building—Environmental Sector Programme, Nicaragua

In the Danish supported Environmental Sector Programme in Nicaragua just referred to, capacity development is understood as an *improvement of the organizational performance and management processes.* Emphasis is put on improved *processes.* In addition, the partner organization expressed a *demand for capacity development.* The major performance indicators for the programme's institutional development are grouped in four broad areas:

- Legal framework
- Institutional framework
- Staff development
- Technical capability

In some cases indicators simply note the presence or absence of particular features (e.g., laws or agencies dealing with specific environmental matters). Other indicators attempt to quantify the effort devoted to environmental matters, e.g., by staff numbers, environmental expenses, etc. Both types of indicators must, however, be used with considerable caution, because institutional development is as much about *quality* as it is about *quantity.* Hence, numerical or presence/absence indicators alone can be very misleading.

To monitor institutional capacity and systems performance, the ESPS has identified a set of indicators within the eight categories included in the capacity definition (Box 7.24). Since capacity building is an objective of the programme, there is much emphasis on the partner organization's commitment and participation, e.g., in discussions on how to monitor the outcome of the institutional capacity building exercise. Thus, *input and participation of the partner organization in decisions on indicators and means of verification is an indicator in its own right.*

Initially the central indicators are concentrated around

- Monitoring institutional capacity and systems performance
- Monitoring of counterpart commitment
- Monitoring of external factors

Methodologically, component and context-specific indicators in these three dimensions will be monitored as follows:

- The 'process indicators' reflecting *institutional capacity* to be based on a few selected interviews at different levels within the organization and focus group discussions with 'clients'—both exercises on an annual basis.
- Indicators on *counterpart commitment* and *external factors* to be reported directly in short qualitative statements in quarterly progress reports.

A monitoring system on institutional capacity building as that proposed for the ESPS thus becomes a key part of building partnership between national institutions and the donor agency. The framework and indicators for measuring and monitoring institutional capacity building is jointly decided; the monitoring framework and indicators are not predetermined, but develop incrementally.

7.4   Impact Monitoring and Evaluation

7.4.1 Impact M&E—Rationality, Causality and Attribution

Impact monitoring and evaluation are increasingly demanded, as they answer the question as to whether aid funds have a reasonable effect. Impact, 'the positive and negative changes produced by a program or project, directly or indirectly, intended or un-intended', is one of DAC's five evaluation criteria: *relevance, efficiency, effectiveness, impact* and *sustainability*. Measured as economic, social, political, technical and environmental change, impact includes effects that can be expected to accrue from the intervention.

The expectation—which comes from politicians and sometimes from the population at large—that development agencies are able to document the impact of their investments, is understandable and legitimate. However, measuring impact is not always as simple as evaluators would like and development agencies make believe. They should be reminded that aid evaluations cannot control all confounding and intervening factors. Aid evaluators need to make a variety of judgements; they cannot be totally value free, though objectivity is aimed for and the premises must be documented.

It is useful to be reminded that probabilistic relations may be as close as we get in aid impact evaluations. Max Weber's concept of *adequate causality* is a reminder that *probabilistic relations* are as far as we may normally go in establishing causal relations in the social sciences (see Box 7.25).

Box 7.25   Adequate Causality—Probabilistic Relations

The critical point in Max Weber's thinking on causality is his belief that because we can have a special understanding of social life (verstehen), the causal knowledge of the social sciences is different from the causal knowledge of the natural sciences. In social science value judgements are necessary.

Weber's thoughts on causality were intimately related to his efforts to come to grips with the conflict between nomothetic and idiographic knowledge. Those who subscribe to a nomothetic point of view would argue that there is a necessary relationship among social phenomena, whereas the supporters of an idiographic perspective would be inclined to see only random relationships among these entities. Weber took a middle position, epitomized in his concept of 'adequate causality'. The notion of *adequate causality* adopts the view that the best we can do in social science is make probabilistic statements about the relationship between social phenomena; that is, if x occurs, then it is *probable* that y will occur. The goal is to 'estimate the *degree* to which a certain effect is "favoured" by certain conditions' (Weber, 1903: 17, 1949: 183).

After Ritzer, 2000: 114.

An aid impact study is hardly concerned with the process of aid delivery—though differences may occur. It is assumed that the monitoring procedures will have yielded adequate information on the delivery process. Rather, aid impact assessment is about *changes* in the lives of poor women and men, in the environment, in the economy and in social and political structures, etc. The focus in impact studies is more on measurable changes than on the factors which cause the changes. However, documenting impact cannot totally avoid the question of *attribution*, i.e., the extent to which observed development effects can be attributed to a specific project or programme in view of the effects of other interventions or confounding factors. Attribution means trying to establish 'adequate causality' of changes, especially the extent to which they can be attributed to aid agencies' specific interventions.

In concrete aid intervention contexts, assessment of the *significance* of observed changes, i.e., impact, is rarely a directly quantifiable measure. Change assessment, therefore, is an area where *participatory* rural research methods are recommended by many organizations, including the World Bank, as the most appropriate (World Bank, 1993).

Oxfam UK, a large international NGO, has introduced a simple monitoring device for impact assessment to encourage reflection and learning from change in Oxfam supported interventions (see Box 7.26):

Box 7.26   Impact Monitoring—Tracking Reflection on Change with Five Key Questions

Oxfam UK encourages the use of five questions to guide reflections:

- What key changes have happened in people's lives? How sustainable are they?
- What changes in equity, in particular gender equity, are occurring at different levels?
- What has changed in the policies and practices, and ideas and beliefs, of those institutions that affect the lives of people living in poverty?
- What has changed in the degree to which people living in poverty have participated in and taken control over programmes, processes and decisions that affect their lives?
- How cost-effective have Oxfam and others been in promoting the above changes?

After Roche, 1999 and 2001.

Core questions as those set out in Box 7.26 capture the tangible and intangible dimensions (ref. the 'Cone', Figure 7.5). They can be answered with different degrees of precision, with the input of different stakeholders, and by using a wide range of methods. Based on the five key questions, decisions still have to be taken about how elaborate the impact assessment will be. Nevertheless, working with core questions helps to structure the often overly ambitious plans for managing large monitoring datasets. For this to be valid, as for all impact studies, conditions are that some records be kept of answers, compared from time to time, shared, and acted on.

7.4.2   Monitoring and Evaluation of Poverty and Well-being Changes

The demand today is less to assess impact in general, than to capture impact in terms of poverty reduction (see also Sections 3.2.3, 5.1.3 and 6.2). As poverty reduction has become the paramount goal of development aid, the expectations of impact studies are to show improvements in the livelihoods of poor people. Thus poverty impact analysis cuts across different types of monitoring and evaluation studies, as several of the cases in this chapter also illustrate.

The multidimensional and constantly changing nature of poverty is a big challenge in practical development work and research. Perhaps because the imbalance between the livelihoods of poor people and the comfortable conditions of development workers and researchers is so striking, there is a particular need to involve the poor themselves in poverty perception studies. A decade ago the first participatory poverty studies—eliciting poor people's own perceptions about poverty and well-being, causes and remedies of deprived livelihoods—were initiated as part of the preparation of poverty eradication strategies, e.g., in Uganda (MFEP, 1996). Leaving aside at this point the ethical problems of such poverty self-assessments (ACPDT, 1995), participation of poor people in planning, implementing and monitoring poverty reduction initiatives followed. In this area, the intentions outweigh the concrete experience as an Operations Evaluation Department, OED, study shows:

An assessment of projects approved by the World Bank showed that there has been an increase from 40 per cent to 72 per cent of projects with primary stakeholder participation between 1992 and 2000. But only 9 per cent of projects approved (1994–98) included participatory monitoring and evaluation, 'which ensures project implementers' accountability to primary stakeholders' (OED, Précis, 2001). These figures are indicative only and participation of poor people is below these figures, since all primary stakeholders cannot be equated with 'poor people'.

Participatory poverty assessments have been fast on the increase after the dominant international aid agencies adopted 'participation' as one of the approaches to their key strategies and policy frameworks. Participation is integral to the Comprehensive Development Framework, CDF, to the development of Poverty Reduction Strategy Papers, PRSPs (Booth and Lucas, 2002), and is being reinforced in the Millennium Development Goals. Some see this as a sign of patronizing by the International Finance Institutions and global development organizations and, consequently, as watering down the meaning of participation. Others apply a pragmatic view and try to learn from and contribute to critical interpretations and analysis of the many studies which appear on this account.

Appreciating that 'who calls the tune' does matter, let us turn to the shift from the project to the *policy level*, which currently pertains to poverty monitoring and evaluation. Guides for Participatory Poverty Assessments (Norton et al., 2001) and Poverty and Social Impact Analysis (World Bank, 2002) are currently being developed to facilitate monitoring and impact assessment of poverty reduction policies. The results are still limited according to Booth and Lucas:

Substantial experience with participatory monitoring and evaluation (PME) is available for project/program level. There, PME has proven to raise ownership and autonomy of primary stakeholders, increase accountability and transparency of service delivery institutions and improve their performance. *However, with regard to participation in policy and policy impact monitoring experience is still very limited* (my emphasis, 2002: 63).

The quote is extracted from a proposal for Participatory Impact Monitoring, PIM, prepared by the World Bank's Social Development Department in 2001. The PIM programme is described in short in Box 7.27.

Box 7.27   Participatory Impact Monitoring, PIM

The Participatory Impact Monitoring, PIM, programme has a double objective:

- to increase the voice and the agency of poor people through participatory monitoring and evaluation, so as to enhance the effectiveness of poverty oriented policies and programmes in PRSP countries, and
- to contribute to methodology development, strengthen the knowledge base and facilitate cross-country learning on the effective use of Participatory Monitoring on policy level, and in the context of PRS processes in particular.

The methodology and conceptual approach of the proposed PIM combines (1) the **analysis of relevant policies and programmes on the national level,** leading to an inventory of 'impact hypotheses', with (2) **extensive consultations at the district/local government level,** and (3) **joint analysis and consultations with poor communities** on their perceptions of change, their attributions to causal factors and their contextualized assessments of how policies and programmes effect their situation.

It is emphasized that this general approach has to be adapted to the specific country situation considering a number of questions and circumstances:

1. **methodological development/integration with quantitative approaches:**

   - How to make best use of qualitative/participatory methods for policy impact monitoring (appropriate design, sampling, generalization)?
   - What should be the specific contribution/added-value of these methods in a national poverty monitoring system?
   - What are the combinations/synergies of PIM with quantitative M&E approaches?

2. **developing suitable institutional arrangements to influence decision-making:**

   - What is the institutional context in which PIM should be integrated, e.g., PRS/poverty monitoring systems or civil society monitoring initiatives?
   - What use can be made of existing PME systems, e.g., of sector Reform or CDD programmes?
   - How can the actual use of PIM results in decision-making be promoted/supported (dissemination seminars, feedback loops, communication channels between local institutions, sub-national and national levels)?
   - How to facilitate institutional learning to deepen the poverty focus of implementing institutions?
   - How to best stimulate informed pubic debate on the effects of PRS?
   - What is the role of civil society, parliament, and the media in disseminating and discussing the results?

After Booth and Lucas, 2002: 64.

The proposed Poverty Impact Monitoring stands out as a reaction to lessons learnt in Booth and Lucas' critical review of PRSP documentation for sub-Saharan Africa. These lessons show that the documents are saying little about how stakeholders will be incorporated into PRSP monitoring arrangements, and how information will be used to improve policy and implementation. Their findings also confirm the need to combine survey data with participatory poverty assessments:

Despite its aura of technical superiority, survey-based analysis of poverty trends can get it badly wrong. Also, for poverty targeting purposes, survey data almost always need to be combined with census and/or PPA results (ibid.: vi).

The challenge of working with a multidimensional phenomenon like poverty has been addressed in several poverty impact studies, in the past with the focus on the 'micro' and 'meso' levels, while the future is likely to see stronger links between Participatory Poverty Assessments, PPAs, and policy making.

The methodology for poverty impact studies today have better access to predetermined and globally comparative poverty indicators, e.g., the Human Development Index, Human Poverty Index and Gender-related Development Index (UNDP/HDR, annual). But when it comes to the identification of locally specific poverty indicators, participatory poverty assessments are required.

The conceptual framework for understanding poverty and social impacts developed by the World Bank is rather straightforward. The main concepts underlying the poverty and social impact analysis, PSIA, are:

(*i*)   What is being analysed—i.e., *impact of what?*
(*ii*)   What is the welfare measure being assessed—i.e., *impact on what?*
(*iii*)   Who is being analysed—i.e., *impact on whom?*
(*iv*)   How are impacts channelled?
(*v*)   How do institutions affect outcomes?
(*vi*)   When do impacts materialize? and
(*vii*)   What are the risks of an unexpected outcome? (World Bank, 2002)

Besides the methodologies developed by the World Bank—in cooperation with partner country agencies—on how to monitor poverty reduction in relation to policies and to the PRSP in particular, the OECD/DAC provides useful guidance on poverty monitoring.

A guide for ways to measure and monitor poverty is included in the DAC's broader Guidelines on Poverty Reduction (OECD/DAC, 2001, see also Section 6.2). 'Measurement is necessary for monitoring the degree to which policy goals have been met, for assessing the impact of particular policies and programmes, and for identifying the poor,' to quote from the DAC guide, which is set out at some length in Box 7.28.

Box 7.28   How Can Poverty be Measured and Monitored?

A key issue is how to measure the diverse dimensions of poverty. Measurement is necessary for monitoring the degree to which policy goals have been met, for assessing the impact of particular policies and programmes, and for identifying the poor. The best practice is to collect data that differentiate according to gender, age and other social categories. The adequacy of various tools for measuring poverty depends on the availability of data and the purpose of measurement.

The less tangible dimensions of poverty are more costly and time-consuming to measure and to quantify. Composite indexes that include both economic and other poverty dimensions may provide more solid comparable

(Box 7.28 contd)

(Box 7.28 contd)

quantitative measures than measures in one dimension only. The most prominent ones have been developed by UNDP in the annual Human Development Report (HDR). They have been vital in drawing attention to the multidimensional and serious problems of poverty. However, to some extent, the choice of indicators and the weights assigned to them is arbitrary, and trade-offs between them are not captured. Thus, discrete poverty measures are still more useful for specific planning purposes.

Figure 2   Measuring Poverty at Different Aggregation Levels

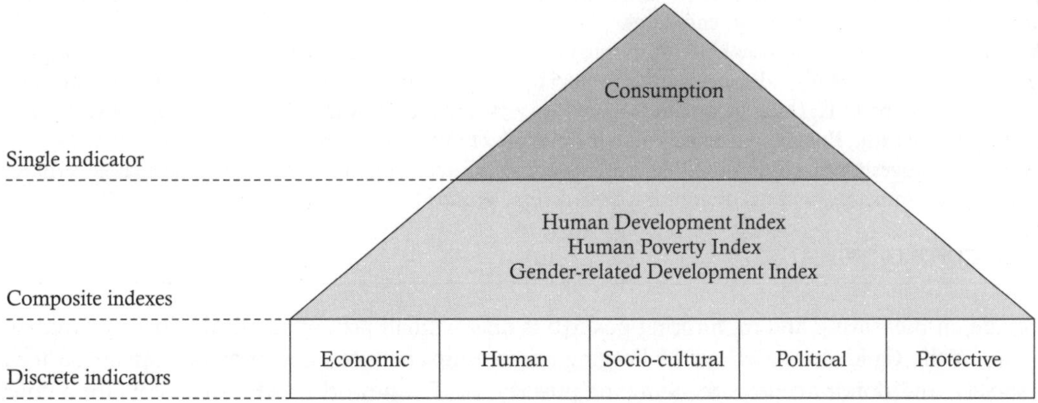

Single indicator

Consumption

Composite indexes

Human Development Index
Human Poverty Index
Gender-related Development Index

Discrete indicators

Economic	Human	Socio-cultural	Political	Protective

Different kinds of measures have their uses: relative, contextual, qualitative and multidimensional indicators are best for understanding a specific situation and intervening in it effectively. But they are less useful for comparisons or for overall poverty monitoring and impact assessments, which require absolute, simple and quantified measures (Figure 2). The top of Figure 2 illustrates the simple consumption or income expenditure measure available from household surveys in a large number of countries. This is useful for comparative analyses of poverty over time in a country and among different countries, and for overall poverty monitoring. In other words, at the top there is a bird's eye view measure of poverty. The middle section represents composite indexes. The bottom section portrays the foundation for measuring poverty in its various dimensions. It is closer to the local community level and so is of more use in detailed planning and monitoring.

National data on human development are routinely collected in surveys and presented in global tables in HDR and the World Development Reports (WDR) from the World Bank. For the remaining dimensions there are no good methods to standardize and quantify measures that would permit comparisons. But several countries have undertaken participatory poverty assessments that provide very useful qualitative and multidimensional information about poverty.

The narrow approach to measuring poverty permits the identification and statistical analysis of those households falling under an absolute poverty line, which is set at a minimum standard of nutrition and consumption. This is necessary for monitoring the numbers as well as the proportion of poor people over time and among countries, and the depth and severity of poverty. The most common poverty lines for international comparisons are US$ 1 a day for low-income countries, US$ 2 for middle-income countries, and US$ 4 for transition

(Box 7.28 contd)

(Box 7.28 contd)

economies. Many countries have their own poverty lines reflecting different social, economic and climatic conditions in determining what is considered an acceptable minimum income.

Having considered the meaning of poverty and how poverty can be measured, the next step in formulating a poverty strategy is to specify indicators and goals. Governments must set poverty reduction targets and identify means of assessing and monitoring them. Goals and benchmark indicators should be specified according to data sources that are available for the period for which they are set. They should conform to the economic, political and socio-cultural realities of each country and specify the precise meaning of poverty reduction objectives. The goals should be related to the MDGs, though countries may have targets of their own for different indicators or for different end dates.

It is vital to dis-aggregate national indicators into others which will distinguish outcomes for different categories of people: for example by gender, age and other social categories, geographic or administrative region, and by rural and urban areas. Tracking inequalities in this way provides early warnings on important poverty factors including conflict risk. Popular participation in the process of setting goals and indicators can generate national consensus on poverty reduction. Good data are essential for analysing outcomes against which governments can be held accountable, and for monitoring how diverse groups of poor people fare.

After OECD/DAC, 2001: 41–43.

The guide on measuring and monitoring poverty is only a small part of the DAC Poverty Guidelines. The core of the Guidelines address: (*i*) Forging partnerships between governments, private sector and civil society, and donor agencies for reducing poverty; (*ii*) Frameworks and instruments for a country programme of poverty reduction strategies; and (*iii*) Policy coherence for poverty reduction. Last, the DAC guidelines propose actions for (*iv*) Institutional change and development for mainstreaming poverty reduction, partnership and policy coherence.

The following cases are examples of poverty impact monitoring and evaluation.

7.4.3 Case 7: Evaluation of Poverty Reduction in Danish Development Assistance

Major questions when evaluating poverty impact relate to methodology, of how to conceptualize 'measurable' poverty and 'experienced' poverty. Poverty is a question of distribution of resources as much as a question of the size of the cake—it is relative and absolute and dynamic, and a cause as well as a symptom. On the one hand poverty is measurable in terms of limited consumption and income. On the other, poverty is experienced as deprivation, isolation and powerlessness. Personally, I was deeply involved in Danida's Poverty Reduction Evaluation in 1995–96 with several colleagues from COWI and evaluators in Uganda and Zimbabwe. The evaluation team got a strong feeling of the challenges involved in *planning and implementing* effective poverty reduction, keeping track of *achievements* through *monitoring* and later *evaluating* the effects and impact of development policies and interventions in specific sectors on poor people's well-being (MFA/Danida, Mikkelsen et al., 1996).

The conceptual framework for country-based poverty assessment of Danida's development assistance appears in Figure 7.7.

Figure 7.7   Framework for Country-based Poverty Assessment of Danida's Development Assistance

Danida's Poverty Evaluation included impact assessment of national policies (macro level), sector-specific interventions (meso level), and impact at community level (micro). Core poverty indicators, *livelihoods, resources, knowledge and rights* were qualified by primary stakeholders as additional indicators—primarily at the micro level.

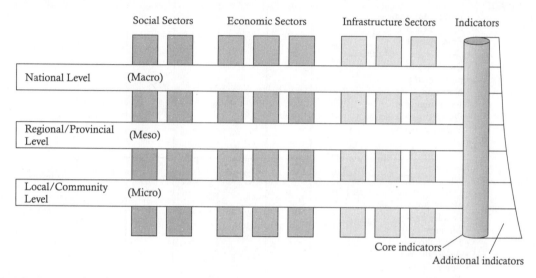

After MFA/Mikkelsen, 1996.

In the poverty impact evaluation we focused on four core indicators: i.e., *livelihoods, resources, knowledge and rights*. These four 'core indicators' were used by ODA (1995) in a theoretical framework that captures 'social change'. The evaluation team for the poverty reduction/impact evaluation departed from a theoretical assumption that poverty reduction is a social process, and hence the four core indicators would be relevant to assess changes attributable to the interventions. The hypothesis was established that people's perceptions about change, which could be at least partially attributed to the interventions under evaluation, would cluster around the four core indicators.

A focus group technique was then used by which primary stakeholders identified what they thought were positive or negative changes, if any, due to the particular interventions being evaluated—irrigation projects, infrastructure, housing, budget support programmes, etc. The hypothesis proved right in that the indicators identified by stakeholders in the focus group discussions could be clustered under the four core indicators. These 'additional indicators' qualified the core indicators. The perceived changes— positive or negative—were then recorded on a simple 5 point scale from very positive change—over no change—to very negative change, in the Change Assessment and Scooring Tool, CAST. The CAST tool is illustrated in Figure 7.8.

Figure 7.8   Change Assessment and Scoring Tool, CAST, for Monitoring Stakeholders' Perceptions of Poverty Related Change Attributable to an Infrastructure Project

Infrastructure/Well-being Monitoring of Roads Interventions

Tentative Indicators

		++ Very positive	+ Positive	No Change	− Negative	− − Very Negative	
Improvement	**Livelihoods:**						**Impoverishment**
	• Income from sale of Agric. Products		√				•
	• Employment		√				•
	• Health status—adult				√		•
	• Child-Health		√				•
	• Food security		√				•
	• Nutrition			√			•
	• Job absenteeism	√					•
	• Ownership of assets (Bicycles, autos)		√				•
	•						
	•						•
Access	**Services:**						**Exclusion**
	• Quantity/quality of transport	√					•
	• Health posts, schools		√				•
	• Pendler jobs	√					•
	• Markets		√				•
	• Local shops				√		•
	• Affordability				√		•
	• Security				√		•
	• Travel time		√				•
	•						•
	•						•
Improvement	**Knowledge/Practice:**						**Reduction**
	• Technical skills	√					•
	• Management skills		√				•
	• Environmental protection			√			•
	• Aids precaution				√		•
	•						•
	•						•
Involvement	**Rights/Participation:**						**Alienation**
	• Private sector Participation	√					•
	• Gender equality			√			•
	• Institutional capacity			√			•
	• Decision processes		√				•
	•						•
	•						•

Target Groups by age and sex

Source: Mikkelsen, own graph.

The advantage of a simple monitoring device like the CAST is that it provides a quick overview of perceived changes by specific groups who are affected by an intervention. These can be groups of women, of men, or mixed groups. Comparing the results from different (target) groups can in itself provide interesting information about women's and men's perceptions.

It is evident that the results of the CAST exercise do not provide the full picture of impact. In the first place, it is difficult to attribute change to a specific development intervention. And in order to take action, more information than what is contained in the CAST tool is needed, not least information about other possibly influential factors from the local and national context at macro and local levels. However, when the Change Assessment and Scoring exercise is supplemented by narrative explanations from the participants in a focus group, a fuller picture of impact can be drawn.

What the poverty reduction evaluation did not manage was to establish a clear link between the core and additional indicators at macro, meso and micro levels, not least due to the limited time available for the evaluation. Nevertheless, there seems to be interesting prospects in working with 'core' and 'additional indicators' (see the right column of Figure 7.7 and Section 5.1.3). Behind the CAST tool, which was applied in Danida's poverty reduction evaluation, is a theoretical framework which maintains that social change processes, hence also of poverty changes, can be captured in the four core indicators *livelihoods, access to resources, knowledge* and *rights* (ODA, 1995, see also Chapter 5). Replication of the framework indicates its relevance, as a similar conceptual framework was applied in subsequent poverty impact studies (for example, Cox et al., 2002).

This chapter has shown that there are a variety of visual monitoring tools. The 'web' is a common way of capturing changes. Figure 7.9 is a web-like monitoring tool—a wheel—on which the spikes are the indicators. The most significant step is to let the 'target group', the participants in the exercise, identify the indicators, or do this in cooperation with the facilitators. Ratings of each indicator as good, fair or poor are given on the spikes. The particular wheel illustrated here has incorporated the 'core indicators' livelihoods, resources, knowledge and rights, as well as additional indicators. Whether one wants to operate with core indicators is of course an arbitrary choice.

Monitoring and evaluation tools like the CAST (Figure 7.8) and the Monitoring Wheel (Figure 7.9) will normally be composed step-wise, from an open brainstorming on indicators which are then structured afterwards, for example under core indicators. The specific context, including the time factor, will influence the degree of prior structuring. The facilitator will need to consider the purpose and the practicalities, but generally the CAST and the Wheel function well as participatory tools, and provide for good discussion on priority indicators, rankings, etc.

To be an optimal monitoring and evaluation tool, the challenge is to compare changes in the 'web' and take action where the 'scores' are not satisfactory.

Figure 7.9 Monitoring Wheel

Poverty/Well-being Monitoring Wheel of Infrastructure/Roads Intervention

Tentative Indicators

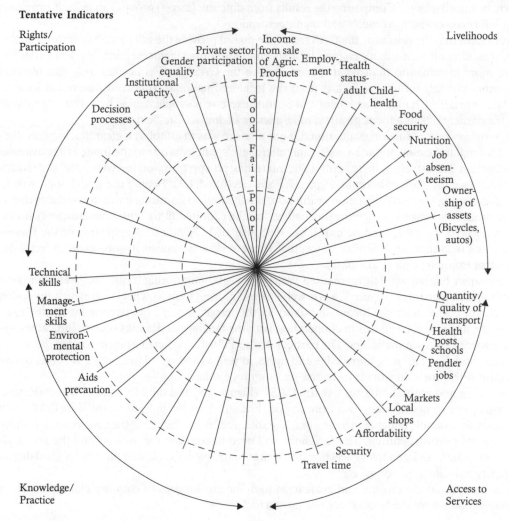

Source: Mikkelsen, own graph.

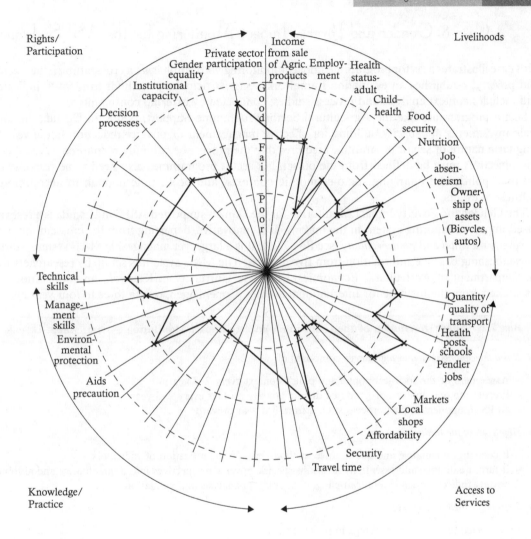

Target Groups by age and sex

Source: Mikkelsen, own graph.

7.4.4 Case 8: Gender and Poverty Impact Monitoring for the ASPS, Uganda

This case illustrates a sector programme impact monitoring with emphasis on crosscutting issues, gender and poverty; establishes an evaluation framework using participatory methods to identify indicators, and includes context analysis and process studies; conducted by external consultants.

Sector programmes like the Agricultural Sector Programme Support, ASPS, in Uganda are large-scale investments in capacity building for effective management of poverty reduction initiatives. The long-term nature of sector programmes requires that the process be carefully monitored. Overall goals and objectives must be defined from the outset, but sector programmes also need to be responsive to national policy and changing socio-economic contexts, and be flexible enough to accommodate unforeseen events.

The Gender and Poverty Impact Monitoring for the Danish-supported ASPS in Uganda is a research-based impact monitoring system in the making. It is innovative, departing from the crosscutting issues of *poverty reduction* and *gender equality* (see Box 7.29). It is a large, yet manageable M&E system, starting by establishing baseline information from five districts. The M&E system is set up by researchers from the Department of Agricultural Economics, Makerere University in Kampala, in cooperation with researchers from the Institute for International Studies, Copenhagen, over a three to four year period.

Box 7.29   Short Description of the Gender and Poverty Impact Monitoring System, ASPS, Uganda

- *It is a three-pronged monitoring strategy* composed of

  - Assessment of the socio-economic and policy context every 2–3 years
  - Preparation and analysis of gendered district poverty profiles every 2–3 years
  - ASPS component impact process studies from 3rd year onwards

- *Highlights of the methodology* are

  - It combines qualitative and quantitative methods, e.g., in identification of indicators
  - It turns qualitative and essentially locations-specific poverty perspectives into a quantitative and absolute poverty index through careful sampling, extrapolation analysis and validation

- *Steps of the methodology* are

  1. Conducting well-being rankings in selected sites
  2. Identifying well-being indicators and determining the extent to which they can be extrapolated
  3. Developing and measuring poverty indicators and constructing a poverty index
  4. Validating the poverty index
  5. Developing a gendered poverty profile.

After MFA/Ravnborg, 2002.

Local Perceptions of Poverty and Well-being

At the heart of the methodology is the inquiry into local perceptions of poverty and well-being through well-being rankings. Well-being rankings of households and of women were undertaken in a total of 30 communities, selected by using a maximum variation sampling strategy. **Sampling factors** were:

(*i*)   agro-ecological zone
(*ii*) population density
(*iii*) ethnicity
(*iv*) health and education facilities and
(*v*)   accessibility

These factors were supposed to capture differences in the perceptions of well-being. In each community three to four informants were asked to rank households according to perceived well-being. Other informants were asked to rank women's well-being as they perceived it. The informants were selected to optimize differences in age, sex, occupation, ethnicity, marital status, etc.

The well-being rankings of households and of women were conducted using the card-sorting methods. Following the card sorting, the informants were asked to describe each of the heaps of cards in terms of well-being. The results from the ranking were subsequently analysed. The first step was to ensure that a reasonable level of agreement existed between the three to four rankings of the households and rankings of the women within each of the communities. This was done using the Spearman rank order correlation test, available in SPSS. The test showed a high validity of the ranking (Danida 2002: 6). Through a prioritization technique, the indicators were then reduced to 13 household poverty/well-being indicators (see Box 7.30).

Box 7.30   Household Poverty Indicators in the Gender and Poverty Impact Monitoring

- land ownership
- non-agricultural sources of income
- day-labouring
- animal ownership
- hiring agricultural labourers
- food security
- quality of diet
- housing quality
- health status
- children's schooling
- dressing
- marital status
- age

The approach to establishing this gender and poverty monitoring system for the ASPS is very thorough, and it is not possible here to do justice to the details involved in data collection and analysis. Several steps follow after the above described well-being ranking. These steps are in brief:

– Translating well-being descriptions into well-being indicators of household and female well-being
– Extrapolation analysis

- Questionnaire survey
- Developing a measure of household poverty
- Household poverty index (see Box 7.31).

Box 7.31   Household Poverty Index

The household poverty index is developed by giving well-being scores to each household. The household poverty index is defined as the average of household well-being scores on the 13 household poverty indicators. For land ownership, for example, each household is ranked according to the following scores (the higher the score, the higher is the level of poverty, everything else being equal):

Land-ownership:

- Own (including leasehold, customary tenure and freehold) more than five acres of land (score 33)
- Own between one and five acres of land (score 67)
- Do not own land or own less than one acre (score 100)

Similar scoring classifications for the other indicators add up to poverty profiles for the households in the 5 districts included.

The poverty profile for Tororo District, for example, is:

Poorest households (36 per cent)
Less poor households (40 per cent)
Best off households (24 per cent)

After MFA/Ravnborg, 2002.

Compared with many other monitoring systems, this system integrates the gender dimension on the assumption that poverty affects women and men differently, and hence has to be addressed differently in the Agricultural Sector Programme Support.

The gendered poverty profile is developed by introducing household gender equality indicators and establishing gender relations indicators between husband and wife. The gender equality indicators are based on local people's perceptions, just like the poverty indicators were.

The key gender equality indicators derived from the scoring exercise are:

- Woman's influence on how to spend income from crop or animal product sales
- Husband's contribution to household expenditures
- Woman's sources of income
- Woman's access to land
- Woman's ownership of animals

The scoring system used to quantify gender relations indicators can be illustrated for the indicator *expenditure* (the higher the score, the more inequitable is the relation between husband and wife, everything else being equal):

- Husband contributes to all of the following household expenditure categories: food, paraffin/soap, salt/sugar, children's education, children's clothes and medical expenditures (score 33)
- Husband contributes to at least one of the following household expenditure categories: food, paraffin/soap, salt/sugar, children's education, children's clothes and medical expenditure (score 67)
- Husband does not contribute to any of the above household expenditure categories or he does not sell crops from own or shared fields or animal products (score 100)

When the scores on each indicator are combined, the result is a profile of gender relations in the five districts—exemplified here with Tororo District:

Inequitable households (39 per cent)
Less equitable households (50 per cent)
Equitable households (12 per cent).

By applying the described methodology, it can already be seen at the initial stage of baseline study that there is no uniform relationship between poverty and gender equality. Relations between husband and wife are more inequitable in the poorest households in three districts, but not in the two other districts. How poverty and gender equality can interact differently is illustrated by the two statements quoted in Box 7.32.

Box 7.32   No Uniform Relationship between Poverty and Gender Equality

The combined result of household well-being and gender relations assessment in the Gender and Poverty Impact Monitoring for the ASPS, Uganda, shows that there was no uniform relationship between poverty and gender equality at the time of the baseline study in 2001. Two contrasting perceptions of female well-being— or lack of the same—are:

(1)
'Some have husbands who have money. They are mostly farmers and business women and they are involved in many women's group activities. Most of their husbands do not interfere with how they spend the income from their projects. Their husbands are very hard working' (*description of women ranked as enjoying a high level of well-being in Matale Kalagala, Kalisizo sub-county, Rakai District*).

(2)
'Husbands are mostly drunkards. Their houses are grass-thatched, and they are always struggling for the survival of the children. The husbands do not care much about their wives. Clothes are out of a very big struggle, some times wearing a cloth for a very long time, like a week, without change' (*description of women ranked as enduring a low level of well-being in Gwanda, Kyebe sub-county, Rakai District*).

After MFA/Ravnborg, 2002.

After the initial phase of establishing gendered poverty profiles in the five participating districts and gathering baseline information about gender relations, the current M&E activities focus on impact process studies.

Impact Process Studies

The process studies aim to document the social processes which are generated when agricultural sector programme support is provided at the community level. The process studies are related to the extension component of the ASPS. They make use of the original questionnaire for constructing gendered poverty profiles, and of complementary interviews.

The analysis goes beyond the basic assumptions on which the ASPS is established and questions some of the assumptions which have more or less become 'holy cows' in development cooperation. The concept 'demand-driven', for example, needs to be reconsidered. Farmers may be tempted to formulate demands according to what they think they might be able to get support for, and not according to their own assessment of the feasibility and relevance of the support. This is not sustainable and leads to a contradictory programme policy. It boils down to trying to empower and control at the same time.

Another assumption being challenged concerns the reach of the ASPS to 'the active poor'. The preliminary process study documents question the concept of 'the active poor', maintaining that it is vague and pragmatic and may serve as a euphemism for people who are not in fact among the poor. This should be taken into consideration and result in adjustments of the programme strategy.

Such critical questions pertaining to the assumptions about a programmes' ability to reach the poor could be a blow to many programmes at a time when poverty reduction is at the core of development aid.

However unwelcome critical information may be to planners and other stakeholders, it is the aim of well-designed M&E programmes to provide additional layers of knowledge, according to which adjustments of interventions and aid programmes can be made. The task of evaluators does not always harmonize well with the interests of funding agencies and other interest groups. (See also Section 7.2.4 about the issue of potential conflicts between evaluators and funding agencies.)

Most of the M&E cases illustrated above address poverty reduction. Poverty measures, monitoring and impact assessments have been subject to much methodological reflection and testing in recent years, including goal-oriented, process and participatory M&E approaches. We shall turn to an illustration of some of the better practices and challenges involved in M&E of poverty and well-being in the following section.

7.4.5 Case 9: Impact Evaluation in an Empowerment Framework

Recent methodological developments of impact studies have moved the balance from the project towards the context of the project. This pertains to the Gender and Poverty Impact Monitoring for the Agricultural Sector Programme Support in Uganda illustrated above. Along this line, the authors of an in-depth impact study of a bio-intensive homestead gardening project in Patuakhali, Bangladesh, the Local Initiatives for Farmers' Training, LIFT, programme implemented by CARE-Bangladesh, observe:

> We believe it is one of the main problems of ordinary evaluation, reviews and impact assessments that they focus entirely on the *intervention,* more or less disregarding the *context* which is crucial for the outcome and impact (Sultana and Folke, 1999: ix).

Hence they design and conduct what is characterized as a *contextualized, tailor-made, in-depth impact study of a development project*. The study works with a very broad understanding of impact, 'denoting any significant change in people's life—positive or negative, intended or unintended, immediate or long-term—brought about by a project' (ibid.: xi). But as there is no clear definition of which changes are significant, they include in the impact concept the *effect* or short-term changes that are more narrowly linked to the project's objectives.

The LIFT impact study in Bangladesh is an example of a goal-oriented evaluation designed as an after study with control group (see Section 7.2.1). It forms part of the worldwide 'Danish NGO Impact Study—A Review of Danish NGO Activities in Developing Countries' commissioned by Danida and Danish NGOs and published in 1999. Under the guidance of Peter Oakley, the NGO Impact Study in its totality was a major contribution to the development of M&E methodology. For the evaluators' brief description of the approach and methodology in the LIFT study see Box 7.33.

Box 7.33   Approach and Methodology of a Contextualized, Tailor-made, in-depth Impact Study

In comparison with ... most impact assessments, this study puts emphasis on the study of the *local context* (whereas the national context is dealt with in the Bangladesh country study of impact of Danish NGOs). Since the outcomes and impact of any intervention are the result of an interplay of factors linked to the intervention and factors rooted in the context, a better analysis of the context will contribute to a deeper understanding of impact. This, moreover, enables us to throw light on the *differential impact* on different individuals and groups of people (e.g., men and women, different ethnic or religious communities, different socio-economic groups, etc.). This is essential for a better understanding of the impact of development interventions, but often not studied owing to lack of time and resources. The present study in particular focuses on the *beneficiary level*, both in order to make a well-founded assessment of impact at this level, which ultimately is the test of success or failure, and in order to solicit the intended beneficiaries' views on the project and the way it has been implemented. As something more unusual, we also identify a sample of non-beneficiaries (neighbours of beneficiaries) in order to find out whether they have been affected—positively (e.g., learning) or negatively (e.g., competition)— by the project. On a small scale they can also serve as a control group.

After Sultana and Folke, 1999: I–II.

The approach includes a number of *core issues* (or cross-cutting issues) which are used as the basis for assessing the broader impact: Poverty, Gender, Environment, Democratization, Partnership and Sustainability. Priority has been accorded to three of these, due to the nature of the studied project:

- *Poverty*—does the project lead to sustainable improvements in poor people's livelihoods?
- *Gender*—what is the impact on gender relations and in particular on women's empowerment?
- *Sustainability*—are the project results sustainable both in a socio-economic and institutional sense?

The prioritization of these three issues makes the approach to the impact study 'tailor-made' to this particular programme.

A major part of the fieldwork was taken up by three central *surveys—of Local Extensionists, Household Farmers and Non-beneficiaries* and additional semi-structured interviews with key informants—in each case tailor-made.

The study has applied a wide range of fairly standard *quantitative* and *qualitative* methods, most of which are different forms of individual and group interviews.

Important methodological lessons recorded by the evaluators are also:

In our view there is no standard recipe to the study of impact of development projects .... In principle we think that each impact study ought to be tailor-made to suit that particular intervention and context. Indeed that is what we have been doing in this case by developing an appropriate approach and based on that an elaborate *study design*, encompassing a number of components (embodying a range of methods) specific to this study. On the one hand *this implies that it is impossible to simply replicate our approach and method in another study. But on the other hand it is certainly possible to learn from this study and design similar contextualised and tailor-made impact studies* incorporating elements of our approach and methodology (Sultana and Folke, 1999: ix–x).

In an *Impact Evaluation Study of Four Training Projects for Farm Women in India*, one of the authors refines the contextualized, tailor-made approach (Folke, 2002). The two key issues are *agricultural extension* and *gender issues*. Concerning gender issues, the study applies the *empowerment framework* developed by Naila Kabeer and inspired by A. Sen (Kabeer, 2002). Empowerment refers to the expansion in people's ability to make strategic life choices in a context where this ability was previously denied. Abilities to exercise choices are seen to be determined by three interrelated dimensions: *resources*—the conditions under which choices are made; *agency*—the ability to define one's goals and act upon them; and *achievements*—the outcome of choices. Together resources and agency make up capabilities or the potentials of achieving valued ways of 'being and doing' (Sen, 1990). The evaluation seeks to distinguish and identify *empowerment processes* at different individual and collective/group levels:

- Individual resources, agency, achievements (self-confidence, pride, negotiation, abilities, etc.)
- Mutually supportive social processes (among women, in families, communities, etc.)
- Collective steps towards changing gender relations (e.g., farm women's groups evolving into a movement of farm women).

Methodologically this impact evaluation study applies questionnaire surveys of a representative, stratified sample of beneficiaries from the four projects (women and men). And in order to provide a proper context analysis for the village-based studies, information is gathered though documentary/policy/statistical analysis and individual and group interviews. A methodology-cum-planning workshop ensures participation by evaluation team members and selected stakeholders.

A lesson from the LIFT impact study, which may be carried over to the impact study of training for farm women in India, is that the combined use of a wide range of methods on balance is positive. The main problem is that of *limited time* and *resources* for planning and applying all the methods in an optimal way—constraints which are familiar to most evaluation teams, and which in the last resort determines which study design is feasible.

7.5   Learning from M&E and Impact Studies

The ultimate purpose of monitoring, evaluation and impact assessment is to learn about what works and what does not work, and how to apply these lessons in the future—short or long term. This pertains to development aid agencies as well as to their partner organizations.

There are a number of well-known bottlenecks to promoting organizational learning. Roche points to staff-turnover, poor systems for recording, storing and retrieving information, and poor linkages between learning and training. This is compounded by lack of rewards or incentives to learn and share learning; as a result, little time is devoted to it. When learning is hived off to specialist evaluation units, staff may see it as the specialists' responsibility, rather than everyone's (see Roche, 1999: 258–60).

Box 7.34 suggests some of the questions that can be explored in order to assess the degree to which the organizational context within which evaluation and impact assessment occur will be conducive to absorbing lessons.

Box 7.34   Questions Related to Organizational Learning from Monitoring and Evaluation

- Who learns in the organization and how?
- What kind of learning is rewarded?
- To what degree are errors admitted and analysed?
- What forms of knowledge are defined as legitimate, and how?
- What constraints are there to learning?
- How does information flow in the organization?
- How is institutional memory constructed; how accessible is it, and for whom?
- What changes occur through self-learning, rather than other ways of learning?
- How does the organization react to learning which challenges its assumptions?
- Is the organization better placed than it was, in the light of what it has learned, to anticipate change in the environment and adapt accordingly?
- What changes are being made to the organization's learning systems?

After Roche, 1999: 259.

What constitutes good practice for M&E and impact assessment has been discussed at length and donor agencies have started to prepare Codes of Conduct for evaluations (see MFA, 2004). A warning has already been sounded and shall be repeated here—that there is a danger in supposing that impact evaluations can solve more than it can be expected to. The value added to impact assessments is linked to other important elements of organizational development such as learning, accountability and reward systems.

However, as we move in the domain of international development cooperation, and increasingly so at the policy and sector programme level rather than at the project level, building national capacity is vital. It is central to improving analytical rigour over time and for strengthened country ownership. Many low-income countries have limited capacity and experience in areas of critical importance to poverty and social impact analysis. These areas range from data collection systems, analytical capacity, monitoring and evaluation systems, the capacity to translate data and analysis into policy, and the capacity for debate on such policy issues. An approach that fosters learning by doing is an obvious case for funding agency assistance.

Concluding Remarks

It seems appropriate to round off this chapter on issues involved in monitoring and evaluation with some lessons that may help practitioners in their considerations of which M&E approach to pursue in a given context. As already pointed out, resources and time will always be parameters of concern, including personnel capacity as well as financial resources. A look at tomorrow's evaluation issues takes inspiration from Cracknell (2000) and Rist (2004) in the following points:

- Search for a modus vivendi between traditional evaluation and the participatory approach.
- Strengthen evaluation capacity with the partner organizations in the developing countries.
- Be flexible in the application of the Logical Framework Approach if application of LFA is at all justified.
- More effective feedback, in particular at policy or strategy level, and fresh ways of synthesizing macro lessons may be required.
- Information flows need to move from vertical to horizontal flows to strengthen organizational learning.
- More qualitative information to support quantitative information flows.
- New evaluation techniques to cope with new kinds of aid. Strengthen the concurrent trends of non-project aid (macro direction) and the trend towards more participatory methods (micro direction).
- Move from evaluation studies to streams.

Last but not least, a call is made for more participation in ongoing debates regarding the future of the evaluation profession.

This concluding chapter addresses the ethical implications of development work and research and of intervention in society, questions which concern all the parties involved. It is pointed out that while the forms of intervention have changed through the ages, images of 'the other' and of 'ourselves' are at the root of our behaviour. The importance for cultural interpretation of the distinction between central and peripheral norms is pointed out, and the reader is reminded of the way basic concepts and language structure may differ in different cultures. Eurocentric definitions of development are questioned, meaningful ways ahead in development cooperation are explored, and ethical principles and dilemmas and codes of conduct are illustrated. Finally all field workers, whether from the North or the South, researchers or practitioners, are called upon to pool their experience and to share the results, the honour and the blame, and to perform their studies with imagination and care.

Intentional Interventions—A Question of Ethics

The topics covered in this book invite a variety of ethical questions. Cooperation between societies for the sake of intervention and change and research into other cultures, and studies of the conditions for international, cross-cultural cooperation raise practical problems which have to be dealt with if co-operation is to function. The ethical questions are much easier to push aside. And after all, is it worthwhile wasting time on ethical headaches for which there is no straightforward cure anyway? Have we not done what is required by suggesting dialogue and participatory approaches to development studies and practice?

The point to be made here is that ethical considerations are fundamental to the approach to development cooperation and research. It is the purpose of the following sections to call attention to ethical issues of intervention and cultural interpretations. At the same time it is maintained that formalized codes of ethics can only provide limited guidance. In contrast to the natural sciences, formalized codes of ethics may even mislead in the social sciences.

It may seem a bit cynical to admit an awareness of the many contradictory claims in which development workers-cum-researches tend to be entangled, without offering a clear-cut approach to the dilemmas. However, it requires the contribution of many people from the South and the North to bring the ethical aspects from the level of debate to concrete action for a new paradigm of international development cooperation.

A few reminders concerning basic cultural interpretations are pertinent. Our cultural ballast, 'Images of the others', i.e., the reciprocal images people carry of each other and themselves, constitutes the context in which specific interventions and field studies take place. 'Developers' may think they have emancipated themselves from stereotypical images of 'the others'. But as Mai Palmberg observes in her thorough documentation, *Encounter Images in the Meetings between Africa and Europe* (2001), at least the missionaries created a consistency, while the developers have not. 'We can easily identify missionary thinking, but we often mistake developmentalism for common sense, and not ideology' (ibid.: 18). Evidence on this point stems from Løngreen, who has analysed information material on development aid published by the Danish International Development Agency, Danida. She talks of a Development Gaze that is very similar to the Tourist Gaze. Both are directed towards features which are pre-modern and which separate them from Western ways of living. The difference is, Løngreen says, that unlike the case of tourism, there is an obvious power relationship between 'Us Here' and 'Them Out There' (2001).

8.1   Images of 'the Others'

8.1.1 Culture Encounters

A British journalist once asked Mahatma Gandhi: 'What do you think about Western civilization?' Gandhi gave the journalist a thorough look and replied: 'I think it would be a good idea.'

This often quoted exchange beautifully illustrates what cultural identity is about: the difference between how 'we' consider ourselves to be the civilized while 'the others' consider us to be barbarians—and vice versa. But culture contact affects reciprocal images. Tvedt expresses it like this. He provides a critical analysis of Norway as 'the World Champion of Aid':

... in an era when the world is being conquered culturally by the West. For the first time in history all countries' problems are being described with common concepts. 'The others' are described, and describe themselves, with measures and concepts forced upon them by the historical development of the West (Tvedt, 1990: 11).

More than a decade after this observation the Western dominance of the global agenda for international development cooperation is stronger than ever, appearing as global consensus on a neo-liberal development discourse. A frightening dimension is that wars are being staged by those in power in the name of their self-declared interpretation of democracy, breaching internationally agreed conventions.

For people in Western societies, the North, it is a rare experience to be subjected to intensive studies by outsiders. People have been totally accustomed to a situation where Western anthropologists and sociologists travel to the South and critically study their cultures. Northerners legitimize their studies with academic degrees, or as necessary inputs to make foreign aid sustainable.

When a student of development studies from the South occasionally comes to the North, it is not to subject the Northern society to a critical study, but to get access to literature and documentation about his/her society which, ironically, have been accumulated in the North but may not be available in the home country. Great was the surprise in Denmark when in 1989 an Indian professor of anthropology came to study life in a Danish village. Danish people were extremely fascinated at being confronted with a foreigner's image of our 'closed' society.

Professor Reddy wasn't just any observer. In contrast to the average Western student of foreign societies, he shared his observations with the public by publishing in the native language, Danish (Reddy, 1992/1993 and 1998/2002). With his professional anthropological approach, he was able to disclose the salient features of a typical Danish village in a highly industrialized society. Half the fascination came from his analysis, which reflected his own totally different cultural background and the culture shock he experienced in the 'isolating' Danish society. The contrast with the typical Danish image of ourselves was obvious; our cultural values are a profound care for each other by means of a highly developed social welfare system. We happily support those in need and respect the individual's rights and entitlements in this small country 'where few have too much, and fewer have too little'. The Danish dilemmas were obvious to Reddy (1998/2002), but hardly noticed by the Danes themselves.

Like Reddy, we have few other possibilities when interpreting other societies and cultures than starting from our own experience. Our concepts cover only the things we know. The ethnocentric perspective that this implies means that the world is interpreted with one's own culture, norms and values at the centre and as the yardstick for other cultures. This is not in itself the problem, as long as we accept the limitations of ethnocentric interpretations. The latter is, unfortunately, rarely the case. The problems start to arise when our interpretations contain values about good and bad, right and wrong, as Herlitz points out (1991: 30).

Herlitz makes a point of emphasizing the importance of a willingness to understand, before value judgements are drawn about certain culture-specific phenomena. A typical Western interpretation of India's holy cows is shown in Box 8.1.

Reddy's observations as an anthropological observer from the South in a Danish village provides a good account of completely irrational behaviour—that Danes would let their homegrown apples rot on the ground and at the same time go to the shop and buy apples! (Reddy, 1993).

The idea of African otherness has occupied a central role in discourses on cultural production in Africa, whether film, literature, music, or the arts. It means that particular criteria and standards are adopted in relation to cultural production in Africa. Increasingly, the claim to African otherness is gaining momentum in the wake of globalization, while it is also being increasingly challenged by a number of contemporary artists in various fields of cultural production in Africa, as illustrated by Erikson Braaz and Palmberg (2001).

8.1.2 Central and Peripheral Norms

The distinction between central and peripheral cultural norms is important for cultural interpretation.

Herlitz illustrates how other cultural practices create deeper conflicts of interpretation than the phenomenon of holy cows. For instance, female circumcision is much more difficult for Westerners to accept, even after an explanation has been given, than for example the 'holy cow' phenomenon. He likens Westerners' refusal to accept the practice of female circumcision to the disgust against our 'Old People's Homes' felt by many immigrants to Scandinavia. It does not matter much that Scandinavians may be able to explain why we isolate our old folks; this is due to our family structure, the labour market, etc. People still feel it is repugnant. Likewise, Westerners may understand the intellectual explanation

---

Box 8.1   Trying to Understand the Phenomenon: Holy Cows

In Scandinavia we use the expression 'holy cow' for irrational loyalty. When people cannot be moved by even the strongest rational argument we talk about 'a holy cow'. The derogatory meaning attached to the expression reflects the typical understanding of India's holy cows: 200 million holy cows, in a country with massive starvation—what a waste of food resources; a waste of fertile land to let them graze all over; a nuisance to the traffic; a health hazard, their droppings left anywhere and to let them die from age! ... all in the name of 'holiness'.

Herlitz elaborates an explanation of this tradition which Scandinavians (and people of most other cultures) find peculiar. He departs from the assumption that there must be a sensible, if not rational, explanation of the cows' holiness, and in a Western cultural tradition he tries to understand the economic significance of the holy cows for India.

1. Draught-animals are indispensable in India's agriculture. From an economic as well as from an ecological point of view it is not desirable to substitute draught power with tractors. A vital function of the holy cows is to provide draught animals.
2. The milk from the cows is vital nourishment, especially for the children.
3. The cows do not compete with people over arable land or food. They graze on the edges of ditches and roads and feed on waste in the rural areas and in the bazaars.
4. Almost all of the 800 million tons per year of cow-dung is recycled as fuel or fertilizer. It does not lie around haphazardly spreading diseases. Dung is a slow-burning fuel, perfect for the Indian way of cooking.
5. Carcasses are recycled; meat is distributed as food for the Scheduled Castes, skins for the tanning industry which is the largest in the world, and bones are turned into glue, etc.
6. India's 15 million oxen give more power than all other power sources together. The oxen provide about two-thirds of all labour on a farm. An estimate is that replacing this source of energy by any other forms would cost some 20 to 30 billion dollars. To substitute dung-fuel with coal would cost a billion dollars.

To sum up, let us quote Mahatma Gandhi again: 'It is no mystery to me that the cows are holy. Without them India would not be possible'.

Gandhi was referring to the enormous importance of the holy cows for India's economy, according to Herlitz. This is not to say that Indians give an economic explanation for the phenomenon of holy cows. Their understanding is likely to relate to reincarnation, while the above explanation is itself a typical trait of Western culture: to look for rational explanations of religious expressions. Nevertheless, Herlitz's explanation is likely to contribute to understanding, rather than condemnation, of the seemingly irrational cultural phenomenon of 'holy cows'.

After Herlitz, 1991: 32–35 (in *KulturGrammatik*).
Reprinted with permission from Konsult forlaget AB (author's translation).

---

of female circumcision—that the custom is one of society's attempts to regulate child spacing and enhance infant survival, besides being a vital link to the past. Understanding is not the same as accepting.

The reason for **immigrants'** resistance to Old People's Homes (also expressed by Reddy, 1992, 1993) and Westerners' resistance to female circumcision is that these customs touch **central** cultural norms. Immigrants to Scandinavia typically come from cultures where strong family ties are very basic. Female circumcision touches the Scandinavians' central norms for protection of the individual against mutilation. In Herlitz's interpretation, the 'holy cow' phenomenon in India touches only Westerners' **peripheral** norms.

8.1.3 Concepts of Space and Time

It is not possible here to enter into a deeper discussion of the basic concepts and structure of languages in different cultures. Only one example: the different concepts of **space and time** will serve to illustrate this very important basis for cross-cultural communication. So deep-rooted is all human beings' perception of the basic structuring features of their culture, that reflection is not required. For Westerners time and space, for example, are taken as eternal and global yardsticks. The example given in Box 8.2 is a reminder to the time-conscious practitioner and to other prospective field workers.

Box 8.2   The Concepts of Space and Time

Space
'How big is your house, Godson?'
Godson Handoma: 'I have house for my ancestors, the wife and God gave me eight children, Bwana.'
'Yes, I understand that, but what is the size of your house?'
GH: 'The house for my family is 15 paces, Bwana.'
'How can a house be 15 paces, Godson? How long is a pace?'
GH: 'The headman, Mr Viyambo, does the pacing in the village, Bwana.'
'What surprises most is to find that various grand generalizations of the Western world, such as time, velocity and matter, are not essential to the construction of a constant picture of the universe' (B.L. Whorf, quoted in Fuglesang, 1982: 34).

Time
In Indo-European languages, there is a time division according to past, present and future .... Time is perceived as an endless stream of time-units. Westerners allocate a pro rata value to time. One piece of time is worth the same as another piece of time. On this basis, we calculate the value of work in man-hours. We make estimates of the future and records and accounts of the past. We use calendars, time graphs or clocks which dismember the experience of time in an endless row or circle of time-units. Time is chopped up like a sausage and sold by the hectogram because time is money. Westerners buy and sell time but have lost the sense of time as a social value in the realm of human experience.

After Fuglesang, 1982: 37 (in *About Understanding*). Reprinted with permission from Andreas Fuglesang.

It is no wonder that the Western planning model based on 'economic time' conflicts with time interpretations which value 'social time'. A different time perspective between development workers and indigenous people is a classic cause of conflict in development cooperation.

There are lots of similar contradictions in interpreting cultural phenomena. They vary from different signals of body language to basic norms of power and gender relations, social cooperation, seniority, etc. An interesting encounter is thoroughly documented by Paul Rabinow, who had his own ethical certainties shaken up during field work in Morocco (1977; Pryke et al., 2003).

Few societies fully share their central and peripheral cultural norms with other societies. Neither do people of the same society share all norms. How this affects the field study situation has been demonstrated in a variety of ways by a group of Indian scholars in a book edited by M.N. Srinivas et al. (1979). The indigenous Indian field researcher, for instance, is often—against his/her political or ideological conviction—challenged to disclose his/her caste affiliation before enquiry can begin. Awareness of the implications of basic caste, class and ethnic differences for the subjects may be even more crucial for the indigenous field researcher than for the expatriate, who is by definition branded as an outsider. As such s/he may be less dangerous if private and sensitive issues are to be disclosed.

8.1.4 Women Field Researchers and Field Assistants

Several female field researchers claim that being a woman is in many instances an advantage in field studies. Panini's collection (1991) contains numerous illustrations, however, of dilemmas faced by women who study their own societies. The approach to data collection itself has to be carefully considered, as illustrated by Palriwala:

> Despite their good intentions, the villagers' perceptions and mine regarding data collection did not always coincide. The villagers, especially the women, would get bored and tired of what appeared to them as repetitious questioning. They saw no need for me to interview so many people and the same people repeatedly. I was unable to explain to them the concept of a sample or its utility. They felt I would be getting the same answers time and again. 'Why not just talk to one or two "knowledgeable" men and women and then relax and gossip with us?', they would ask. Their idea of gossiping with me was to find out more about me! All through the period I was collecting data for my research, I was also being thoroughly researched. I was questioned about my life, my hopes and future prospects and my reactions to their life style. They sought out my opinion on many customs and practices. To most of the women I was the closest contact with the wider world about which they had vaguely heard or had only dimly seen (Palriwala, 1991: 32).

While different interests between researcher and researched prevail, it is important that the researcher permits time to be researched herself. To talk about dialogue would otherwise be meaningless.

Does the topic of study affect women and men field researchers differently? Yes, and sometimes in a contrary direction to what might be expected. Thus, Silberschmidt found, in a sensitive study on men's changing roles and perceptions of gender relations, that men felt much more at ease being interviewed by women than by men: 'They did not need to show off and protect their image to women as they did to interviewers of their own sex' (Silberschmidt, 1991: 26). Finding outside indigenous women for whom it is appropriate and possible to live and work in the field is difficult in some societies (Arn, 1986). A better solution may be to look for assistants in the local community and provide the required training and sharing of ideas.

It is not only with regard to sensitive issues that the role of the interviewer has tremendous significance, be the interviewer the analyst him/herself or an assistant. For outsiders who are new both to the **culture** and to the **language** of the people studied, the assistant—or interpreter—is the filter of information. Barley's accounts of the analyst-assistant relationships are telling illustrations of this (Boxes 8.3, 8.4 and 8.5).

Box 8.3   Hiring an Assistant

'I was pre-empted by one of the preachers being trained at the Poll mission who knew what I was looking for; it so happened that he had 12 brothers. With rare entrepreneurial flair he swiftly mobilized them, marched them in from the village 20 miles out in the bush and presented them to me. This one, he explained, was a good cook and very cheerful. Alas, he did not speak French. This one could read and write, was a terrible cook, but very strong. This one was a good Christian and told stories well. Each, it seemed, had great virtues and was an outstanding bargain. In the end, I agreed to hire one on trial, nobly settling for one who could not cook but spoke the best French, and could read and write. I realized at the time that the preacher himself was the man I should have taken on but his present employment prevented that. He was subsequently thrown out of the mission because of his promiscuous tendencies.'

After Barley, 1986: 45 (in *The Innocent Anthropologist*).

Box 8.4   Picking up the Language

'The first priority was to find an assistant and settle down to learning the language. The anthropologist's assistant is a figure who seems suspiciously absent from ethnographic accounts. The conventional myth seeks to depict the battle-scarred anthropologist as a lone figure wandering into a village, settling in and 'picking up the language' in a couple of months; at the most we may find references to translators being dispensed with after a few weeks. Never mind that this is contrary to all known linguistic experience. In Europe, a man may have studied French at school for six years and with the help of language-learning devices, visits to France, and exposure to the literature, and yet find himself hardly able to stammer out a few words of French in an emergency. Once in the field, he transforms himself into a linguistic wonderworker. He becomes fluent in a language much more difficult for a Westerner than French, without qualified teachers, without bilingual texts, and often without grammars and dictionaries. At least, this is the impression he manages to convey. Of course much may be done in pidgin or even in English, but as often as not, this isn't mentioned either.'

After Barley, 1986: 44 (in *The Innocent Anthropologist*).

Box 8.5   An 'Unsuitable' Partner

'An important feature of "collecting the mail" was that it provided me with a break from my assistant. I had never in my life spent so much time in the uninterrupted company of one person and had begun to feel like one married against his will to a most unsuitable partner.'

After Barley, 1986: 68. Reprinted with permission from Penguin Books Ltd.

Devereux and Hoddinott (1992) argue that if you were to draw up a job description for an ideal research assistant, it would probably include:

> communication skills, good knowledge of English (or French, or Spanish) as well as the local language(s), a perceptive intelligence, inexhaustible patience, unfailing dependability, and an ability to get along with all elements of the local population (quoted in Scheyvens and Storey, 2003: 131).

Inherent in the suggested profile is: be aware of the many possible distances between a native research assistant and ordinary people! While it may seem impossible to find someone who fits all dimensions of the profile, there will always be individuals who, despite a lack of one or two of the above qualities, will make excellent research assistants.

The assistant/interpreter issue is here illustrated by individual anthropological field studies. Its significance multiplies in relation to participatory approaches and underscores the importance of adequate local cooperation, with local researchers, NGOs, field assistants, officials and community members (Hansen and Vaa, 2004).

Another sensitive issue in field studies is the utility of the studies and possible benefits to the subjects. It is an age-old ethical dilemma, as shown in what follows.

8.2   Interventions, Interference and Agents of Change

Implicit in the foregoing discussion are a number of questions concerning interventions, i.e., interventions by whom, for whom, which type, how and why? These questions are increasingly being discussed under the heading International Development Ethics[1] (Clair, 2004) as *ethics of interventions* in general, ethics of certain *disciplines*, and ethics of *personal conduct* (cf. Gullestrup, 1992), or as *research ethics* and *researcher ethics* (Ruyter, 2002).

8.2.1   Ethics and Development Interventions

From the documentation by Lappé et al. (1980) of 'Aid as Obstacle' to helping the hungry, to sources which incorporate historical trends of development aid and research like Eriksen (1987), Tvedt (1990), Nielsen and Vilby (1992), Wilson (1992) and Dichter's (2003) account of 'Why Development Assistance to the Third World has Failed', evidence has built up which calls serious attention to this whole field.[2]

---

[1] International Development Ethics has given name to the Association, IDEA, which defines international development ethics as ethical reflection on the ends and means of local, national and global development. IDEA is forging a consensus on the tasks and methods of this new discipline, adhering to specified 'Levels of Value Issues' and 'Types of Value Inquiry'.

[2] The sceptics of development aid include unavoidable texts with emphasis on causes of failure, for example, Escobar (1995) stresses, 'The making and un-making of the third world', Hancock (1997) emphasizes 'The freewheeling lifestyles, power, prestige and corruption of the multibillion dollar aid business', and for Sachs (1996), 'The idea of Development stands today like a ruin in the intellectual landscape. Its shadow obscures our vision.'

Partly in allegoric form, partly based on critical conceptual analysis, Wilson (1992) delivers a penetrating attack on current development work and research in the Working Paper entitled 'Faust: the Developer'. Referring to Berman's (1988) rewriting of Goethe's Faust in order to situate the rise of modernity and the emergence of the new world of ambiguity that it brought, the parallels between Faust the representative of the transformation to modernism, and 'Faust the Developer' of today are brought out. Results are what matter to Faust. It is Mephisto who secretly clears the way for development as Faust's brutal agent. Wilson quotes Berman that this 'is a characteristically modern style of evil: indirect, impersonal, mediated by complex organisations and institutional roles.' (You recognize a current development issue.) Why this drive to destroy all that is in the way of development? 'It stems from a collective, impersonal drive that seems to be endemic to modernisation: the drive to create a homogeneous environment, a totally modernised space, in which the look and feel of the old world have disappeared without trace' (Berman, quoted in Wilson, 1992: 4).

One of Wilson's questions is: Are present-day developers just as ambiguous and potentially destructive as the early modernizers? Surely, she says, developers, by changing their goals and vocations, have altered their dubious image for the better. Have the 'good developers', whether from governmental or non-governmental aid bureaucracies, not struggled hard to address the needs of the poor? Made serious attempts to set up smaller projects concerning basic needs, and listened to what people want? Indeed, some contemporary developers no longer **do** development as such; instead they see themselves as facilitators or brokers, advocating the interests of the poor to distant governments and aid bureaucracies. Yet, are the individuals still not moulded by modernist thought? 'Or have we become post-modernist enough to see everything as relative and conjunctural?' (ibid.: 6–7).

Wilson leaves the important debate about the ethics of intervention with a polemic reference to the motto coined by personnel in a Scandinavian aid agency: 'We aim to reach the poor—in comfort'. The next step would have been to recommend other forms of international cooperation. However, to elaborate ideas for alternative ways of cooperation was not what Wilson set about doing.

Nielsen and Vilby (1992) also take a critical stance on the Eurocentric definitions of development which have removed people's 'right to own development'. They consider aid interventions in the form of 'projects' as particularly patronizing, not least in rural contexts. Like many other contemporaries, including verbal statements by aid bureaucrats, they advocate a **process approach** which paves the way for planned change on conditions set by people themselves. But exactly how planned change and the process approach may correspond is yet—a decade later—to be worked out. Several methodological hints have been given in this book. What we know today is that development takes expedient and people-centred methods and approaches, but these cannot substitute for political will and commitment.

After Wilson's devastating criticism of the 'developer', which includes the development researcher, and Nielsen and Vilby's (1992), Dichter's (2003) and many others' denunciation of 'projects', the question arises as to where the meaningful ways ahead in international development cooperation are to be found.

Let us recollect some meanings of intervention and interference before turning to ethical questions which relate more directly to research and specific disciplines: There is a distinction between spontaneous development and change on the one hand, and induced or planned development on the other. Aid projects and programmes, for example, are purposive interventions used for directing and accelerating economic and social development, also when there is an insistence on 'putting people first' in planned development interventions (Cernea, 1991). Development projects offer broad scope for intensive, applied development studies. As direct or indirect, applied or action inputs, studies are also interventions and field studies are interference (see Box 8.6).

There is a common understanding that an anthropological study, no matter how theoretically it may be defined, inevitably is an intervention in the social context that is being studied. This has led to the new understanding that anthropology and other development studies must be seen both as a means of intervention and as a means to understand the nature of change. Regardless of whether it is interference through research or through development work, opinions differ on the 'blessings' (see Box 8.7). Interference can still be threatening.

Box 8.6   The Threatening Interference

The notion of change can be threatening. The very presence of the field workers—with their cassette machines, their motorcycles, the trousers they wear, and their inevitable 'modern' habits, is bound to add to the disruption of traditional life. In addition, the changes that our interactions generate are geared to a pace faster than normal mechanisms can cope with. The arts should reflect the outlook of the community, as well as signalling the acceptance of new ways. Our attention to the artistic life of the village accords respect to the culture as well as supporting it in a time of stress, and counts on its support in turn for a deeper acceptance of the changes we may suggest.

After Mauro, 1991.

Box 8.7   Parasite or Agent of Change?

'During my time in Cameroon I met many such specialists, some of whom reproached me bitterly for being a "parasite on African culture". They had come to share knowledge, to change people's lives. I was only there to observe and might, by my interest, encourage pagan superstition and backwardness. Sometimes, in the silent watches of the night, I too wondered about that, just as in England I had wondered about the point of an academic life. However, when it came to the crunch they seemed to accomplish very little. For every problem they solved they created two more. I rather felt that it was people who claimed to be the sole possessors of the truth who should be ill at ease for the disruption they caused in others' lives. At least one can say of the anthropologist that he is a harmless drudge, it being one of the professed ethics of the trade to interfere directly as little as possible in what one observes.'

After Barley, 1986: 25.

While elaborate systems have been developed by aid organizations for induced or planned development, guidelines on the ethics of planned interventions are slowly entering the discourse under the name of 'corporate social responsibility' (e.g., DFID, 2003) where investments are involved. These and Quality Management or Quality Assurance, QA, Systems, are measures applied by aid donors for controlling—or inducing self-assurance—in the increasing number of consultants and multidisciplinary teams who act as 'developers' on behalf of the development cooperation organizations (e.g., www.cowi.dk/

about_cowi/quality_management.asp). Ethical codes are all-encompassing regulations of agencies' and corporations' performance, while QA systems address the technical standards.[3]

8.2.2 Ethics of Specific Disciplines

Anthropology, more than any other social science discipline, has been conscious of ethical questions. The nature of the anthropologist's work partly explains why (see Box 8.8). The urge to intervene and take action, in this case in her own society, in accordance with knowledge gained during field studies, is expressed as a series of ethical dilemmas by the Indian anthropologist Palriwala (Box 8.9).

Box 8.8   The Anthropologist's Subjective Involvement

'In a discussion with my friend, the spirit-medium, about why rural development was not taking off, he suggested that social scientists no longer regard it as their responsibility to change society. His observation reinforced the question that had bothered me since the time I entered the field. Every morning as I got ready to make my visits, I asked myself, "What right do I have to ask these people any questions?" In most cases the peasant men and women challenged me by wanting to know what they should expect to get from answering my questions and from helping me achieve my objective. Others wanted to know what good my knowledge was going to do to them. Such attitudes and misgivings made me realize that there was no reason why I should expect the peasant men and women to be involved with my research problems. Through my daily contacts with different men and women, observing their poverty, their lack of information and their helplessness, I felt very strongly that it was not enough just to be an anthropologist. I realized that "free" research in which the researcher goes in, absorbs as much as he or she can, and then gets out cannot be justified.'

After Tadria, 1991: 96.

There is still a divide between development research and practice on the one hand and 'interventions against oppression' of those being researched on the other, but there are channels through which the researcher/practitioner can express his or her solidarity as a civil person. Actions are, for example, initiated as advocacy work by a number of civil society organizations and NGOs for putting more than face value on involving poor people in the Poverty Reduction Strategy Process. An example is an advocacy experience from Nicaragua attracting development practitioners, where the NGO Ibis initiated a PRSPcito (mini-PRSP) in response to frustrations over the exclusion of poor people (Cranshaw, 2003).

Some ethical codes remain while others are adjusted as the disciplines become more involved in applied studies.

Anthropology's grand old lady, Margaret Mead, shares her experience of the shift in ethical questions which resulted from anthropology becoming an applied discipline, in an article on 'The Evolving Ethics

---

[3] In line with many aid agencies the Danish Ministry of Foreign Affairs, MFA, is in the process of introducing Codes of Conduct—for Management Conduct, for Staff Conduct, and for Evaluation (2004), and a Quality Assurance Department has recently been established.

Box 8.9   The Urge to Intervene against Oppression

'The villagers would often ask me what benefit they would get out of my work. Why should they sit and talk about their life and cooperate with me? I would weakly answer that once the 'book' I was writing was complete, it could be used to demand certain facilities, certain changes and improvements in the conditions of their life. They were never totally convinced of this argument, and since I myself knew that it was hollow I never felt very comfortable with the answer.

As a person emotionally and intellectually attached to the fight against the oppression of people including that of women, I strongly felt the injustice of many customary practices, of certain prevalent beliefs and of several events which occurred in the village. In the normal circumstances, instead of remaining a silent spectator, I would have tried to get something done. However, traditionally, in anthropology, we have been told we must remain neutral and not express our own ideas, especially if they are critical of existing practices, as this would distort the responses we would get. We must certainly not act on our own ideas as it would change the reality being studied, limit our mobility, and create difficulties in collecting 'objective' data.

This raises many philosophical and political questions for the researcher. Does one's own research interest take precedence over honesty and openness and over organized action when the situation demands it? Will the expression of my ideas have any positive impact, or is this just a form of self-indulgence? Will it necessarily weaken the validity of the data I obtain, or in the long run will not the reverse be true? Is not keeping quiet when particular events occur, as good as condoning and participating in them? Would not 'participatory' or 'activist' research be a more truthful approach through which I could arrive at fuller or better data?

These are the doubts and questions which I often faced in the field, but I could not do much in getting the right answers .... My power and ability to experiment in field work practices were limited by various factors, especially time.'

After Palriwala, 1991: 33.

---

of Applied Anthropology' (Mead, 1978). She reminds us that the ethical considerations which guide the work of applied anthropologists are those of the entire discipline.

For those of us who a little less than a century later are engaged in applied development studies, it is good to be reminded of history's influence and recurrence of issues. Mead reminds us of the situation when she started her active life as an anthropologist in the 1920s:

Ethical questions revolved around the obligation, with limited equipment and limited funds, to preserve as much as each of us could of the small scraps of old beliefs and practices that remained among acculturated, but identifiable peoples, and of the whole range of cultural behaviour (ibid.: 427).

A number of other ethical imperatives followed:

• the need for good records of all aspects of a culture because culture was a 'whole'
• the race against time
• an obligation to the people themselves because the anthropologist had the means of studying their cultures which they lacked
• an obligation to colleagues, whom one could help with data collection

- involvement in the material and psychological well-being of the people studied
- ethical problems also revolved around the ways in which findings were reported
- respect for and protection of individuals
- caution in reporting practices which might bring individuals and communities into conflict with the laws of the superordinate powers
- the extent to which the field workers should engage in struggles dictated by knowledge of the culture and concern for the people whom no outsiders would know equally well
- the level of the anthropologist's engagement in battles over land, hunting, or mineral rights, the kinds of education and citizenship that were being offered or withheld from primitive people
- activism, which closed the way to further studies was poor scientific strategy, while
- putting the interests of the discipline over and above 'a given people's hunger' and need was poor performance for any member of the human race! (ibid.: 427–28).

There is considerable likeness between Margaret Mead's ethical imperatives and those embedded in Merton's CUDOS norms (1973—see below) and in ethical issues of field work, which Punch condenses as: *'privacy, harm, identification, confidentiality, and spoiling the field'* (Punch, 1986: 44), and others include *deception* (disclosed or false name of the research) and issues of *power* (the tendency to study the powerless) (Bryman, 2001; Neuman, 2000).

8.2.3 Regulations and Codes of Conduct

The ulterior motives for which applied social sciences have sometimes been used first raised serious concern for the anthropological profession. Margaret Mead, with her anthropologists' organizations, saw the need for an ethical struggle like that of other professions: that is, 'if applied anthropology is to become a profession and not simply a collection of random activities .... As interventionists we became practitioners and needed professional ethics, just as the medical or legal professions.' The result was the 'Statement on Ethics' passed by the Society for Applied Anthropology in 1962. Since then other associations have followed and their statements of professional principles are frequently accessible on the Internet. Some of the most useful codes of ethics can be found at Internet addresses.[4]

Statements on Ethics were first formulated in medical sciences. It has proved difficult for the social sciences to follow the ethical models of other disciplines, since the scope of work and the methodologies differ considerably between the disciplines. The ethical codes of medicine and bio-medicine, for example, must reflect controlled experiments involving human beings as one of the disciplines' primary methodologies.

A central principle in bio-medical codes of ethics is *'informed consent'*, in which subjects should be aware of the fact and accept that they are being investigated. Further, 'that the potential research subjects

---

[4] British Sociological Association (BSA): Statement of Ethical Practice: http://www.britsoc.org.uk/about/ethic.htm. Social Research Association (SRA): Ethical Guidelines: http://www.the-sra.org.uk/ethics.htm. American Sociological Association (ASA), Code of Ethics: http://www.asanet.org/ethics.htm.

understand the intention of the research and sign an 'informed consent' form, which incidentally must specify that the subject may withdraw from the research project at any time' (Punch, 1986: 36). If followed strictly in the social sciences, this principle would seem to ban covert research entirely and abolish a great deal of participant observation research while, ironically, serving to protect the powerful.

It could be argued that planned development interventions—aid assistance—likewise make people subject to 'experimentation' to which they have not given their consent. A difference is the degree of bodily involvement, while methods of 'people's participation' are anticipated to ensure consent concerning aid interventions. This assumption certainly cannot be verified in many cases, but attention to the reflexivity of practitioners' own role and to the pitfalls of participatory methods are now issues in the development discourse.

Both the social and the medical sciences bear witness to numerous cases where ethical codes—whether written or anticipated to be shared codes—have been violated in Third World contexts. Cases of dumping medicines prohibited in Western countries and experimentation with dangerous drugs in the name of family planning in poor countries are numerous. Another type of breach of social science research ethics is the Camelot Project for projecting political unrest in Latin American states, initiated in 1964 by the Special Operations Research Office (SORO) of the US Army (Horowitz, 1967). Without their knowledge, least of all consent, many researchers involuntarily contributed field research data.

Experimentation and interventions in physical, cultural and social contexts require regulations of conduct. Changing technologies in the bio-medical sphere, changing development issues cutting across environmental, technical, natural and social science disciplines make ethical concerns a continuous imperative. That is, regulations and codes of conduct cannot be formulated once and for all for specific disciplines and activities, research or development work, even if core elements have eternal validity.

The norms or ethical principles for social science, first formulated in 1942, are habitually used as a reference point under the acronym CUDOS (admiration/prestige), formed by putting together the initial letters from the four norms that constitute Merton's original ethos of science:

- **C**ommunalism—research results are public property
- **U**niversalism—independence of gender, race, colour or creed and essentially international
- **D**isinterestedness—results should not be manipulated to serve personal profit or ideology
- **O**rganised **S**cepticism—criticism and self-criticism of research process and results

The revival and rephrasing of ethical codes comes at a time, Ernø-Kjølhede (2000) argues quoting Latour, when we are going through *a transition period from a culture of science to a culture of research:*

Science is certainty; research is uncertainty. Science is supposed to be cold, straight and detached; research is warm, involving and risky. Science puts an end to the vagaries of human disputes; research creates controversies. Science produces objectivity by escaping as much as possible from the shackles of ideology, passions, and emotions; research feeds on all of those to render objects of inquiry familiar (Latour, 1998: 208).

It is easy to accept some regulation of conduct in research, and it certainly also would be so in connection with development interventions. Punch has, however, convincingly shown a number of drawbacks of codes of ethics. It is necessary to accept some moderate measure of field-related deception, provided the interests of the subjects are protected, and provided, above all, that it produces good research. It is agreed that a professional code of ethics is beneficial as a *guideline* that alerts researchers and development workers to the ethical dimensions of their work, particularly *prior* to entry. The ethical implications of one's activities, from choice of topic to the methods used, must be considered throughout the process from the earliest possible stage (Punch, 1986; see also Alver and Øyen, 1997).

8.3   Dilemmas of Topics and Methods, and Reminders on Conduct

8.3.1 Unintended Consequences of Codes of Conduct

It is not always possible to separate topic from method of study when ethical issues are considered. The Camelot project mentioned earlier, for example, was planned to make extensive use of anthropologists and sociologists for the study of ulterior political motives.

Action and dialogue research risks stirring unrest since interest conflicts are likely to remain between different groups of participants. In action and dialogue studies, topics and methods are closely intertwined.

The dilemmas concerning topics of field study and the adequate methods of analysis tend to differ from the researcher to the development practitioner (see Wilson, 2004), though it is argued throughout this book that the tool-box is largely the same. In most cases the researcher has more influence over the choice of subject and methodology, whereas the practitioner often starts his/her job after an agency has decided the topic and time-frame of the study. At best the decisions have been taken together with local planners. The dilemma is accentuated in situations where strict separations are maintained between phases and functions in the project or programme cycle. In the name of avoiding nepotism, many organizations retain the strict separation between project planners, implementers, reviewers and evaluators, to the detriment of accumulation of experience, and perhaps dedication.

To ensure better continuity, donor organizations would have to relax their regulations, but first of all procedures must be developed for how to involve a larger variety of potential users in choices of topics, issues, or problems to be studied, and by which methods.

Consultants and other practitioners are likely to experience increasing conflicts over field study topics. Sensitive issues including forced transmigration and resettlement have already caused unease amongst consultants who refrain from participating in the planning for political and ethical reasons. The right to pull out of politically sensitive studies with ulterior motives should be claimed by all practitioners. For example, the current trend of developing personal registry programmes at the national level must be critically analyzed and even rejected if there is any risk of such programmes being used for the political registration of citizens. The risk is not fictitious, unfortunately.

It is likely that many environmental studies will cause concern on the part of the affected population, as such studies may relate to their basic livelihood, evidenced for example by people on the fringes of national parks (Schmidt, 2004; CARE, 2000). Even if people do not absolutely refrain from providing information, the analyst must at least be aware of the possibility of receiving misleading information. The researcher and practitioner are constantly reminded that their roles cannot be completely neutral. The question—who studies what on whose behalf?—remains valid.

A brief recollection of the central development issues outlined in previous sections suggests that they give rise to value judgements as soon as analysis and action upon them are initiated. Concepts like power relations, empowerment, poverty, human rights and democracy inevitably raise ethical questions once they become the subject of study or direct intervention. Ironically, codes of conduct as exemplified in corporate social responsibility can disadvantage the poor, as stated by DFID (2003):

Corporate social responsibility can disadvantage the poor:

- socially responsible practices should not replace local laws, let alone prevent businesses complying with them. Ultimately it is effective institutional, regulatory and legal frameworks, including appropriate tax systems, which will deliver the greatest benefit to most poor people
- prescriptive corporate codes of conduct, or sudden action which does not involve suppliers, may not be appropriate for local conditions
- in the worst cases, inappropriate codes of conduct become a form of protectionism that prevents goods from the South being sold in the North
- many non-government organizations, consumers and investors have put pressure on multinational enterprises to withdraw from countries with poor human rights records. Instead of withdrawing investments, principled engagement can help poor people and so help to bring about change.

If the social context is guarded by restrictions on speech, on freedom of movement, on freedom of the press, etc., unintended consequences may arise for the socially conscious corporation, and the analyst is particularly apt to become entangled in dilemmas of field study.

8.3.2 Ethics and Methods—The Power of Interviewing

The legitimacy of development interventions has been questioned as unethical interference—interference in national policies, in cultures, in community life, in individuals' integrity, through a variety of means and methods applied by development practitioners. The legitimacy of contemporary participatory methods, for example, has been questioned by different scholars as discussed in Chapter 2. Here, a reflection on interviews—the most distinct technique of field studies—is pertinent.

Interviews are interventions placing the interviewer in a role for which an ethical framework is needed. Interviews can become confessions. People will tell you things they never intended to tell anyone. Some will make up stories to please the interviewer, or just for the sake of good stories. Lonely people will prolong the interview, longing for the company of someone to talk to. There may be pressure on you as an interviewer to answer a lot of questions, to give your opinion and judgement, and a temptation to take over the role as interviewee. Dilemmas of interviewing are illustrated in Boxes 8.10 and 8.11.

Box 8.10   Ethical Dilemmas of Interviewing

'The interviewer, in establishing rapport, is not a cold slab of granite, unresponsive to the human issues, including great suffering and pain, that may unfold during an interview. In a major farming system's needs assessment project to develop agricultural extension programmes for distressed farm families, I was part of a team of 10 interviewers (working in pairs) who interviewed 50 farm families. Many of these families were in great pain. They were losing their farms. Their children had left for the city. Their marriages were under stress. The two-hour interviews traced their family history, their farm situation, their community relationships, and their hopes for the future. Sometimes questions would lead to husband-wife conflict. The interviews would open old wounds, lead to second-guessing decisions made long ago, or bring forth painful memories of dreams never fulfilled. People often asked for advice—what to do about their crops, their children, government subsidy programmes, even their marriages. But we were not there to give advice. We were there to get information that might, or might not, lead to new programmes of assistance. Could we do more than just ask our question and leave? Yet, as researchers, could we justify in any way intervening? Yet again, our interviews were already an intervention. Such are the ethical dilemmas that derive from the power of interviews.'

After Patton, 1990: 354 (in *Qualitative Evaluation Methods*).

Box 8.11   Cultures of Conversation and Interviews

To begin with I was distressed to find that I couldn't extract more than 10 words from Dowayos at a stretch. When I asked them to describe something to me, a ceremony, or an animal, they would produce one or two sentences and then stop. I would have to ask further questions to get more information. This was very unsatisfactory as I was directing their answers rather more than sound field method would have prescribed. One day, after about two months of fairly fruitless endeavour, the reason struck me. Quite simply, Dowayos have totally different rules about how to divide up the parts of a conversation. Whereas in the West we learn not to interrupt when somebody else is talking, this does not hold in much of Africa. One must talk to people physically present as if on the telephone, where frequent interjections and verbal response must be given if only to assure the other party that one is still there and paying attention. When listening to someone talking, a Dowayo stares gravely at the floor, rocks backwards and forwards and murmurs, 'Yes', 'It is so', 'Good', every five seconds or so. Failure to do so leads to the speaker rapidly drying up. As soon as I adopted this expedient, my interviews were quite transformed.

After Barley, 1986: 67.

The power of interviewing is particularly blatant in qualitative inquiry:

> Because qualitative methods are highly personal and interpersonal, because naturalistic inquiry takes the researcher into the real world where people live and work, and because in-depth interviewing opens up what is inside people—qualitative inquiry may be more intrusive and involve greater re-activity than surveys, tests, and other quantitative approaches (Patton, 2002: 407).

8.3.3 Ethical Issues of Field Studies

As a starting point in thinking through ethical issues in design, data collection, and analysis, Patton (2002) presents a checklist, acknowledging that many others have contributed to these points:

1. **Explaining purpose.** How will you explain the purpose of the inquiry and methods to be used in ways that are accurate and understandable? What language will make sense to participants in the study? What details are critical to share? What can be left out? What is the expected value of your work to society and to the greater good?

2. **Promises and Reciprocity.** What is in it for the interviewee? Why should the interviewee participate in the interview? Do not make promises lightly, such as promising a copy of the tape recording, the report or photos taken. *If you make promises, keep them.*

3. **Risk assessment.** In what ways, if any, will conducting the interview put people at risk? Psychological stress? Legal liabilities? In evaluation studies, continued programme participation (if certain things become known)? Ostracism by peers, programme staff, or others for talking? Political repercussions? How will you describe these potential risks to interviewees? How will you handle them if they arise?

4. **Confidentiality.** What are reasonable promises of confidentiality that can be fully honoured? Know the difference between confidentiality and anonymity. (Confidentiality means you know but won't tell. Anonymity means you don't know, as in a survey returned anonymously.) What thing can you not promise confidentiality about, for example, illegal activities, evidence of child abuse or neglect? Will names, locations, and other details be changed? Or do participants have the option of being identified? Where will data be stored? How long will data be maintained?

5. **Informed Consent.** What kind of informed consent, if any, is necessary for mutual protection? Politically sensitive situations, e.g., party affiliation, and private issues such as income data, family affairs, tax avoidance, etc., may require avoidance of these issues in public. Consider a public or private place for the interview. Possible agreement on duration of interview.

6. **Data Access and Ownership.** Who will have access to the data? For what purposes? Who owns the data? Who will benefit economically from published data? Be clear about this in the contract of funding and clarify if respondents so wish. Who has right of review before publication?

7. **Interviewer Need for Debriefing.** How are you and other interviewers likely to be affected by conducting the interviews? If interviews are conducted by an assistant and not the researcher personally, debriefing by the assistant must be a routine for sharing of data. Assistants may need to let off steam, depending for example on the sensitivity of data collected, harassment from respondents, etc. What will they hear or see that may merit debriefing and processing? Who can you talk to about what you experience without breaching confidentiality?

8. **Confidant and Advisor.** Who will be the researcher's confidant and counsellor on matters of ethics during a study? Not all issues can be anticipated in advance. Think of agreement with a confidant in advance.

9. **Data collection boundaries.** How hard will you push for data? What lengths will you go to in trying to gain access to data you want? What won't you do? How hard will you push interviewees to respond to questions about which they show some discomfort?

10. **Ethical versus legal.** What ethical framework and philosophy informs your work and ensures respect and sensitivity for those you study, beyond whatever may be required by law? What disciplinary or professional code of ethical conduct will guide you?

(*After* Patton 1990 and 2002).

To the above points of ethical issues for field studies we can add one more:

11. **Permission to undertake research.** The entrance to the field is as important as the exit. In most countries there are regulations for obtaining permission to conduct research. A breach of these has resulted in researchers being expelled from the field and from the country. Procedures differ considerably from country to country and over time, sometimes requiring many months. It is important to check the specific regulations through the relevant embassies well in advance.

8.3.4 Reciprocity

In the case of the farm family interviews (Box 8.10), the research team coped with the ethical problems by sharing prepared information. They decided to leave each family a packet of information about resources and programmes of assistance. To avoid having to decide which families really needed such assistance, the team left information with all families. When interviewees asked for advice during the interview, the team could tell them that they would leave them referral information at the end of the interview.

All development studies are associated with expectations of later interventions—at best to the benefit of the poor, at worst as an untimely intrusion in the interest of a rich few or outsiders. It is virtually impossible not to raise expectations, whether false or real. The danger is probably higher in connection with participatory methods, except that the dialogue which arises may further the level of information to sufficiently counter false expectations.

Experience shows that very often no observable results follow, and if at all, only much, much later than the study. From where should people's motivation to participate in a study then come? Fortunately obstruction or lack of interest is not an everyday problem in development studies. However, the question of reciprocity and remuneration is relevant. Reciprocity can never fully exist in the field study situation between the researcher and the researched. It is basically a give and take situation.

The common interest in a study may be more obvious in action research, provided the participants are fully part of major decisions. The language barrier itself creates an uneven relationship, to the disadvantage of the analyst and the validity of information. And other obsessions and social insensitivities on the part of the analyst may obstruct information—e.g., obsession with privacy (see Box 8.12).

Paying for interviews has always been considered bad practice in social research—it may bias the interviewee and cause replies to become pleasing. This is a sound principle, but like other principles it needs to be assessed in the light of new developments. People in the South frequently complain that

---

Box 8.12   Westerners' Obsession with Privacy

'On one occasion, I trekked up into the mountains to the outermost confines of Dowayoland. Many of the children had never seen a White man before and began to scream with terror until comforted by their elders who explained that this was the White chief from Kongle. We all laughed good-naturedly at their fright and smoked together. Normally I do not smoke, but found it useful to be able to do so to share tobacco and so create a social bond between us. As I left, one of the girls burst into tears and I heard her snivel, 'I wanted to see him take his skin off'. I made a mental note to ask about it later; normally, such expressions turned out to be the result of a misinterpreted tone or an unknown homonym. When asked about it, however, my assistant showed acute embarrassment. I went into a jollying-along routine I had had to develop for precisely this sort of situation and gave him all my attention. Dowayos are frequently mocked by surrounding tribes for their 'savagery' and will clam up at the least sign that they are not being taken seriously. Reluctantly, he confessed that Dowayos believed that all White men who lived for extended periods in Dowayoland were reincarnated spirits of Dowayo sorcerers. Underneath the white skins we had managed to cover ourselves with, we were black. When I went to bed at night, I had been seen to take off my white skin and hang it up. When I went to the mission with the other White men, we drew the curtains at night, locked the door and took our white skins off. Of course, he declared somewhat sniffily, *he* did not believe this, looking me up and down as if afraid that I would revert to my black colour on the spot. The belief explained Westerners' obsession with privacy.'

After Barley, 1986: 54–55.

---

their role has been reduced to delivering 'raw material' in research also, while Western researchers go back and earn their credentials on the basis of that material. This is an unfortunate division of labour which takes time to alter, even through programmes for building research capacity in the South.

The spread of participatory methods puts the question of remuneration in a different light. More field data are generated by communities who spend time in workshops, with social mapping, area walks, ranking exercises, in-depth interviews, etc.

It has now become legitimate to introduce payment for the costs incurred to communities that host PRA workshops, for example. What constitutes normal practice in a given area should be sought out from collaborating researchers or other key people. Some try to retain some reciprocity by other incentives, e.g., giving gifts appropriate for particular situations: a blackboard for the school, food and drink, buying goods in the village shop, etc. It is impossible to give clear guidelines on which type of remuneration is appropriate. It is wise to carefully consider not only what, but also how to show appreciation in order to comply with protocol (see Box 8.13).

Box 8.13   Errors of Protocol

'Customs can vary from village to village, and unfamiliarity led to one or two early errors of protocol. The desire, indeed expectation, of the griots to be remunerated, and the question of how to go about it, e.g., the provision of beer and dance customs and later food for a communal meal for the actors, were all much discussed with the field workers (who were all of them Bobo), and with the management (who were not), but nobody realized how treacherous was the ground until hindsight showed it. When we agreed to provide a bicycle for the griots so that they could travel to Bangassi to sign, we discussed it with the village chiefs, but failed to make the handover into a ceremonial gesture by delivering it to the village chief to be passed on to the recipient. We had offended the dignity of the chief, and aroused the jealousy of the farmers who thought we were favouring the griots. In another village this may have been overlooked as a minor aberration; in Tana it was grave and took months to resolve. If this had happened recently, it would have appeared in the plays (put on by the villagers), and no doubt we would have been able to avert some ill-feeling.'

After Mauro, 1991.

Conclusion

A few messages have hopefully been transmitted, if not explicitly stated. For example:

- Development work and research have far-reaching ethical implications, stemming from interventions in social and cultural processes. We do not like to be compared with missionaries of former times or the Faust-like 'developers', but the reflection is imperative.
- Appropriate field study methods reflect the purpose and the time and resources available. Suggestions have been given and newer participatory methods, techniques and tools presented to facilitate studies using methodological pluralism, method combinations, flexibility and iterative research processes, but first of all to adjust development studies 'as if people matter'.
- The 'messages' are written by a Northern scholar with a major concern for improving field studies involving Northerners in the South. The risk of a Eurocentric perspective prevails, since full honour has been far from paid to excellent studies undertaken by scholars from the South in their own societies. The best way to honour their work would be to invite them to come to the North and undertake critical studies here. That would be a fair basis for genuine dialogue. Till then the call to all field workers—from North and South—is:

Share the experience, the results, the honour and the blame!
and
Perform field studies with imagination and care to prevent spoiling the field for others—
and for yourself.

Glossary

Accountability: In development work accountability would typically be the process by which development organizations are accountable to their partners and poor and marginalized groups. It entails greater participation and transparency in organizations' work.

Advocacy: Is pursuit of influencing outcomes—including public policy and resource allocation within political, economic and social systems and institutions that directly affect people's lives—e.g., a struggle for a goal or an agenda such as gender equality, fair trade, etc.

Analysis: Breaking down something into its component parts. Involves examination of data for trends, comparisons, relationships and themes. *Qualitative analysis* seeks to answer questions like what, how and why something happened, using methods of analysing and interpreting data like participatory methods, meetings, open-ended interviews, maps, observations. *Quantitative analysis* seeks answers to questions like how much, how many, how often; analyse and interpret data using numerical or statistical methods, graphs and charts. In development studies quantitative and qualitative analysis often complement each other.

Attribution: The ascription of a causal link between observed (or expected to be observed) changes and a specific intervention, in view of the effects of other interventions and conditions which may influence the changes.

Baseline study: A collection of data about the characteristics, for example of a population or an area before a programme or project is set up. The data can be compared with a study of the same characteristics carried out later in order to see what has changed. See *monitoring* and *evaluation*.

Capacity: The ability of individuals and organizations to perform functions effectively and efficiently. Resources (people, money, assets) skills, knowledge and organization required to carry out a particular task.

Capacity building: The process through which capacity is created—e.g., in organizations, amongst stakeholders, in groups. Increasingly an aspect of poverty alleviation interventions.

Community participation: A wide range of ways local people are involved in external development interventions, from token and passive involvement to more empowerment-oriented forms of local decision-making.

Diagram: A model that presents information in an easily understandable form. Different types of diagrams are, for example, pie charts, web charts, histograms, maps, transects, seasonal calendars, time lines, daily routine diagrams, flow diagrams, causality diagrams, Venn diagrams.

Effect: Intended or unintended change resulting directly or indirectly from a development intervention.

Effectiveness: The extent to which the development intervention's objectives were achieved, or are expected to be achieved, taking into account their relative importance; the merit or worth of an activity.

Efficiency: A measure of how economically resources and inputs for a specified intervention are converted to results.

Empowerment: Refers to the expansion in people's ability to make strategic life choices in a context where this ability was previously denied to them.

Evaluability: Extent to which an activity or a programme can be evaluated in a reliable and credible fashion.

Evaluation: A systematic (and as objective as possible) examination of an ongoing or completed project, programme or policy, its design, implementation and results. It aims to answer specific management questions, and judge the overall value of an endeavour and supply lessons learned to improve future actions, planning and decision-making. Evaluations commonly seek to determine the efficiency, effectiveness, impact, sustainability and the relevance of an intervention's objectives. An evaluation can involve the definition of appropriate standards, the examination of performance against those standards, an assessment of actual and expected results, and the identification of relevant lessons.

Gender (roles, relations): Refers to the social roles and relations between women and men. This includes the different responsibilities of women and men in a given culture or location. Unlike the sex of men or women, which is biologically determined, the gender roles of women and men are socially constructed, and such roles can change over time and vary according to geographic location and social context for the gender mainstreaming strategy.

Gender analysis: Helps to frame questions about women's and men's roles and relations in order to avoid making assumptions about who does what, when and why. The aim of gender analysis is to formulate development interventions that are better targeted to meet both women's and men's needs and constraints. Gender analysis has been established as a basic requirement for the mainstreaming strategy.

Gender mainstreaming: The consideration that attention to gender equality is a central part of all interventions, including analyses, policy advice, advocacy, legislation, research and the planning, implementation, monitoring and evaluation. Gender mainstreaming is an approach, gender equality is the goal.

Impact: Positive and negative, primary and secondary long-term effects produced by a development intervention, directly or indirectly, intended or unintended; the changes in the lives of people affected by a development intervention, as perceived by them and their partners, to which the intervention has contributed.

Indicator: Qualitative or quantitative factor or variable that provides a simple and reliable means to measure achievement, reflect changes connected to an intervention, or help assess the performance of a development actor. Indicators are proxies used to *indicate* the characteristics of a state of affairs and to measure change. For example, the height of a child would be an indicator of growth (a quantitative indicator). The possibility of sleeping in a different room than the farm animals would be an indicator of well-being in some societies (a qualitative indicator). Indicators can be combined into composite indicators, e.g., the Human Development Index, composed of life expectancy at birth, adult literacy rate, combined first-, second- and third-level gross enrolment ratio and GDP per capita. There are indicators of objectives, of process, of achievement, of outcomes, of performance, of impact. Ideally indicators should be SMART. See *objectives*.

Intervention: In international development cooperation this refers to external support, for example to policy formulation, budget support, a sector programme (e.g., agriculture, education, health, infrastructure), a project, involving a series of activities agreed between partners (donor and non-donor).

Monitoring: A continuing function that uses systematic collection and analysis of data on specified indicators to provide management and the main stakeholders of an ongoing development intervention with indications of the extent of progress and achievement of objectives. Meant to assist timely decision-making, ensure accountability and provide the basis for evaluation and learning.

Objectives (development objectives): Intended impact contributing to physical, financial, institutional, social, environmental, or other benefits to a society, community, or group via one or more development interventions; are specific, time-bound and measurable goals for projects or programmes, which contribute to achieving the longer-term aims of the *intervention*, for example to achieve 80 per cent immunization coverage in the next five years in district X. Essential characteristics of an objective should be that it fulfils the criteria SMART— Specific, Measurable, Achievable, Relevant, Time-bound.

Observation: Direct observation means observing objects, events, processes, relationships or people's behaviour systematically, and recording these observations. Observation is a useful qualitative research method.

Participation: Common meanings of *participation* and *participatory* are; voluntary contributions by people in development activities; sensitization of people to increase their receptivity to development interventions; an active process where a group of people take initiatives; fostering of dialogue between stakeholders, between those with more and less decision-making power; voluntary involvement of people in self-determined change. Associated with different degrees of voluntarism or coercion.

Participatory approaches: When staff, partners, people affected (stakeholders) by an intervention or piece of work, and others involved with the work participate directly in planning and carrying out a study, an assessment, a review, monitoring or evaluation exercises.

Participatory evaluation: Representatives of agencies and stakeholders, including people being affected by an intervention, work together designing, carrying out, and interpreting and possibly following up an evaluation. The primary focus may be the information needs of stakeholders rather than the donor's. There is a distinction between participatory evaluations and participatory evaluation methods. An evaluation may use participatory methods and tools, and still not qualify as a fully participatory evaluation.

Participatory methods: For collecting information and analysis, for dialogue, communication and awareness raising; involve different stakeholders in addition to the researcher; include many different techniques, some *space related*, others *time related*, while some methods are *relational*. Participatory methods are often characterized as *qualitative methods*, but the latter need not be participatory.

Participatory rural appraisal (PRA); participatory learning and action (PLA): Investigations involving people affected by an intervention in order to gain a common understanding of a situation and agree on relevant actions. A form of qualitative research using participatory techniques and tools are, e.g., those mentioned under *diagrams*.

Partners: The individuals and/or organizations that collaborate to achieve mutually agreed upon objectives. Partnership connotes shared goals, common responsibility for outcomes, distinct accountabilities and reciprocal obligations. Partners may include governments, civil society, non-governmental organizations, universities, professional and business associations, multi- and bilateral development organizations.

Qualitative research: A flexible approach of building up an in-depth picture of a situation, community, etc., often combining a variety of methods, observation, discussion, open-ended and semi-structured interviews, mapping and other *participatory approaches and tools*. In development studies quantitative and qualitative research often complement each other. (See *analysis*.)

Quantitative research: Is used to collect data which can be analysed in a numerical form. Often makes uses of questionnaires, and questions are asked according to a defined questionnaire so that the answers can be coded and analysed numerically. In development studies quantitative and qualitative research often complement each other. (See *analysis*.)

Ranking: Placing something in order. Ranking can be used to help identify the main preferences of people and to compare their priorities.

Reflexivity: The social researcher's awareness of the possible implications and biases of his/her choice of methods, values, decisions, and of the researcher's mere presence in the very situation being investigated.

Relevance: The extent to which the objectives of a development intervention are consistent with the priorities of those it was supposed to benefit. Relevance is also often defined as consistency with country needs, global priorities and partners' and donors' policies. The issue of relevance often important when it comes to the question of whether the objectives of an intervention or its design are still appropriate, given changed circumstances.

Reliability: Consistency or dependability of data and judgements, with reference to the quality of the instruments, procedures and analyses used to collect and interpret data. Information is reliable when repeated observations using the same instrument under identical conditions produce similar results.

Rights-based approach, RBA: Approaches to programming aim to make people's human rights a reality. RBA builds on the belief that all human beings have certain rights which cannot be taken away from them, and which enable them to make claims on others when their rights are being denied or violated. These rights are set out in international law, where they are presented as standards and norms that all societies should aim to achieve. All *rights-holders* have entitlement to their rights, and can legitimately claim them.

Sample/Sampling: The selection of a representative part of a population in order to determine parameters or characteristics of the whole population. A sample can be purposively chosen to represent only smaller sections of a population. Related concepts are *probability sampling, non-probability sampling, random sample, quota sample.*

Stakeholders: Are all those who have an interest in an intervention or are likely to be affected by it—positively or negatively. Stakeholders include people implementing the activities, external service providers, financial sponsors, and the wider public. A stakeholder analysis identifies who the stakeholders are and their different and perhaps conflicting interests in the intervention.

Target group: The specific individuals, group or organization for whose benefit the development intervention is undertaken.

Theoretical sampling: Used mainly in relation to *grounded theory* to refer to sampling carried out so that emerging theoretical considerations guide the selection of cases and/or research participants. Theoretical sampling is supposed to continue until a point of *theoretical saturation*, the point when emerging concepts have been fully explored and no new insights are being generated.

Triangulation: Use of a variety of sources, methods and types of information (or field team members) to verify and substantiate an assessment; to cross-check and validate data and information to limit biases.

Validity: The extent to which the data collection strategies and instruments measure what they purport to measure.

Validation: The process of cross-checking to ensure that the data obtained from the use of one method are confirmed by the data obtained from using a different method.

Bibliography

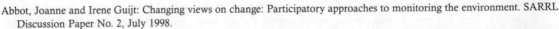

Abbot, Joanne and Irene Guijt: Changing views on change: Participatory approaches to monitoring the environment. SARRL Discussion Paper No. 2, July 1998.

ACPDT/Africa Community Publishing and Development Trust: The Suffering Are the Cornerstone in Building a Nation. Community views on poverty, poverty alleviation and wealth creation. For Government of Zimbabwe and UNDP, 1995.

ActionAid/IIED: 'From Input to Impact: Participatory Rural Appraisal' for ActionAid, the Gambia, March 1992.

Adesida, Olugbenga and A.O. Oteh (eds): African Voices—African Visions. The Nordic Africa Institute, Uppsala, 2004.

Agarwal, Bina: 'Participatory Exclusions, Community Forestry, and Gender: An Analysis for South Asia and a Conceptual Framework'. *World Development*, Vol. 29, No. 10, pp. 1623–48, 2001.

Agrawal, A.: 'Dismantling the divide between indigenous and scientific knowledge'. *Development and Change*, Vol. 26, pp. 413–39, 1995.

Albaek, Erik: 'Knowledge interests and the many meanings of evaluation: A development perspective', *Scandinavian Journal of Social Welfare*, Vol. 7, 1998.

Aldenderfer, Mark and H.D.G. Maschner: *Anthropology, Space and Geographic Information Systems*. Spatial Information Systems Series, Oxford University Press, New York, 1996.

Alex, Gary and Derek Byerlee: Monitoring and Evaluation for AKIS Projects. Framework and Options. The World Bank Rural Development Family, December 2000.

Allott, Philip: 'Eunomia: New Order for a New World', 1990, in Steiner/Alston, *International Human Rights in Context. Law, Politics, Morals*, Oxford University Press, Oxford, 2000.

Altrichter, Herbert: 'Do we Need an Alternative Methodology for Doing Alternative Research?' In O. Zuber-Skerritt (ed.), *Action Research for Change and Development*, Avebury, 1991.

Alver, Bente G and Ø Øyen: Forskningsetikk I forskerhverdag. Vurderinger og praksis. (Research ethics in day to day research. Assessments and practice). Tano Aschehoug, Oslo, 1997.

Alvesson, Mats and Kaj Sköldberg: Tolkning och reflection. Vetenskapsfilosofi och kvalitativ metod (Interpretation and reflection. Meta science philosophy and qualitative methods). Studentlitteratur, Lund, 1994.

Anacleti, Odhiambo: 'Research on Local Culture and its Implications on Participatory Development'. GAPP Conference on Participatory Development, Goldsmith College, July 1992.

Andersen, Ib: Den skinbarlige virkelighed—vidensproduktion inden for samfundsvidenskaberne (The incarnate reality—knowledge production in the social sciences). Samfundslitteratur, Copenhagen, 2002.

Andersen, Ida E. and Birgit Jaeger: 'Scenario workshops and urban planning in Denmark'. In PLA Notes 40, 2001.

Anderson, M.B.: An Analysis of Operational Experience in Integrating Women into Development, 1970–1991, UNIFEM, SWID/1991/WP 2.

Anderson, M.B. and P.J. Woodrow: *Rising from the Ashes: Development Strategies in Times of Disaster.* Westview Press, UNESCO, Paris, 1989 and Lynne Rienner Publishers, 1998.

Andersson, Bengt-Erik: Som man frågar får man svar—en introduction i intervju- og enkätteknik. (As you ask questions you get answers—an introduction to interview and survey technique) Raben & Sjögren. Tema Nova, Stockholm, 1992.

Andreassen, Maria Dyhr and Britha Mikkelsen: Bibliography on Participation and Participatory Methods in Development Work and Research. Institute for International Studies, Copenhagen, February 2003.

Ankersborg, Vibeke: I Erslevs fodspor—en lærebog I kildekritik som savfundsvidenskabelig metode (In Erslev's footprints—a reader in critical source analysis methodology in the social sciences). Forlaget Politiske Studier, Copenhagen, 2002.

Arn, Ann Lisbet: 'Noakhali Villages. A Description of the Socio-Economic Conditions in Four Villages in Noakhali District, Bangladesh', CDR Research Report No. 6. Copenhagen, 1986.

Arnfred, Signe: 'Questions of Power: Women's Movements, Feminist Theory and Development Aid'. In Sida Studies No. 3, 2002.

Baden, Sally, Shireen Hassim and Sheila Meintjes: 'Country Gender Profile: South Africa', for Sida, 1998.

Bamberger, Michael, Mark Blackden, Lucia Fort and Violeta Manoukian: Gender. Chapter 10. In Jeni Klugman (ed.), *A Sourcebook for Poverty Reduction Strategies*, World Bank, 2001.

Barley, Nigel: *The Innocent Anthropologist. Notes from a Mud Hut*. Penguin Books, 1986.

Bauer, Martin W. and George Gaskell (eds): *Qualitative Researching with Text, Image and Sound. A Practical Handbook*. Sage Publications, London, 2002.

Bauer, Martin W.: 'Classical Content analysis: A Review'. In Bauer and Gaskell (eds), *Qualitative Researching with Text, Image and Sound. A Practical Handbook*, Sage Publications, London, 2000.

Baulch, Bob: 'Editorial. The new poverty agenda: a disputed consensus', *IDS Bulletin* Vol. 27, No. 1, pp. 1–10, 1996.

Bellon, M.R.: *Participatory Research Methods for Technology Evaluation: A Manual for Scientists Working with Farmers*. CIMMYT, Mexico, 2001.

Berman, Marshall: *All That is Solid Melts Into Air. The Experience of Modernity*. Penguin Books, 1988.

Biggs, S. and G. Smith: 'Beyond methodologies: Coalition-building for participatory technology development', *World Development*, Vol. 26, No. 2, pp. 239–48, 1998.

Bijker, W.E. and J. Law: *Shaping Technology/Building Society—Studies in Socio-technical Change*. Cambridge Mass., MIT Press, 1992.

Bijker, W.E., T.P. Hughes and T.J. Pinch (eds): *The Social Construction of Technological Systems—New Directions in the Sociology and History of Technology*. Cambridge Mass. MIT Press, 1987.

Bilgi, Meena: 'Entering Women's World Through Men's Eyes—A Participatory Rural Appraisal at Boripitha, Netrang', Aga Khan Rural Support Programme, India, 1992.

Blackburn, James, R. Chambers and J. Gaventa: 'Mainstreaming Participation in Development', OED WP 10, World Bank, 2000.

Boolsen, Merete Watt: Kvalitative analyser i praksis. (Qualitative Analysis in Practice). Forlaget Politiske Studier, Copenhagen, 2004.

————: *'Jeg spø'r, får svar og handler. Men hvad mente jeg egentlig?'* (I ask, get anwers and act. But what did I actually mean? In Charlotte Paludan (ed.): *Pas på pædagogikken (Watch the Pedagogic)*. Reitzels Forlag, Copenhagen, 1997.

Boolsen, Merete Watt, Jill Mehlbye and Lisbeth Sparre: Børns opvækst uden for hjemmet (Children Growing Up Outside Home). AKF, Copenhagen, 1986.

Boolsen, Merete Watt: Struktur, teknologi og produktivitet. (Structure, Technology and Productivity), Doctoral Thesis, University of Copenhagen, 1977.

Booth, David and Henry Lucas: 'Good Practice in the Development of PRSP Indicators and Monitoring Systems'. Working Paper, No. 172. ODI, London, 2002.

Botchway, Karl: 'Paradox of Empowerment: Reflection on a Case Study from Northern Ghana'. *World Development*, Vol. 29, No. 1, pp. 135–53, 2001.

Bourdieu, Pierre and L.J.D. Wacquant: *An Invitation to Reflexive Sociology*. Chicago University Press, 1992.

Bredsdorff, Niels: Diskurs og konstruktion—En samfundsvidenskabelig kritik af diskursanalyser og socialkonstruktivismer. (Discourse and construction—A social science critique of discourse analysis and social constructivisms), Forlaget Sociologi, Frederiksberg, 2002.

BRIDGE: *Gender and Participation. Cutting edge pack*. Institute of Development Studies, Sussex, August 2001.

Brown, David, Mick Howes, Karim Hussein, Catherine Longley and Ken Swindell: *Participation in Practice: Case Studies from the Gambia*. ODI, London, 2002a.

————: 'Participatory Methodologies and Participatory Practices: Assessing PRA use in the Gambia'. AgREN Network Paper No. 124, ODI, London, July 2002b.

Brown, David: 'Professionalism, participation, and the public good: Issues of arbitration in development management and the critique of the neo-populist approach'. In M. Minogue, C. Polidano and D. Hulme (eds), *Modern public management: Changing ideas and practices in governance*, Edward Elgar, Cheltenham, London, 1998.

————: 'Rhetoric or reality? NGOs as agencies of grassroots development', in AERDD Bulletin, No. 28, pp. 3–10, 1990.

Brownlie, Ian and Gut S. Goodwill-Gill (eds): *Basic Documents on Human Rights*. Oxford University Press, 2002.

Bryman, Alan: *Social Research Methods*. Oxford University Press, London, 2001.

Buch-Hansen, Ellen: 'Are partnership and participation "magic wands" for promoting sustainability, democratisation, equity and poverty reduction?' Paper for Aid Impact Forum seminar on Partnership, Participation and Empowerment in Development Cooperation—A Role for the Poor—or Legitimizing Devices?, CDR (now DIIS), Copenhagen, 21 October 2002.

Buhler, William, S. Morse, E. Arthur, S. Bolton and J. Mann: *Science, Agriculture and Research. A Compromised Participation?* Earthscan, London, 2002.

Burr, V: *An Introduction to Social Constructionism*. Routledge, London, 1995.

CARE-Uganda: QEPACCP Project Document, CARE Danmark, CARE Uganda, 2000.

Campbell, J.R.: 'Interdisciplinary research and GIS—Why local and indigenous knowledge are discounted'. In Sillitoe et al.: *Participating in Development. Approaches to Indigenous Knolwedge*. Routledge, London, 2002.

CAPEQM: Guideline on Spatial Planning for Sustainable Development, CAPEQM, Khon Kaen, October 2003.

CAPEQM: 'A Sourcebook for Participatory Local Planning, A Guide for Managers and Planners—Integrating environmental, economic and social goals to improve Thai peoples' quality of life', by Charles Pendley, COWI, for CAPEQM, Khon Kaen, September 2003.

Carney, D. (ed.): *Sustainable Rural Livelihoods. What Contribution Can We Make?* DFID, London, 1998.

Carrión, Diego M.: 'Democracy and social participation in Latin American cities', *Development in Practice*, Vol. 11, Nos. 2&3, May 2001.

Casley, D.J. and D.A. Lury: *Data Collection in Developing Countries*. Clarendon, 1981.

Cernea, Michael M.: *Putting People First. Sociological Variables in Rural Development*, New York, Oxford University Press, 1991.

Chambers, R.: *Participatory Workshops. A Sourcebook of 21 Sets of Ideas and Activities*. Earthscan, London, 2002a.

————: 'Relaxed and Participatory Appraisal: Notes on practical approaches and methods for participants in PRA/PLA—related familiarisation workshops', IDS, Sussex, January, 2002b.

————: *Whose Reality Counts? Putting the First Last. Intermediate Technology Publications*, London, 1997.

————: 'Paradigm shifts and the practice of participatory research and development', in Nici Nelson and Susan Wright, *Power and Participatory Development—Theory and Practice*, pp. 30–42, IT Publications, London, 1995.

————: *Poverty and Livelihoods: Whose Reality Counts?*, IDS, Brighton, UK, 1995.

————: 'Participatory Rural Appraisal (PRA): Challenges, potentials and paradigm', *World Development*, Vol. 22, No. 10, pp. 1437–54, 1994.

————: 'Rural Appraisal: Rapid, Relaxed and Participatory', IDS Discussion Paper 311, IDS, Sussex, 1992.

Christiansen, L. et al.: 'Comparing village characteristics derived from rapid appraisals and household surveys: A tale from Northern Mali', *Journal of Development Studies*, Vol. 37, No. 3, pp. 1–20, 2001.

Christoplos, I.: 'Representation, Poverty and PRA in the Mekong Delta'. Research Report No. 6. EPOS Environmental Policy and Society, Linköping University, Sweden, 1995.

Clair, John St.: 'What is Development Ethics?' International Development Ethics Association, IDEA, 2004. http://www.development-ethics.org.

Cleaver, Frances: 'Institutions, Agency and the Limitations of Participatory Approaches to Development'. In Cooke and Kothari (eds), *Participation: The new tyranny?* Zed Press, London, 2001.

Cohen, J. and N. Uphoff: 'Participation's place in rural development: Seeking clarity through specificity', *World Development*, No. 8, pp. 213–35, 1980.

Collins, Tara, L. Pearson and C. Delany: 'Rights Based Approach' (Discussion Paper), The Senate of Canada, April 2002.

Connelly P., T. Li, M. MacDonald and J.L. Parpart: 'Feminism and Development: Theoretical Perspectives'. In J.L. Parpart et al. (eds), *Theoretical perspectives on Gender and Development*, IDRC, Ottawa, 2000.

Conway, G.R.: *Agro-ecosystem Analysis for Research and Development*, Winrock International, Bangkok, 1986.

Cooke, Bill and U. Kothari (eds): *Participation: The new tyranny?* Zed Press, London, 2000.

Cooperrider, David: 'Positive image; positive action: The affirmative basis of organising'. In S. Srivastva and D.L. Cooperrider (eds), *Appreciative management and leadership*, pp. 91–125, Jossey-Bass, San Francisco, CA, 1990.

Cornwall, Andrea: 'Making Spaces, Changing Places: Situating Participation in Development', IDS Working Paper 170, October 2002.

————: 'Beneficiary, Consumer, Citizen: Perspectives on Participation for Poverty Reduction', Sida studies No. 2, 2000.

Cornwall, A, I. Guijt and A. Welbourn: 'Acknowledging Process—Challenges for Agricultural Research and Extension Methodology', IIED/IS Workshop on 'Beyond Farmer First. Rural People's Knowledge. Agricultural Research and Extension Practice', IDS, Sussex, October 1992.

COWI: 'Guide to Evaluation', Prepared by Claus Rebien, Lyngby, Denmark, March 2000.

COWI Development Fund: 'Capacity Development—How Do We Measure It?' Lyngby, Denmark, May 2002.

COWI: 'Water Prices in CEE and CIS Countries. A Toolkit for Assessing Willingness to Pay, Affordability and Political Acceptability'. By Peter Christensen et al., for Danish Ministry of the Environment, DEPA and the European Bank for Reconstruction and Development, EBRD, 2002.

———: 'Review of Monitoring and Indicators in Relation to MDGs and PRSPs'. By Anette Aarestrup and Niels E Olesen, for Ministry of Foreign Affairs/Danida, April 2004.

———: 'District Road Network Support Program in Lira, Uganda', COWI, Denmark, 2000–ongoing.

———: Interviewbaserede kvalitative undersøgeler. Retningslinier og gode råd (Interview based qualitative studies. Guidelines and advice). COWI Division 1, May 2004.

———: 'Quality Management'. See www.cowi.dk/about_cowi/quality_management.asp.

Cox, Aidan, Steen Folke, Lau Schulpen and Niel Webster: Do the Poor Matter Enough? A Comparative Study of European Aid for Poverty Reduction in India. Concept Publishing House, New Delhi, 2002.

Cracknell, Basil Edward: Evaluating Development Aid. Issues, Problems and Solutions. Sage Publications, New Delhi, 2000.

Cramb, Rob and Tim Purcell: 'How to Monitor and Evaluate Impacts of Participatory Research Projects: A Case Study of the Forages for Smallholders Project', CIAT Working Document No. 185, October 2001.

Cranshaw, Martha Isabel: 'So, We Are Making Progress. The Northern León "PRSPcito". An Advocacy Experience from Ibis in Nicaragua', Ibis, Guatemala, 2003.

CROPnewsletter. International Social Science Council, Oslo, Recurrent.

DAC Working Party on Aid Evaluation: Glossary of Evaluation and Results Based Management Terms, DCC/DAC/Ev(2001)3, OECD, Paris, November 2001.

Dahler-Larsen and H.K. Krogstrup (eds): Tendenser I Evaluering (Trends in Evaluation). Odense University Publishers, Denmark, 2001.

Danida: Ligestilling I dansk udviklingsbistand—Strategi (Gender Equality in Danish Development Cooperation—Strategy), MFA, Copenhagen, 2004.

———: 'Women in Development', Danida's WID Policy Towards the Year 2000, MFA, Copenhagen, 1993.

Dahl-Østergaard, D. Moore, V. Ramírez, M. Wenner and A. Bonde: 'Community-Driven Rural Development. What Have We Learned?', SDD, Technical Papers Series, Inter-American Development Bank, 2003.

Davies, R.J.: 'An Evolutionary Approach to Facilitate Organisational Learning: An Experiment by the Christian Commission for Development in Bangladesh'. In David Mosse et al. (eds), Development as Process: Concepts and Methods for Working with Complexity, Routledge, London, 1998.

DAWN: 'Marketisation of Governance: Critical Feminist Perspectives from the South' (compiled by Vivien Taylor), SADEP, University of Cape Town. Available at www.dawn.org.fj, DAWN, 2000.

DCA, DanChurchAid: 'Promoting Gender Equality in Palestine', DCA Political Space Programme in Palestine, DCA Copenhagen, 2004.

DGIS/Netherlands: Integrated Rural Water Supply/Sanitation Project, IRWS/S, Karnataka, 1992.

Degnbol-Martinussen, John and Poul Engberg-Pedersen: Aid—Understanding International Development Cooperation. Zed Books, 2003.

Denscombe, Martyn: The Good Research Guide for small-scale social research projects. Open University Press, Philadelphia, Second Edition, 2003.

Denzin, Norman K. and Y.S. Lincoln: Handbook of Qualitative Research. Sage Publications, Thousand Oaks, USA, 1994, new edition 2000.

Deshingkar, Priya and A.J. James: 'Participatory Rural Appraisal (PRA): Some Concerns from the Field'. In IFAD, Enhancing Ownership and Sustainability. A Resource Book on Participation, Rome, 2001.

Devereux, S. and J. Hoddinott (eds): Fieldwork in Developing Countries. Harvester, New York, 1992.

Department for International Development (DFID): DFID and corporate social responsibility. Could corporate social responsibility disadvantage the poor? DFID, UK, 2003.

Department for International Development (DFID): *Realising Human Rights for Poor People. Strategies for Achieving the International Developing Targets.* DFID, London, 2000.

———: *Sustainable Livelihoods Guidance Sheets.* London, 1999.

Dichter, Thomas W.: *Despite Good Intentions, Why Development Assistance to the Third World Has Failed.* University of Massachusetts Press, Amherst and Boston, 2003.

Donnelly, Jack: *Universal Human Rights in Theory and Practice.* Cornell University Press, Ithaca, N.Y., 1989.

Dunn, E., P. Atkins and J. Townsend: 'GIS for development: A contradiction in terms?', *AREA*, Vol. 29, No. 2, pp. 151–59, 1997.

Durkheim, Emile: *The Rules of Sociological Method.* The Free Press, NY, 1964.

Eide, W.B.: 'Nutrition Research in Developing Countries—"Data Imperialism" or a Tool in the Fight against Hunger and Malnutrition?', Paper for 5th Nordic Congress of Nutrition, Reykjavik, Iceland, 14–17 June 1992.

Elle, Morten: Byøkologiske fremtidsbilleder (Visions of Future Urban Ecology), Danish Board of Technology, 1992.

Elliott, Charles: *Locating the Energy for Change: An Introduction to Appreciative Inquiry.* International Institute for Sustainable Development, Cambridge, 1999.

Enderud, Harald: Hvad er organisations-sociologisk metode? Den 3die bølge i metodelæren (The Third Wave of Methodological Interpretations), Bind 1 og 2, Samfundslitteratur, 1984.

Epstein, Scarlett T., A.P. Suryanarayana and T. Thimmegowda: *Village Voices. Forty Years of Rural Transformation in South India.* Sage Publications, New Delhi, 1998.

Epstein, Scarlett T., J. Gruber et al.: *A Training Manual for Development Market Research (DMR) Investigators.* BBC World Service, UK, 1991.

Epstein, Scarlett T.: *A Manual for Culturally-Adopted Market Research (CMR) in the Development Process.* RWAL Publications, UK, 1988.

Eriksen, Tore Linné (ed.): Den vanskelige bistanden (The Difficult Aid. Trends in Norwegian Development Aid). Universitetsforlaget, Oslo, 1987.

Erikson Braaz, Maria and Mai Palmberg: *Same and Other. Negotiating African Identity in Cultural Production.* The Nordic African Institute, Uppsala, 2001.

Ernø-Kjølhede, Erik: 'Scientific norms as (dis)integrators of scientists?', Working Paper 14/2000, Department of Management, Politics and Philosophy, CBS, Copenhagen, 2000.

Escobar, Arturo: *Encountering Development. The Making and Unmaking of the Third World.* Princeton Studies in Culture/Power/History, Princeton University Press, 1995.

Estrella, Marisol and John Gaventa: 'Who Counts Reality? Participatory Monitoring and Evaluation: A Literature Review', IDS WP No. 70, IDS, Brighton, 1998.

Estrella, Marisol (ed): Learning From Change. Issues and Experiences in Participatory Monitoring and Evaluation. IT Publications, London, 2000.

European Commission, EC: *Gender Equality in Development Co-operation. From Policy to Practice.* Brussels, 2003.

———: 'Thematic Evaluation of the Integration of Gender in European Commission Development Co-operation with Third Countries, by Mary Braithwaite et al., Brussels, 2003.

European Commission and Sida: 'Integrating Gender Equality into Development Cooperation. Drawing Lessons from the Recent Evaluations by Sida and the EC'. Brussels, November 2003. By Mary Braithwaite and Britha Mikkelsen et al., EC and Sida (forthcoming working paper), UTV, Sida, Stockholm, 2004.

Ferguson, C: *Global Social Policy Principles: Human Rights and Social Justice.* DFID, London, 1999.

FAO: *Participatory Monitoring and Evaluation. Handbook for Training Field Workers.* Bangkok, 1990.

FAO/Sida: 'Community Forestry, Rapid Appraisal. Forests, Trees and People', Community Forestry Note 3, Rome, 1989.

Feuerstein, Marie-Thérese: *Partners in Evaluation. Evaluating Development and Community Programmes with Participants.* Macmillan, London, 1988.

Flyvbjerg, Bent: *Rationality and Power: Democracy in Practice* (in Danish, Akademisk Forlag, Copenhagen, 1992). University of Chicago Press, 1998.

———: *Making Social Science Matter. Why social inquiry fails and how it can succeed again.* Cambridge University Press, 2001.

Folke, Steen, with Susanne Possing: 'Evaluation/Impact study of four training projects for farm women in India (WYTEP, TANWA, TEWA, MAPWA)', Approach Paper, Centre for Development Research, June 2002.

Foucault, M.: *Discipline and Punish. The Birth of the Prison*. Translated by A. Sheridan, Vintage Books, New York, 1978 version.

Francis, P.: 'Participatory Development at the World Bank: The Primacy of Process'. In B. Cooke and U. Kothari (eds), *Participation: The new tyranny?*, pp. 72–87, Zed Press, 2001.

Frank, Leonard: 'The Development Game'. *GRANTA*, Special Issue on Travel Writing, No. 20, Penguin, 1986.

Fransman, Jude (ed.): 'Learning and Teaching Participation in Higher Education', Report of the International Workshop by Learning Participation, a global dialogue on learning and teaching, www.ids.ac.uk/ids/particip/networks/learnparticip, April 2003.

Freydenberger, K.: 'The use of RRA to inform policy: Tenure issues in Madagascar and Guinea'. In J. Holland (ed.): *Whose Voice? Participatory Research and Policy Change*, pp. 67–79, Intermediate Technology, London, 1998.

Friis-Hansen, Esbern and B. Sthapit (eds): *Participatory Approaches to the Conservation and Use of Plant Genetic Resources*. IPGRI Rome and Centre for Development Research, Denmark, 2000.

Fuglesang, Andreas: *About Understanding—Ideas and Observations on Cross-cultural Communication*. Dag Hammarskjöld Foundation, Uppsala, 1982.

Gaskell, George: 'Individual and Group Interviewing'. In Bauer and Gaskell (eds), *Qualitative Researching With Text, Image and Sound. A Practical Handbook*. Sage Publications, London, 2000.

Gaventa, J. et al. (eds): 'Making Rights Real: Exploring citizenship, participation and accountability', *IDS Bulletin*, Vol. 33, No. 2, IDS, Brighton, UK, 2002.

Gill, Rosalind: 'Discourse Analysis'. In Bauer and Gaskell (eds), *Qualitative Researching With Text, Image and Sound. A Practical Handbook*, Sage Publications, London, 2000.

Goonesekere, Savitri. 'A Rights-Based Approach to Realising Gender Equality', Paper prepared with the United Nations Division for the Advancement of Women. As posted on http://www.un.org/womenwatch/daw/news/savitri.htm, 20 October 2003.

Gosling, Louisa, with Mike Edwards: *Toolkits. A practical guide to planning, monitoring, evaluation and impact assessment*. Save the Children, UK, 2003.

Graham, Carol and Stefano Pettinato: *Happiness and Hardship. Opportunities and Insecurity in New Market Economies*. Brookings Institution Press, Washington DC, 2002.

Grandin, Barbara: *Wealth Ranking for Smallholder Communities: A Field Manual*. ITDG, London, 1988.

Green, Maia: 'Social Development: Issues and Approaches'. In Kothari and Minogue (eds), *Development Theory and Practice. Critical Perspectives*, Palgrave, 2002.

Grinspun, Alejandro (ed.): *Choices for the Poor. Lessons from National Poverty Strategies*. UNDP, 2001.

Grootaert, Christian and T. van Bastelaer: 'Understanding and Measuring Social Capital—A Multidisciplinary Tool for Practitioners', *Directions in Development*, World Bank, 2002.

Grundahl, J.: 'The Danish consensus conference model', in S. Joss and J. Durant (eds), *Public Participation in Science: The Role of Consensus Conferences in Europe*, Science Museum, London, 1995.

Guba, Egon and Yvonna S. Lincoln: *Fourth Generation Evaluation*. Sage Publications, Beverly Hills, 1989.

————: 'Competing Paradigms in Qualitative Research'. In Guba and Lincoln (eds), *Handbook of Qualitative Research*. Sage Publications, Thousand Oaks, USA, 1994.

Guijt, I. and M. Kaul Shah: 'Wake up to power, conflict and process'. In I. Gujit and M. Kaul Shah (eds), *The myth of community: Gender issues in participatory development*, London, IT Publications, 1998.

Gullestrup, Hans: Kultur, kulturanalyse og kulturetik—eller hvad adskiller og forener os? (Culture, Culture-analysis and Culture ethics—Or What Separates and What Unites Us?), Akademisk Forlag, Denmark, 1992.

GTZ: *Methods and Instruments for Project Planning and Implementation*. Eschborn, June 1991.

Habermas, Jürgen: *Theory of Communicative Action*. Boston, 1987.

Hancock, Graham: *Lords of Poverty*. Arrow Books, 1997.

Hanghe, Ahmed Artan: *Folktales from Somalia*. Nordic Africa Institute, Uppsala, Sweden, 1988.

Hannan, Carolyn: 'Gender Mainstreaming: Reflections on Implementation of the Strategy'. In EC/Sida, *Integrating Gender Equality into Development Co-operation*, Report of EC/Sida joint seminar, Brussels, November 2003.

Hansen, Karen Tranberg and Mariken Vaa (eds): *Reconsidering Informality. Perspectives from Urban Africa*. The Nordic African Institute, Uppsala, 2004.

Hansson, Finn: 'How to evaluate and select new scientific knowledge? Taking the social dimension seriously in the evaluation of research quality', *VEST, Journal for Science and Technology Studies*, Vol. 15, Nos 2&3, pp. 27–52, 2002.

Hardt, Michael and Antonio Negri: Imperiet (The Empire). Informations Forlag, Copenhagen, 2003 (Empire, Harvard University Press, 2000).

Hartoft, Caroline: 'Study of Returned Development Workers'. COWI, for Danish Association for International Cooperation, 2003.

Hastrup, Kirsten: Det antropologiske project (The Project of Anthropology—About Amazement). Gyldendal Intro. Denmark, 1992.

Häusermann, Julia. 'The Realisation and Implementation of Economic, Social and Cultural Rights'. In R. Beddard and D.M. Hill (eds), *Economic, Social and Cultural Rights: Progress and Achievement*, London, Macmillan, 1992.

HDR: Human Development Report 2003. UNDP, New York, 2003 and annual.

Herlitz, Gillis: Kultur Grammatik. Kunsten at mode andre kulturer (Grammar of Culture. The Art of Meeting Other Cultures). Munksgaard, Copenhagen, 1991.

Hildyard, N. et al: 'Pluralism, Participation and Power: Joint Forest Management in India'. In Cooke and Kothari (eds), *Participation—the New Tyranny?* Zed Books, 2001.

Hill, Polly: *Development Economics on Trial: An Anthropological Case for a Prosecution*. CUP, Cambridge, 1986.

Hornstrup, Carsten and J. Loehr-Petersen: Appreciative Inquiry—en konstruktiv metode til positive forandringer (A Constructive Methods for Positive Changes). Jurist- og Oekonomforbundets Forlag, Copenhagen, 2003.

Horowitz, Irving (ed.): *The Rise and Fall of Project Camelot: Studies in the Relationship between Social Sciences and Practical Politics*. Cambridge, Massachusetts, MIT Press, 1967.

House, Ernest R. and Kenneth R. Howe: 'Deliberative Democratic Evaluation'. *New Directions for Evaluation*, No. 85, 2000.

Human Rights Council of Australia: *The Rights Way to Development—A Human Rights Approach to Development Assistance—Policy and Practice*, The Human Rights Council of Australia, Maroubra, 2001.

Hvalkof, Søren: 'GIS, Remote Sensing and Participatory Approaches', Danish Institute for International Studies, DIIS, Copenhagen, August 2003.

Hvalkof, Søren (ed.): *Dreams Coming True. An Indigenous Health Programme in the Peruvian Amazon*. Karen Elise Jensen Foundation and NORDECO, Copenhagen, 2004.

Hvalkof, Søren: 'Progress of the Victims. Political Ecology in the Peruvian Amazon'. In Aletta Biersack and James B. Greenberg (eds), *Imagining Political Ecology*, Ecologies for the Twenty-First Century Series, Duke University Press. Forthcoming, 2004.

Hvidt, Martin: Projektbistand—om projektet som medium for overførsel af bistand til 3. verdens landdistrikter (Project Aid—The Project as a Medium for Transfer of Aid to Rural Areas in the Third World), University of Aarhus, 1987.

IDS Policy Briefing: Poverty Reduction Strategies: A Part for the Poor? No. 13, IDS, Sussex, 2000.

IFAD: *Enhancing Ownership and Sustainability. A Resource Book on Participation*. Rome, 2001.

————: *Managing for Impact in Rural Development. A Guide for Project M&E*. Rome, 2002.

IPDET: International Program for Development Evaluation Training. Carleton University, Ottawa, and World Bank. Recurrent.

Jacobsgaard, Mette: Street-children evaluate their own project, Ghana. COWI, Denmark, 2002.

Jenkins, Richard: *Pierre Bourdieu*. Key Sociologists, Routledge, 1992.

Jungk, R. and N. Müllert: Haandbog I fremtidsvaerksteder (Handbook in Future Workshops), Politisk Revy, Copenhagen, 1984.

Kabeer, Naila: *Reversed Realities: Gender Hierarchies in Development Thought*. Verso, London, 1994.

————: 'Resources, Agency, Achievements: Reflections on the Measurement of Women's Empowerment', *Development and Change*, Vol. 30, pp. 435–64, 1999. Adjusted in Discussing Women's Empowerment—Theory and Practice. Sida Studies No. 3, 2002.

Kaplan, R.S. and D.P. Norton: 'Transforming the balanced scorecard from performance measurement to strategic management'. University of South Florida, 2001.

Kapoor, Ilan: 'Deliberative Democracy or Agonistic Pluralism? The Relevance of the Habermas-Mouffe Debate for Third World Politics', *Alternatives*, Vol. 27, pp. 459–87, 2002.

Karlsson, G. (ed.): Sociologiska Metoder (Sociological Methods), Nordisk Forlag, Copenhagen, 1961.

Kelle, Udo: 'Computer-Assisted Analysis: Coding and Indexing'. In Bauer and Gaskell (eds), *Qualitative Researching With Text, Image and Sound. A Practical Handbook*, Sage Publications, London, 2000.

Kenny, Charles and David Williams: 'What Do We Know About Economic Growth? Or, Why Don't We Know Very Much?' *World Development*, Vol. 29 No. 1, pp. 1–22, 2001.

KIDP: Mutomo Soil and Water Conservation Project—Social Perceptions and Management Issues, Danida, 1991.

Kjaer, Louise (ed.): Local Partnerships in Europe. An Action Research Project. The Copenhagen Centre, 2003.

Kollapen, Jody: Keynote speech included in European Commission, 'Human Rights and Democratisation in Sub-Saharan Africa—Report of the EIDHR Regional Meeting', Cape Town, April 2003.

Kothari, Uma and Martin Minogue (eds): *Development Theory and Practice. Critical Perspectives.* Palgrave, 2002.

Kotler, Philip and E.L. Roberto: *Social Marketing—Strategies for Changing Public Behaviour.* FP, London, 1989.

Krogstrup, H.K.: Tendenser i evaluering (Trends in Evaluation), Odense University Publishers, Denmark, 2001.

Kumar, Ranjit: *Research Methodology. A Step-by-Step Guide for Beginners.* Sage Publications, London, 1999.

Kumar, Somesh: *Methods for Community Participation. A Complete Guide for Practitioners.* Vistaar Publications, New Delhi, 2002.

Kumar, Krishna: Conducting Group Interviews in Developing Countries. AID Program Design and Evaluation Methodology Report No. 8, USAID, April 1987.

Kusek, Jody Z. and Ray C. Rist: *Ten Steps to a Results-Based Monitoring and Evaluation System: A Handbook for Development Practitioners.* The World Bank, 2004.

Kvale, Steinar: *InterViews. An Introduction to Qualitative Research Interviewing.* Sage Publications, USA, 1996.

Laier, J. Koch: 'Et problematisk parforhold (A problematic relationship)'. *Den Nye Verden (The New World)*, Vol. 3, Danish Institute for International Studies, DIIS, Copenhagen, 1999.

Lairap-Fonderson, Josephine: 'The Disciplinary Power of Micro-credit: Examples from Kenya and Cameroon'. In Parpart, Rai and Staudt, *Rethinking Empowerment*, mimeo, 2000.

Lappé, Frances Moore, J. Collins and D. Kinley: Aid as Obstacle. Twenty Questions about Our Foreign Aid and the Hungry. IFDP, USA, 1980.

Latour, Bruno: 'From the World of Science to the World of Research?' *Science*, Vol. 280, No. 5361, pp. 208–9, April 1998.

Launsø, Laila and O. Rieper: Forsking om og med mennesker (Research about and with People—Research Types and Research Methods in the Social Sciences). Nyt Nordisk Forlag Arnold Busck, Copenhagen, 2000.

Laws, Sophie with C. Harper and R. Marcus: *Research for Development. A Practical Guide.* Sage Publications, London, 2003.

Learning Participation Network. IDS, UK 2002—ongoing.

Levy, C.: Training Materials for Gender Planning, Danida, 1990–92.

Liakopoulos, Miltos: 'Argumentation Analysis'. In Bauer and Gaskell (eds), *Qualitative Researching With Text, Image and Sound. A Practical Handbook*, Sage Publications, London, 2000.

Lightfoot, Clive, R. Ramirez, A. Groot, R. Noble, F. Shao, D. Kisauzi, and I. Bekalo: Learning Our Way Ahead: A linked local learning approach to decentralisation, International Support Group, NL, November 2000.

Lindqvist, Sven, P. Brock, et al.: Grav hvor du star—Håndbog I at udforske et arbejde (Dig where you stand—Handbook for exploring a job), SOC, Copenhagen, 1982.

————: Gräv där du står (Dig where you stand). Bonniers, Stockholm, 1978.

Lipton, M. and S. Maxwell: *The New Poverty Agenda. An Overview.* ODA, London, 1992.

Little, Daniel: *Varieties of Social Explanation. An Introduction to the Philosophy of Social Science.* Westview Press, 1991.

Long, C.: *Participation in Development: The Way Forward.* Draft. Boston: Institute for Development Research, 1999.

Løngreen, Hanne: 'The Development Gaze. Visual Representation of Development in Information Material from Danida'. In Mai Palmberg (ed.), *Encounter Images in the Meetings between Africa and Europe*, The Nordic Africa Institute, Uppsala, Sweden, 2001.

Longwe, Sarah H.: 'The evaporation of policies for women's advancement'. In Noeleen Heyzer (ed.), *A Commitment to the World's Women. Perspectives on Development for Beijing and Beyond*, UNIFEM, New York, 1995.

————: 'The evaporation of gender policies in the patriarchal cooking pot', *Development with Women*, Oxfam Publications, Oxford, 1999.

Lundquist, Lennart: Det vetenskapliga studiet av politik. (The scientific study of politics). Studentlitteratur, Lund, 1993.

Macdonald, Laura: 'NGOs and the Problematic Discourse of Participation: Cases from Costa Rica'. In Wolfgang Sachs (ed.), *The Development Dictionary. A Guide to Knowledge as Power*, Zed Books, 1995.

March, Candida, Ines Smyth and Maitrayee Mukhopadhyay: *A Guide to Gender-Analysis Frameworks*. Oxfam, 1999.

Marris, P. and A. Somerset: *African Businessmen: A Study of Entrepreneurship and Development in Kenya*. Routledge and Kegan Paul and East African Publishing House, 1971.

Marshall, C. and G.B. Rossman: *Designing Qualitative Research*. Sage Publications, 1989.

Mauro, A.: Development Theatre—A Way to Listen. Report on the Development Theatre Programme. Community Environment Project (CEP), Tominian, SOS SAHEL, Mali, April 1989–June 1991.

McCracken, Jennifer A., Jules N. Pretty and Gordon R. Conway: *An Introduction to Rapid Rural Appraisal for Agricultural Development*. IIED, London, 1988.

McGee, Rosemary: 'Participating in Development'. In Kothari and Minogue (eds), *Development Theory and Practice. Critical Perspectives*, Palgrave, 2002.

McGee, R.: Participation in Poverty Reduction Strategies: A synthesis of experience with participatory approaches to policy design, implementation and monitoring. IDS WP No. 109, Sussex, 2000.

McNeill, Desmond: 'The State of Development Research'. Annual Conference of the Norwegian Association for Development Research, Oslo, 1992.

Mead, Margaret: *The Evolving Ethics of Applied Anthropology*. Quoted in Elizabeth M. Eddy and William M. Partridge (eds), *Applied Anthropology in America*, Columbia University Press, NY, 1978.

Mearns, R., D. Shombodon, G. Narangerel, U. Turul, A. Enkhamgalan, B. Myagmarzhav, A. Bayanjargal and B. Bekhsuren: 'Direct and indirect Uses of Wealth Ranking in Mongolia'. In RRA Notes, No. 15, IIED, London, 1992.

Merton, Robert K. (ed.): The Sociology of Science. Theoretical and Empirical Investigations. (Includes the CUDOS paper from 1942). The University of Chicago Press, 1973.

MFA, Ministry of Foreign Affairs: Udenrigsministeriets effektiviseringsstrategi (The Strategy for MFA's Effectiveness), Copenhagen, March 2004.

MFA Ministry of Foreign Affairs, Danida: A World of Difference. The Government's Vision for New Priorities in Danish Development Assistance 2004–2008, June 2003.

———: *Evaluation—Danish Support to Mine Action*. By Cecilia Ljungman et al., COWI, for Danida, Copenhagen, 2003.

———: Survey on the independence of evaluation teams (Draft), AMI/Ementor, January 2003.

———: Evaluation of Business Sector Support Programme, Tanzania, Copenhagen, 2003.

———: Gendered district poverty profiles and monitoring of ASPS outcomes, Kabarole, Masaka, Pallisa, Rakai and Tororo districts, Uganda (by DAE, Makerere University and IIS, Ravnborg et al, Copenhagen), June 2002.

———: MEMA, Natural Woodland Management Project and Udzungwa Mountains Forest Management Project. Beneficiary Assessment (by S.S. Rasmussen, COWI), Copenhagen, June 2002.

———: Evaluation—In the Wake of a Flagship. Ex-post Impact Study of the Noakhali Rural Development Project in Bangladesh (by Steen Folke et al.), Copenhagen, 2001–5.

———: Indicators for Institutional Capacity Building in Relation to Nicaragua ESPS, ESPS Discussion Paper (by Rasmus Ødum, COWI), January 2001.

———: Denmark's Development Policy, Partnership 2000. Copenhagen, 2000.

———: Danish Support to Promotion of Human Rights and Democratisation, Evaluation. Vol. 5, Participation and Empowerment, Copenhagen, 1999/11.

———: Evaluation Guidelines, Copenhagen, February, 1999.

———: Guidelines for Sector Programme Support (Including Project Support), 1996 and 1998.

———: Evaluation—Poverty Reduction in Danish Development Assistance. Copenhagen (by Britha Mikkelsen et al, COWI), 1996/14.

———: Capacity Development Evaluation. By Boesen, Christensen and Therkildsen, 2002–ongoing.

MFEP: The Poverty Eradication Strategy, DRAFT, Kampala, Uganda, 1996.

Mikkelsen, Britha, T. Freeman, B. Keller et al.: Mainstreaming Gender Equality. Sida's Support for the Promotion of Gender Equality in Partner Countries. A Sida Evaluation Report 02/01, Stockholm, 2002.

Mikkelsen, Britha: 'Behind Participation' in the Development Discourse. A reaction to 'Professionalisation' of Public Participation. Roskilde University, 1998.

———: *Methods for Development Work and Research. A Guide for Practitioners*. Sage Publications, New Delhi, 1995.

Miles, M.B. and M. Huberman: *Qualitative Data Analysis. An Expanded Sourcebook*. Sage Publications, Thousand Oaks, 1994.

Mills, Wright C.: *The Sociological Imagination*. Penguin, 1959.

Minogue, Martin: 'Power to the People? Good Governance and the Reshaping of the State'. In Kothari and Minogue (eds), *Development Theory and Practice. Critical Perspectives*, Palgrave, 2002.

Minot, Nicholas (IFPRI) and B. Baulch (IDS): Poverty Mapping with Aggregate Census Data: What is the Loss of Precision? IDS, Sussex, UK, 2003.

Mlama, Penina Mihando: *Culture and Development. The Popular Theatre Approach in Africa*. SIAS, Uppsala, 1991.

Molyneux, M.: 'Mobilisation without Emancipation? Women's Interests, States and Revolution in Nicaragua', *Feminist Studies*, Vol. 11, No. 2, 1985.

Moore, M., M. Choudhary, and N. Singh: How can we know what they want? Understanding local perceptions of poverty and ill-being in Asia. IDS Working Paper No. 80, UK, 1998.

Moser, Caroline and Andy Norton: *To Claim our Rights: Livelihood security, human rights and sustainable development*. Overseas Development Institute, 2001.

Moser, Caroline: *Gender Planning and Development. Theory, Practice and Training*. Routledge, London, 1993.

———: 'Gender Planning in the Third World: Meeting Practical and Strategic Gender Needs', *World Development*, Vol. 17, No. 11, 1989.

Mosse, D.: 'The Making and Marketing of Participatory Development. A Sceptical Note'. In Cooke and Kothari (eds), *Participation: The New Tyranny?* Zed Books, London, 2001.

Mosse, David, J. Farrington and Alan Rew (eds): *Development as Process: Concepts and Methods for Working with Complexity*. Routledge, London, 1998.

Mosse, D. with KRIBP Project Team: People's knowledge in project planning: The limits and social conditions of participation in planning agricultural development. AgREN Network Paper No. 58. London, ODI, 1995.

Mosse, D.: Authority, gender and knowledge: Theoretical reflections on the practice of Participatory Rural Appraisal. AgReN Network Paper No. 44, London, ODI, 1993.

MS, Danish Association for International Cooperation: Impact Monitoring Without Indicators. MSC Pilot Study in Mozambique. Draft Report, Copenhagen, June 2001, MSC Pilot Study in Zambia, Draft Report, Copenhagen, 2001.

Mukherjee, Neela: *Participatory Learning and Action—With 100 Field Methods*. Concept Publishing Company, New Delhi, 2002.

———: 'Villagers' Perceptions of Rural Poverty Through the Mapping Methods of PRA', RRA Notes, No. 15, IIED, London, 1992.

Müller, Jens: 'Global Technological Transformations. Conceptual and Methodological Framework'. In John Kuada (ed.), *Culture and Technological Transformation in the South—Transfer or Local Innovation?* Samfundslitteratur, Denmark, 2003.

Narayan, Deepa, R. Chambers, M.K. Shah and P. Petesch: *Voices of the Poor. Crying Out for Change*. Oxford University Press, 2000.

Narayan, Deepa with R. Patel, K. Schafft, A. Rademacher and S. Koch-Schulte: *Voices of the Poor. Can Anybody Hear Us?* Oxford University Press, 2000.

Narayan, Deepa and Patti Petesch (eds): *Voices of the Poor. From Many Lands*. Oxford University Press, 2002.

Nelson, N. and S. Wright: 'Participation and Power'. In N. Nelson and S. Wright (eds), *Power and participatory development: Theory and practice*, IT Publications, London, 1995.

Neuman, W. Lawrence: *Social Research Methods—Qualitative and Quantitative Approaches*. Allyn and Bacon, 2000 and 2003.

Nichols, Paul: 'Social Survey Methods. A Fieldguide for Development Workers'. Development Guidelines, No. 6, Oxfam, 1991.

Nielsen, K Aagaard: 'Aktionsforskning som—forskning i—læreprocesser (Action research as—research in—learning processes)'. In Kirsten Weber, *Laering på livstid? (Learning for Life?)*, Roskilde University, 2002.

Nielsen, H.K. and Knud Vilby: Ret til egen udvikling? Mål, midler og modsætninger i udviklingsbistanden (Right to Own Development? Goals, Means and Contradictions in Development Aid), Reitzel's, Copenhagen, 1992.

Nielsen, H.A.: *Monitoring the Development Intervention: An alternative Approach to Impact Evaluation*, Aalborg University, Denmark, 1990.

Nilsson, Per-Ulf and P. Woodford-Berger: Using Participatory Approaches in Bilateral Development Co-operation. Sida, Div. for Policy and Socio-Economic Analysis. Stockholm, 2000.

NORAD: *Handbook in Human Rights Assessment*. Oslo, 2001.

NORAD: *The Logical Framework Approach (LFA). Handbook for Objectives-oriented Project Planning*. Oslo, 1990 and 1999.

Norton, Andy with B. Bird, K. Brock, M. Kakande and C. Turk: *A Rough Guide to PPAs—Participatory Poverty Assessment. An Introduction to Theory and Practice.* ODI, GB, 2001.

Oakley, Peter and D. Marsden (eds): 'Evaluating Social Development Projects'. Development Guidelines No. 5, 1991.

ODA: A Guide to Social Analysis for Projects in Developing Countries, HMSO, London, 1995.

OECD/DAC: Gender Equality Tipsheets. Paris, 2003 and www.oecd.org/dac/gender.

———: The DAC Guidelines. Poverty Reduction, Paris, 2001.

OECD-DAC/DCC: Gender Training Programme, 1998.

OED/World Bank: Annual Report on Evaluation Capacity Development, 13 June 2002.

OED/World Bank: Précis—Participation in Development Assistance. No. 209, Fall 2001.

Office of the High Commissioner for Human Rights, Regional Representative for Aisa-Pacific: 'OHCHR Human Rights Roundtable No.1: Rights Based Approaches to Development', Meeting Summary, Bangkok, 4 October 2002.

Office of the High Commissioner for Human Rights: 'Draft Guidelines. A Human Rights Perspective to Poverty Reduction Strategies', UN, NY, September 2002.

OHCHR Website: http://www.unhchr.ch/.

Olesen, Virginia L: 'Feminisms and Qualitative Research At and Into the Millennium'. In Norman Denzin and Yvonna S. Lincoln (eds), *Handbook of Qualitative Research.* Second Edition, pp. 215–56, Sage Publications, Thousand Oaks, 2000.

Olsen, Henning: Kvalitative kvaler. Kvalitative metoder og danske kvalitative interviewundersøgelsers kvalitet. (Qualitative Queries. Qualitative Methods and the Quality of Danish Studies Using Qualitative Interviews). Akademisk Forlag. Copenhagen, 2002.

Olsén, Peter, B.S. Nielsen and K. Aa Nielsen: Demokrati og bæredygtighed. Social fantasi og samfundsmæssig rigdomsproduktion. (Democracy and sustainability. Social Fantacy and Social Well-being Production), Roskilde University, 2003.

Orkin, Martin: *Drama and the South African State.* Manchester University Press, 1991.

Palmberg, Mai (ed.): *Encounter Images in the Meetings between Africa and Europe.* The Nordic Africa Institute, Uppsala, Sweden, 2001.

Palriwala, Rajni: 'Research and Women: Dilemmas of a Fieldworker in a Rajasthan Village'. In M.N. Panini (ed.), *From the Female Eye. Accounts of Women Fieldworkers Studying Their Own Communities,* Hindustan Publishing House, Delhi, 1991.

Paludan, Charlotte (ed.): *Pas på pædagogikken (Watch the Pedagogic),* Reitzels Forlag, Copenhagen. 1997.

Panini, M.N. (ed.): *From the Female Eye. Accounts of Women Fieldworkers Studying Their Own Communities.* Women in Development Series, Vol. 2 (Series Editor T.S. Epstein), Hindustan Publishing House, Delhi, 1991.

PANOS: *Reducing Poverty. Is the World Bank's Strategy Working?* London, 2002.

Parellada, A. and S. Hvalkof (eds): *Liberation through Land Rights in the Peruvian Amazon.* IWGIA Doc. No. 90, IWGIA, Copenhagen, 1998.

Participation Resource Centre at IDS, UK www.ids.ac.uk/ids/particip/.

PARTICIPLAN—Package for workshop facilitation—www.participlan. www.stefduplessis.com/participlan.html.

Patton, Michael Quinn: *Qualitative Research and Evaluation Methods.* Third edition, Sage Publications, Thousand Oaks, 2002.

———: *Utilization-Focused Evaluation. The New Century Text.* Sage Publications, Thousand Oaks, 1997.

———: *Qualitative Evaluation Methods.* Sage Publications, USA, 1990.

Pendley, Charles, Morten G. Poulsen and Maja Naur: Urban Poverty Study, Bhutan. COWI study sponsored by Danida, 2002.

Picciotto, Robert (ed.): Evaluation and Development. Proceedings of the 1994 World Bank Conference—Postscript. OED/WB, 1995.

Pimbert, M. and Wakeford: 'Reclaiming our right to power: Some conditions for deliberative democracy'. In PLA Notes 40, IIED, London, 2001.

PLA Notes 40: 'Deliberative democracy and citizen empowerment', IIED, London, 2001.

Poole, Peter (ed.): 'Geomatics: Who needs it?', Special edition of *Cultural Survival Quarterly,* Vol. 18, No. 4, Winter, 1995.

Pretty, J. and I. Guijt: 'Primary Environmental Care: An Alternative Paradigm for Development Assistance', *Environment and Urbanisation,* Vol. 4, No. 1, 1992.

Pretty, J., I. Scoones, I. Guijit and J. Thompson: *Participatory Learning and Action. A Trainer's Guide.* IIED, London, 1995.

Pretty, J. and I. Scoones: 'Institutionalizing adaptive planning and local level concerns: Looking to the future'. In Nici Nelson and Susan Wright, *Power and participatory development: Theory and practice,* IT Publications, London, 1995.

PROWWESS: Taking the Pulse for Community Management in Water and Sanitation, UNDP, NY, 1990.

Pryke, Michael, Gillian Rose and Sarah Whatmore: *Using Social Theory. Thinking through Research*. Sage Publications, London, 2003.

Punch, Maurice: *The Politics and Ethics of Fieldwork*. Sage Publications, London, 1986.

Putnam, Robert D.: 'The Prosperous Community—Social Capital and Public Life', *The American Prospect*, Vol. 13, pp. 35–42, 1993.

Rabinow, Paul: *Reflection on Fieldwork in Morocco*. The University of California Press, Berkeley, CA, 1977.

Ragin, C.C.: *Constructing social research*. Pine Forge Press, Thousand Oaks, USA, 1994.

———: *The Comparative Method. Moving Beyond Qualitative and Quantitative Strategies*. University of California Press, 1987.

Rahman, Hossain Zillur and M. Hossain (eds): *Rethinking Rural Poverty: A Case for Bangladesh*. Sage Publications, New Delhi, 1995.

Rahnema, Majid: 'Participation'. In W. Sachs, *The Development Dictionary*, Zed Books, 1992.

Rasmussen, Søren Skou: *Poverty Reduction Strategy Planning and Decentralisation at District Level, Ghana*. COWI, Denmark, 2004.

———: Why and how to negotiate an environment for participation. Paper for Conference on 'Debating Participation: Actors Shaping Sustainable Urban Development', Danish University Consortium for Environment and Development, Industry and Urban Areas, June 2003. Available from the author ssr@cowi.dk.

———: Beneficiary Assessment, COWI Consult, DK, 2003.

———: Review of Anthropology in Afforestation and Reforestation Project in the Northern State, Sudan. COWI Consult, Copenhagen, 1992.

Rasmussen, Søren Skou et al.: *Ghana Poverty Reduction Initiative*. For Government of Ghana and European Commission, COWI Denmark, 2001.

Ravnborg, Helle Munk: Resource Poor Farmers: Finding Them and Diagnosing Their Problems and Opportunities. Proceedings of 12th Annual Farming Systems Symposium, Michigan State University, September 1992.

Reddy, G. Prakash: 'Danish Dilemmas. Perspectives of an Indian Anthropologist on Values in Danish Society'. Department of Anthropology, Sri Venkateswara University, Tirupati, India, 2002.

———: *Danske Dilemmaer*. Grevas, Denmark, 1998.

———: *Danes Are Like That! Perspectives of an Indian Anthropologist on the Danish Society*. Grevas, Denmark, 1993.

———: *Sådan er Danskerne!* Grevas, Denmark, 1992.

Ribot, Jesse C.: *Democratic Decentralization of Natural Resources—Institutionalising Popular Participation*. World Resources Institute, 2002.

Richards, M, J. Davies and Gil Yaron: *Stakeholder Incentives in Participatory Forest Management. A Manual for Economic Analysis*. TIDG Publishing, London, 2002.

Richey, Lisa: 'Development, Demographic, and Feminist Agendas: Depoliticizing Empowerment in a Tanzanian Family Planning Project'. In Jane Parpart, Shirin Rai and Kathleen Staudt (eds), *Rethinking Em(power)ment, Gender and Development*, pp. 41–60, Routledge, London, 2000.

Rist, Ray C.: 'Rethinking the Utilization Debate. From Studies to Streams'. Paper for Danish Society for Evaluation Annual Conference, 2002.

Ritzer, George: *Sociological Theory*. McGrawHill, 2000.

Robb, Caroline M.: *Can the Poor Influence Policy? Participatory Poverty Assessments in the Developing World*. IMF/WB, Washington DC, 2002.

Roche, C.: Paper for Aid Impact Forum Workshop, Centre for Development Research, Copenhagen, April 2001.

———: *Impact Assessment for Development Agencies. Learning to Value Change*. Oxfam, Oxford, 1999.

Rosander, Eva Evers: 'People's Participation as Rhetoric in Swedish Development Aid'. In G. Dahl and A. Rabo (eds), *Kamap or Take-off. Local Notions of Development*, Stockholm Studies in Social Anthropology, Stockholm, 1992.

Rowlands, Jo: 'Empowerment examined'. In Oxfam, *Development with Women*, Oxfam Publications, Oxford, 1999.

———: *Questioning Empowerment*. Oxfam, Oxford, 1997.

RRA Notes No. 13 and No. 15, IIED, London.

Rubin, H.J.: 'Applied social research'. Columbus, OH: Charles E Merrill, 1983. Quoted in W.L. Neuman, *Social Research Methods*, Allyn and Bacon, 2000.

Rundstrom, R.: 'GIS, indigenous peoples, and epistemological diversity', *Cartography and Geographic Information Systems*, Vol. 22, No. 1, pp. 30–44, 1995.

Ruyter, Knut W.: Forskeretikk og forskningsetikk (Researcher ethics and research ethics). Den nasjonale forskningsetiske komité for medicine, Oslo, 2002.

Sachs, Wolfgang (ed.): *The Development Dictionary. A Guide to Knowledge as Power.* Zed Books, London, 1996.

Salmen, Lawrence F.: The Voice of the Farmer in Agricultural Extension. AKIS Discussion Paper, World Bank, Washington DC, 2000.

———: *Beneficiary Assessment—An Approach Described.* World Bank, 1995.

———: *Beneficiary Assessment—An Approach Described.* Poverty and Social Policy Division, The World Bank, Working Paper No. 1, February 1992.

Scheyvens, Regina and Donovan Storey (eds): *Development Fieldwork. A Practical Guide.* Sage Publications, London, 2003.

Schmidt, Kasper: On the Right Track? An impact assessment of the Queen Elisabeth Protected Area Community Conservation Project—Uganda. MA Thesis, unpublished, Department of International Development Studies, Roskilde University, Denmark, 2004.

Sellamna, N.: Relativism in agricultural research and development: Is participation a post-modern concept? Working Paper No. 119, ODI, London, 1999.

Sen, Amartya K.: *Development as Freedom.* Alfred A. Knopf, New York, 1999.

———: 'Gender and Co-operative Conflict'. In I. Tinker (ed.), *Persistent Inequalities*, Oxford University Press, Oxford, 1990.

———: 'Rights and Capabilities'. In A.K. Sen (ed.), *Resources, Values and Development*, Blackwell, Oxford, UK, 1984.

———: *Poverty and Famines.* Clarendon Press, Oxford, 1981.

Sen, Ghita and C. Grown, DAWN: 'Development Crises & Alternative Visions'. In *Third World Women's Perspectives*, Earthscan, 1985.

Shah, Parmesh and D. Youssef: 'Voices and Choices at a Macro Level: Participation In Country-Owned Poverty Reduction Strategies'. A Workshop Report. Action Learning Program Dissemination Series No. 1, SDD, World Bank, 2002.

Sida: Reflection on Experiences of Evaluating Gender Equality. UTV Working Paper (by Britha Mikkelsen et al., COWI), Stockholm, 2003.

———: Perspectives on Poverty, Stockholm, October 2002.

———: Mainstreaming Gender Equality. Sida's support for the promotion of gender equality in partner countries, by Britha Mikkelsen et al. A Sida Evaluation Report 02/01, Stockholm, 2002.

———: Discussing Women's Empowerment—Theory and Practice. Sida Studies, No. 3, 2002.

———: Using Participatory Approaches in Bilateral Development Cooperation—Some Sida Experiences 1980–2000, by Per-Ulf Nilsson and Prudence Woodford-Berger. Stockholm, September 2000.

———: Sida's Action Programme for promoting equality between women and men in partner countries. Stockholm, 1997.

———: Evaluation Manual for SIDA (by E. Lewin). Stockholm, 1994.

Sigsgaard, Peter: 'Monitoring without indicators: and ongoing testing of the MSC approach', *Journal of Evaluation*, New series, Vol. 2, No.1, August 2002.

Silberschmidt, Margrethe: 'Rethinking Men and Gender Relations. An Investigation of Men, Their Changing Roles within the Household, and the Implications for Gender Relations in Kisii District, Kenya', CDR Research Report 16, Copenhagen, 1991.

Sillitoe, Paul: 'Participant observation to participatory development: Making anthropology work'. In Sillitoe, Bicker and Pottier (eds), *Participating in Development. Approaches to Indigenous Knowledge*, Routledge, London, 2002.

Sillitoe, Paul, Alan Bicker and Johan Pottier (eds): *Participating in Development. Approaches to Indigenous Knowledge.* ASA Monographs 39, Routledge, 2002.

Sklair, Leslie: *Sociology of the Global System.* John Hopkins University Press, Baltimore, 1991.

Skutsch, Margaret M.: Gender in Energy Training Pack. Occasional Paper No. 9. Technology and Development Group, Twente University, Netherlands, 1997.

Slim, Hugo: 'Making Moral Ground. Rights as the Struggle for Justice and the Abolition of Development', in *Praxis, The Fletcher Journal of Development Studies*, Vol. XVII. As posted on http://fletcher.tufts.edu/praxis/xvii/Slim.pdf, 23 October 2003.

Sørbø, Gunnar M.: 'Aid and Academia: An Uneasy Relationship', *Forum for Development Studies*, No. 2, pp. 309–28, 2001.

Sørbø, Gunnar M., Bente Herstad, et al.: Report from Conference on Poverty, Development and Environment. Chr. Michelsen Institute, Bergen, Norway, 2002.

Sørensen, Pernille, Gertrude Halkjaer, Selome Bekele, Kiros G/Egizabher Berhe, et al.: Various reports for The Impact Study Group of the Joint Ethio-Danish Development Programme in North Wollo, DIIS, Copenhagen, 2000–4.

Srinivas, M.N. et al. (eds): *The Fieldworker and the Field. Problems and Challenges in Sociological Investigation*. Oxford University Press, Bombay, 1979.

Srivastva, S. and D.L. Cooperrider (eds): *Appreciative management and leadership*. Jossey-Bass, San Francisco, CA, 1990.

Steiner, Henry and J. Philip Alston: *International Human Rights in Context. Law, Politics, Morals*. Second Edition, Oxford University Press, Oxford, 2000.

Stepputat, Finn: 'Beyond Relief? Life in a Guatemalan Refugee Settlement in Mexico'. Ph.D Thesis, University of Copenhagen, 1992.

Stiefel, Matthias and Marshall Wolfe: *A Voice for the Excluded. Popular Participation in Development. Utopia or Necessity?* Zed Books, London, 1994.

Stirrat, J.: 'The new orthodoxy and old truths: Participation, empowerment and other buzz words'. In S. Bastian and N. Bastian (eds), *Assessing participation: A debate from South Asia*, pp. 67–92, Konark Publishers, Delhi, 1996.

Storgaard, Birgit: 'Etnografi og udviklingsbistand. En case fra Indien' (Ethnography and Development Aid. A Case from India). In Klaus Khan Baba, *An Ethnographic Kaleidoscope for Klaus Ferdinand*, Aarhus University, 1991.

Strauss, Anselm and Juliet Corbin: *Basics of Qualitative Research, Grounded Theory Procedures and Techniques*. Sage Publications, Newbury Park, 1990 and 1996.

Sumner, Andrew: Economic Well-being and Non-economic Well-being. A Review of the Meaning and Measurement of Poverty. Research Paper No. 2004/30, WIDER, Helsinki, 2004.

Sultana, Parvin and Steen Folke: Bangladesh in-Depth Study. Project Impact at the Local Level —A Study of LIFT—Patuakhali. The Danish NGO Impact Study. A Review of Danish NGO Activities in Developing Countries. Centre for Development Research, Denmark, September 1999.

Tadria, H.M. Kabushenga: 'Challenges of Participation and Observation: Fieldwork Experience Among Some Peasants of Uganda'. In M.N. Panini (ed.), *From the Female Eye. Accounts of Women Fieldworkers Studying Their Own Communities*, Hindustan Publishing House, Delhi, 1991.

Taguchi, Lynne: *Case on Participation in Thailand. For Organizing for Development*. International Institute, ODII, 1996.

Tendler, Judith: *Good Government in the Tropics*. John Hopkins University Press, 1997.

Tesch, R.: *Qualitative Research. Analysis Types and Software Tools*. Falmer, NY, 1990.

Theis, Joachim and H.M. Grady: *Participatory Rapid Appraisal for Community Development. A Training Manual Based on Experiences in the Middle East and North Africa*. IIED and Save the Children, 1991.

Theis, Joachim: 'Brief Introduction to Rights-based Programming', Save the Children, Sweden, August 2003.

Thomsen, Thomas J.: Reflections on Rural Finance Study, COWI, 2002, Unpublished.

Tomaselli, K.G. (ed.): 'Encounters in the Kalahari', Special Issue, *Visual Anthropology*, Vol. 12, Nos 2&3, Routledge, 1999.

Tostensen, Arne, Lise Rakner and Lars Svåsand: *The Participatory Aspects of Poverty Reduction Strategies in Malawi and Zambia*. For NORAD, October 2002.

Toulmin, S.E.: *The Uses of Arguments*. Cambridge University Press, 1958.

Tvedt, Terje: Bilder af 'De Andre'. Om utviklingslandene i bistandsepoken (Images of 'The Others'. About Developing Countries in the Epoch of Aid). Universitetsforlaget, Norway, 1990.

UNDESA (United Nations Department of Economic and Social Affairs). 'Integrated and Coordinated Implementation and Follow-up of Major United Nations Conferences and Summits: A Critical Review of the Development Indicators in the Context of Conference Follow-up'. Geneva, 1999.

UNDP: Human Development Report, 2000, 2001, 2002, 2003 and annual.

———: Choices for the Poor. Lessons from National Poverty Strategies. By A. Grinspun, UNDP, NY, 2001.

UNICEF: 'A Human Rights Approach to UNICEF Programming for Children and Women: What it is and Some Changes it will Bring', 1998. As posted on http//coe-dmha.org/Unicef/HPT_Introreading01.htm on 20 October 2003.

———: *Human Rights for Children and Women: How UNICEF Helps Make them a Reality*. UNICEF, New York, 1999.

UNIFEM: *Gender Budget Initiatives. Strategies, Concepts and Experiences*. UNIFEM, NY, 2001.

———: *The World's Women*. Recurrent.

United Nations: Gender Mainstreaming—An Overview. Office of the Special Adviser on Gender Issues and Advancement of Women, NY, 2002.

———: 'Second Interagency Workshop on Implementing a Human-Rights-based Approach in the Context of UN Reform', Workshop Report, Stamford, 5–7 May 2003.

———: 'The Human Rights Based Approach to Development Co-operation—Towards a Common Understanding Among the UN Agencies'. Statement of Common Understanding, output of the UN Interagency Workshop on Human Rights Based Approach in the Context of UN Reform, 5 May 2003.

Uphoff, Norman, M.J. Esman and A. Krishna: *Reasons for Success. Learning From Instructive Experiences in Rural Development.* Kumarian Press, 1998.

Uphoff, Norman: *Learning from Gal Oya: Possibilities for Participatory Development and Post-Newtonian Social Science.* IT Publications, London, 1996.

Uvin, Peter: 'On High Moral Ground: The Incorporation of Human Rights by the Development Enterprise', *Praxis, The Fletcher Journal of Development Studies*, Vol. XVII. As posted on http://fletcher.tufts.edu/praxis/xvii/Uvin.pdf on 23 October 2003.

Vaa, Mariken: 'Mali—The position of women and a dual commitment', *News from the Nordic Africa Institute*, No. 1, pp. 7–10, Uppsala, Sweden, 2001.

———: On Quality in consulting: Reflections from a researcher. Unpublished. Nordic Africa Institute, Uppsala, Sweden, 1997.

———: 'Gender relations and the environment of urban poverty'. In SAREC, Tropical Diseases, Society and the Environment, Conference Report 1995, No. 2, SAREC, Stockholm, 1995.

Vansina, Jan: *Oral Tradition as History.* Heinemann, Kenya, 1985.

van Weerelt, Patrick: 'A Human Rights-based Approach to Development Programming in UNDP. Adding the Missing Link', August 2001.

Wallace, Helen: 'The Issue of framing and consensus conferences'. In PLA Notes 40, 2001.

Watkins, Jane Magruder and Bernard J. Mohr: *Appreciative Inquiry—Change at the Speed of Imagination.* Jossey-Bass/Pfeiffer, 2001.

Weber, Max, in Roscher and Knies: *The Logical Problems of Historical Economics.* Free Press, New York, 1975.

Webster, Neil: Notes on Political Space. For LPPD workshop, DIIS, Copenhagen, June 2004.

Webster, Neil and Lars Engberg-Pedersen (eds): *In the Name of the Poor. Contesting Political Space for Poverty Reduction.* Zed Books, London, 2002.

Weiner, D., T. Warner, T. Harris and R. Levin: 'Apartheid representations in a digital landscape: GIS, remote sensing and local knowledge in Kiepersol, South Africa', *Cartography and Geographic Information Systems*, Vol. 22, No. 1, pp. 45–57, 1995.

Wennerholm, Carolina Johansson. *The Feminisation of Poverty—the Use of a Concept.* Sida, 2002.

White, Howard: 'Combining Quantitative and Qualitative Approaches in Poverty Analysis', *World Development*, Vol. 30, No. 3, pp. 511–22, 2002.

Whitney, Diana and A. Trosten-Bloom: *The Power of Appreciative Inquiry—a practical guide to positive change.* Berrett-Koehler Publishers, 2003.

Wilkie, David S. and J.T. Finn: *Remote Sensing Imagery for Natural Resources Monitoring. A guide for first-time users.* Methods and Cases in Conservation Science Series, Columbia University Press, NY, 1996.

Wilson, Fiona: 'From Humanitarianism to Good Governance? Reflections on a Danish-Ethiopian Aid Model'. Article for Aid Impact book, forthcoming from Danish Institute for International Studies, DIIS, 2004.

———: Faust: The Developer. CDR Working Paper 92.5, Center for Development Research, Copenhagen, 1992.

———: 'Development Studies Between the Disciplines'. In S. Arnfred et al., *The Language of Development Studies*, New Social Science Monographs, Roskilde University Centre, RUC, 1990.

World Bank: Qualitative Poverty and Exclusion Study, QPES, Guatemala. By David Moore et al., COWI, Denmark, 2002.

World Bank, Poverty Reduction Group and Social Development Department: A User's Guide to Poverty and Social Impact Analysis, Work in Progress, 19 April 2002.

World Bank: A Sourcebook for Poverty Reduction Strategies. By Jeni Klugman ed., Washington DC, 2002.
———: Engendering Development. Through Gender Equality in Rights, Resources, and Voice. A World Bank Policy Research Report. 2001.
World Bank/CDD: Participation and Civic Engagement Team, Proposed Work Program, 10/15/2001.
World Bank: World Development Report 2000, Washington DC, 2000.
———: The World Bank Participation Sourcebook, Washington DC, 1996.
———: Expanding OED's Program of Impact Evaluations: Proposed Principles and Procedures, Report of Interim Working Group, 1993.
———: www.worldbank.org/poverty/strategies.
World Bank/ESSD: Safeguard Policies: http://Inweb18.worldbank.org/ESSD/sdvext.nsf/52ByDocName/SafeguardPolies.
www.cowi.dk/about_cowi/quality_management.asp .
www.seacsn.net/publications/bulletin/oct-dec2002/focus.htm.
www.iaia.org/siaguide/: Guidelines and Principles for Social Impact Assessment, US Department of Commerce, 1994.
www.scolari.co.uk and www.scolari.com.
Yin, Robert K.: Case Study Research. Design and Methods. Sage Publications, USA, 1989 and 2002.

Index

About the Author

Britha Mikkelsen is a senior social science, research and quality assurance specialist with the international consultant firm COWI, Denmark. During her rich and varied career in research and development, she has conceptualized and been in charge of multidisciplinary studies from planning to design, review, and evaluation. She is particularly interested in community participation, poverty and gender analysis, impact and evaluation methodology, cross-cultural perspectives, and ethics. Her experience has been gained from many sectors such as rural infrastructure, education and vocational training, HRD, primary health care, small enterprise, poverty and social capital assessments. She has served on international and Danish research councils and has participated in policy and strategy formulation for international and bilateral agencies and NGOs. Dr Mikkelsen is also a facilitator and lectures frequently in Denmark and abroad. Her previous publications include *Mainstreaming Gender Equality. Sida's Support for the Promotion of Gender Equality in Partner Countries* (2002); *Behind Participation in the Development Discourse* (1998); and *Poverty reduction in Danish Development Assistance* (Ministry of Foreign Affairs, Copenhagen, 1996).